SAMS Teach Yourself

Microsoft®
Project 2000

in 24 Hours

Tim Pyron

 **SAMS**   201 West 103rd St., Indianapolis, Indiana, 46290 USA

Sams Teach Yourself Microsoft® Project 2000 in 24 Hours

Copyright © 2000 by Sams Publishing

International Standard Book Number: 0-672-31814-8

Library of Congress Catalog Card Number: 99-067006

Printed in the United States of America

First Printing: April 2000

04 03 02   6 5 4 3

Trademarks

All terms mentioned in this book that are known to be trademarks or service marks have been appropriately capitalized. Sams Publishing cannot attest to the accuracy of this information. Use of a term in this book should not be regarded as affecting the validity of any trademark or service mark.

Warning and Disclaimer

Every effort has been made to make this book as complete and as accurate as possible, but no warranty or fitness is implied. The information provided is on an "as is" basis. The authors and the publisher shall have neither liability nor responsibility to any person or entity with respect to any loss or damages arising from the information contained in this book.

ACQUISITIONS EDITOR
Betsy Brown

DEVELOPMENT EDITOR
Jon Steever

MANAGING EDITOR
Charlotte Clapp

PROJECT EDITOR
Andy Beaster

COPY EDITOR
Kate Givens

INDEXER
Sheila Schroeder

PROOFREADER
Candice Hightower

TECHNICAL EDITOR
Connie Myers

TEAM COORDINATOR
Amy Patton

MEDIA DEVELOPER
Jason Haines

INTERIOR DESIGNER
Gary Adair

COVER DESIGNER
Aren Howell

COPYWRITER
Eric Borgert

PRODUCTION
Lisa England
Steve Geiselman
Brad Lenser

Contents at a Glance

Contents

About the Authors

TIM PYRON (tpyron@txdirect.net), besides writing for Sams and Que, is an independent consultant and trainer for Microsoft Project. His previous Microsoft Project books include, among others, *Using Microsoft Project 4, Special Edition Using Microsoft Project 98, Special Edition Using Microsoft Project 2000*, and *Sams Teach Yourself Microsoft Project 98 in 24 Hours*—all of which have together sold more than 250,000 copies. He is also Contributing Editor to *Woody's Project Watch*, a free newsletter for Project users. To subscribe, go to http://www.woodyswatch.com/wpw/.

IRA BROWN (ibrown@projectassistants.com) is the senior vice president of Project Assistants, Inc., a Microsoft Project Solution Provider specializing in training, consulting, and custom software development for Microsoft Project. He has extensive project management and application development experience, and is recognized as a leading authority in integrating Microsoft Project with other products utilizing VBA, specializing in integration with the Microsoft Office suite of applications. He also has significant experience in helping an organization implement Microsoft Project across an enterprise, utilizing the workgroup features, Web publishing, and multiple project consolidation capabilities of the software.

Several Project Assistants, Inc. employees also contributed to this new edition:

PETER MARCH (pmarch@projectassistants.com) is currently performing project management and process and software development consulting at a Fortune 100 company in their Web site development division. In addition, he has many years of experience in consulting with events, marketing, facility, and construction management. He lives in Atlanta, Georgia and is a graduate of Georgia Southern University.

LENA DIXON (ldixon@projectassistants.com) is currently providing project management and process consulting at a Fortune 100 company in their e-business division. She has many years experience consulting in the Finance/Banking and Healthcare/Beauty industries. She is a graduate of The University of Washington in Seattle, Washington, and lives in Atlanta, Georgia.

LAURIE SOSLOW (lsoslow@projectassistants.com) is an expert at technical writing for computer-based tools and education. She creates user documentation, online help systems, and custom training materials for Microsoft Project, as well Project Commander and TeamWork, the popular add-on products for Microsoft Project. She received her Bachelor of Arts degree in English and Political Science from the University of Vermont, and her Master's Degree in English and Creative Writing from Boston University.

MICHELLE WILEY (mwylie@projectassistants.com) has extensive experience in the project management field. She also has an extensive technical background in networking. She has acquired several industry certifications from both Microsoft and Compaq. Working as a consultant with one of the world's largest web integrators, She provides project management leadership and expertise in areas of process development and project support. She is a graduate of The University of South Carolina with a double major in MIS (Management Information Systems) and Marketing and a minor in French. She lives in Atlanta, Georgia.

For more information about Project Assistants, visit their Web site at www. projectassistants.com. Projects Assistants, Inc. employees can also be contacted by phone at (800) 642-9259, or by fax at (302) 477-9712.

BARBEE DAVIS (barbeedavis@home.com) owns Davis Consulting, a provider of Project Management workshops and a Microsoft Project add-on tool, "Process Bridge." A former owner of ExecuTrain of Nebraska, she has provided training in all Microsoft desktop and technical applications. Her B.A. in Education, an M.A., and a Professional in Human Resources accreditation (PHR) led to writing corporate handbooks, management development programs, and sales training. She has written and facilitated training for IBM Corporation, ExecuTrain, and designed and implemented large project roll-outs in a variety of industries.

JO ELLEN SHIRES (jshires@cscservices.com) is the owner of Common Sense Computing, a Portland, Oregon-based company that exclusively serves Microsoft Project users. She began her programming and training careers in 1974 and holds a B.S. in Economics and an M.S. in Biometry. A noted lecturer at regional and national gatherings and founder of the Portland Project Users Group, she contributed to the previous edition of this work as well as the 98 and 2000 editions of *Special Edition Using Microsoft Project*. She serves as an advisor to the Project development team at Microsoft and is participating in the launch of the Project certification testing program.

Dedication

In appreciation for all our parents...

Acknowledgments

Even a small book owes its existence to many more people than the one whose name appears as author. I am immensely grateful to the other writers who jumped in to help complete this book and who contributed a great deal to the text: **Jo Ellen Shires**, **Ira Brown**, and **Barbee Davis**. **Jon Steever** has done a masterful job of ferreting out the meaning that the other authors and I intended, all the while tactfully suggesting that clarity is considered a virtue by Sams' readers. Technical errors, though unintentional, are still a sin in technical writing. Connie Myers expertly pointed out both the sins of commission and of omission, and she even exorcised some of the devils found in the details herself. Those errors that remain are entirely my responsibility.

Writing, especially writing against intense deadlines, takes a toll on the writer's family. The family and pets always sacrifice more than the writer is aware of (even though occasional hints may be dropped from time to time). I know I speak for the other writers when I thank our families for their patience and forbearance. My wife, Gerlinde, could write a book of her own on the topic. Hopefully, she will leave it in private circulation.

Tell Us What You Think!

As the reader of this book, *you* are our most important critic and commentator. We value your opinion and want to know what we're doing right, what we could do better, what areas you'd like to see us publish in, and any other words of wisdom you're willing to pass our way.

You can email or write me directly to let me know what you did or didn't like about this book—as well as what we can do to make our books stronger.

Please note that I cannot help you with technical problems related to the topic of this book, and that due to the high volume of mail I receive, I might not be able to reply to every message.

When you write, please be sure to include this book's title and author as well as your name and phone or fax number. I will carefully review your comments and share them with the author and editors who worked on the book.

Email: feedback@samspublishing.com

Mail: Mark Taber
         Sams Publishing
         201 West 103rd Street
         Indianapolis, IN 46290 USA

Introduction

Is This the Book for You?

Absolutely…if you have to plan how to coordinate a lot of different activities and people to reach a specific goal—and if you're already planning to use Microsoft Project 2000 to help you do it. If you're still undecided about using project management software, or about which software to use, then this book will show you how instrumental Microsoft Project 2000 can be to the success of your project. This book is as much for those who support the manager of the project as it is for the manager.

Almost every adult has to organize a project at some time. It's common enough in the workplace: planning conferences and conventions, a move to a new office, the introduction of a new product, the construction of a skyscraper, a landing on the moon, that sort of stuff. I've even known people to use Microsoft Project to plan weddings and the remodeling of their homes. (The wedding was great, thank you; the remodeling is finally just a painful memory.) And if the stars on *Touched by an Angel* don't whip out a laptop on camera, you can bet the producers do to coordinate all the details that go into filming the travails of those heart-warming souls. Hey! How do you think She pulled off a Creation in just seven days? But, I digress…

Microsoft Project is a great friend to have if you are responsible for putting together a plan of action for reaching a goal (or if you are the one who supports the person with that responsibility). It helps you block out the big picture and then fill in and organize all the details that must be completed if the goal is to be reached. Of course, you have to provide the inspiration; but Project helps you capture your thoughts in an organized way so that you can turn them into a workable plan. Working with Project you can easily estimate completion dates for each task or phase of the project, ensuring that you complete your project on time.

If you assign people and other resources to the tasks, Project will show you who's working when, and how much the project is going to cost, and it will alert you when someone's assignment schedule is beyond reason—the stuff that a micromanager's dreams are made of.

When work finally gets started on your project, you can update the schedule with the actual dates as tasks are started and completed, and Project will recalculate the schedule, showing you the implications when tasks are finished late or early.

Finally, and maybe most importantly, if you use Microsoft Project you will be able to print reports throughout the planning and production stages that illustrate and explain your plan and the progress that's being made. As you know, if more than one person is involved, good communication is essential to success.

This book is designed to help you gain control quickly of the planning, implementation, and recording of your project. All the essentials for using Microsoft Project 2000 effectively are included, but I've omitted as much theory as possible, giving you only as much as you need to make good choices. If you need more details, you should see my comprehensive guide *Special Edition Using Microsoft Project 2000*, published by Que.

Many of the lessons in this book contain references to sample Project files, and solutions to exercises. These helpful files can be found on the Macmillan USA Web site dedicated to this book. To download the files, go to http://www.mcp.com/product_support/. Enter this book's ISBN—0672318148—in the Book Information and Downloads text field and click Search.

How This Book Is Organized

Part I, "Getting Started with a Project" (Hours 1 through 3), gets you up and running quickly with Microsoft Project 2000. You learn early how to manage the main screen that displays project data, how to start a new project, and how to put together the list of tasks or things to do in the project.

Part II, "Developing a Timeline" (Hours 4 through 7), shows you how to give Microsoft Project the information it needs to turn the list of tasks into a reasonable schedule of dates for working on the tasks.

Part III, "Displaying and Printing Your Schedule" (Hours 8 through 10), shows you some of the alternative ways you can view a project in Microsoft Project 2000 and then shows you how to get printed reports and copies of the project that look the way you want them to look.

Part IV, "Assigning Resources and Costs to the Tasks" (Hours 11 through 15), is where you learn how to let Project know who is going to do the work, when they are available, the other resources they need to do the work, and how much it all is going to cost. This section also deals with how changes in resource availability and assignments can affect your schedule.

Part V, "Finalizing and Publishing Your Plan" (Hours 16 through 19), covers the steps you should take to review and optimize your plan. You will also see how to generate reports that explain the project in varying levels of detail, including how to publish your project on Web pages.

Part VI, "Managing and Tracking the Project" (Hours 20 and 21), explains how to track progress after the work is underway and how to analyze the progress to help keep things on track.

Part VII, "Beyond One Project, One Application" (Hours 22 through 24), expands your horizons to include combining multiple project plans into a master plan, using the workgroup features of Project to communicate changes and progress via email and the Internet, and exchanging data between Microsoft Project and other software applications.

Conventions Used in This Book

This book uses the following conventions:

Text that you type and text that you see onscreen appear in `monospace type`:

`It will look like this.`

A **Note** presents interesting information related to the discussion.

A **Tip** offers advice or shows you an easier way of doing something.

A **Caution** alerts you to a possible problem and gives you advice on how to avoid it.

 New terms are introduced using the New Term icon.

PART I

Getting Started with a Project

Hour

HOUR 1

Getting Started with Microsoft Project 2000

You might be reading this because you just found out that you have to organize a project of some kind or because you work for someone who has to get one organized—meaning you have to do much of the work yourself. On the other hand, if you're like most people who have come to my Microsoft Project classes, you're already into a project of some kind and realize that you need to get a grip. You need to take charge of your project, now! And that's what this hour is about.

In this hour, you will learn:

- About project management as a process
- How to use Project's built-in tutorials and on-online help
- What the Project views are telling you and how to navigate around the Project interface
- How to exit Project 2000

The Life Cycle of a Project

Most of the hour-long lessons in this book parallel the process that you would normally go through using Microsoft Project to help you plan and manage a project. Have the big picture in mind as you start so that you can understand how one lesson leads into the next. The following sections give you a brief overview of Project's features and how they can help you track and manage your projects.

Clarifying the Goal of the Project

Start by writing down the objective or goal of your project in a short sentence or two. It's essential that you clarify what you hope to accomplish with this project before you start the planning process. If you don't know where you're going, you're likely to wind up in a strange place. You have a chance to record the goal when you start a project file so that you have it handy if you need to explain the project to anyone.

Be specific about what exactly has to happen in order for the people who have a stake in the project to judge it a success. The following are a few questions to answer before beginning a project:

- What must be delivered or accomplished by the project? Be specific not only about what has to be produced or what the outcome must be, but also about the quality standards that must be met to satisfy those who commissioned the project.
- Are there deadlines that must be met?

  When must the work start or when must it be finished?
- What are the budget constraints that you have to consider?

Planning the Schedule

Next, do some brainstorming and put together a list of the major phases of activity—the blocks of work that must be completed. After you have identified the major blocks of work, you can start filling in the details, listing the tasks that fall under each of the major phases. Hour 3, "Starting a New Project and Working with Tasks" will show you how to build and organize the task list.

After you have the list of tasks organized, Project can help you organize the task list into a schedule of work with calendar dates. Of course, you still have to do most of the work—Project just helps you get it together and puts it all into time frames so that you can see when things start and finish. The following are some ideas to consider when preparing your schedule:

1

- You need to estimate how long you think it will take to complete each task. Hour 4, "Starting the Scheduling Process" will show you how to enter your estimates of how long tasks will take.

- You need to check the calendar that comes with Project and record any holidays or other non-working time that Project needs to work around in its scheduling. Hour 5, "Defining When Project Can Schedule Tasks" will show you how to set up the calendar.

- You will use links between tasks that must follow one another in a required sequence so that Project won't schedule the cart before the horse. You will learn about "Linking Tasks in the Correct Sequence" in Hour 6.

- You should also take note of any deadlines that must be met during the project. Hour 7 covers "Working with Deadlines and Constraints."

- If you want, you can assign tasks to people or other resources. Project can schedule tasks around vacations and other off-days that you've defined for the resources that are assigned to a task. You will learn all about assigning resources to tasks during the 5 Hours of Part IV, "Assigning Resources and Costs to the Tasks."

Organizing a task list into a schedule takes work, but after it's done, Project will have calculated when each task needs to start, how long it is to take, and when it is to finish so that the next task can get under way. Also, Microsoft Project will have calculated when you can expect the project to be completed, based on the start date and other information you have provided, or when it must start in order to be completed on time if you have provided a fixed finish date.

If the calculated schedule is not acceptable, you need to rethink some of the assumptions you've entered about what should happen. (By the way, Project includes a number of tutorials and wizards to help you with the planning process. I'll show you how to use those later in this hour.)

Publishing the Schedule

After your plan is complete, you will want to print copies of the schedule and distribute it to other people. You probably need to get the plan approved; you definitely need to show it to those you've assigned to do the work; and you may need to explain to other people in the organization (or in the community) what's going to happen and when. Indeed, the ability to print meaningful and helpful reports is the main reason some people use Microsoft Project. Project makes it relatively easy to publish reports on both paper and on Web pages for the Internet or an organizational intranet. You will see how to present your project in several Hours of this book: Hour 10, "Finalizing and Printing Your Schedule"; Hour 17, "Printing Resource Details and Customizing Reports"; and Hour 19, "Publishing Projects on the Web or an Intranet."

Tracking Progress and Adapting to Change

After the work starts on the project, you can use Microsoft Project to record the actual dates when work begins and ends on individual tasks. As you enter these dates, Microsoft Project notes any differences between the scheduled dates and the actual dates and automatically reschedules the remaining tasks in the project if you are ahead or behind on the planned schedule. In this way, you get an early warning if deadlines are in jeopardy of not being met, and you can give resources advance notice of necessary changes in the schedule. Hour 20, "Tracking Work on the Project," shows you how to record actual work and costs.

If you record costs for your project, your tracking efforts can give you a heads-up when it begins to look like costs are going over budget. This gives you time to find ways of reducing the remaining costs to stay on target.

Wrapping up the Project

At the end of the project, you will want to submit a report glorifying its successful completion (or putting a good spin on what went wrong). Microsoft Project can help you prepare good looking, informative descriptions and analyses of the project. After all, if you don't objectively report on your work, who's going to give you the credit you deserve?

Using Project 2000's Tutorials and Help Features

The first thing to do with any new software is to get used to the user interface—the screens, menus, and toolbars that you use to run the program. Microsoft Project offers an impressive array of learning aids, starting with the opening window. When you start Microsoft Project, the Welcome! window offers immediate access to tutorials and guides for using Project to develop and manage a project plan.

The Welcome! window (see Figure 1.1) appears each time you start Project (unless you clear the check box labeled Display Help at Startup). This is also the main Help window you will see when you choose Help, Contents and Index from the menu. It displays a number of built-in help features you can use to become more proficient with Microsoft Project. Even if you are an experienced Project user, the items in the Help window will be useful as you learn this version of Project. Use the Close button in the upper-right corner of the Welcome! window if, for the time being, you just want to close it without selecting any of the learning aids.

FIGURE 1.1

The Welcome! screen offers six different kinds of help for getting started with Microsoft Project 2000.

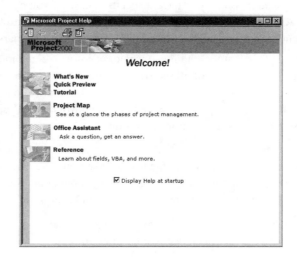

Each of the items in the Help window is a link to a help feature in Microsoft Project. When you position the mouse pointer on a feature name, the pointer changes to a hand. Click on the feature name to access the help information. The following list briefly describes the choices in the Microsoft Project Help window:

- *What's New.* A brief description of the most significant new features in Project 2000 with hyperlinks to more extensive explanations of each feature.
- *Quick Preview.* A short presentation (5 screens) that provides an overview of the major functional benefits of Microsoft Project.
- *Tutorial.* A series of lessons designed to introduce project management and Microsoft Project to users. The emphasis is on understanding the basic concepts necessary to use Microsoft Project.
- *Project Map.* Though it may appear to be similar to the Tutorial, the Project Map is in fact quite different. The Project Map is really designed for experienced project managers and people already familiar with the information presented in the Tutorial. The Project Map is a more detailed look at project management concepts and how to use Microsoft Project to accomplish your project management requirements.

The Project Map outlines the three main phases of any project—Build a Plan, Track and Manage a Project, and Close a Project. Under each phase you'll find specific topics to guide you through completing that phase.

- *Office Assistant*. When you have a specific question you need answered, use the Office Assistant. For example, when you type **create calendars** in the Office Assistant search box, a list of help topics relating to calendars appears.

- *Reference*. This feature contains a wealth of information about Microsoft Project, including: descriptions of all the fields, troubleshooting tips, mouse and keyboard shortcuts, assistance with using Visual Basic for Applications (VBA) in Microsoft Project, a glossary of project management and Microsoft Project terms, and the Microsoft Project specifications and limits.

Using most of these features are self-evident after you click on the feature name. Blue-colored hyperlinks are embedded in the text to take you to related topics or to drill-down for more information on a topic. I am going to say more about the Office Assistant, however, because it is an alternative way to delve into help information.

Microsoft Project has many esoteric terms that may be new to you. Make frequent use of the on-line Glossary to help you become familiar with new terms.

To Do: Viewing the On-line Glossary

To find the definition of a new term, check for it in the Glossary

1. Choose Help, Contents and Index.
2. On the Contents tab click the plus-sign outline icon next to Reference to display the topics.
3. Click Microsoft Project Glossary.
4. Use the alphabet letters at the top to jump to the initial letter for the term you want to examine. Then scroll to find the term.

Using the Office Assistant

The Office Assistant is one of the quickest ways to get help in Microsoft Project. If the Office Assistant is not active, press the F1 key or choose Help, Microsoft Project Help from the menu. The Office Assistant will help find answers to your questions, by interpreting the questions you ask it. It can interpret questions you type in your own, nontechnical words and provide a list of Help topics that might be relevant to your question. This is often the quickest way to find relevant references within the help files.

Additionally, the Assistant works closely with Project's Planning Wizard (see the next section) to help explain problems and offer shortcuts on working more effectively with

Microsoft Project. If the Office Assistant is active, the suggestions and warnings offered by the Planning Wizard will be displayed through the Office Assistant. If you close the Office Assistant, the Planning Wizard will use its own standard dialog boxes to display the messages.

Working with the Planning Wizard

The Planning Wizard is a Microsoft Project feature that continuously monitors your use of the program and suggests tips for easier ways to do things. It also warns you about potential problems you might create for yourself as a result of your current action and offers you solutions for avoiding the problems. For example, the message in Figure 1.2 appears when Planning Wizard detects that a task is being moved to a non-working day and suggests appropriate ways to complete the procedure. The Planning Wizard is automatically "turned on" in Microsoft Project.

FIGURE 1.2
The Planning Wizard monitors your work and offers suggestions to improve your use of Microsoft Project.

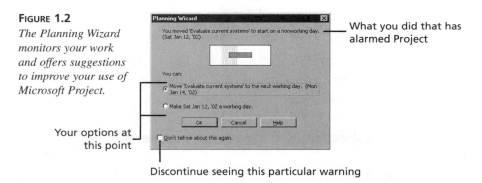

What you did that has alarmed Project

Your options at this point

Discontinue seeing this particular warning

Using Other Sources of Help

The Help menu also offers the standard Windows Contents and Index access to the help files. You can look up answers by:

- Browsing through the Contents tab, where topics are organized into book volumes
- Searching the alphabetized index of help topics on the Index tab
- Using the Answer Wizard tab like you ask questions of the Office Assistant

Choose What's This? on the Help menu to turn the mouse pointer into a question mark. Then, click a screen element like a toolbar button, a menu choice, or a part of the data display in order to see a description of the object that you clicked. This is a great way to gain familiarity with the screen.

Choose Office on the Web from the Help menu to open Internet sites that offer everything from technical support and free software for Microsoft Project to links to Microsoft Office and other helpful sites.

Exploring the Microsoft Project Window

Figure 1.3 shows the Project window after closing the Welcome! screen and Office Assistant. The major components of the window are identified in the following list:

- The title bar at the top of the screen indicates the name of the project file on which you are working.
- Below the title bar, you see the menu, toolbars, and an entry bar for typing and editing data.
- Running down the left side of the screen is the View bar, which provides a quick way to choose the display format for the project data.
- Running across the bottom of the screen is the status bar.
- You view the project data in the center of the screen.

Each element of the window is described in the following sections.

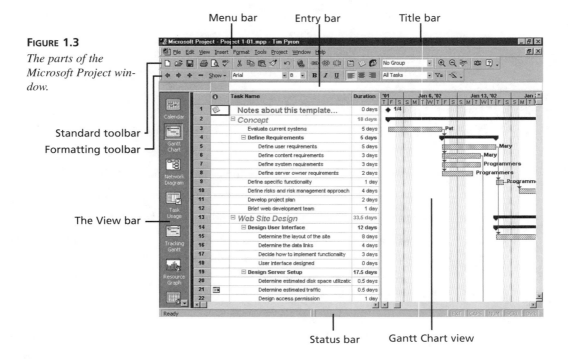

FIGURE 1.3

The parts of the Microsoft Project window.

The Menu Bar

The menus listed on the Microsoft Project Menu bar are very similar to the menus in other Microsoft Office products (Word, Excel, PowerPoint, and Access). The menus and the commands they display are defined and described in detail in later sections as the functions they perform are discussed.

The Toolbars

The toolbar buttons provide shortcut access to frequently used menu choices or special functions. The individual tools are described as you encounter them in the following sections. A brief description (called a *ScreenTip*) appears beneath a tool if you position the mouse pointer over the tool for a second or two.

For more complete descriptions of the tools, use the What's This? command on the Help menu. Choose Help, What's This? (or simply press Shift+F1) and then click a tool. A mini help screen provides you with additional information about that tool.

Microsoft Project 2000 provides 12 toolbars. The two that are displayed initially are the Standard toolbar and the Formatting toolbar. You can add and remove toolbars to the Project window, or create your own custom toolbars. For a detailed description of all the Project toolbars, choose Help, Contents and Index. On the Contents tab, select Microsoft Project Reference (it's toward the bottom of the list), select Toolbars and Buttons, and finally, select Toolbars. This help screen lists all the toolbars. Clicking one of the toolbar names displays its tool buttons with descriptions of the tools.

To show additional toolbars, or to hide one that is currently displayed, choose View, Toolbars from the menu. Toolbars that are checked are currently displayed (see Figure 1.4). Click a checked toolbar to hide it; click an unchecked toolbar to display it.

The shortcut menu is a quick way to show or hide toolbars. Position the mouse over any visible toolbar and right-click to display the shortcut menu. Toolbars that are checked are currently displayed. Choose a checked toolbar to hide it; choose an unchecked toolbar to display it.

Figure 1.4
*Display or hide tool-
bars by clicking them
in the Toolbars list.*

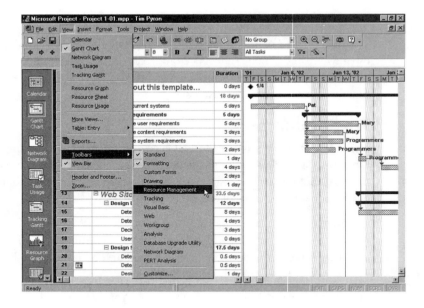

The Entry Bar

The entry bar is on the line below the toolbars. The entry bar performs several functions:

- The left end of the entry bar displays progress messages that indicate when
  Microsoft Project is engaged in calculating, opening, and saving large files, and so
  on.

- The center of the entry bar contains an entry area where data entry and editing
  takes place. During Entry and Editing modes, Cancel and Enter buttons appear.

Use the entry area to enter data in a field or to edit data previously placed in a field.

When the entry bar is active, many features of Microsoft Project are unavailable. Most menu commands, toolbar buttons, and shortcut keys are also
unavailable. Make sure that you close the entry bar by pressing Enter after
entering or editing data in a field.

The Status Bar

The *status bar* is located at the bottom of the window. It shows the status of special keys
and displays advisory messages (see Figure 1.3). At the left end of the status bar is the
mode indicator. This indicator displays Ready when Microsoft Project is waiting for you

1

to begin an operation. The mode indicator displays Enter when you initially enter data, and it displays Edit when you edit a field where you have already entered data. The mode indicator is also used to provide information for some actions that are in progress, including messages while displaying a dialog box, opening or saving a file, and previewing the document before printing.

The middle of the status bar displays warning messages when you need to recalculate and when you've created circular relationships while linking tasks. The far right end of the status bar indicates the status of special modes or keys: Extend (EXT), Caps Lock (CAPS), Num Lock (NUM), Scroll Lock (SCRL), and Insert (OVR). When you press one of these keys to activate it, the key name changes from gray to black on the status bar. Choose Help, Contents and Index and use the Index tab to look up status bar for more information on these keys.

The View Bar

The View bar displays a column of icons that represent the select set of *views* that are listed on the View menu. You can display any of the views represented on the View bar by simply clicking its icon. If a view icon appears depressed, the active view is displayed. The scroll arrow at the bottom of the View bar displays additional view icons.

To show or hide the View Bar, choose View, View Bar. Similar to the way views and toolbars are checked, choose the checked View Bar to hide it; choose the unchecked View Bar to display it.

Use the shortcut menu to show or hide the View bar. Simply right-click in front of the bar to display the shortcut menu, and click next to View Bar to toggle its display status on and off.

Understanding Views

Microsoft Project provides 26 predefined formats or views for viewing project information, and this book explores all the most frequently used views. The only views I do not explore are those that are for advanced topics or those that have been superseded by improved views.

Help has a good review of all the views. Choose Help, Contents and Index, Reference. Choose the topic Views, Tables, Filters, and Groups. Select Views to see descriptions of the Available Views.

The View menu includes eight of the most commonly used views for quick access, and then provides a More Views command for selecting the rest of the views. These are the same views that are represented by icons on the View bar.

> *View* is the term Microsoft Project uses to describe the way in which the project data is displayed on the screen and in printing. Figure 1.3 is an example of a view: it displays part of the information in a spreadsheet-like *table* on the left side and additional information in a bar graph under a *timescale* on the right side. A view can also contain a *form*, which has the advantage of presenting a lot of information about one task in a compact way. *Combination views* are made up of two separate views that are coordinated to present even more information in one display. You can create your own views to add to the set provided by Microsoft.

A Sampling of the Major Views

If you examine the next five figures (Figure 1.5 to Figure 1.9), you see how different the views in Microsoft Project can be. Each of these views draws on the same set of data, but presents it differently to stress particular aspects of the project or to help managers analyze the project in different ways. Learning to make good use of the different views is an important key to the successful use of Microsoft Project.

FIGURE 1.5

The Gantt Chart view of the project shows how tasks fit into the outline and also how they fit into the timeline.

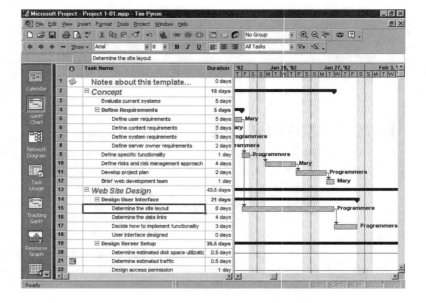

FIGURE 1.6

The Calendar view of the project presents a traditional calendar format for the scheduled activities and is most effective when focused on a subset of tasks—for example, showing the assignments for just one resource.

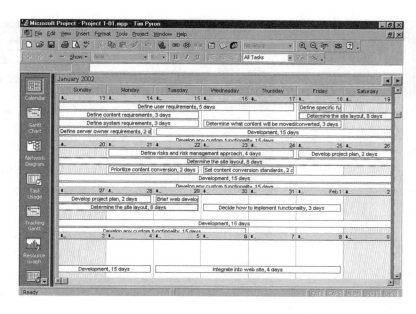

FIGURE 1.7

The Network Diagram view of the same project is like a flow chart, and the connecting arrows emphasize very effectively the planned sequence of tasks.

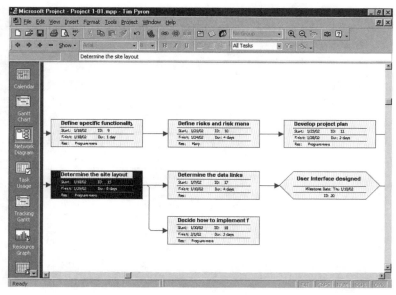

FIGURE 1.8

*The Resource Sheet is
like a spreadsheet with
columns and rows.
Sheet views provide
lots of information in
the compact table for-
mat preferred by many
for data entry.*

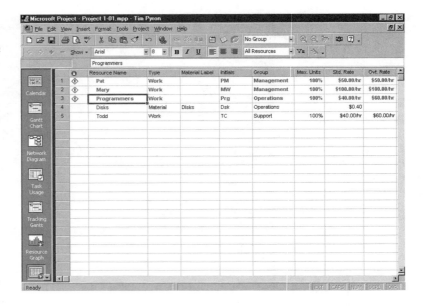

FIGURE 1.9

*The Resource Usage
view displays the task
assignments for each
resource along with the
amount of work that is
scheduled each day.*

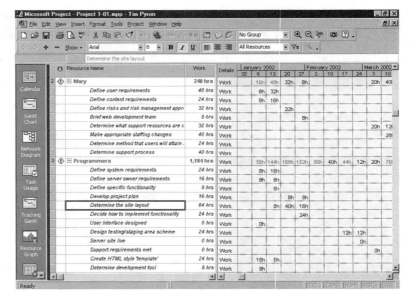

1

Learning to make use of the different views is a key to successful use of Microsoft Project. Each of these views draws on the same set of data, but presents it differently.

- In the Gantt Chart in Figure 1.5, the task named Determine the Site Layout is selected.

- In the Calendar in Figure 1.6, the task named Determine the Site Layout begins on January 18th and extends into future dates.

- In the Network Diagram of Figure 1.7, you see that the same task must finish before either of the tasks, Determine the data links or Decide how to implement functionality, can start.

- In the Resource Sheet in Figure 1.8, you see defining information about the resources such as their cost rates and the groups they belong to.

- In the Resource Usage view of Figure 1.9, you see that this is one of several tasks assigned to the Programmers. You also see how many hours of work are assigned during specific time periods.

Using Views in Combination

You can use the Window, Split command with any view to split the window into a top pane and bottom pane. If the view in the top pane is a task view, the default view in the bottom pane is the Task Form. (Figure 1.10 shows the Gantt Chart in the top pane and the Task Form in the bottom pane.)

The view in the bottom pane always displays only information related to the selection in the top pane. For example, Figure 1.10 shows the Gantt Chart in the top pane and the Task Form in the bottom pane. The task Define User Requirements is selected in the top pane, and the Task Form shows details about the task in the bottom pane.

Combination views are extremely useful for reviewing details about one task in the bottom pane while seeing how the task fits in with the rest of the project in the top pane.

You can remove the split view by choosing Window, Remove Split. You learn more about managing split views in Hour 2, "Becoming an Instant Project Guru."

FIGURE 1.10

Splitting the window in the Gantt Chart produces the Task Entry view, with the Gantt Chart in the top pane and the Task Form in the bottom pane.

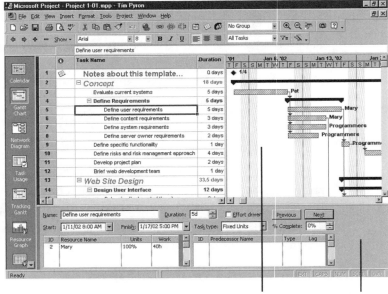

Gantt Chart view   Task Form view

Exiting Microsoft Project 2000

You can exit Microsoft Project by choosing File, Exit, or you can click the application's close button in the upper-right corner of the window.

When you exit the application, all open project files close. If any changes have been made in a project file since you last saved it, a dialog box prompts you to save the changes before closing the file. Choose Yes to save the changes, choose No to close without saving the changes, or choose Cancel if you want to return to work on the project.

> If the Planning Wizard asks you about saving a baseline when you save a file, just click OK for now—you don't need a baseline this early in the game. See "Tracking Work on the Project" in Hour 20.

Summary

In this hour you've seen how the project cycle evolves, from the conception of a goal through presenting final reports. You've also seen how to use the extensive Help system and tutorials. In addition, you've been introduced to the display in the Microsoft Project window and you've developed a passing acquaintance with Project's views.

Q&A

Q I deselected Display Help at Startup on the Help screen when I started Microsoft Project, but now I'd like to have that screen back. How can I do this?

A Use the Project menu and select Tools, Options. Select the General tab and fill the check box next to Display Help On Startup.

Q Are there any other personalities as alternatives to Clipit, the (paper-clip) Office Assistant?

A Yes! To try out a whole gallery of interesting characters, click the Office Assistant tool and choose the Options button. In the Office Assistant dialog box, click the Gallery tab and use the Next button to view each of the personalities. When you find the one you like, click OK. (My favorite is Einstein; but, don't bother asking him about the Theory of General Relativity in this application.)

Exercises

1. Work your way through the Tutorial on the Welcome! Help screen.

2. Choose Reference on the Welcome! Help screen and then choose and then choose Microsoft Project Specifications to see the number of tasks you can have in a project, the number of resources, and so on.

3. Open an existing project file if you have one and use the View bar to look at different views. You won't understand them all yet, but you'll start getting used to the look and feel of Microsoft Project.

HOUR 2

Becoming an Instant Project Guru

In this hour, you learn how to read what the primary Microsoft Project display indicates about a project plan, and you learn techniques, tips, and tricks to make Project display the plan the way that you want to see it.

You may be anxious to start putting a task list together, but some of you have already been given a project file to make sense of and start using right away. Besides, after this hour you are better prepared to start building the task list because you are familiar with the workspace.

In this hour, you will learn:

- How to create a new project file
- How to identify the essential elements of a Gantt Chart
- What a Gantt Chart timescale represents and how to modify it
- Navigation techniques for moving through a Gantt Chart
- Methods for viewing basic Project task information

Practicing with a Sample File

You get the most benefit from this hour if you can display a project file onscreen that is already developed. I recommend that you open the file I use as the basis for my illustrations. It's one of the Project 2000 templates that is copied to your hard disk when you install Microsoft Project. If you already have a project file that you are going to be working with, you can open it also and try things out with both files.

To Do: Creating a Project from a Template File

To create a new file based on a supplied Project template, do the following:

1. Choose File, New from the menu.

2. In the New File dialog box, select the Project Templates tab.

FIGURE 2.1

A variety of supplied templates can help you start a new project.

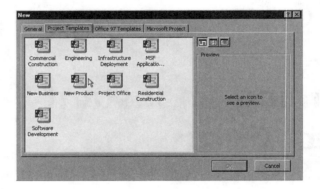

3. Select the New Product template.

4. Click OK.

5. If Project displays a Project Information dialog box requesting date and scheduling information, simply click OK to close the box.

Figure 2.1 shows the template files in the Project Templates category. Notice that there is also a Microsoft Project category and an Office Template tab. The Microsoft Project category was created automatically at installation of Project 2000 because templates from earlier versions of Project were already installed on my hard drive. The Office templates come from my workgroup template list.

If you also want to look at your own file during these exercises, you can open it now. Then you can switch back and forth between your file and the New Product example by opening the Window menu and selecting the file that you want to activate from the numbered list at the bottom of the menu.

Because you're going to be experimenting in ways that could permanently change the display of the project, save the open file with a different name to create a working copy. By doing so, you won't run the risk of accidentally saving the results of our experiments over the original.

To Do: Making a Working Copy of the New Product Template

2

To save a new file, do the following:

1. Choose File, Save As from the menu. In the Save as Type drop-down list, you'll notice that Project assumes the saved file will be a normal Project file, and not a template.

2. In the Save In drop-down list, Project assumes you want to save your file in the folder where all Project files are saved by default. You can Change the location for the file in the Save In list box or change the name of the file in the File Name text box—or do both. You now have a separate, working copy of the original project file.

3. The Planning Wizard may prompt you for a decision about Baseline information. When, why, and how to set a baseline for your project will be discussed in detail in Hour 20, "Tracking Work on the Project." For now, select the default option to save without a baseline and click OK.

You should do the same thing to create a working copy for your own file if you have opened one.

Understanding What You See

Figure 2.2 shows the New Product project screen (with a few changes I've made for illustration purposes). The display consists of a listing of task names on the left and a timeline with horizontal taskbars on the right. Details of a project can be displayed many other ways, but this is the display, the Gantt Chart view, that is most often used in Microsoft Project.

Long ago, Henry Gantt introduced the use of graphical bars drawn on a timeline in his studies of industrial management. It's such an easily understood way to compare and contrast the timeframe for events that it's not only widely used by project managers, but also by historians and scientists who want to explain time relationships. Microsoft Project has paired Gantt's chart with a spreadsheet-like table and called it the Gantt Chart view.

Now, let's start poking around in the Gantt Chart view. Before you get too adventurous, however, let me warn you that the Gantt Chart view is a dangerous place for click-and-drag fiends. The mouse can do powerful things in Microsoft Project, and you need to be especially careful about using click-and-drag until you know what it does. I'll show you those techniques later. For now, just say no.

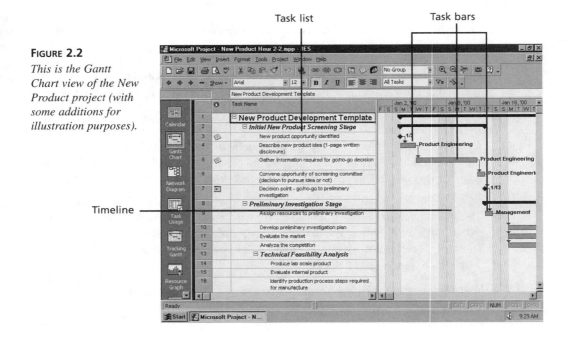

FIGURE 2.2
This is the Gantt Chart view of the New Product project (with some additions for illustration purposes).

The Task Table

The spreadsheet on the left of the view (see Figure 2.3) contains a table that displays the list of tasks that are to be completed for the project. The table has rows, columns, and cells where data is entered and displayed, just like a spreadsheet. Each row represents a project task. Each column displays information from one of Microsoft Project's database fields.

The row numbers on the left are the ID numbers for the tasks. Graphical icons or indicators appear in the second column. The indicators provide important information about the task. If you pause your mouse pointer over an indicator cell, a ScreenTip shows you the meaning of the indicators for that task. For Figure 2.3, some conditions have been set in a sample file so that indicator icons will appear in the second column. For example, the figure shows the ScreenTip for the indicators for Task 5. You can now see the meaning of the indicator icons: the small grid warns you that Task 5 has a Finish No Later

Than constraint set for 1/13/00, and someone has noted that the task will require two team meetings.

FIGURE 2.3
You can review the meaning of an indicator by displaying its ScreenTip.

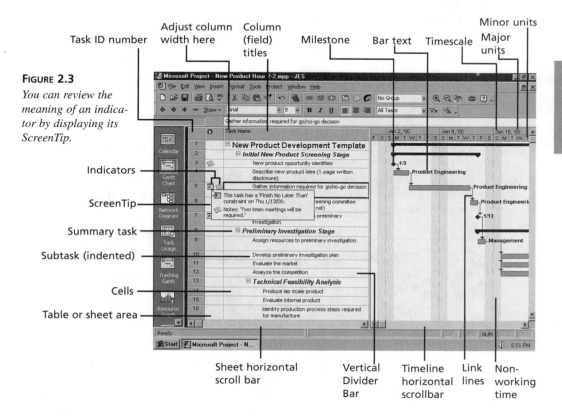

Outlined Task Lists

NEW TERM The Task Name column shows the name of each task. If the task list is outlined, the display is indented to show the outline hierarchy. If a task name is indented, it is a *subtask* belonging to the *summary task* under which it is indented. An outline symbol (a small icon with a plus or minus sign in it) appears to the left of summary task names.

NEW TERM A *summary task* summarizes the important details for its subtasks (those that are indented under it). For instance, the start and finish dates for the summary task span the time between the earliest start and latest finish of any of its subtasks. The cost of the summary task is based on the sum of the cost of all its subtasks.

You can do the following with the minus sign and plus sign outline symbols:

- Click a minus sign outline symbol to hide the summary task's subtasks, leaving only the summary task displayed. The minus sign changes to a plus sign.
- Click a plus sign outline symbol to display a summary task's hidden subtasks (and to restore the minus sign icon).

Hiding the subtask details in order to focus on the larger task groups is a great way to view a summary of what happens in a project. (You learn more about outlining in Hour 3, "Starting a New Project and Working with Tasks.")

Viewing the Other Columns

The table has more columns, but the timeline area on the right hides them. Use the scroll bar below the table, or use the right arrow key, to bring those columns into view. I describe the data that's displayed in these columns later in this hour in the section "Working with the Task Table."

 You can also drag the Vertical Divider bar that separates the sheet and timeline areas to change how much of the window is devoted to each area (refer to Figure 2.3).

The Timeline

The right side of the screen in the Gantt Chart view is sometimes called a *timeline*. It includes the *timescale* (the grid or ruler of time units located at the top) and the bars and other symbols underneath the timescale. Microsoft Project locates the Start and Finish dates for each task row in the timeline area and connects those end points with a line or bar in that task row. This device enables you to see at a glance how the start and finish dates for different tasks are related to each other, and how long each task will take. The vertical shading represents nonworking days like weekends and holidays.

The Timescale

The default timescale displays weeks divided into days. The weeks are the *major time units*, and their dividing lines extend vertically all the way down the timeline. The days are *minor time units*. You can easily display different time units and different labels for those time units. By default the week starts on Sunday, and it is the Sunday date that is used to label each week (refer to Figure 2.3.)

Task Bars

By comparing a task bar to the timeline above, you see when an event begins and ends. Longer bars generally appear to identify the events with longer duration. That can be a little misleading because the bars may include nonworking days, as you will see in the description of Duration.

The task bar for a summary task is black and it spans all the task bars for its subtasks; thus, it shows the overall duration of that group of subtasks.

When a task is represented by a diamond shape in the timeline (see Tasks 3 and 7 in Figure 2.3, for example), the task is a milestone, not really a task with work to be done. Milestones mark important events in the project, such as completion of a significant phase of the project.

NEW TERM   *Milestones* are flags or reference points that mark significant events or accomplishments in the project. Although they are entered as tasks, they typically have no work associated with them directly and are instead markers indicating turning points in the project.

Use the scroll bar beneath the timeline to scroll to later or earlier dates and view other task bars and milestones.

Bar Text

You can display text next to the task bars. For instance, Task 3 is a milestone, and by default Project displays the date next to the diamond shape for milestones. Also, the standard Gantt Chart shows resource names to the right of task bars. Some standard resource types were already assigned in the New Product template.

> You are not limited to the standard Gantt Chart formatting. You might want to change task bar colors, the milestone marker shapes, or what text is printed next to the task bars. See Hour 9, "Formatting Views," for a complete discussion of Gantt Chart formatting.

Link Lines

The lines with arrow points that connect tasks represent *links* between tasks that define the order in which they must be executed. For example, the arrow drawn from the finish of Task 4 points to the start of Task 5. That means that Task 4 must be finished before Task 5 can start. Task 4 is said to be the *predecessor* of Task 5.

NEW TERM   *Links* are used to define the sequence in which tasks must be scheduled. When two tasks are linked, one is called the *predecessor* and its schedule determines the schedule for the other task (called the *successor*).

Displaying the link lines is optional. If you don't want the lines cluttering up the space you can hide them. Choose Format, Layout from the menu to display the Layout dialog box (see Figure 2.4) and select the first button in the Links group. Click OK.

FIGURE 2.4
You can govern the display of task link lines with the Layout dialog box.

Working with the Timeline

Now that you know a little more about what the Gantt Chart view displays, let's look at the techniques for moving around in the view to see different parts of the project and for changing the way the information is displayed. You'll start with the timeline on the right side of the screen and then move back over to the table in the sheet area.

Scrolling the Timeline

Use the horizontal scroll bar below the timeline to scroll back and forth in time from the start date to the finish date of the project. If you drag the scroll button, a ScreenTip indicates what date is displayed at the left edge of the timescale when you release the button. Drag the horizontal scroll button all the way to the left to go to the beginning of the project and all the way to the right to go to the end of the project.

The following are some handy keyboard alternatives for scrolling the timeline in the Gantt Chart view:

- Alt+Home jumps to the start date for the project.
- Alt+End jumps to the finish date for the project.
- Alt+Right arrow and Alt+Left arrow scroll right and left, one day at a time.
- Alt+Page Down and Alt+Page Up scroll right and left by one screen at a time.

Additional keyboard shortcuts are listed and described under the Help topics. To locate the Help screen, choose Help, Contents, and Index from the menu. On the right side of the Help display, click the icon next to Reference. In the Reference area, point to the underlined phrase, keyboard shortcut. Click to display a categorized list of possible keyboard shortcuts. You might want to print a list and keep it handy. You can print the list of keys by choosing Options, Print Topic.

If you drag the horizontal scroll button all the way to the right (or press Alt+End), you are at the finish of the project. You probably have to scroll down the task list to find the tasks whose task bars appear in this date range.

Finding a Task Bar or a Specific Date in the Timeline

 If you have selected a task in the table and you want to see its task bar in the timeline, click the Go To Selected Task tool on the Standard toolbar. Project scrolls the timeline to show the beginning of the task bar.

Use the Edit, Go To command (Ctrl+G) to display the Go To dialog box (see Figure 2.5) if you want to jump to a specific date in the timeline. Enter a date in the Date box or click the down arrow in the Date box to display the date-picker calendar. You can scroll the months with the arrows at the top of the little calendar and then click a date to select it. Click OK to jump to that date in the timeline. You can also type in just a number to jump to that date in the current month. For example, if the current date is October 20, 2000 and you want to go to October 3, 2000, just type in the number **3**.

The Date box also accepts the words "today", "tomorrow", and days of the week, and jumps to those dates. This is especially helpful for those of us who don't know what day it is.

FIGURE 2.5

Use the Go To command to jump to specific dates in the timeline.

Adjusting the Units on the Timescale

The timescale has two rows. The top row is called the *major scale* and its tick lines run all the way down the screen. The bottom row subdivides the major scale and is called the *minor scale*. You can customize the amount of time encompassed by the units on each of the scales and you can change the labels that appear in the units. The following techniques provide quick adjustments to the timescale.

You can quickly zoom in to see smaller time units (for example days instead of weeks or hours instead of days) or zoom out to see longer time periods compressed in the display area. Clicking the Zoom In tool on the Standard toolbar (the magnifying glass with the plus sign) expands the timescale so that task bars become longer, and you see more detail in the same area of the screen. If you get carried away clicking the Zoom In tool you can display time units as small as 15-minute intervals. You could micromanage restroom breaks with this display.

If you want to compress the timescale, so that you see less detail and a longer span of time on one screen, click the Zoom Out tool (the magnifying glass with the minus sign). You can zoom out so far that you see seven or eight years at once, each divided into two half-year periods.

Project can adjust the timescale so that your entire project fits tidily in the space that is currently available on the screen. To do this, you need to choose the View menu, and select the Zoom command to display the Zoom dialog box (see Figure 2.6). Select Entire Project and then click OK. The Reset button in the Zoom dialog box returns you to the default timeline (weeks divided into successive days).

FIGURE 2.6

Use the Zoom command to have Project compress the timescale and display the entire project.

For ultimate control over the timescale, double-click over the timescale itself to display the Timescale dialog box (or choose Format, Timescale from the menu). In Figure 2.7, I have changed the Major Scale Label to spell out the month and I've changed the Minor Scale Label to display the month/day number instead of the day letter. You can see the results in the background in Figure 2.8.

Major Scale settings

FIGURE 2.7

The Timescale dialog box enables you to customize every part of the timescale.

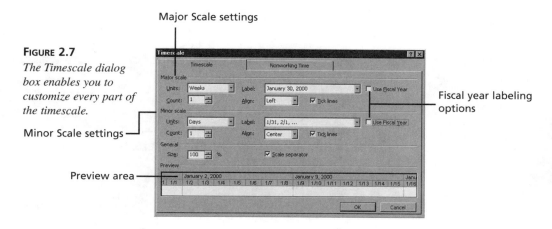

Minor Scale settings

Fiscal year labeling options

Preview area

Here's a trick question: When is June not the 6th month of the year? Answer: when the "year" is a fiscal year that does not start on January 1. You can set the beginning of your fiscal year in Project, if it does not match a calendar year, and then set Project to display time periods (such as months and quarters) with the appropriate fiscal year label. Choose Tools, Options, Calendar, and change the Fiscal year starts in month setting. Then, in the Format, Timescale dialog box, turn on the options for major or minor scale labels to reflect the fiscal year instead of the calendar year.

For example, suppose your company's fiscal year begins July 1. InTools, Options, Calendar, set the Fiscal Year Starts in month to July. In Figure 2.8, I've chosen to display Quarters on the major timescale and Months on the minor timescale. The major scale has also been set to label the time periods according to the fiscal year. So here you have activity for the month of June accurately labeled as occurring at the end of the 4th quarter. A calendar year label would show June as the end of the 2nd quarter.

The Nonworking Time tab enables you to control how the shading is displayed for nonworking days. In Figure 2.9, I've chosen to display the shading in front of the task bars. Many people prefer this because it hides the nonworking parts of task bars, and the visible length of the bar more accurately reflects the duration. The shading also avoids agitating a work force that would otherwise see task bars stretching across Thanksgiving and Christmas holidays, creating the impression that people would have to come in to work on those days. By placing the shading in front, it's obvious that work is not scheduled for those nonworking days.

FIGURE 2.8

Timescale Labeling options allow you to see time periods according to Fiscal Years, whenever the fiscal year begins.

Fiscal Year labeling option

Calendar Year labels

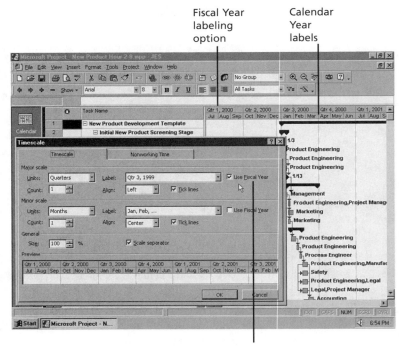

Fiscal Year labels

FIGURE 2.9

You can also control the display of shading for nonworking days with the Timescale dialog box.

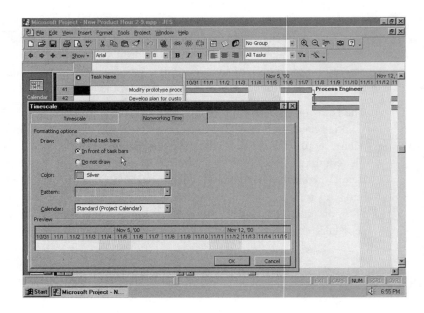

Working with the Task Table

In this section you look at some techniques for finding information quickly in the table and for changing the way the data is displayed.

As pointed out earlier, you can drag the vertical divider bar right and left to change the amount of the table that you see. If the divider bar falls in the middle of a column, you can double-click the divider bar to make it snap to the nearest column border.

With the vertical divider bar moved out of the way in Figure 2.10, you can see all the columns in the task table.

FIGURE 2.10

View columns of inter-est by positioning the vertical divider bar on the Gantt Chart.

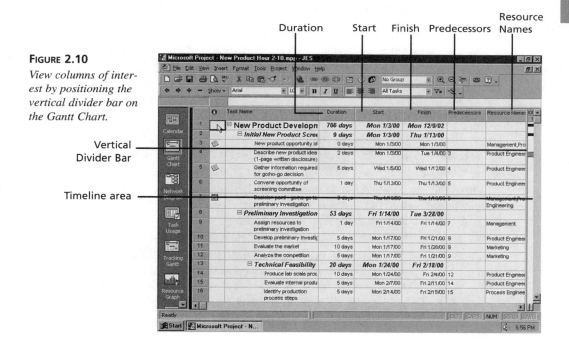

The following list provides a brief description of each additional column:

- *Duration.* Duration is the number of hours, days, or weeks during which work is going on for the task. The duration for Task 5 is six days. Notice from Figure 2.2 that the task bar extends over and seems to include the weekend days; however, those days are shaded to indicate that they are nonworking days.

- *Start.* The Start column shows the scheduled start date for the task.

- *Finish.* The Finish column contains the scheduled finish date for the task.

- *Predecessors.* This column shows the ID number for a task's predecessors—other tasks that need to go before this task. (You look at linking tasks into predecessor sequences in Hour 6, "Linking Tasks in the Correct Sequence.")
- *Resource Names.* If resources have been assigned to work on tasks, their names appear here.

> To change the width of a column, place the mouse over the right edge of the column title (over the line dividing the column title from the column title to the right). When the mouse turns into a single vertical line with arrows pointing left and right, drag the dividing line left or right. If you double-click the dividing line, Project adjusts the column on the left of the dividing line to accommodate the widest cell entry in that column. In the case of some columns, such as the Predecessor column in Figure 2.10, the widest entry is the column title itself.

Navigating Through the Task List

The vertical scroll bar at the far right of the window adjusts the rows of the table that you see, and consequently the section of the timeline that you see also. If you drag the scroll button, a ScreenTip indicates the ID number and name of the task that appears at the top of the screen when you release the scroll button. Dragging the scroll button all the way to the bottom of the scroll bar displays the last task in the task list.

> You can also use the keyboard to move through the task list, as described in the following list. Using the keyboard, however, actually moves the cell selection, whereas using the scroll bar enables you to look at a different part of the task list without changing the cell that is selected and, consequently, losing your place.

The Up and Down arrow keys move through the task list a row at a time. The Page Up and Page Down keys move whole screens at a time. Alternatively, other keystroke combinations enable you to move quickly through the table.

- Ctrl+Up arrow jumps to the first task row but keeps the selection in the same column in which you start.

- Ctrl+Down arrow jumps to the last task row keeping the selection in the same column in which you start.
- Ctrl+Home jumps to the first task row and selects the first column.
- Ctrl+End jumps to the last task row, but it selects the last column. You need to press Home to scroll the task name for the row into view.
- Home jumps to the first column of the task row in which you start.
- End jumps to the last column of the task row in which you start.

> The Go To dialog box used earlier in this hour to move quickly to a specific date can also be used to move quickly to a specific task. Choose Edit, Go To (or press function key F5), and supply the ID number of the task to move to.

Finding Tasks by Name

If your project has a long list of tasks, you may find it helpful to search for a task by name. For that matter, you can search any of the columns for a particular value, but finding task names is the most common objective.

Note that your selection doesn't have to be in the column that you want to search. You can tell Project which field to look in. The search commences, however, from the row your selection is in and proceeds down the list. After the search reaches the last task, it continues from the top of the task list until it reaches the task row in which you started. You also have the option of reversing the direction of the search, to search up from the starting row. After the search reaches the first task, it continues from the bottom of the list until it reaches the starting point.

To Do: Finding a Task

To find a task in the New Product project that has the word "decision" in its name, follow these steps:

1. Choose Edit, Find from the menu to display the Find dialog box (see Figure 2.11).
2. Type the word or series of letters for which you are searching in the Find What text box. I've typed in **decision**.
3. The Look In field box displays the field (column) Name by default. This is the actual name of the data field displayed in the Task Name column. You can change the field to be searched by selecting a different field name. For example, if you want to search task notes, you would click the Look In field box and select the Notes field.

FIGURE 2.11

Use the Find command to locate tasks by keywords in their names.

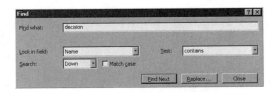

4. The entry in the Test box determines the type of comparison that is to be made between your search value and the values Project finds in the search field. The default test is "contains" because it is the most commonly used. This test finds any task name that contains the letters "decision" anywhere in the name. Other tests are available, but you and I only have 24 hours, so I have to pass on explaining them.

5. Change the direction of the search, if you prefer, by clicking Up or Down in the Search box.

6. If you want to find only instances that match the exact upper- and lowercase letters that you typed in, fill the Match Case check box. Leave it unchecked to accept either case.

7. To initiate the search, click the Find Next button. If a match is found, the cell containing the match is selected. Click Find Next again until the match for which you were looking is found. You can also close the dialog box after the first match is found and press Shift+F4 to continue searching in the direction you chose. That way, the dialog box is not in the way when you look at the selected cells.

Changing the Date Format

The default format for dates is the mm/dd/yy pattern, and this is the format that you see in the Start and Finish columns of the New Product project. You can add the time of day to the display, or switch to any one of a number of date format options. Be aware, however, that the display will be the same for all date fields throughout all the views in Microsoft Project, and it applies to all the project files that you view. While looking at some projects you may want to include time of day, for example, and for others you might want to include the day of the week.

To Do: Changing the Date Display Format

To change the date formatting throughout the Project file, do the following:

1. Select Tools, Options from the menu to display the Options dialog box.

2. On the View tab, select the format that you want in the Date format box (see Figure 2.12).

FIGURE 2.12

Select the format for dates in the Options dialog box.

2

3. Click the OK button to make the change effective.

4. If any cells in the Start or Finish columns display all # signs, you need to widen the column to display the new format. Simply double-click the column divider line to the right of the title for the column you want to adjust. For example, if the Start column needs to be adjusted, double-click the line separating the titles Start and Finish.

For international changes in date and time formats, you must use the Regional Settings applet in the Microsoft Windows Control Panel (Start, Settings, Control Panel, Regional Settings).

Using Wordwrap to See Long Task Names

NEW FEATURE
One way to see more columns in the table or sheet portion of the Gantt Chart is to reduce the width of the Task Name column, but then you usually can't see all the task name text. The solution is to increase the height of the rows; Microsoft Project automatically wraps the entries in each cell. In Project 2000, the row height can be set for each individual row; a mixture of row heights on a single table is now allowed.

To Do: Wrapping Long Task Names

To control the display of long cell entries follow these steps:

1. Move the mouse pointer over the line dividing any two row numbers in the task ID column.

2. When the pointer's shape changes to a single horizontal line with arrows pointing up and down, drag the dividing line up or down to the new row height that you want to use.

   You can increase the height to any size you'd like, but you cannot shrink it to the point of hiding the task. There is a minimum height that can't be changed.

3. Adjust the width of the Task Name column and Microsoft Project automatically wordwraps any entry that needs more than one line to display.

To change the height for more than one row at a time, select several rows first, and then change the height for one of them; they will all change together.

Changing the Columns

Sometimes, you may want to change the column titles to match common usage within your organization, or you may even want to change the contents of a column. For example, you could change the title of the Name column to "What has to be done," or you could display the Notes field in place of the Resource Names field in the last column. To modify the column, simply double-click the column title and Project displays the Column Definition dialog box (see Figure 2.13). The following list describes the options in the Column Definition dialog box.

- If you want to change the content of the column, select a different field in the Field name box.
- Change the entry in the Title box to modify the column title. If you don't supply an entry in the Title box, Project displays the field name as the column title.
- You can select the alignment (left, center, or right) for the title with the Align title box and for the data with the Align data box.
- Clicking the OK button installs the changes you have selected.
- Clicking the Best Fit button installs the changes just like the OK button does, but it also adjusts the column width to accommodate the longest cell entry.

FIGURE 2.13

Change what is displayed in a column by double-clicking the title itself.

Many, if not most, of the fields listed in the Field Name drop-down list are probably unfamiliar to you. The complete list of Project's database fields is available through Help. Choose Help, Contents, and Index. On the right side of the Help screen, click on the Reference icon. On the Reference screen, scroll down to the Reference content in Help section, and choose Fields Reference.

If you don't care to see a column, you can delete it from the sheet without losing the data that it displays. Simply click the column title to select the entire column and then press the Delete key.

To insert a new column in the table, select the column title that is now in the place you want the new column to be and press the Insert key. The Column Definition dialog box appears, and you can select the column options as described previously.

Inserting, deleting, and modifying columns as described in this hour permanently changes the way a table looks. For information on how to keep your current table as it is and create another, similar table, see Hour 18, "Creating Custom Views."

Viewing More Task Details

The Gantt Chart view packs a lot of information. You can see even more details about individual tasks with either the Task Information dialog box or by splitting the screen and viewing the Task Form. You look at both of these ways to view more information before wrapping up this hour.

Using the Task Information Dialog Box

Click the Task Information tool on the Standard toolbar to display a dialog box that includes many details about the selected task (see Figure 2.14). You can also open the Task Information dialog box by right-clicking on a task name and choosing Task Information, and most of the time you can simply double-click on a task to open this box (there are some exceptions to this method, though).

The five tabs in the dialog box provide access to many additional fields. If you have a summary task selected, the Summary Task dialog box is displayed. Some fields are dimmed and unavailable on the Summary Task dialog box because those fields are calculated by Project from the subtasks for the summary task and can't be changed manually.

For now, just note that in any view where you can select a task, you can see all of these fields by selecting the Task Information tool—even if the fields are not normally displayed in the view with which you are working. Also note that the last tab, the Notes tab, contains the full text of the Notes field. You can go directly to this tab for the selected task by clicking the Task Notes tool on the Standard toolbar.

NEW FEATURE In Project 2000, you can also select a task by clicking once on its Gantt Chart bar. The toolbar buttons for the Task Information dialog box and Task Notes tool are also available by selecting the bar in this way, instead of selecting a cell on the table side of the view.

FIGURE 2.14

The Task Information dialog box provides a great deal of information about a selected task.

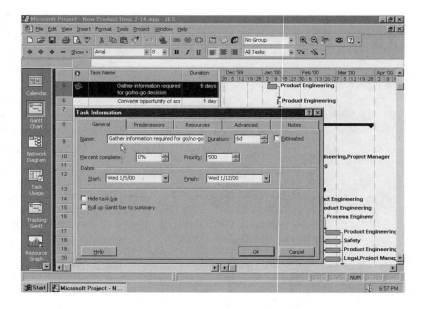

Using Combination Views

One of the most useful and powerful display techniques that Microsoft Project provides is the capability to split the screen in half and see two different views of the project simultaneously. Choose Window, Split to split the screen. You can also double-click the split box, which is located immediately below the arrow at the bottom of the vertical scroll bar (see Figure 2.15).

2

FIGURE 2.15

The combination view of the Gantt Chart and the Task Form shows the essential details for the task that is selected in the top pane.

Gantt Chart

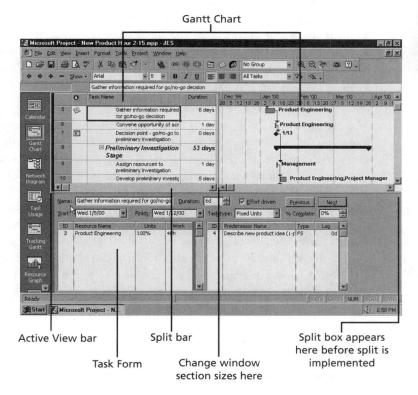

Active View bar

Task Form

Split bar

Change window section sizes here

Split box appears here before split is implemented

The window is split into two panes: the top pane shows the view with which you were working and the bottom pane shows either the Task Form (if you started with a task view) or the Resource Form (if you started with a resource view). Because the Gantt Chart is a task view, the bottom pane is the Task Form (see Figure 2.15). You can remove the split just as easily: choose Window, Remove Split or double-click the split box, which is now at the center of the screen. Drag the Split bar up or down to change the division of the screen between the top and bottom panes. You can also change the sizes of all sections of the screen at one time: pause the mouse at the intersection of the vertical divider bar in the Gantt Chart and the horizontal split bar; when the mouse pointer becomes a four-headed arrow, click and drag the intersecting lines to change the proportions of all sections on the screen.

Task 5, "Gather information required for go/no go decision," is selected in the top pane in Figure 2.15, and that is the task whose details appear in the bottom pane. By default, the bottom form displays all the fields that I've been discussing from the columns of the Gantt Chart table. This split arrangement enables you to see those field values and more of the timeline at the same time. You are also able to see additional fields—Effort Driven, Task Type, and % Complete—as well as much more detail about resources and predecessors. Altogether, this split screen is a very efficient way to view the tasks in a project. You can see how the task fits into the overall scheme of things in the top pane, and you can see many significant details in the bottom pane.

You can enter task information in either pane, but you must activate the pane before you can use it. To activate the bottom pane, simply click anywhere in the bottom pane. You can also use the F6 function key to toggle back and forth between the panes. The pane that is active at the moment displays a darker shade in its half of the Active View bar.

The two mini-tables at the bottom of the Task Form initially display resource and predecessor details. You can select different details to display in this area. First, activate the bottom pane. Then choose Format, Details from the menu to see a cascading list of details you can display. (You can also right-click the bottom pane to display the list of available details). For example, if you choose Notes, you see the full text of the Notes field. You can then move down the task list in the top pane and read the notes attached to each task in the bottom pane. It's a good way to review all the notes.

Summary

You've covered a lot of ground in this hour. You've learned how to interpret the standard project display (the Gantt Chart) and how to make changes in the way it displays the project data. You've also learned how to move through the project task list and timeline with ease. Finally, you've discovered ways to view more details about the project with the Task Information dialog box and the Task Form.

Q&A

Q **I split the screen to look at the Gantt Chart and the Task Form. Now I want to look at one of the other views, but I want it to fill the screen. Is there a quick way to do that?**

A Glad you asked! If you have a combination view on the screen and want to display a new view as a full-screen view, just hold down the Shift key as you click the View icon on the View Bar (or as you select the view from the View menu). Similarly, if you have a full-screen view and would like to add another view in the lower pane, do the same thing: hold down the Shift key as you select the new view and it appears in the bottom pane.

Q **If you delete a column in the table on the left side of the Gantt Chart, do you lose all that data?**

A No, the data is secure. Deleting a column merely removes the display of that field from the current view; it doesn't delete the information.

Q **I dragged the vertical divider bar over to see more columns. How do I get my timeline back?**

A A common problem. Drag the mouse slowly toward the right side of the screen. When the mouse is over the divider bar, the pointer shape will change to two vertical parallel lines with arrows pointing right and left. You won't be able to drag the divider bar back to the left unless the mouse pointer changes to the appropriate shape.

Exercises

Your manager has suggested you open a supplied Project template to see if it can be a good starting point for your own software development project. In the following steps, you create a new file based on a template and examine its contents a variety of ways. See the Introduction for instructions to access the solutions for this exercise on the book's Web page.

1. Create a project file based on the Software Development template.

2. Navigate through the project to answer the following questions:

    How many tasks are in the project?

    How many tasks are milestones?

    What is the scheduled start date of the first task in the list?

    What is the scheduled finish date of the last task in the list?

3. Change the timescale to display Months over Weeks. Change the bottom label to a month/day display (mm/dd).

4. Increase the row height and wordwrap the task names for Tasks 2–5.

5. Investigate Task 8, "Conduct needs analysis." Split the screen to display a form at the bottom. Does Task 8 have any resources already assigned to it? If so, who? Also, does Task 8 have any predecessor tasks? If so, which one?

HOUR 3

Starting a New Project and Working with Tasks

In this hour, you begin the new document for your project. If you've been given a project file to work with, you can use it to work through the features presented here. This hour covers preparing for your first project file, starting the project file, and putting together the list of things to do in the project—the task list. Hours 4, "Starting the Scheduling Process," 5, "Defining When Project Can Schedule Tasks," and 6, "Linking Tasks in the Correct Sequence," show you how to turn that list of tasks into a schedule or timeline.

In this hour, you will learn:

- How to start and document a new project
- General concepts for creating a task list
- What information to enter when creating a task list
- How to modify a task list and give it an outline structure
- What steps to take to password protect your Project files

Things to Do When Starting a New Project File

It's ironic that many people adopt Microsoft Project to help them get organized, but then don't want to bother with an organized approach to using Project. There are three things I urge you to do at the beginning of any new project:

- Set the start or finish date for the project, which gives Project a peg on which to base its schedule calculations.
- Record the goal or objective of the project to guide your planning. It will prove invaluable in keeping you focused on the end result.
- Change any of the critical default options that govern how Microsoft Project calculates the schedule for your project.

You can do these things after you've already started a project file, and you can change them as often as you want, but it saves time to take care of them up front.

Starting a New Project File

When you start a new project document, you need to define for Microsoft Project the start or ending date for the project—usually the date on which work will begin or a deadline date by which the project must be completed. Project schedules your tasks based on the fixed start or finish date. You should also record the project goal when you start the new document and select any of the option settings that you want to change for that project.

Setting the Start or Finish Date for the Project

When you start a new project document, Microsoft Project displays the Project Information dialog box. In this dialog box you are expected to tell Project whether a fixed start date or a fixed finish date governs the schedule. Project schedules all work from the date you select.

New Term   If you know when you want work to start on your project, and you don't have a deadline by which it must be finished, enter the date you want work to start and let Project calculate a schedule from that date forward. The project is said to be scheduled from a *fixed start date*.

If your project has a deadline date by which it must be finished, enter that date as the project's finish date and let Microsoft Project calculate a schedule backward from that date that guarantees all tasks will be completed by the finish date. The project is said to be scheduled from a *fixed finish date*.

Although it sounds tempting to back-schedule from a finish date, it isn't the best technique. We tend to think and plan by looking ahead, not backward. Similarly, Project's scheduling capabilities are at their best when it schedules going forward in time. Your goal is to put all required tasks into a schedule and then see if the schedule will meet your requirements. Your job as project manager is to review and maintain the project schedule, letting Project tell you where the plan has gotten off track and by how much.

You should pick a start date and let Project schedule tasks from that date. Project schedules all tasks to be started as soon as possible after that date based on other information you enter, including the order in which tasks ought to occur, any intermediate deadlines that have to be met, and the availability of resources assigned to work on the tasks. The schedule that Project calculates will produce a finish date for the project.

If your project is required to be finished by a deadline date over which you have no control, you can enter that finish date and tell Project to schedule the project to be finished by that date. Project schedules all activity to be completed by the fixed finish date. The schedule Project calculates will produce a project start date that tells you when work has to begin, or should have begun, to finish by the deadline.

To Do: Starting a New File and Defining Start or Finish Date

To begin scheduling a new Project file, do the following:

1. Choose File, New from the menu to base your plan on a supplied Project template, or click the New tool on the Standard toolbar to open a new project document. Project displays the Project Information dialog box (see Figure 3.1).

2. In the Schedule From box, select Project Start Date or Project Finish Date, depending on your requirements.

   If you select Project Start Date, the Start date box is accessible and the Finish date box is dimmed. If you select Project Finish Date, the Start date box is dimmed and the Finish date box is accessible.

3. Enter the project start date or finish date in the appropriate box.

FIGURE 3.1

Settings in the Project Information dialog box determine whether the project is scheduled from a fixed start date or to meet a fixed finish date.

▼

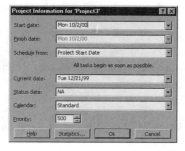

▼   Click the down arrow in the date box if you want to select the date from a pop-up
      calendar. Change months with the scroll arrows on either side of the calendar's title
      bar, and click on the date you want to be entered in the box.

> Project also stores the time of day as part of these dates, even if you are not
> displaying one of the date formats that include the time of day.
>
> If you enter a project start date, Project includes the default start time you
> enter in the Calendar tab of the Options dialog box. If you enter a project
> finish date, Project includes the default end time as part of the date. If this
> project is to begin or end at a non-default time, be sure to include the time
> with the date you enter.
>
> For example, if you have set the default end time to be 5:00 p.m., but you
> want this project to end by noon on January 4, 2001, you would enter
> **1/4/01 12:00 p.m.** in the Finish date box.

▲   4. Click OK to close the dialog box.

You can access the Project Information dialog box at any time by choosing Project,
Project Information from the menu. You can change the start or finish date as needed,
and you can change whether the project is to be scheduled from a fixed start date or a
fixed finish date.

Record the Goal and Scope of the Project

NEW TERM When starting a new project, one of the first things you should do is to state
clearly the project's objective or goal.   The goal must include a well-defined
deliverable, or final result, something that can be measured to determine whether the
project is meeting or has met its objectives. There should be a clear statement of any
important assumptions or limitations, such as time and budget constraints or the quality
of the final product. You should show this statement to all parties with an interest in the
project outcome and protect yourself against future misunderstandings by getting an
agreement from them that this statement of the objective is accurate.

The goal or objective statement for the project doesn't have to be a lofty, superbly
crafted statement. It just needs to state clearly in a few sentences what the project is
designed to accomplish. If you don't have this goal clearly in mind, your plans are going
to lack the direction and clarity of purpose they need to succeed.

A good place to record the project goal is in the Comments box of the Properties dialog
box. This dialog box is also the place to enter items such as the project's title, the com-

pany or organization's name, and the project manager. It's important to supply these entries because they can be used in headers and footers on printed reports to identify the project.

To Do: Recording Document Properties

To Do

To include the project goals and other key information in the file, do the following:

1. Choose File, Properties from the menu to display the Properties dialog box. Be sure the Summary tab is selected (see Figure 3.2).

FIGURE 3.2

Supply general information about the project in the Properties dialog box.

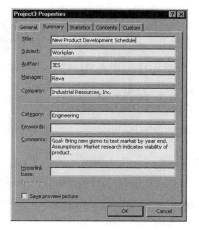

3

2. In the Title box, enter the project title that you want to appear on printed reports. Project places the filename in this box until you type something of your own there.

3. Your username should appear automatically in the Author box. Change it if necessary to the spelling you want to appear on reports.

4. Place the project manager's name in the Manager box. This information is also commonly used in reports.

5. Place the company or organization name, also for use in reports, in the Company box.

6. Place the project goal in the Comments box. This box can hold several thousand characters, but the typical goal statement is much shorter than that.

▲ 7. When finished, click the OK button.

Choosing Microsoft Project's Operating Defaults

The first time you use Microsoft Project you should take the time to set the options that
govern Project's default assumptions and behavior. A few of these options are critical
because they affect the data values that Project records when you add to or edit the project document. I'm going to suggest the settings I think are best in this hour, and show
you how to make them the standard settings for all your future work. However, I'll defer
any thorough explanation of them until later hours where the operations they affect will
be discussed.

NEW FEATURE You now have more control over one important aspect of Project that is not a
scheduling feature: where your Project files are saved by default and whether
you want Project to automatically save your work for you every few minutes.

To Do: Setting Default Values for Critical Options

To change underlying settings for your Project files, including default file storage location and file saving options, follow these steps:

1. Choose Tools, Options from the menu to display the Options dialog box (see
   Figure 3.3).

2. Select the General tab and clear the check box for Automatically Add New
   Resources and Tasks. You'll see why in Hour 11, "Defining Resources and Costs."

   Click the Set as Default button to make this the default for all future projects.
   Otherwise, you will be changing the settings just for the current project.

FIGURE 3.3

*The Options dialog
box is your control
panel for determining
critical features of
Project's calculations.*

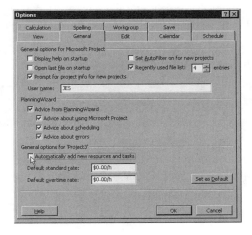

▼   3. Select the Calendar tab and set the values in each box described in the following list to match your organization's work schedule. These are critical options that determine how Project interprets the data you enter, so it's important that they reflect your organization's practices.

- Set Default *Start* Time to the time people normally begin work in your organization. The default is 8:00 a.m., but if your organization's hours are from 7:00 a.m. to 4:00 p.m., for example, change this entry to 7:00 a.m.

- Set Default *End* Time to the normal end of the working day for your organization.

- Set Hours per *Day* to the normal hours for employees in your organization. The default is 8 hours a day. If your organization lets people work four 10-hour days a week, with three days off, you should enter 10 in this field. This value determines how Project interprets this information when you set the length of a task in "days."

- Set Hours per *week* to match the total hours employees work per week. The default is 40. This value determines how Project interprets this information when you set the length of a task in "weeks."

Click the Set as Default button to make these Calendar options the default for all future projects.

4. Select the Schedule tab and clear the check box for the option Autolink Inserted or Moved Tasks. This option will be explained in Hour 6.

Click the Set as Default button to make this setting the default for all future projects.

5. Select the Save tab and turn on the option to Auto Save either the active file or all open files. Work will be saved every 10 minutes, by default, but you can change that value to any number between 1 and 120 minutes.

Experimenting is part of the power of Project; be sure to also turn on the Prompt Before Saving option to give you more control over what is saved.

Change the default storage folder for your files by clicking on the Projects line in the File Types section and then clicking the Modify button.

▲   Click the Set as Default button to make this setting the default for all future projects.

When you start a new project document from now on, these default values will be in place.

Now that you have entered the information that defines the project, the next step is to start defining the major tasks or groups of tasks for the project.

Starting the Task List

You can put together the list of activities or tasks for the project in several ways. The most common method is to build an outline of the work that has to be done on the project. Start by listing the large blocks of activity or major phases of the project. Then break down each phase into greater detail by listing more narrowly defined tasks, known as *subtasks*, that contribute to completing the major phase. Continue to break down the work into subtasks until you have identified all the activities you want to keep track of in the project.

 NEW TERM   A *subtask* is a detail item that is part of a larger task. If Relocate Wall is a task in a remodeling project, one of its subtasks might be Tear Down Existing Wall and another one could be Frame New Walls.

If you were remodeling a house, for example, the phases or major tasks might be Relocate Walls, Painting, and Carpeting. Each phase or major task can be broken down into smaller tasks. Subtasks for the Relocate Walls task might be Tear Down Existing Wall, Frame New Wall, Install New Wiring, Install New Plumbing, and so forth.

> It's an art deciding how finely detailed your task list should be. For the Relocate Walls example, subtasks such as Tear Down Existing Wall, Frame New Wall, and Install New Wiring might be reasonable. However, breaking the list down to the level of Pull Out Old Nails and Carry Debris Outside is too detailed to be useful.

Don't list every little thing that has to be done, but list everything you want to monitor to be sure it's completed. The smallest tasks—the lowest level of the outline—should be fairly short in duration (compared to the overall duration of the project) and should be easily observed or monitored.

It's also possible to create the task list by importing an already prepared task list from another source. You can start with a template like those supplied by Microsoft Project during installation, or you can import into Project a task list that was created in some other application like Excel or Word. You learned how to open a template in the last hour. In this hour, you'll first build a list from scratch, but then I'll also show you how to import a prepared task list.

One final note: I'm going to concentrate in this hour on building and editing the task list and defer until later the discussion of how you turn that list into a schedule with start and finish dates. After you know how to use Project, you might prefer to combine some of these techniques and enter scheduling details as you create the task list.

As you add tasks to the list, Project is going to fill in some scheduling information in its calculated fields. You will see a default Duration of "1 day" or "1 day?" appear as soon as you enter the task name. You can change that entry if you want, but I will defer discussing duration and other scheduling issues until the next hour. You will also see default Start and Finish dates appear, which are both initially set to the project's fixed start or finish date. Don't worry about them for now. You'll give Project better information for calculating those dates in the next hour.

Creating the Initial List

The easiest way to build the task list is to start brainstorming and list the top-level tasks in the table on the left side of the Gantt Chart view. Click in a cell in the Task Name column and type in the name of a major phase or top-level task for the project. You can use any characters on the keyboard as part of the task name, including numbers and spaces. Names do not have to be unique, so you can have, for example, several tasks named "Stop to Assess Progress."

When you press Enter, Project automatically fills in a default Duration (1 day or an estimated 1 day) and schedules the task to start and finish on the project's fixed start date (or fixed finish date). Project then moves the selection to the cell below so you can enter the next task.

Project 2000 assumes your duration entry for a new task is really a "guestimate." By default, it enters a value 1 day for the duration, followed by a question mark to indicate that the value has not been confirmed by your project team and is subject to change. If you would rather Project not make this assumption, and have it simply insert a 1 day default duration, choose Tools, Options, Schedule tab and clear the setting for New Tasks Have Estimated Durations. See Hour 4 for more information regarding duration values.

You can leave blank rows in the list where you plan to fill in detail later, or you can wait and insert blank rows when you get ready to type in the details.

Keeping Notes About Tasks

It's an excellent idea to attach notes to tasks to remind yourself of important ideas. Notes also explain to others why you've done particular things in the project plan. The notes can also be included in printed reports you prepare for the project.

To add a note to a task, select the task and click the Task Notes tool on the Standard toolbar. The Task Information dialog box will appear with the Notes tab selected (see Figure 3.4). Type the note directly in the Notes box.

You can enhance the note's text with the formatting controls at the top of the Notes box. The usual buttons are available for font formatting, text alignment, and creating bulleted text. Also, a graphics control lets you insert an image, such as a logo, into the Note field.

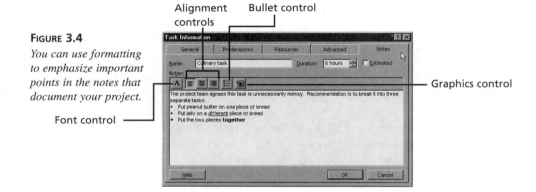

FIGURE 3.4
You can use formatting to emphasize important points in the notes that document your project.

Click OK to close the Task Information dialog box. Tasks that have Notes attached also have an icon in the Indicators column that resembles the icon on the Notes toolbar button.

Entering Milestones

As you build the task list, you will probably want to include some checkpoints or *milestones*. Usually these are points in the life of the project that signal significant events or the completion of major phases. You enter a milestone just as you do any other task except that you change its *duration* to zero. Project treats any task with a zero duration as a milestone and represents it with a diamond shape instead of a bar on the Gantt Chart.

Editing the Task List

If you are a perfect typist, you will never have typos to correct; but who among us is perfect? Also, you will most likely decide at some point to change the name of a task, or to go back and insert a task, or change the order of the tasks in some way. You can easily type over old names with new ones, and you can insert, delete, move, and copy tasks to your heart's content.

Undoing Changes

Before you start changing the task list, remember that you can usually reverse the last change you have made in a project with the Edit, Undo command or by clicking the Undo button on the Standard toolbar. The shortcut key is Ctrl+Z. Microsoft Project does not have a separate Redo command. If you use Undo to reverse a change, using Undo again reverses the reversal. Remember, it's only the most recent change that you can undo.

Editing Cell Contents

To edit the content of any cell, you first must select the cell by clicking on it once, and then change into Edit mode. Click once on the editing bar to begin editing. Or you can also now edit a cell directly. If you pause for just a moment, and then click the cell a second time, you will change Project into Edit mode, as shown in Figure 3.5. The blinking insertion point will be visible inside of the cell, ready for you to use the arrow keys and the Backspace and Delete keys to move around in the cell and make your changes. Also, the word Edit will appear in the lower-left corner of the screen, and the red X and green check mark will be visible on the editing bar. Be sure to press Enter to lock in your changes and move away from the cell.

FIGURE 3.5
Edit fields directly in cells and copy cell contents with the Fill feature.

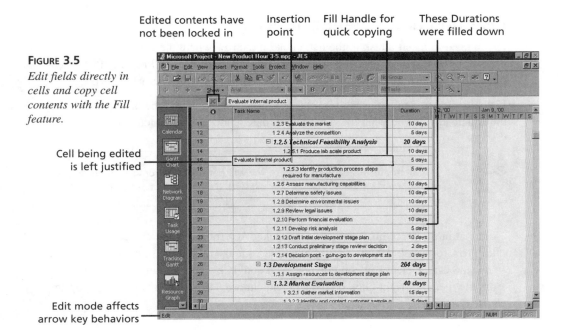

Edited contents have not been locked in

Insertion point

Fill Handle for quick copying

These Durations were filled down

Cell being edited is left justified

Edit mode affects arrow key behaviors

If you click a second time on the cell too quickly, Project will treat it as a double-click and will act accordingly, probably by opening the Task Information dialog box. Be sure to pause briefly between the click to select a cell and the click to edit it.

Another handy cell-editing feature is the ability to quickly copy cell contents to several other adjacent cells in one step. There is a little square in the lower-right corner of the box surrounding the selected cell—the Fill Handle. If you pause your mouse pointer over the square, the pointer shape becomes a small cross. Click on the square Fill Handle and drag down to copy the cell contents to all the cells you cross in the selection. Release the mouse and old values are replaced with the copied values.

You might use this fill-handle feature to copy task names; you could copy a task name like Submit Draft 1 to other tasks and then edit the Draft numbers, rather than retyping the task names. It may be more common to copy and fill numeric values like dates or durations—you could change a series of 1 day? estimated durations to another value like 5 days. Type the 5 days duration in a field first, and then drag the fill-handle square to copy it down the Duration column.

Inserting and Deleting Tasks

If you need to insert a task in the list, click on the row where the new task should go and press the Insert key (or choose Insert, New Task from the menu). Project will create a blank row by pushing down the task that was in that row and other tasks below.

If you decide to remove a task from the list, click on any cell in the task's row and press the Delete key. If you want to go the menu route, choose Edit, Delete Task.

 Watch out! Pressing the Delete key will permanently remove the *entire task* you were on when the key was pressed. (Don't forget about Undo!)

Note that in the preceding paragraph the Delete key (or the menu choice) removes the entire row for a task. If you want to clear the contents of just the selected cell, you need to use the Ctrl+Delete key combination. You could also choose Edit, Clear, Contents from the menu, or right-click on the cell and choose Clear Contents from the pop-up shortcut menu.

Rearranging the Task List

You can rearrange the order of the tasks by moving tasks into new positions on the list. In general, you should list the tasks in the approximate order in which you want the work to be scheduled. It isn't necessary, but it makes your task list easier to understand.

You can also copy a task from another location in the list. You may have more than one task named Submit Report, for example. Save yourself some time by copying and pasting the task rather than inserting blank rows and re-typing it.

To Do: Moving or Copying Tasks

To edit the task list by moving or copying tasks, do the following:

1. Select the row for the task (or tasks) you want to move or copy by clicking on the row numbers (the task ID numbers). It is very important that you select the entire row for the task, not just a cell in the row.

2. Click the Cut (or Copy) Task tool or choose the Edit, Cut (or Copy) Task command. Note that the ScreenTip for the tool and Edit command on the menu reads cut or copy *cell* if you *haven't* selected the entire task.

3. Select the row, or a cell in the row, where you want the moved or duplicated task or tasks to be placed. You do not have to insert a blank row ahead of time to receive the new task(s).

▲ 4. Click the Paste tool or use the Edit, Paste command to paste in the task(s).

> If the selection is not the entire task row when you move or copy a task, you will be moving or copying only the cell or cells that were actually selected. Always click the task ID number to select the entire task before using the Cut or Copy command if you want to use the entire task.

Arranging Tasks with an Outline

After the top-level tasks are defined, you can use the outline tools to start filling in the details under each phase of the project. You insert blank rows beneath a top-level task, list the subtasks in the blank rows, and then indent the subtasks under the top-level task. When you indent tasks, Project turns the task they are indented under into a *summary task*.

Summary tasks serve to summarize many aspects of their subtasks. A summary task's bar in the Gantt Chart spans all the task bars of its subtasks so you can see the life span of that part of the project. Later you will see that if you assign resources and costs to tasks, the cost of a summary task is based on the combined cost of all its subtasks.

Indenting and Outdenting Tasks

To indent one or more tasks, select the task—selecting either a single cell or a task ID number works here—and choose the Project, Outline, Indent command, or click the Indent tool on the Formatting toolbar. Project shifts the display of the subtasks to the right and changes the task immediately above into a summary task.

You can reverse this process, also. If you decide that a task should not be a subtask under its summary task, you can shift the task leftward, or "outdent" it, with the Project, Outline, Outdent command, or by clicking on the Outdent tool on the Formatting toolbar.

Working with Summary Tasks

Summary tasks "contain" the subtasks beneath them. Anything you do to the definition of the summary task is also done to its subtasks.

- If you indent or outdent a summary task, its subtasks move with it and are further indented or outdented also.
- If you delete a summary task, you also delete its subtasks.
- If you move a summary task, its subtasks go right along with it, in a subordinate position, to the new location.
- If you copy a summary task, you also copy its subtasks.

If you want to delete a summary task without deleting its subtasks, you must first outdent its subtasks so that it is no longer a summary task. Then you can delete it without losing its former subtasks.

Hiding Subtasks

One advantage of outlining is the ability to collapse the outline to show only high-level tasks or to expand it to show all the details. By default, Project displays a small icon to the left of summary task names that both identifies them as summary tasks and also indicates whether their subtasks are hidden or displayed. Each summary task can be collapsed or expanded separately.

A small plus sign icon, similar to the Show Subtasks tool on the Formatting toolbar, means that there are hidden subtasks. Click the plus sign icon, or select the summary task and click the Show Subtasks tool, to display the subtasks. You can also select the summary task and then use the Project, Outline, Show Subtasks command to display its subtasks.

A small minus sign icon similar to the Hide Subtasks tool means that all the subtasks immediately under the summary task are currently showing and that clicking the icon will hide them. You can also select the summary task and click the Hide Subtasks button or use the Project, Outline, Hide Subtasks command.

Show ▾ The new Show feature on the Formatting toolbar allows you to collapse the outline down to a specific level of detail without having to select and hide details under each summary task. If you want to collapse the entire outline to top-level tasks only, click the Show tool, and choose Outline Level 1. To show and print one more level of detail, choose Show, Outline Level 2. And so on, up to 9 levels of the outline (which can contain 65,535 outline levels per project!). To quickly display all tasks, choose Show, All Subtasks. These Show level options are also available under the Project, Outline, Show cascading menu.

Selecting the Display Options for Outlining

You can choose options for how summary tasks are displayed or decide if you want them displayed at all. If you choose to hide the display of summary tasks themselves, the task list shows only non-summary tasks (tasks with no subtasks under them).

It is also handy to choose to display a summary task for the entire project. You do not have to create this task; Project can calculate it and display it at the top of the task list as a task with ID number zero. The task bar for the project summary task stretches from the project's start to its finish, and its cost measures the total cost of the project.

To Do: Changing Outline Display Options

To view or hide outline formatting features, such as the outline numbering system, follow these steps:

1. Choose Tools, Options from the menu to display the Options dialog box (see Figure 3.6).
2. Click the View tab. The options for outlining are on the bottom of the dialog box.
3. Clear the Show Summary Tasks check box to suppress all summary tasks in the view. By default, this option is on.

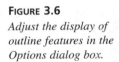

FIGURE 3.6

Adjust the display of outline features in the Options dialog box.

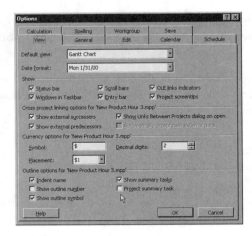

4. Fill the Project Summary Task check box to display an overall summary of the project at the top of the task list; it will show as task ID zero.

5. Clear the Indent name check box to suppress the outline hierarchy format. All task names will appear lined up against the left margin.

6. Fill the Show Outline Number check box to display numbers next to each task name. The numbering system will be the legal numbering system as illustrated in Figure 3.7. You can tell by the outline number where a task lies in the project plan. If the number is "3.2.4," it means this is the fourth subtask under the second subtask under top-level Task 3.

7. If you don't want the outline icons to appear next to task names, clear the Show Outline Symbol check box.

You may be familiar with the term Work Breakdown Structure (WBS). If your company uses a numbering or lettering scheme to identify what type of work is required for each task in the project, you don't need to fill a separate field to track this structure. Project automatically places the task's outline number into the WBS field. However, if this scheme doesn't fit your needs, you can enter your own values in the WBS code field for each task. Select a task, display the Task Information dialog box, and move to the Advanced tab to view and edit the WBS field.

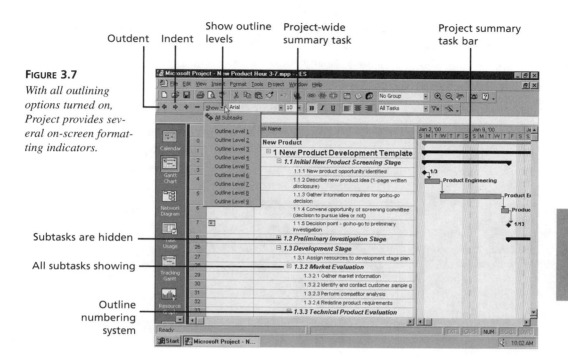

FIGURE 3.7

With all outlining options turned on, Project provides several on-screen formatting indicators.

Outdent Indent Show outline levels Project-wide summary task Project summary task bar

Subtasks are hidden

All subtasks showing

Outline numbering system

NEW FEATURE Also, you can now create custom work and outline numbering codes. The intricate details of creating custom outline codes and Work Breakdown Structure masks are outside of the scope of our 24 hours together. However, I'll get you started. Luckily, the online help for both of these features is quite complete:

- To create a custom outline code unlike the legal numbering system supplied by Project, choose Tools, Customize, Fields. Select Outline Code in the Type drop-down list, and then click Define Outline Code. In the Outline Code Definition dialog box, click Help to go directly into the online help for outline code creation.

- To create a customized Work Breakdown Structure, choose Project, WBS, Define Code. The WBS Code Definition dialog box will be displayed and Help for this feature is available directly from the box.

Entering Recurring Tasks

If you have an activity such as a regularly scheduled meeting that you want to include in the task list, you can create a *recurring task*. When you enter a recurring task, Project asks for the *duration* of each occurrence of the task and how often the task occurs. The default time unit for duration is one day (d). You can also use minutes (m), hours (h), weeks (w), and months (mo) as time units. Project then schedules each of the occurrences and creates a summary task for the series of events.

To Do: Creating Recurring Tasks

To schedule tasks which repeat during the project, do the following:

1. Select the task row where you want the task to go.

2. Choose Insert, Recurring Task from the menu to display the Recurring Task Information dialog box (see Figure 3.8).

FIGURE 3.8

The Recurring Task Information box gives you great flexibility in defining recurring events.

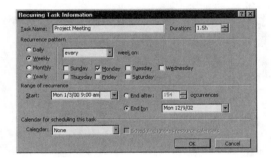

3. Enter a name for the task in the Task Name box.

4. Enter how long each event will be in the Duration box. For example, if the event is to be scheduled for 1.5 hours each time, enter **1.5 hrs** in the Duration box.

5. In the Recurrence pattern section, select the recurring time period (Daily, Weekly, Monthly, or Yearly). Your choice of pattern determines the options that appear to the right for your next selection.

6. If you selected Daily occurrences, choose the frequency of the event in the list box and select either Day or Workday. For example, the events might take place "every other" Workday.

   If you select Weekly occurrences, choose the frequency and the day of the week.

   If you select Monthly occurrences, you can define the frequency in terms of the day number in the month or in terms of a specific day of the month. For example, you could select Day 1 of every month or the third Thursday in every month.

▼   If you select a Yearly occurrence, you can define the event as a specific date in the year or as a specific weekday in a particular month. For example, you could select April 15 of each year or the last Wednesday in July.

7. Finally, you need to define how many times the event (task) will take place. You must specify the date for the first event in the Start date box. If the task takes place at a particular time of day, be sure you add the time of day to the date in the Start date box. In Figure 3.8, the meeting is set to start at 9:00 a.m. every Monday.

   You can then specify the last date this event will occur in the End By date box, or enter a specific number of occurrences in the End After box. Project supplies the finish date for the project as a default End By date, but you can change that if needed.

8. When you have completed your choices, click OK and Project will attempt to schedule all the events. If any of the occurrences fall on a weekend or other non-working day, Project warns you with the alert dialog box. Your options are to let Project reschedule those occurrences that fall on nonworking days to the next working day, or to have Project omit scheduling those few occurrences. You can also Cancel the recurring task at that point.

   For example, if you scheduled weekly meetings for Monday mornings, some of those Mondays may be part of 3-day weekends. Should those meetings be moved
▲   to Tuesdays, or should those meetings be cancelled for that week?

On the Gantt Chart, if you show the subtasks for this new summary task, you can see each event is a separate task. Instead of a continuous bar for the summary task, each of the individual events is *rolled up* to display on the summary task row. Figure 3.9 shows a weekly project meeting scheduled at the top of the New Product project. Note the circular icon in the indicator column for this task. Also notice the task ID numbers: 1, 2, and 156(!). If you expanded the Project Meeting summary task, you would see 155 new, individual meeting tasks added to my plan.

If you want to modify a recurring task, select the task and choose Project, Recurring Task Information (or simply double-click the recurring task) to display the dialog box again and modify any of the selections.

3

FIGURE 3.9
FIGURE 3.9

Enter regularly repeat-
ing events as recurring
tasks.

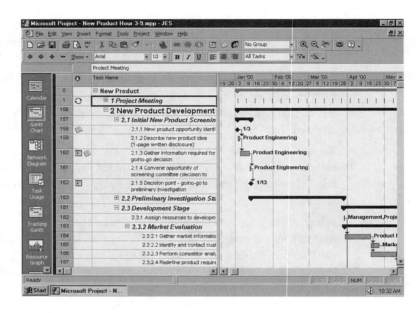

Copying a Task List from Another Application

There is another way of creating a task list that I want to mention because you might find it very helpful in getting started. If you already have a list of tasks in another application, such as a word processor or spreadsheet, you can copy the task list from that application and paste it into Project. However, you should be aware that you cannot import an outlined task list with this method. Even if the task list is outlined in the word processor, it will not be outlined in Project. You will have to indent tasks to create the outline once you get the tasks into Project.

In Hour 24, "Exchanging Project Data with Other Applications," you will see more elaborate ways to move data between Project and other applications.

To Do: Copying a Task List from Another Application

To bring in a list of tasks from another software application, do the following:

▼ To Do

1. Select the task list in the other application. In a spreadsheet, the task names must each be in a separate cell in a column. In a word processor, each task name must be on a separate line in the text.

   Choose Edit, Copy to copy the task list

3. Select a cell in the Task Name column of the Project document. It does not have to be the first row.

4. Choose Edit, Paste or click the Paste tool on the Standard toolbar to copy the list into the Project sheet.

▲

Getting a Simple Printout of the Task List

3

If you're like me, you still want to see it on paper. There are several ways to print data from your project. The most common method is to get the screen to look the way you want it to look on the printed copy and then print that view. There are also some supplied reports that emphasize various aspects of the project. To get a simple copy of the task list, your best bet is to simply print the Gantt Chart.

Adjust the vertical divider bar, the column widths, and the Timescale settings as you did in Hour 2, "Becoming an Instant Project Guru," to get the look you want on paper. Because I have focused on the task names and the outline this hour, the remaining columns in the table and the Gantt Chart are not very interesting. You might prefer to widen the Task Names column a bit and hide the other columns behind the chart.

If you hide subtasks on the screen, they will be hidden in the printed copy. For example, you could print just the top-level tasks or any combination of summary and subtasks.

 To print the Gantt Chart view, you simply need to click the Print tool on the Standard toolbar and Project will print the current view. By default, Project prints all the tasks in the project that have not been hidden under their summary tasks. You will learn how to customize the printout in Hour 10, "Finalizing and Printing Your Schedule."

Saving the New File

You can save Microsoft Project data in a variety of formats, but the standard format uses the file extension .mpp.

To Do: Saving a Project Document

To save your work to disk, do the following:

1. Choose File, Save from the menu or click the Save tool on the Standard tool-bar to display the Save dialog box (see Figure 3.10). If the file has already been saved, but you would like to save it with a different name or in a different folder, choose File, Save As instead.

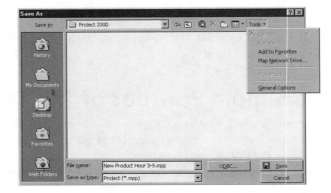

2. The Save In box suggests the default folder. Select the folder you want to use.

   Like the other Microsoft Office products, Microsoft Project uses a default directory for saving and opening files. You can specify the name and location of default folders under Tools, Options, Save, as discussed earlier in this hour.

3. Provide a name for the project in the File Name box.

4. If you want to provide password protection for the file, click the Tools button and choose General Options to display the Save Options dialog box (see Figure 3.11).

Type a password in the Protection Password box if you want to keep people who don't know the password from opening the file. Type a password in the Write Reservation Password box if you want to allow people to open and modify the plan but not be able to save changes over the original without knowing the password.

▼   Both of these passwords can contain up to 17 characters and are case-sensitive. Be
            sure you write down the passwords you use and store them in a safe place. You
            must remember the password to be able to use the file.

        5. Click OK to close the Save Options dialog box.

▲   6. Click Save to save the file.

Summary

In this hour, you learned to set critical options that will apply to all the new project documents you start. You've also seen how to establish the fixed start or finish date on which
Project will base the schedule, and how to document your project. Finally, you now
know how to build the task list with the structure of an outline and how to create a variety of tasks: summary tasks, subtasks, recurring tasks, and milestones. And don't forget
to save (or at least let Project remind you every few minutes.)

Q&A

**Q I have several old project files that were created before I set the defaults rec-
ommended in this hour. Have those settings been changed in those files also?**

A No, setting the defaults only changes the settings in the template that Project uses
    as the default for new files (the file named GLOBAL.MPT). You will have to open
    those files and change the option settings in each one if you want to apply the new
    settings to those files.

**Q Do tasks have to be entered in the list in the order in which they need to be
performed?**

A No, the order in the list has no effect on the order in which they will be scheduled.
    In the next hour, you will see how to define the scheduling order. However, it does
    make it easier to understand the schedule if tasks within the major summary tasks
    are approximately in the order of execution.

Q Do I have to follow these steps and create my major tasks first?

A Absolutely not. Many people prefer the "brain dump" method: open a file and list
    all the tasks you can think of for your project. Then use the copy, move, insert and
    delete techniques to put your tasks in a logical order. But do create an outline hier-
    archy at some point; the benefits of outlining are enormous.

3

Exercises

You'd like to be an entrepreneur. You've met with some possible partners and compiled a list of activities they believe are required to start a new project. You need to see it in print and submit the plan for their review. In the exercises below, you will create a new file, document it, and create an outlined task list. The completed exercise can be seen in the file, "New Business Hour 3-Exercise.MPP." See the Introduction for instructions to access the sample files and exercise solutions on this book's Web page.

1. Create a new project file. Schedule the project from a start date of October 2, 2000.

2. Give the project a descriptive name, identify yourself as the project manager, and enter your proposed company name. Briefly summarize the goal for this project.

3. Enter the following first 10 ten tasks for your plan, letting Project supply an estimated duration of 1 day for each task.

   Self-assessment

   Define business vision

   Summarize findings in writing

   Identify available skills, information, and support

   Decide whether to proceed

   Define the opportunity

   Research the market and competition

   Interview owners of similar businesses

   Identify needed resources

   Submit findings to partners

4. Task 5, "Decide whether to proceed," and Task 10, "Submit findings to partners," are important markers. Make them milestone tasks.

5. Task 3, "Summarize findings in writing," is out of logical order. Make it the next-to-the-last task.

6. Make Task 1, "Self-Assessment," and Task 5, "Define the Opportunity," summary tasks.

7. Turn on the outline numbers for this plan.

8. Print the plan, with the Task Name and Duration columns showing.

9. Save your work.

PART II
Developing a Timeline

Hour

HOUR 4

Starting the Scheduling Process

In Hour 3, "Starting a New Project and Working with Tasks," you put together the list of tasks that need to be completed in your project, but that list is not a workable *schedule* until you attach realistic dates showing *when* work on each task is expected to start and finish. Hour 5, "Defining When Project Can Schedule Tasks," gives you an overview of the factors Project considers in calculating dates for tasks. You learn in this and the next hour how to control these factors with your instructions. However, the story will not be complete until Hour 12, "Mastering Resource Scheduling in Microsoft Project," where you look at how changing resource assignments affects the schedule.

Although Microsoft Project assigns defaults, in this hour, you will learn how to:

- Select a default format for dates
- Set your own start and finish dates
- Define duration units
- Control the working hours in a day and a week

Understanding How Default Dates Work

Microsoft Project automatically calculates default start and finish dates when you first enter tasks (see Figure 4.1), but that schedule calls for everything to start at once, like horses racing out of the starting gate. You have to give Microsoft Project instructions for calculating a more meaningful schedule.

Tasks initially have a tentative duration estimate default of 1 day

Tasks are scheduled on the first working day of the project

FIGURE 4.1

In the initial task list, the tasks are lined up at the start date and ready to race off to the finish line all at once.

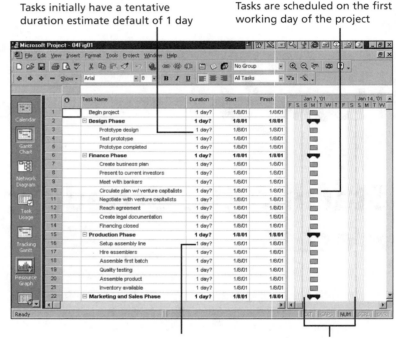

Question marks indicate this duration is a tentative estimate

Nonworking days are shaded

Before I start discussing dates, you should be aware that almost every date field in Microsoft Project also includes the time of day. If you want to see both the time and date for scheduled events, change the display format for dates to include the time of day. However, you will usually have to widen the date columns to display this format, which takes much space onscreen (see Figure 4.2). Still, it can be a helpful temporary aid in troubleshooting problems.

If you want dates to include the time of day, you can change the default display for all dates in Microsoft Project with the Options dialog box.

FIGURE 4.2

Dates have a time component, but the format for date and time takes a lot of screen space.

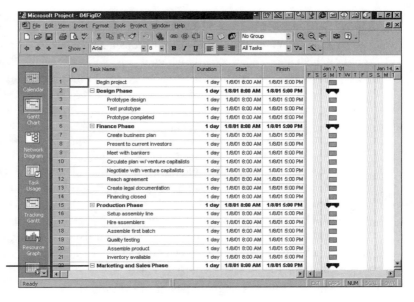

Time of day added to the date format

To Do: Selecting a Default Format for Dates

To select the default format for dates, follow these steps:

1. Choose Tools, Options from the menu to display the Options dialog box. Make sure that the View tab is displayed.

2. Click the list arrow in the Date Format list box and select the format you want to use (see Figure 4.3). The first choice in the list displays both the date and time of day.

3. Click the OK button to close the dialog box.

FIGURE 4.3

Sometimes displaying the time of day with dates helps you understand peculiarities in the schedule.

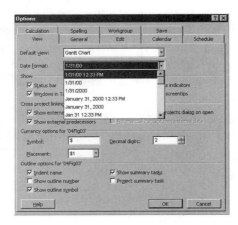

4

Understanding How Tasks are Scheduled

As soon as you enter a new task in your project, Microsoft Project immediately places it on the schedule calendar. Exactly where it gets placed depends on whether your project is scheduled from a fixed start date or from a fixed finish date. These and the other factors controlling the scheduling of tasks are in the following list, which includes several new terms. They will be defined more precisely in the extended coverage for each factor—in most cases, later in this hour.

- Tasks are usually scheduled to start *as soon as possible*, which means as soon after the start of the project as the other factors listed here will allow. (You learned how to set the start date for the project in the previous hour.) If your project is scheduled from a fixed finish date, tasks are scheduled to finish *as late as possible*, which means as close to the end of the project as possible. For example, if you start a new project file and give the project a fixed start date of January 8, 2001 (see Figure 4.1), then as you add tasks they are all initially scheduled to start as soon as possible after January 8, 2001.

- Microsoft Project includes a built-in *calendar* that defines *working days* and *non-working days* (such as weekends and holidays). The calendar also defines the *times of day* when work can be scheduled. For the most part, tasks are scheduled only during the working times defined in the calendar. The Gantt Chart shades the non-working days in the timeline area. As you can see in Figure 4.4, if you select a start date for your project that falls on a Saturday, Project schedules tasks to start on the following Monday, the first working day after the start of the project. Similarly, if you entered a time of day for the start of your project that is not a working hour on the calendar, Project would schedule tasks to begin in the first working hour thereafter. You will see more about working times in this hour.

- Some tasks take longer to complete than others, and you give Project that information by your entry in the *Duration* field. When you first create a task, Project assigns a default duration of one day, and schedules the finish date at the end of one full working day. If you later enter a different duration estimate for the task, Project reschedules the finish date. If, however, your project has a fixed finish date then Project would not adjust the finish date, but would move the start date to an earlier time period.

  In Figure 4.5, the duration estimates for the project have been entered. Some task bars are longer, others are shorter, and the task finish dates reflect the duration values.

FIGURE 4.4

Tasks are scheduled only on working days.

Project start date is a nonworking Saturday

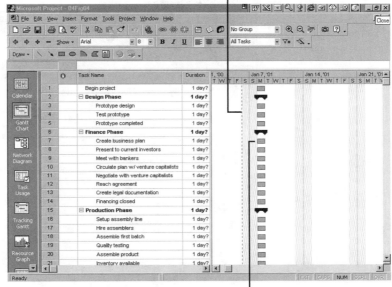

Tasks are scheduled
on the first working
day after the project
start date

4

- Normally, Project assumes that once work begins on a task, it continues uninterrupted (except for nonworking days) until the task is finished. However, you can introduce arbitrary *splits* that interrupt the scheduled work on a task. In other words, you can schedule a task to start, stop, and start again at intervals of your choosing, and as often as you choose. For example, if an employee is unavailable or a piece of equipment breaks down (hopefully not vice versa), you could interrupt the task schedule until a replacement is available. In Figure 4.5, Task 13 shows a split that was introduced because the person doing that task will be away at a conference during that time.

- If there is a *fixed date* defined for the individual task, it overrides Project's attempt to schedule the task as soon or as late as possible. For example, in the project in Figure 4.5, the start date for Meet with bankers (Task 9) has been fixed at January 15, 2001, because the business plan created in Task 7 won't be finished until that date. After you add this fixed *date constraint* to the Task, its scheduled start date shifts to the fixed date. Using constraints is covered in Hour 7, "Working with Deadlines and Constraints."

FIGURE 4.5

Adding duration esti-mates to tasks causes Project to adjust their scheduled dates.

Durations affect the finish dates

Task with a fixed date

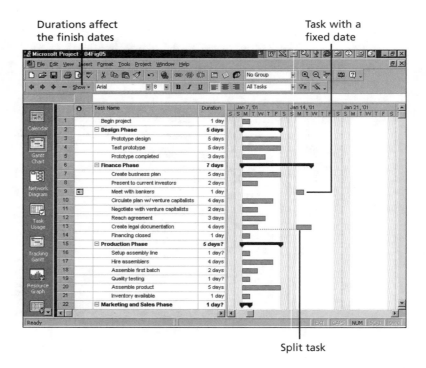

Split task

- Most of the time, the start or finish of a task is *dependent* on the start or finish of some other task. For example, in a residential construction project, the start of the Frame Walls task must wait until the finish of the Prepare Foundation task. You define this dependency in Project by *linking* tasks. In Figure 4.6, Task 18 (Assemble first batch) is linked to Task 4 (Test prototype) and should not be started until Task 4 is finished; you shouldn't attempt to start assembling your new product until the prototype testing is successfully completed. Linking tasks is covered in Hour 6, "Linking Tasks in the Correct Sequence."

- When you *assign resources* to work on tasks, it can affect the schedule in a number of ways. Changing the number of people or machines assigned to a task can affect the task's duration and, therefore, the task's finish date. For example, if you double the number of people working on a task, it usually means the task is finished more quickly. The availability of the resources also affects the schedule for the task; work must be scheduled around vacations and other nonworking times for the resources, which could lengthen the schedule for the task. And, if the same resource is assigned to two overlapping tasks, you might have to *delay* the work on one task while the resource works on the other task. Resource assignments are covered in Hours 11, "Defining Resources and Costs," 12, "Mastering Resource Scheduling in Microsoft Project," and 13, "Assigning Resources and Costs to Tasks."

Task 4

FIGURE 4.6

The appropriate sequence for working on tasks is defined by linking tasks.

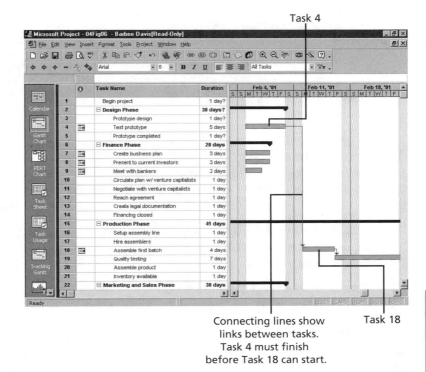

Connecting lines show
links between tasks.
Task 4 must finish
before Task 18 can start.

Task 18

4

In the following sections, you learn how to control all but the last three items in the preceding list. You also learn how to link and constrain tasks in Hours 6 and 7, and how to manage resource assignments starting in Hour 11.

Setting the Start or Finish Date for the Project

As you saw in Hour 3, "Starting a New Project and Working with Tasks," all projects are scheduled from a fixed start date or a fixed finish date. New projects are, by default, scheduled from the beginning of the work day on the current date (your computer's internal clock date) as a fixed start date. So, if you start Microsoft Project at 3:00 p.m. on June 1, 2001, and start entering tasks in the new document (project1.mpp), the tasks are scheduled to start at 8:00 a.m. on that date—unless you change the project's fixed start date or finish date.

Even if you don't display the time of day in the date format, Project attaches the default time for the start of the work day (normally 8:00 a.m.) to the fixed start date or the default time for the end of the work day (normally 5:00 p.m.) to the fixed finish date. The section "Adjusting the Default Working Day" in the next hour shows you how to change these default times.

Project assigns new tasks a default duration of 1 day (normally, that means the task will require 8 hours of work) and schedules an initial start and finish for each new task. If the project is scheduled from a fixed start date, Project schedules a new task to start as soon as possible after the start of the project and to finish at the end of one working day.

If the project is scheduled from a fixed finish date, new tasks are scheduled to finish at the end of the project finish date. The task's start date is then calculated as one working day before the task's finish.

You must set the fixed start or finish date for the project because the rest of the project schedule is pegged to this date.

To Do: Setting the Fixed Start or Finish Date

To set the fixed start or finish date for the project, follow these steps:

1. Choose Project, Project Information from the menu to display the Project Information dialog box.

2. Click the arrow in the Schedule From list box and choose either Project Start Date or Project Finish Date.

3. If you chose Project Start Date, click the Start Date field to enter the fixed start date for the project. If you chose Project Finish Date, click the Finish Date field to enter the fixed finish date. Either type in the date or click the arrow to the right of the field and select the date from the calendar control.

4. Click the OK button to close the Project Information dialog box.

When you want to enter today's date or a date within the next 7 days, you can type in the words today, tomorrow, or the name of any day of the week, either spelled out or abbreviated (for example, Friday or Fri). Project will replace your text with the full date for the day you typed. For day names, Project uses the next occurrence of that name after the current date. For example, if the current date is Thursday, January 4, 2001, and you type in **9am Monday**, Project will supply **1/8/01 9:00 AM**.

▼ Even if the time of day is not displayed in the current date format, Project attaches the default start time of day (normally 8:00 a.m.) to your entry in the Start Date field or the default finish time of day (usually 5:00 p.m.) to your entry in the Finish Date field.

If you want to specify a time of day that differs from the default time of day, type in the time of day either before or after the date. For example, to be sure that the project starts at 7:00 a.m. on January 8, 2001, you could type **1/8/01 7:00 AM** into the Start Date field or you could type **7am January 8, 2001** (See Figure 4.7). Default times will be discussed in more detail later in this hour.

FIGURE 4.7

You should define the date from which the project starts or must finish when you start a new document.

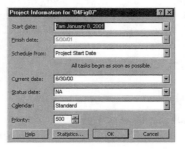

4

If the date and hour you define for the project to start or finish is not a working day and hour, tasks are scheduled on the nearest working date and hour. The next section shows you how to determine the working days and hours. In Figure 4.7, the start of the project is being set to 7:00 a.m. If the first working hour on the base calendar is 8:00 a.m., the

▲ tasks are actually scheduled to start at 8:00 a.m.

Estimating Task Duration

When scheduling tasks, Microsoft Project needs to know how long each task will take to complete. In other words, Project needs to know how much time should be allowed between the start and finish dates for the task. You supply an estimate of that time in the task Duration field.

NEW TERM The term *duration* is used to refer to the amount of working time it will take to finish a task. Duration can be measured in minutes, hours, days, weeks, or months, and it always means the amount of time during which work on a task actually takes place. Duration units, such as "day" and "week," mean the amount of work done in a day or a week. Project places a default value of 1 day in the Duration field for each new task, but that means a working day, usually 8 hours, not the 24 hours defined in the dictionary. This is a tentative duration estimate that you will replace with your own duration estimate.

 NEW FEATURE A question mark follows the default duration of 1 day to show it is only a tentative estimate, a new feature in Microsoft Project 2000 (see Figure 4.1). You can type a new duration over the default value Project supplies, or you can use the spin control in the Duration field to increase or decrease the number for the existing duration units. After you overwrite the duration default value with your own more realistic estimate, the question mark indicating it is a tentative estimate will go away.

> You can use the question mark with your own duration estimates. If you want to enter a tentative duration value (your "best guess" estimate at the time) and change it later, you can add a question mark to your entry as a reminder.

Defining Duration Units

Duration values are entered and displayed in any one of five time units (minutes, hours, days, weeks, or months), and you can spell out the units, use an abbreviation, or use an initial. For example, a duration of 2 weeks could be displayed as 2 weeks, 2 wks, or 2 w. Project automatically changes the unit to plural form when appropriate. You control how duration units are displayed with settings in the Options dialog box.

To Do: Controlling the Display of Time Unit Labels

To control the display of time unit labels, follow these steps:

1. Choose Tools, Options to display the Options dialog box and select the Edit tab.

2. Use the list arrow in each field (Minutes, Hours, Days, Weeks, Months, and Years) to select the initial, abbreviation, or word as the default label for that unit.

3. Fill the check box next to Add Space Before Label to separate the label from the number value.

4. Click the Set As Default button to apply these defaults to all new project documents in the future. (see figure 4.8)

 The "year" unit is not used in the Duration field. It's used when entering an annual salary for a resource's cost rate.

FIGURE 4.8

Control the display of time unit labels for all tasks in the Options dialog box.

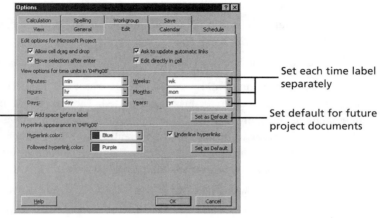

Set each time label separately

Separate number from label

Set default for future project documents

If you enter a number in the Duration field without including the unit label to indicate whether the number represents minutes, hours, days, weeks, or months, Project adds the default time unit, which is days. If you would prefer a different default duration unit, change the setting in the Options dialog box.

To Do: Changing the Default Unit for Duration

To change the default unit for duration, follow these steps:

1. Choose Tools, Options to display the Options dialog box, and select the Schedule tab. (see figure 4.9)

FIGURE 4.9

The default time unit for duration values is "Days," but you can change that.

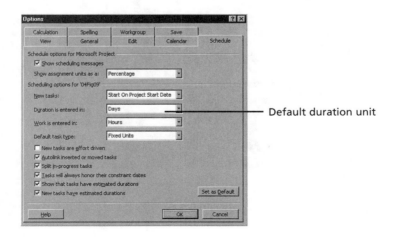

Default duration unit

4

▼ 2. In the Duration Is Entered In list box, select one of the five units: Minutes, Hours, Days, Weeks, or Months.

   3. If you want to use this default unit for all future project documents, click the Set As Default button.

▲ 4. Click OK to save the new setting.

If a task has a duration of 40 hours, that means that it will take 40 hours of time spent working on the task before the task is completed. The terms minutes and hours are unambiguous, meaning that they have a universal definition. However, if someone says "It'll take me a week to finish," you don't really know for sure what that means in terms of hours, although you can be fairly certain that it *doesn't* mean working continuously for 7 days and nights—168 hours.

Therefore, Project requires that you define, using the unambiguous unit *hours*, what you mean by a "day" of work and a "week" of work. The default values are 8 hours in a day of work and 40 hours in a week of work (see Figure 4.10). These are fairly standard expectations of employees, at least in the United States. So, when you estimate the duration of a task to be a week, Project thinks you mean a *working* week, or 40 hours, spread over 5 days with 8 hours of work each day. If your organization has different standards for the number of hours worked in a day or a week, you need to change the definitions in Project so that you can use the terms in Project the way you use them in conversation on the job.

FIGURE 4.10

Change the default start and end of daily working times to match your workplace.

Default end of the day

Default hours per week

Default start of the day

Default hours per day

Default days per month

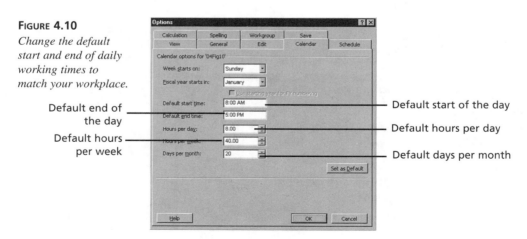

To Do: Defining the Working Hours in a Day and a Week

Follow these steps to define the working hours in a day and a week:

1. Choose Tools, Options to display the Options dialog box, and select the Calendar tab (see Figure 4.10).

2. Enter the hours in a day in the Hours Per Day field.

3. Enter the hours in a week in the Hours Per Week field.

4. Enter the days in a month in the Days per Month field.

5. Click OK to close the dialog box.

> The working hours in your Standard calendar should be defined to match these entries in the Hours Per Day and Hours Per Week fields. The calendar is *not* automatically changed to match these definitions of days and weeks (See Hour 5).

When you enter the duration for a task, Project schedules the duration of the task in the calendar, using the working times the calendar makes available. For example, if you estimate the duration of a task to be 2 days (16 hours) and work starts on the task at 8:00 a.m. on a Friday, Project calculates that the work will continue for the next 16 hours of available working time. At the end of the day on Friday, there will still be 8 hours of work to do (assuming you're using the default calendar). Because Saturday and Sunday are nonworking days, work will resume on Monday and continue to the end of that day. If the Monday in this example was a nonworking holiday, the task would be scheduled to continue through the end of the day on Tuesday.

The Special Case of Continuous Working Time

The usual meaning of duration presumes that you can stop and start work on a task without difficulty. For example, if the task is to assemble a complex machine or to develop an architectural plan, you can stop when 5:00 p.m. comes along, and start back the next morning—you can even go home for the weekend if you're not finished. The time you spend on these tasks doesn't have to be *continuous* time.

Some tasks, however, require continuous time—after the task starts, the work must continue uninterrupted until the task is finished. For example, pouring concrete in a form in a construction project is a continuous process; after you start, you have to stay with it until you have completely filled the form and the concrete has dried and hardened successfully. Not only will the concrete go on drying out and hardening if the 5:00 whistle blows, but workers will need to stay and tend it to be sure it doesn't dry too quickly. This process can't be stopped after it's started. For tasks like this, you need for Project to schedule the task with continuous time, right through the nonworking times in the calendar. In Microsoft Project, you enter elapsed duration units to signal that continuous time is required.

NEW TERM Like duration, *elapsed duration* is a measure of the number of working minutes, hours, days, or weeks required to complete a task. Unlike regular duration, however, elapsed duration time units are the same as those used by people in normal conversation. An "elapsed day" is 24 hours, and an "elapsed week" is 7 elapsed days or 168 hours. Project schedules elapsed duration around the clock, in the calendar's working and nonworking hours and days alike.

To enter an elapsed duration, you simply add the letter *e* before the units label. For example, the duration for a task that should take 24 continuous hours would be entered as "24 ehrs" or "1 eday."

Letting Project Calculate Duration For You

In some cases, you might not know the exact duration for a task, but you have other information that can be used to calculate it. Suppose you have been given a list of tasks to work with that includes start and finish dates for each task. You can import the list of tasks and their predetermined dates into Project, and Project can use those dates to calculate the duration. See Hour 24, "Exchanging Project Data with Other Applications," for instructions on importing data into Project.

If you know how much work a task involves and you also know how many resources you plan to assign to the task, Project can calculate how long it will take the resources to complete the work (that is, the duration). There are settings you can use at the time you assign the resources that cause Project to calculate duration for you. See Hours 12 and 13 for guidelines and the steps to take to get Project to do this for you.

Finally, if you have enough experience with the tasks to be able to give reasonable estimates of the longest possible duration, the shortest possible duration, and the most likely duration, you can use Microsoft Project's PERT analysis tools to calculate a statistically likely duration.

 PERT analysis is beyond the scope of this book, but you can learn how to use it in Chapter 5 of my book *Special Edition Using Microsoft Project 2000* (published by Que).

Summary

In this hour, you have learned how to set the parameters within which Project schedules your tasks and how to establish the fixed start or finish of the project. Now you also know what the Duration field is used for and how to enter duration estimates. In Hour 5, you learn how to use the Calendar.

Q&A

Q   I have a task with a duration of 1 day, but the task bar seems to extend over 2 days. Why?

A   There could be several reasons why this happened. The task might not start at 8:00 a.m., in which case its 1-day duration will require some time in the second day. You should display the Start and Finish fields with time of day to see if the times are what you intended. You might also have some nonworking time in the calendar for the day in question. That means it will take more than one calendar day to do a "day" of work.

Q   My task lasts 2 weeks and 3 days, so how do I enter the duration?

A   You can't enter a task using a combination of units, such as weeks and days. For two weeks and three days (two five-day work weeks, plus 3 days) enter a duration of 13 days.

4

Exercises

Try some of these exercises to build your proficiency with starting the scheduling process.

1. Go into the Project Information dialogue box and set either your start date or your finish date.

2. Go to the Options dialogue box and change your time unit labels.

3. Start with the Tools drop down menu, and change the default unit for duration in your Project from Days to Weeks.

4. Find the way to change the default working hours and set them for your project.

HOUR 5

Defining When Project Can Schedule Tasks

In Hour 4, "Starting the Scheduling Process," you began learning the instructions you can give Project to impose terms and conditions on how it calculates the schedule for you. You saw how to set the project start or finish date, and how to control certain default settings, such as start and finish times for tasks, how much work a day or week contains, and what labels to use for units of time. You were also introduced to entering estimates of task duration for both regular working hours and for continuous or elapsed time.

In this hour, you continue to look at the underpinnings of scheduling in Project. Specifically you will examine the following:

- Creating calendars for the project
- Identifying which days work can be scheduled, and which days are nonworking
- Setting specific hours when work can be scheduled
- Creating a calendar for individual tasks
- Sharing calendars with other Project files

Elements of Project Scheduling

Project is a scheduling tool. It makes sense that there are a number of factors that can influence the scheduling of a task—just as in real life. Before introducing new Project features, let's summarize the underlying scheduling elements; some have already been discussed in earlier hours, several are covered in this hour, and one will be postponed until a later hour.

- The overall project must have a fixed start or fixed finish date (choose Project, Project Information).
- Project needs to know what work values your company uses to define working hours per day, working hours per week, and working days per month (choose Tools, Options, Calendar).
- Knowing that Project schedules and tracks tasks to the minute, you can enter start and finish dates at that level of detail. But if you don't want to get that specific, Project needs to know what to assume for you as task start or finish times (choose Tools, Options, Calendar).
- After the defaults have been set, a company calendar identifying work days and days the office is closed needs to be considered or created. See the section in this hour titled "Defining Work Days on the Standard Calendar."
- On the company calendar, for days when work can be performed, you set actual times during the day when Project can schedule activity. See the section in this hour titled "Setting Working Time in the Standard Calendar."
- Tasks with unique scheduling requirements—exceptions to the normal company calendar—need to be assigned to calendars all their own. See the section in this hour titled "Creating and Applying Base Calendars for Special Scheduling Needs."
- The last calendar type to effect scheduling is the working time availability for each resource (see Hour 11, "Defining Resources and Costs").

Adjusting the Default Working Day

If you define the fixed start or finish date for the project, or if you type in a date for an individual task to start or finish, and you don't include the time of day with the date, Microsoft Project adds the default start time to any start date entry and the default end time to any finish date entry. This feature can create a nuisance for you if the default values don't match the actual start and end of the workday for your organization.

Recall from Hour 4 that the start and end times Project uses for working days can be modified by choosing Tools, Options, and clicking the Calendar tab. Figure 5.1 should look familiar.

FIGURE 5.1

Change the default start and end of daily working times to match your workplace.

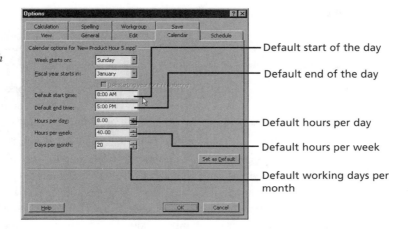

Default start of the day

Default end of the day

Default hours per day

Default hours per week

Default working days per month

When you change the default start and finish times of day, Microsoft Project does not apply those new times to any existing task dates or calendar definitions in the project file. That's why you should make sure these times are set correctly for your organization and make them the default for all future project documents early in your career with Microsoft Project.

How Calendars Are Used in Scheduling

NEW TERM Microsoft Project bases its schedule for tasks on the working days and times defined in a *base calendar* to which the project is linked. At least, that's the case until you assign a resource to work on the task; then, the calendar for the resource determines when work can be scheduled. However, each resource calendar is also linked to a base calendar, usually the same one the project is linked to. The resource calendar just has additional nonworking days and times (like vacations, scheduled sick leave, or special working hours) that apply only to that resource.

Most new project documents start out as copies of the Global project template (the file named GLOBAL.MPT), and that template initially contains three base calendars supplied by Microsoft Project—one named the *Standard calendar*. Initially, all new projects and all newly defined resources are linked to the Standard calendar in their project file as their base calendar.

The features of the three base calendars supplied by Microsoft Project are described in the following list. Any one of them can be used as the base calendar for your project or as the basis for the calendars governing working times for groups of employees. They

5

can all be edited and adapted to your organization. Remember, these calendars are just copies of those in the template—these copies reside in the file for your project. If you edit them, you are not editing the originals in the template. I'll show you how to copy your adapted calendar back to the template later in this hour.

- The *Standard* calendar has Mondays through Fridays as working days, with Saturdays and Sundays as nonworking days. The working hours on Mondays through Fridays are 8:00 a.m. to 12:00 p.m., and then 1:00 p.m. to 5:00 p.m. There are no holidays defined in this or the other calendars listed here.

- The *24 Hours* calendar has 24 hours of working time every day, with no nonworking days defined. Use this calendar as the base calendar for your project if the project involves continuous, around-the-clock operations. You would also use this as the base calendar for any resources that can be scheduled around-the-clock (like equipment and other non-human resources, or human resource groups that are staffed around the clock). You would not use this as the base calendar for a human resource who works only part of the day.

- The *Night Shift* calendar's working hours are from 11:00 p.m. to 8:00 a.m. the next morning. Use this calendar, or a modification of it, as the base calendar for resources who work the night shift. If the project will be worked on exclusively by the night shift workers, make this the base calendar for the project also, so that unassigned tasks are scheduled in the same working hours.

You should adapt the Standard calendar to fit your organization, and generally use it as the base calendar for your projects, but you can also create customized base calendars. This is frequently done when a group of resources have unique scheduling requirements (like the night shift workers mentioned in the preceding list). For example, if your organization hires students on work-study programs, you might create a custom base calendar to use for those resources. If a project was worked on by those resources only, you could also name that custom base calendar as the base calendar for the project.

To Do: Selecting the Base Calendar for the Current Project

▼ To Do

To select the base calendar for the current project, do the following:

1. If you are going to use a customized base calendar, create the calendar first. See the section, "Creating and Applying Base Calendars for Special Scheduling Needs," for instructions.

2. Choose Project, Project Information from the menu to display the Project Information dialog box.

3. In the Calendar field, use the list arrow to display the base calendars that are already defined. If you have defined resources already, their calendars are listed here also.

▼

▼ In Figure 5.2, the base calendars provided by Project are displayed.

FIGURE 5.2

You can select the base calendar for your project in the Project Information dialog box.

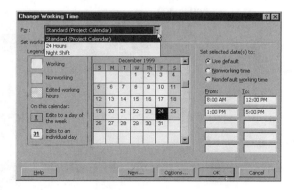

4. Select the calendar you want to use as the base calendar for the current project.

▲ 5. Click OK to save the selection and close the dialog box.

Remember, if you change the default start and end of the working day in the Tools, Options dialog box, you will also need to edit the working hours in your calendars to use these start and end times.

Defining Work Days on the Standard Calendar

You can adjust the working days (and hours) for any calendar with the Change Working Time command. The original calendars have no holidays, so you must supply them yourself. For example, in Figure 5.3, July 4, 2000 is selected and has been set as a nonworking day.

To Do: Changing the Working Dates

To define calendar days as working or nonworking time, follow these steps:

1. Choose the Tools, Change Working Time command from the menu to display the Change Working Time dialog box (see Figure 5.3).

2. Select the calendar you want to modify in the For list box.

3. Click the arrows on the scrollbar in the calendar to change the month and year. There's no quick way to go directly to a specific month or year. (And dragging the scroll box will move you a great distance in time with a small movement of the mouse!)

▼

5

▼ To Do

Select the   Select a day of the   Change status of
calendar to edit   week (for all months   selected date(s)
                        and years)

FIGURE 5.3

*Adapt calendars to
your organization's
work schedule with the
Change Working Time
dialog box.*

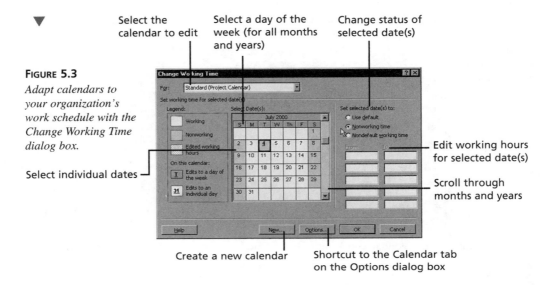

Select individual dates

Edit working hours
for selected date(s)

Scroll through
months and years

Create a new calendar   Shortcut to the Calendar tab
                               on the Options dialog box

4. Click on a specific date whose working status you want to change:

   • Use the click, CTRL key, click technique for selecting dates not next to each other.

   • Click and drag to select a series of dates.

   • If you drag down between 2 weeks, say from Wednesday to Wednesday, be aware that the weekend dates are included in the selection. Any changes you make will affect the weekends, too.

   • To change a day of the week for all weeks (for example, to change all Fridays), select the letter for the day of the week at the top of the day's column. Note that you will be changing that day of the week for all months and all years in the calendar.

5. Use the radio buttons to the right of the calendar to change the status for the date or dates you have selected.

   • Select Nonworking time to make the selected date(s) nonworking dates.

   • Select Nondefault working time to change the selected dates into working dates with the default hours for that day of the week (usually 8:00 a.m. to 12:00 p.m. and 1:00 p.m. to 5:00 p.m.).

     Don't let the name of this option throw you: the logic is, if you select a default nonworking day, like Saturday, and need to make it a day when Project can schedule tasks, click the Nondefault working time option—*any* working time on a Saturday is considered "nondefault".

▽

- Select Use Default to return the selected date(s) to the default status after they've been edited. Mondays through Fridays will become working days with the default working hours; Saturdays and Sundays will become non-working days.

▲

6. When you're finished editing calendars, click the OK button to save your changes and close the dialog box.

> The legend on the left side of the Change Working Time dialog box shows how you can tell the status of a date. Working days with the default times are clear, Nonworking days are shaded, working days with Edited times are striped, and any date that has been edited has an underscore under the label (either on an individual day or on a label for the day of the week).

Setting Working Time in the Standard Calendar

Identifying a date on the base calendar as a working day merely tells Project that there is *some* time during that 24-hour period when work can be scheduled. But which hours are available for scheduling and which aren't? And do the work hours change from day to day? Many companies are experimenting with a modified workweek to ease the commute for employees, among other reasons.

For example, say your company will now work the following hours: Monday through Thursday, 8 a.m. to 6 p.m., and Friday, 8 a.m. until noon. The working days are the same as the Standard base calendar, but the working times aren't. The calendar needs to be modified to reflect this workweek.

To Do: Changing Working Hours on a Base Calendar

To specify exactly which hours tasks can be scheduled, follow these steps:

1. Select Tools, Change Working Time. This is the same dialog box you used to identify working and nonworking days.

2. Select the days that need to be altered. To create the example discussed previously, start by clicking on the M for Monday and dragging across through the Th for Thursday.

3. In the From and To areas on the right side of the dialog box, type in the specific start and finish working times to be applied to the selected days. (Continuing our example, working times for Monday–Thursday would be From 8 a.m. To 12 p.m., and on the next line, From 1 p.m. To 6 p.m.) See Figure 5.4.

▽

To Do (side tab)

5 (side tab)

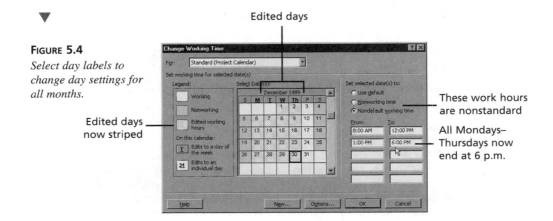

Edited days

FIGURE 5.4
Select day labels to change day settings for all months.

Edited days
now striped

These work hours
are nonstandard

All Mondays–
Thursdays now
end at 6 p.m.

4. To continue making working time changes (and our example needs some adjustment for Fridays), click anywhere on the displayed calendar to lock in the working time entries and turn off the current selection.

5. When finished making changes, click OK to close the dialog box and save your changes automatically.

Notice that you can change the working hours for selected dates by defining up to five "shifts" or working periods per day in the From and To boxes. You must fill these pairs of times from the top down. For example, you can't enter times in the second row if the first row is empty.

Also notice the formatting changes applied to the modified dates. There is now a diagonal striping applied to the days with changed working times, and the date numbers themselves (or the labels for the day of the week) have been underlined. In addition, on the top right of the dialog box Project has automatically selected the Nondefault Working Time option for these dates.

If you've simply lost track of your changes you can start over with a plain Standard calendar. Select all days by clicking on the S for Sunday and dragging across through the S for Saturday, and then click the Use Default option. Project will warn you that it is about to reset the calendar to its original settings, and that all changes will be lost. You can choose to continue or not. Be clear that this resets *everything* back to the Monday through Friday, 8 to 5 workdays, and that any holidays you had marked will have to be changed again.

Creating and Applying Base Calendars for Special Scheduling Needs

Now that you've had a look at changing the day and working time settings on the Standard calendar, the settings for the other two supplied base calendars will probably mean more to you. Open the Tools, Change Working Time dialog box while following this section.

On the Change Working Time dialog box, choose the 24 Hours calendar in the For drop-down list. You will see that every day of the calendar has been changed somehow; all dates show a diagonal pattern, each day label is underlined, and the Nondefault working time option is on. What is different about this calendar? Look in the working hours From and To section. This company schedules work around the clock, 12 midnight to 12 midnight. That explains the name, 24 Hours.

Now use the For drop-down list to see the Night Shift calendar. Again, every day has been modified. And this wasn't a simple change. Select any Monday on the calendar and look at the working times; 11 p.m. to midnight. Where is the rest of the shift? It doesn't actually happen until after midnight, which really makes the working hours early Tuesday morning. Select a Tuesday and look at the working hours. Midnight to 8 a.m. completes the shift (with a one-hour break between 3 a.m. and 4 a.m.), but the next shift begins again that night at 11 p.m. Again, it's a different working shift, but you have to think calendars when creating shifts. The bottom line: Project does not, will not, schedule "shifts" in one step if they span midnight.

Creating Additional Base Calendars

The two supplied base calendars just discussed illustrate the usefulness of creating additional calendars to meet nonstandard scheduling needs. When creating special calendars, you can start with a copy of the Standard calendar (or other base calendar) so that most of your organization's holidays will already be in place, or you can start with a fresh calendar with default working times but no holidays.

To Do: Creating a New Base Calendar

For special calendar needs, create a new base calendar by doing the following:

1. In the Change Working Time dialog box, click the New button to display the Create New Base Calendar dialog box (see Figure 5.5).

FIGURE 5.5

You can create a new calendar by starting with a copy of an existing calendar to keep from having to enter all the holidays.

2. Enter a name for this calendar in the Name field.

3. If you want to start from scratch, choose Create New Base Calendar.

   If you want to start with a copy of another calendar that has holidays and other exceptions already entered, select the calendar you want to copy in the Make a copy of field.

4. Click OK to return to the Change Working Time dialog box. Be sure the name of your new calendar is selected in the For area of the dialog box.

5. Change the new calendar as needed. After the changes are complete, click OK to save the new calendar.

> If your project will not be scheduled according the Standard calendar, you need to tell Project which base calendar to use instead. Select Project, Project Information—the same dialog box where the fixed start or finish date was set. In the Calendar drop-down list on the dialog box, choose the name of the overall project base calendar to be used.

Special Calendars for Special Tasks

I've been discussing base calendars that affect all tasks by default, and that affect all resources based on them. But sometimes a task just doesn't fit the normal workweek schedule. For example, suppose there is a special plotter in your company for printing large diagrams or schematics, but your department only has printing access to it between 4 p.m. and 7 p.m. weekdays. Tasks requiring that printer could start at 4 p.m. but the Standard calendar would only allow 1 hour of printing that day (until 5 p.m.) and then schedule the rest of the printing to begin the next workday at 8 a.m. That isn't acceptable.

Another example of special task scheduling would be the need to schedule equipment maintenance. If you know your production line must stop every Friday from noon until 3 p.m. for maintenance, and the downtime is significant to your plan, you should schedule around it. But what a hassle to continuously maintain stop and start times within individual tasks.

NEW FEATURE Project 2000 includes a feature to solve these scheduling problems. Each task is scheduled around a base calendar, which is the Standard calendar by default. But you can create another base calendar, with working days and times to account for the special scheduling, and tell Project to schedule certain tasks by this modified base calendar. It is a two-step process: create a new base calendar, and then assign the affected tasks to this new calendar.

To Do: Creating and Assigning Calendars for Special Tasks

To accommodate tasks with special scheduling requirements, follow these steps:

1. First, create a new base calendar with the realistic working and nonworking days and times, as described previously in "Creating a New Base Calendar."

   Figure 5.6 shows a new base calendar named DOWNTIME with Friday work time changed to include a 3-hour midday break for maintenance.

FIGURE 5.6

Create a new base calendar to use for individual task scheduling.

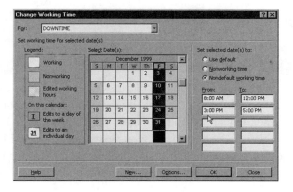

2. Select the task that needs to be scheduled by the new calendar.

3. Click the Task Information button on the Standard toolbar to open the dialog box for the task (see Figure 5.7).

FIGURE 5.7
Schedule a selected
task according to a
special base calendar.

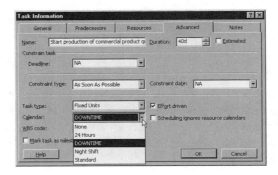

4. Move to the Advanced tab.

5. In the Calendar drop-down list, select the base calendar you just created.

6. Click OK to close the dialog box and reschedule the selected task according to the new working times.

Allowing for this type of downtime or task scheduling restriction will probably cause a change in start or finish date (or time) for the affected task. Project will reschedule the finish date for the task if the project is scheduled from a fixed start date, or will recalculate the task start date if the project is back-scheduled.

Managing Your Calendars

When you edit or create a calendar, the changes exist only in the calendars in the project document that is currently active. If you edit the Standard calendar, for instance, you aren't changing the Standard calendar in other project files. If you want the changes to be included in other project documents, you must copy the revised Standard calendar into those projects and replace their version of the Standard calendar. If you want the changes to be included in all new projects, you must copy the revised calendar into the Global template file (the file named GLOBAL.MPT).

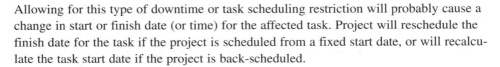

I recommend that you edit the Standard calendar early in your career with Microsoft Project and enter all holidays and other details that apply to your organization. Do that for several years into the future, and then copy this revised Standard calendar to the Global template so all new project files have the Standard calendar already set up for your organization.

Use the Organizer to copy calendars from one project file to another. If you are copying calendars to other project documents, they must be opened (using File, Open) before you start the Organizer.

To Do: Copying a Calendar to Another File

To make customized calendars available to other Project files, follow these steps:

1. Be sure that the file containing the new calendar (the source) and the file you want to copy it to (the target) are both open in Project. The Global template is always open while you work in Project.

2. Choose Tools, Organizer from the menu to display the Organizer dialog box.

3. Select the Calendars tab. The GLOBAL.MPT file will be selected in the list box at the bottom of the dialog box on the left, the one labeled Calendars Available In.

   The project file that was active when you started the Organizer will be selected in the list box on the right, also labeled Calendars Available In. A list of all the calendars contained in each file will appear above the selected filenames.

4. If you want to change the file that is selected, use the arrows in the list boxes to display the names of all files that are open (plus the GLOBAL.MPT). Be sure that both the source file (the one containing the revised calendar) and the target file (the one you want to copy the calendar into) are displayed.

   In Figure 5.8, the GLOBAL.MPT on the left is the target, and the file on the right named New Product Hour 5.MPP is the source.

5

Calendars tab   Copy the selected calendar
                to the other file

FIGURE 5.8
Copy calendars from one project file to another with the Organizer. Filename whose calendars appear above.

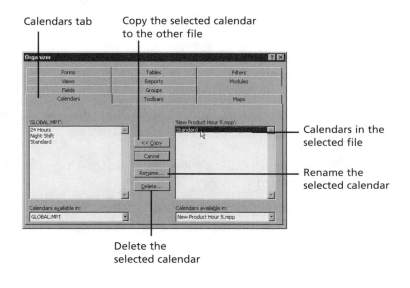

Calendars in the
selected file

Rename the
selected calendar

Delete the
selected calendar

▼ 5. Select the calendar name to be copied in the source file. In the example, the
      Standard calendar is selected.

      The Copy button will automatically point from the source file to the target file.

   6. Click the Copy button.

   7. If a calendar with the same name is already listed in the target file, you will be
      asked if you want to replace the old version (see Figure 5.9).

FIGURE 5.9

*You must decide what
to do when the target
file contains a calen-
dar with the same
name as the one being
copied.*

   • Click Yes to replace the old version with the revised calendar.

   • Click No to cancel the copy operation.

   • Click Rename to copy the revised calendar into the target file with a new
     name. If you click Rename, Project provides a Rename dialog box (shown
▲   later in Figure 5.10).

In a networked environment, it is possible, even probable, that each Project
user will have his own GLOBAL.MPT file installed in his user working directory, and therefore his own list of customized calendars. But you can create
and maintain a company-wide calendar. Someone should be made responsible for the calendar, updating it with holidays and closures as necessary, and
then posting the calendar to a file in a shared Project directory on the network. As needed, send a message to all users to open the shared file (which
will typically *not* be named GLOBAL.MPT) and then use the Organizer to
copy the updated company calendar to their own Global templates.

You must also use the Organizer if you need to rename or delete a calendar. Think of it
as a housekeeping tool.

To Do: Deleting or Renaming Base Calendars

To permanently remove calendars from a file or to rename a calendar, do the following:

   1. Open the Organizer by choosing Tools, Organizer from the menu and select the
      Calendars tab.

   2. Select the calendar to be deleted or renamed.

▼   3. Perform the desired action:

         • Click the Delete button to delete the selected calendar. When asked to confirm the deletion, click Yes.

         • Click the Rename button to rename the selected calendar. Supply the new name in the Rename dialog box and click OK.

▲   4. Click the Close button to close the Organizer.

FIGURE 5.10

Rename new calendars to a name Project doesn't use.

Printing the Calendar Details

If you want to review the working and nonworking dates and times in your base calendars, print the Working Days report. It prints a separate page for each base calendar in the current project file, showing the standard working days and hours and listing all the exceptions, such as holidays, unusual hours, and so forth.

To Do: Printing a Working Days Report

To Do

To get a printed copy of the base calendar working and nonworking day and hour settings, do the following:

1. Select View, Reports.
2. Double-click on the Overview category.
3. Double-click on the Working Days report.

▲   4. At the top of the Preview screen, choose Print.

For detailed instructions on printing this report, see Hour 10, "Finalizing and Printing Your Schedule," especially the section on the Working Days Report.

5

Summary

In this hour, you completed your look at the underlying settings that control scheduling in Project. Default times can be set for those situations where you don't specify exact start or finish times for tasks. A base calendar, typically the Standard base calendar, instructs Project which days to use as working days, and which times within those days can be used for scheduling work. There is even a feature to handle tasks with minds of their own—make that calendars of their own. You've completed the discussion of how tasks relate to calendar settings; in the next hour you learn how tasks relate to each other.

Q&A

Q **I've marked Saturday and Sunday to be nonworking days, but my task bars on the Gantt Chart show work on those days. Why?**

A It's an optical illusion. If Saturday and Sunday are drawn in gray on the Gantt Chart, they are in fact nonworking days. But you need to change a format setting to make it look like no work takes place on the weekends. Select Format, Timescale and choose the Nonworking Time tab. In the Formatting options section, set the Draw option to In Front of Task Bars. Now the task bars will appear to stop at each weekend and other nonworking days.

Q **Most of our staff starts work at 7 a.m. and stops at 4 p.m. I've changed the default options to these start and end times, but the Standard base calendar is still scheduling work hours from 8 a.m. until 5 p.m. Do I have to change the calendar, too?**

A Yes you do. These two features serve different functions and don't really "talk" to each other. The default start and end times (under Tools, Options, Calendar) tell Project what times to use for task scheduling unless the calendar says something else. In your case, the Calendar is controlling the schedule. You need to change both the default and calendar settings to get the results you want.

Q **I have created a copy of the Standard calendar, named it the Business calendar, and made holidays nonworking days. Project still schedules tasks to start, finish, and continue through those days. What's wrong?**

A Did you tell Project not the use the Standard base calendar and to use your Business calendar instead? Select Project, Project Information and look in the Calendar field on the dialog box. If you are using a base calendar for your project that is *not* named Standard, use the drop-down list to choose the correct calendar.

Exercises

You've started a new project and want to be sure all the underlying scheduling elements are set so that Project will schedule your project as you expect. But there are so many elements, you'd like to make sure you understand their effects yourself. In the following Exercises, you will make changes to the task default start and end times, to the project base calendar, and to a specific task that requires special scheduling, and observe the effects of each change. Begin with the file, "New Product Hour 5.MPP." Solutions to the exercise can be found in the file, "New Product Hour 5-Exercises.MPP." See the Introduction for instructions to access the sample files and solutions for these exercises on the book's Web page.

1. Open the project file and change the way Project displays Start and Finish dates so that you can also see time values.

2. Set the project start time to 7 a.m. Then set the task default stop time to 7 a.m. Did *any* tasks change to a 7 a.m. start time? Did *all* tasks change to a 7 a.m. start time?

3. Change the Standard base calendar to start working time for Monday through Friday at 7:00 a.m. Did the Start fields for the remaining tasks change?

4. Task 14, "Produce Lab Scale Product," requires special scheduling. The lab is reserved for R&D department use exclusively on Mondays, so that time is not available to you. Create a base calendar, named Lab, that marks Mondays as non-working and assign Task 14 to the new calendar.

5. Before assigning it to a special calendar, Task 14 had a Duration of 10 days, Starting January 3, 2000 at 7:00 a.m. and Finishing January 13, 2000 at 4:00 p.m. Did applying a task calendar change the task Duration? Did the Start day or time change? Is the Finish the same? Can you explain why?

5

HOUR 6

Linking Tasks in the Correct Sequence

In Hours 4, "Starting the Scheduling Process" and 5, "Defining When Project Can Schedule Tasks," you began learning the instructions you can give Project to impose terms and conditions on how it calculates the schedule for you. You saw how to define the times when tasks can be scheduled and how to enter estimates of task duration for both regular working hours and for continuous or elapsed time. You also saw how to create and modify an essential scheduling element—base calendars, for the entire project and for exceptional tasks.

Although the calendar and duration estimates are essential, you didn't see much change in the schedule in the last two hours. In this hour, you will see dramatic changes. You will look at specifying the order in which tasks should be scheduled, which is called *linking tasks*.

In this hour, you will learn:

- How linking tasks changes your plan
- The four types of task linking relationships
- How to create task links
- How to delete or modify task links
- How to schedule overlapping tasks

Linking Tasks

Most of the tasks in your project should probably be done in a definite order. For example, it usually makes a significant difference whether you frame the walls of a new house before or after you lay the foundation. One way to put the tasks in order is to go through the task list and enter start dates for each task manually, making sure that tasks like "frame walls" start after "lay foundation" tasks. But that's the hard way to do it, and it's definitely not the best way. If you later found that you had left out a task toward the beginning of the sequence, or that you didn't allow enough time for one of the early tasks, you would have to enter all the subsequent dates again. Furthermore, you will learn in the next hour that by entering dates for tasks, you are setting up constraints that keep Project from rescheduling tasks freely.

The best way to ensure that tasks are scheduled in the requisite order is to *link* the tasks and let Project calculate the start and finish dates for each task. Then, if you need to insert another task early in the process or revise the duration estimate for a task, Project can recalculate the dates much faster than you could.

 Linking tasks is defining the order in which they should be scheduled. The task links are represented in the Gantt Chart with lines that connect (link) the tasks.

 Do not use linking to make one task follow another so that a resource can work on both tasks. You will look at better ways to handle that problem in the section on resources starting in Hour 11, "Defining Resources and Costs."

Understanding Task Links

The basic idea of linking tasks is easy enough to grasp—you link the tasks, like stringing beads or hooking up railroad cars, in the order in which you want them to be scheduled. Sometimes you link tasks because the laws of nature decree that one task follow the other in time; the link allows you to teach Project a physics lesson. The example of framing the walls after laying the foundation is a case in point, as is applying the final coat of paint after applying the primer coat.

Other times, you link one task to follow another because it just *ought* to be that way. In the New Product project example you saw back in Hours 4 and 5 (see Figure 6.1), Task 6 indicates the screening committee should meet to decide whether to pursue the new product. This should take place only after you have gathered enough information to make an informed decision, as scheduled in Task 5. Without links between tasks, Microsoft Project has no way of knowing the order in which tasks ought to be scheduled.

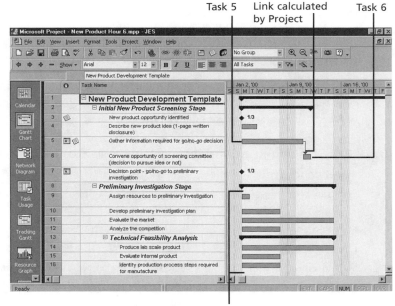

FIGURE 6.1
Without linking, tasks loiter around the start date of the project, all ready to start up the minute the project starts.

However you arrive at the decision of which tasks to link, linking means you tell Microsoft Project to schedule a task first, and then calculate the schedule for the next task so that it can start the moment the first task finishes, if you are scheduling the two tasks end to end. A task whose schedule depends on another task is called a *dependent task*. Microsoft Project automatically recalculates the scheduled dates for the dependent task when anything changes the scheduled dates for the task on which it depends.

6

NEW TERM The terms *predecessor* and *successor* are usually applied to linked tasks, with *predecessor* designating the task whose schedule must be calculated first and *successor* designating the task whose schedule is calculated only afterward.

Defining Types of Dependency Relationships

In most dependency relationships between tasks, the finish date for the predecessor determines the start date for the dependent (successor) task. That's the case, for example, with the foundation–frame walls sequence. This is called a *finish-to-start* relationship (see Table 6.1) because you link the finish of the predecessor to the start of the successor.

The finish-to-start link is only one of several possible links, however. For example, you can also link tasks so that they can start together or finish together. Table 6.1 (and Figure 6.2) show the four possible linking relationships. In each case, the name of the relationship is made up of the predecessor's connecting start or finish date and then the successor task's dependent start or finish date.

Project also uses a shorthand code for each type of relationship. The first letter in the code refers to the predecessor's linking date (start or finish) and the second letter refers to the successor task's linked date (start or finish).

TABLE 6.1   Linking Relationships Available in Microsoft Project

Dependency Type	Code	Description
Finish-to-Start	FS	The predecessor's finish determines when the successor can start
Start-to-Start	SS	Both tasks can start when the predecessor starts
Finish-to-Finish	FF	Both tasks can finish when the predecessor finishes
Start-to-Finish	SF	The start of the predecessor determines when the successor can finish

When you link summary tasks, you can use only the Finish-to-Start or Start-to-Start type links; in other words, you can link the start of a summary task to a predecessor, but you can't link the finish of a summary task to a predecessor.

If you need to use the Finish-to-Finish or Start-to-Finish link types for summary tasks, you must apply the link directly to the subtasks under the summary task.

FIGURE 6.2

The types of dependency relationships are built around the schedule for the predecessor.

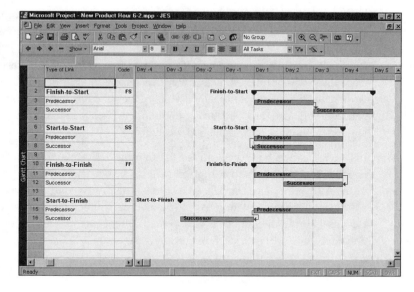

Linking a summary task has the effect of applying the same link to all its subtasks. So, be careful when you link both the summary task and one of its subtasks to predecessors outside the summary task group—it's easy to create conflicting or redundant links.

Everyone seems to understand how two tasks can be linked Finish-to-Start, with one task not able to start until another is finished, and most people have no trouble understanding how two tasks might be linked Start-to-Start and Finish-to-Finish so that they are scheduled to start together or finish together. However, many people have a hard time understanding why you have the Start-to-Finish link, when a task is scheduled to finish when another task starts. Why not just use the Finish-to-Start link—both link types place the tasks end to end, as you can see in Figure 6.2.

The difference lies in which task *drives* the other task. In the Finish-to-Start link, the task that comes earlier determines the schedule dates; in the Start-to-Finish link, the task that comes later calls the shots and its schedule is calculated first.

For example, in the home construction task, laying the foundation determines when you can frame the walls—it is the predecessor to framing the walls. Framing the walls requires lumber, however, and you can't start framing until you get the lumber. Therefore, a case could be made for making Get Lumber the predecessor to Frame

Walls, but you need to get the lumber only because you're planning to use it in framing, and there's no need getting it until it's needed. Doesn't it make more sense to see when the framing can take place and then schedule the lumber delivery just in time for the framing? That way, for instance, if rainy weather interrupts and keeps the foundation from finishing on time, you can enter that information in Project as you're tracking the work, and Project can automatically delay the scheduled start of framing the walls and consequently also delay acquiring the lumber. Then you won't have to provide dry storage for the lumber during the bad weather.

Figure 6.3 shows both scenarios of the framing walls example. With good weather, the tasks will take 10 days to complete. (So, it's a small house, a bungalow.) In the bad weather scenario, I've introduced a split starting on Wednesday when the rains came. The split extends the completion of the foundation, which delays the start of the framing. Because getting the lumber is tied to the framing task, it's also delayed so that it's not delivered too early and left lying around in the rain.

FIGURE 6.3

If bad weather forces a delay in framing, you want the lumber delivery delayed also.

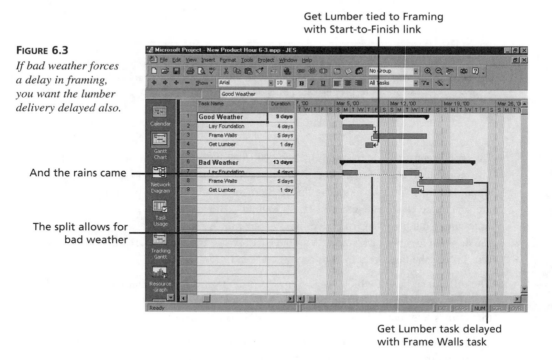

The same principle is used to save storage costs and interest on the money used when ordering materials and parts for manufacturing processes. Parts are ordered just in time for the assembly process that will use them. "Just in time" scheduling has become an important cost-saving tool in many industries, and that's precisely what the Start-to-Finish link describes.

Allowing for Delayed and Overlapping Links

Frequently, the successor task cannot start immediately on the finish date of the predecessor. For example, when the foundation is poured in the construction task, you really should wait a day or two for the concrete to harden completely before you start framing the walls. Or, imagine the tasks in painting the exterior of a house. First, there should be a primer coat, then you apply the final coat, and finally you have to clean up (see Figure 6.4). In reality, however, you have to let the first coat dry before starting the final coat.

FIGURE 6.4

Lags and Leads give added realism and flexibility to the schedule.

Lag time creates a gap between FS tasks

Lead time creates an overlap of FS tasks

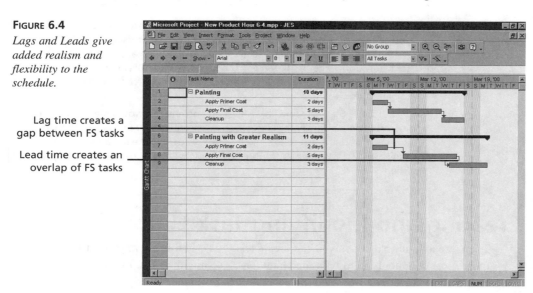

In both scenarios in Figure 6.4, these tasks are linked in Finish-to-Start relationships. In the second scenario, however, Painting with Greater Realism, the Final Coat does not follow immediately on the heels of the Primer Coat; there's time allowed for drying. Because the first coat of paint needs to dry for 2 days (2 *elapsed* days, mind you), I have built a *lag* into the link between the tasks. I told Project to start the successor Task 2 elapsed days after the predecessor task finishes.

NEW TERM *Lag time* is extra time allowed between the dates that link the predecessor and successor tasks. The effect is to delay the scheduled date for the successor.

6

This is actually Project's formula for calculating successor schedules:

```
Predecessor linked date + Lag time = Successor linked date
```

In Figure 6.4, I also decided that the Cleanup task could actually start a little before the Final Coat is completed. So, I built in some *lead time* for the Cleanup task by telling Project to start the successor task one day earlier than the link would otherwise dictate.

NEW TERM *Lead time* is used to move the scheduled date for the successor task to a little earlier time. The effect is usually to overlap the linked tasks. Lead time is entered as negative lag time in Microsoft Project (see the formula in the preceding definition of Lag).

> Lags and Leads are usually entered as time units (for example, 2 days), but you can also enter them as a percentage of the predecessor task's duration. A 10 percent Lag means delay the successor by 10 percent of the predecessor's duration value. A 10 percent Lead (entered as **-10%**) means start the successor earlier by an amount of time equal to 10 percent of the predecessor's duration value.
>
> Therefore, a Start-to-Start link with a 10 percent Lag would mean "start the successor only after the predecessor has started and 10 percent of the work is done." And a Finish-to-Start link with a 10 percent Lead would mean "start the successor when the predecessor is within 10 percent of being finished."

Creating and Modifying Task Links

There are a number of ways you can create task links. In this book, you'll look only at those most commonly used with the Gantt Chart—using the Link Tasks tool, the Task Information dialog box, the mouse, or the Task Form in the lower pane of a split window. For some of these methods, you actually create the default Finish to Start link first, being careful to correctly identify the predecessor and the successor; then you can edit the link to change the type or to add Leads or Lags.

Linking and Unlinking Tasks with the Toolbar

The simplest and easiest way to link tasks is to select the tasks in the task list and then click the Link Tasks tool on the Standard toolbar, or choose Edit, Link Tasks from the menu. If the task bars are visible in the timeline, you will see the linking lines appear immediately.

There's no limit to the number of tasks you can select for linking before you click the Link Tasks tool. You can link just one predecessor and one successor at a time, or you can link all the tasks in the project in the same operation.

If you select the tasks for linking by dragging to select adjacent tasks, tasks higher up on the task list (with lower ID numbers) are always the predecessor to tasks lower in the selection (with higher ID numbers), no matter which direction you drag the mouse in the selection. However, if you use the Ctrl key to select tasks that aren't adjacent, the task you click first is the predecessor to the next task you click. For example, if you hold down the Ctrl key and click Tasks 5, 2, and 12 in that order and then click the Link Tasks tool, Task 5 will be the predecessor to Task 2, and Task 2 will be the predecessor to Task 12.

 If you find a link between tasks is no longer necessary, you need to remove the current link. There are several ways to remove links. You can unlink tasks by using the menu or toolbar. Select the tasks you want to unlink in the task list in the top pane, and click the Unlink Tasks tool on the Standard toolbar or choose Edit, Unlink Tasks from the menu.

> If you select a single task and then click the Unlink Tasks tool or choose Edit, Unlink Tasks, Project removes all predecessors and successors for that task—it is no longer involved in any linking relationships.

If you select multiple tasks and then choose Edit, Unlink Tasks or click the Unlink Tasks button, Project removes all links between any pair of the *selected* tasks. To remove all links from the project, select all tasks by clicking the Select All area above the task ID numbers and then choose Edit, Unlink Tasks or click the Unlink Tasks button.

Linking Tasks in a Dialog Box

Many Project users get accustomed to working in the Task Information dialog box. You can create, modify, and delete links in the dialog box, but there is one mental adjustment you need to make. Project asks you to think backwards using this technique. The tab in the dialog box is named Predecessors—you must tell Project which tasks *precede* the one you selected before opening the Task Information box.

In Figure 6.5, Task 5, "Gather information required for go/no-go decision," was selected and its Task Information box opened by double-clicking on the task name. Then the Predecessors tab was selected. All current predecessors are listed by ID number and by name in the Predecessors section. The link Type and any Lag (or Lead) time is also shown. In this example, selected Task 5 can start when Task 4, "Describe new product idea," has finished (FS link type) and there is no gap or overlap between the two tasks (0d Lag).

Task Information
Predecessors tab   Link type

Selected task name ────────

Current predecessors
to selected task

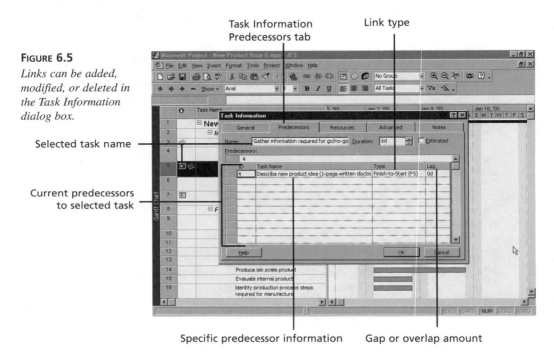

Specific predecessor information   Gap or overlap amount

The Task Information dialog box is particularly handy when you need to create links to several preceding tasks at once, and when those preceding tasks have nothing to do with each other so no series of links exists between them. Just remember to select and work with the successor task in the dialog box.

To Do: Linking Tasks with the Task Information Dialog Box

To create or change task links in the Task Information dialog box, follow these steps:

1. Select a task that will be the successor in one or more linking relationships.

2. Display the Task Information dialog box by double-clicking the task Name or choosing the Task Information button on the Standard Toolbar.

3. Move to the Predecessor tab (shown in Figure 6.5).

4. Click in the Predecessors section to add, delete, or modify links:

      • To add a predecessor to the list, enter its task ID number or choose its name from the in-cell drop-down list in the Task Name area.

      • To change the link type, click in the Type area and select a link type from the in-cell drop-down list.

      • To create a gap (positive amount) or overlap (negative amount) between the predecessor and the selected task, enter a value in the Lag field (start negative values by first typing the minus sign).

      • To break a link between tasks, select a predecessor and press the Delete key, or choose None as the link Type.

   5. Continue making additions or changes to as many predecessors as necessary.

   6. Click OK when finished. Project will draw, or re-draw, the appropriate link lines on the Gantt Chart.

Creating Links Using the Mouse

For the graphically inclined, you can use the mouse to link task bars on the timescale side of the Gantt Chart. You can also use the mouse to edit the linking relationship.

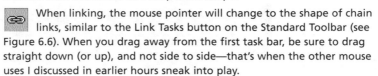

Be careful! Clicking the mouse pointer in these views can produce strange and wondrous results. It's easy to accidentally reschedule the task, change its duration, or mark the task as being partially complete if you're not careful. Watch the shape of the mouse pointer carefully after you start dragging because each action has its own pointer shape.

When linking, the mouse pointer will change to the shape of chain links, similar to the Link Tasks button on the Standard Toolbar (see Figure 6.6). When you drag away from the first task bar, be sure to drag straight down (or up), and not side to side—that's when the other mouse uses I discussed in earlier hours sneak into play.

If you start dragging the mouse from a task bar to link it to another task and the mouse does *not* change into the chain-links shape, you can abort the operation (with or without colorful epithets) by releasing the pointer in an open area of the Gantt Chart.

6

Dragging the mouse pointer from the middle of one task bar to another task bar always establishes the default Finish-to-Start link between the tasks. The task you start on is the predecessor, and the task you drag to is the successor task.

To Do: Linking Tasks with the Mouse

To create a Finish-to-Start relationship between two tasks, do the following:

1. Scroll the task list so that the *predecessor task* is visible onscreen. (This entire technique is easiest when both the predecessor and successor task bars are visible on the screen.)

2. Position the mouse pointer over the middle of the predecessor task. It's not necessary to select the row for the task in the Gantt Chart table. In Figure 6.6, the mouse was over Task 4, "Describe new product idea" when the button was pressed to drag.

Link information box   Tasks to be linked   Predecessor task
                               identified

FIGURE 6.6

Drag from the predecessor task bar to the dependent (successor) task bar to establish a Finish-to-Start link.

Successor task ——

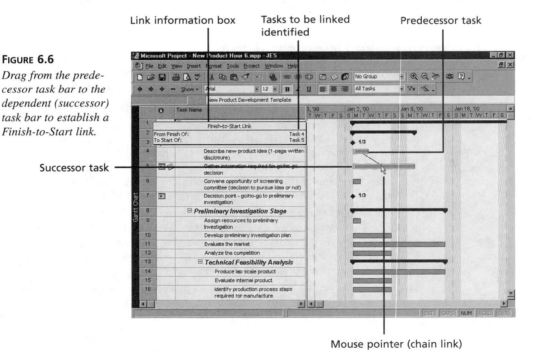

Mouse pointer (chain link)

3. Click and drag toward the middle of the successor task ("Gather information required" in the figure). The mouse pointer should change to the chain-links shape when you drag straight down toward the successor. If it doesn't, you weren't in the

▼ middle of the task bar when you started dragging, or you dragged slightly to one side before dragging down. You should stop your attempt to link by releasing the mouse in any open area on the timeline part of the chart.

A Finish-to-Start Link information box will identify the predecessor task you started on and the dependent task bar you have positioned the mouse over (see Figure 6.6). If the dependent task you're seeking is off the screen, move to the edge of the screen, and Project will scroll the task list or the timescale to bring the task bar into view.

▲ 4. When in position over the successor task, release the mouse button.

Editing and Removing Links Using the Mouse

The dependency type created by dragging the mouse is always a Finish-to-Start relationship. You can change the link type, add a Lag or Lead, or even delete the link in the timescale with the mouse.

To Do: Modifying a Link with the Mouse

To modify existing task links, using the mouse, follow these steps:

1. Position the tip of the mouse pointer on the line connecting the tasks whose link you want to delete or change; it helps to actually point at the linking arrowhead.

2. Double-click the linking line. The Task Dependency dialog box appears.

3. Change the type of link in the Type list box (see Figure 6.7).

FIGURE 6.7

Change or delete a dependency relationship with the Task Dependency dialog box.

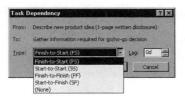

4. Edit the Lag or Lead in the Lag box.

5. To remove the link, set the link Type to None or click the Delete button (hidden from view in Figure 6.7)

▲ 6. Click the OK button to complete the deletion or change and close the dialog box.

Editing Links with the Task Form

Another approach to viewing and editing task links is to split the window and display the Task Form beneath the Gantt Chart. Here you can view details of the linking relationships in the bottom pane (see Figure 6.8).

6

FIGURE **6.8**

The predecessor and successor details in the Task Form display link information for review or editing.

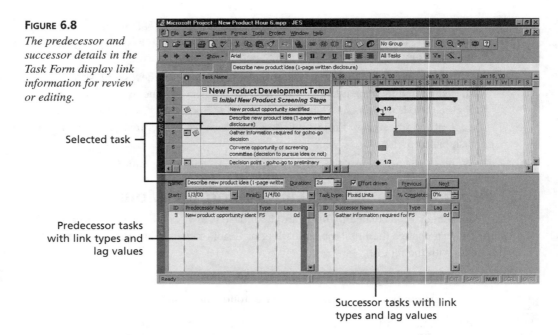

Selected task —

Predecessor tasks with link types and lag values

Successor tasks with link types and lag values

To Do: Displaying Predecessor and Successor Details

To see a list of both predecessors and successors for a task, display the screen as follows:

1. Display the Gantt Chart and split the window with the Window, Split command. The Task Form will be displayed in the lower pane.

2. Activate the lower pane by clicking anywhere in it.

3. Choose Format, Details, Predecessors & Successors from the menu.

   Predecessors for the task that's selected in the top pane are detailed on the left, and successors for that task are detailed on the right.

Working in the Task Form is very similar to editing links in the Task Information dialog box discussed earlier in this hour. You can delete a link in the Task Form by clicking anywhere in the row for the link and pressing the Delete key. Then click OK on the Form to complete the change in the task. You can also modify the link types and the Lag (or Lead) values directly on the Task Form.

Working with the Automatic Linking Option

Microsoft Project's *Autolink* feature will keep chains of linked tasks intact when you delete or insert tasks within the chain—but only if tasks in the chain are linked Finish-to-Start. Autolink is enabled by default, but you can disable it on the Options dialog box.

This is a time-saving feature if you need to re-order tasks that have already been linked together. If you move a group of linked tasks, Project maintains their connections to each other and to other portions of the project, if the moved tasks were in Finish-to-Start relationships. Otherwise, all bets are off and you must recreate any SS, FF, or SF links.

To Do: Disabling or Enabling Autolink

To turn the Autolink feature on or off, follow these steps:

1. Choose Tools, Options to display the Options dialog box and select the Schedule tab (see Figure 6.9).

2. Deselect the Autolink Inserted or Moved Tasks check box. This disables Autolink. To turn it back on, select the check box again.

FIGURE 6.9

Autolinking controls how Project handles links in moved or added tasks.

3. To set the option status as a global default for all new projects, click the Set as Default button. Otherwise, the change you make will affect only the active project document.

4. Click the OK button to close the dialog box.

Reviewing Your Task Links

The project schedule is heavily influenced by the linking relationships you establish among tasks. You should review the link relationships carefully before committing to the project schedule. Accidental or omitted links could easily skew the project's finish date.

You should also review the links with an eye toward shortening your project schedule. Identifying task relationships where overlap between tasks is possible is one of the best ways to shorten the overall time it takes to finish a project. So look for opportunities to use Start-to-Start and Finish-to-Finish links or to use Leads and Lags to overlap tasks.

When you link tasks, you create task sequences or chains of events. The longest chain in a project, the chain with the latest finish date, determines the finish of the project. The way to shorten the project is to shorten that chain of tasks by decreasing the duration of individual tasks or by overlapping tasks. Because shortening projects is often one of the big chores of project management, Project identifies those tasks that are on the longest chain by labeling them as *critical tasks*, and the chain itself is cryptically called the *critical path*. (You can call it "the longest chain of events.")

You will see more about critical tasks, critical paths, and shortening the project in Hour 16, "Fine-Tuning the Project Plan."

The Gantt Chart shows the task links as arrows connecting the task bars, with the arrow always connecting the linked dates and pointing to the dependent (successor) task. Also, as you create and modify task links, Project fills cells in the Predecessors column on the Gantt Chart table. After you have the logic down, you can manually enter your task links in this column if you are more comfortable with the row and column format.

In Figure 6.10, the Predecessors column has been exposed from the example used in Figure 6.4. The logic is this: numbers in the column are the predecessors to the tasks where they are entered. That is, Task 2 is a predecessor to Task 3. But what type of link is it? Because there are no letters following the task number in the cell, the link is the default Finish-to-Start type. Notice that the entry for Task 8's predecessor looks a bit different. Tasks 7 and 8 are in a Finish-to-Start relationship (7FS) but there is a two-day lag (+2 days) between the finish of 7 and the start of 8.

Other views are useful, too, when reviewing the links defined in a project. You saw in Figure 6.8 that the Task Form can be used to review the links for each task. You can also review your task links in the Network Diagram view. The Network Diagram view concentrates on linking relationships by representing each task as a box with arrows from predecessor to successor tasks (see Hour 8, "Working with the Other Task Views").

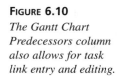

FIGURE 6.10
The Gantt Chart Predecessors column also allows for task link entry and editing.

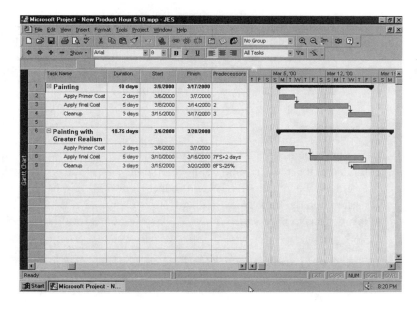

Summary

In this hour, you learned about the real heart of scheduling: linking tasks to determine the order in which they are scheduled. The default relationship, Finish-to-Start, creates a stepping stone pattern on the Gantt Chart. This is the link type created by linking tasks using the toolbar or mouse. Three other link types are available—Start-to-Start, Finish-to-Finish, and the less-used Start-to-Finish. Both the Task Information dialog box and the Task Form provide convenient layouts for adding, deleting, and modifying task links.

Q&A

Q I linked two tasks and accidentally got the wrong task as the predecessor. How do I swap predecessor and successor?

A Sorry, but you can't reverse the roles of the linked tasks. You must delete the link and create it again.

Q When I try to link tasks with the mouse, the screen scrolls too fast for me to find the successor task. What can I do?

A When linking tasks that are not close to each other on the screen, it's often simpler to select the tasks by clicking with the Ctrl key and then using the Link Tasks tool.

Q I have two tasks linked FS and want to change the link to be SS. No matter where I double-click on the link line, the Task Dependency box doesn't display the task names of the two I want to work with. What am I doing wrong?

6

A It isn't you; it's the way the link lines are drawn on the screen. The problem you're having is caused by two or more link lines being drawn on top of each other, so Project makes its best guess as to which pair of tasks you are interested in. Use another method, such as working in the Task Information dialog box for the successor task in the pair you want to modify.

Exercises

You have the first 25 tasks listed for your New Product development plan. It's time to link tasks together and find out how long this part of the project will take to complete. Begin by opening the file, "New Product Hour 6.MPP." The solution to the exercises can be found in the file, "New Product Hour 6-Exercise.MPP." See the Introduction for instructions to access the sample files and solutions for these exercises on the book's Web page.

1. The following groups of tasks should be scheduled in "normal" Finish-to-Start sequences.

   Tasks 3–7

   Tasks 9–12

   Tasks 14–16

   Tasks 20–25

2. Your team has concluded that Tasks 17, 18, and 19 ("Assess manufacturing capabilities," "Determine safety issues," and "Determine environmental issues," respectively) can all start when Task 10, "Develop preliminary investigation plan," has finished. Create these three sets of paired tasks.

3. You also know that Tasks 17, 18 and 19 must finish before Task 20, "Review legal issues," can start. Create these three links.

4. The "Initial New Product Screening Stage" (Task 2) must be finished before you can start the next phase, "Preliminary Investigation Stage" (Task 8). Link these two summary tasks.

5. So far, the "Technical Feasibility Analysis" summary at Task 13 is not linked into your decision milestone at Task 25. Assign this an FS link.

6. Tasks 14 and 15 are already linked together, but further review indicates that they can in fact start together. Task 15 is actually dependent on the beginning of Task 14, not its finish. Change this link to be a Start-to-Start type.

7. What is the project end date, displayed to the right of the Task 25 milestone marker? Now make a change. Task 18 is now estimated to require 15 days; change its duration. What is the date next to the Task 25 milestone now?

HOUR 7

Working with Deadlines and Constraints

In Hour 6, "Linking Tasks in the Correct Sequence," you examined the essential task scheduling tools. Four types of task links are available for your use in connecting tasks: the default Finish-to-Start, plus Start-to-Start, Finish-to-Finish, and the less-used Start-to-Finish. With these links in place, Project can show you the effects of changes in the schedule if one or more tasks must be rescheduled. The tasks can move freely within the limits of the task links.

However, you may not want some tasks to move about in the schedule. If your contract includes a penalty for not starting a task on time, for example, you will want to keep a close eye on that particular task. Project includes two features to help you monitor tasks that must not vary from a specific date. In this hour, you will look at how to handle tasks that must not move around in your schedule, or at least have Project issue a warning if an important task is rescheduled.

In this hour, you will learn:

- How to connect a task to a specific date
- How to set a deadline date for a task
- The different uses for task constraints and task deadlines
- How to apply constraint and deadline filters to the task list

Working with Constraints

In Hour 5, "Defining When Project Can Schedule Tasks," you looked at the case where a task must be scheduled according to a modified base calendar in order to accurately reflect downtime or other work interruptions. Another category of special scheduling instructions you provide to Microsoft Project are those that tell Project about deadlines and fixed dates for individual tasks or groups of tasks.

 A *constraint* is a limitation on the range of dates when a task can be scheduled.

When you add a new task to a project that is scheduled from a fixed start date, Microsoft Project automatically assigns the default constraint that the task is to be scheduled as soon as possible after the start of the project. When you add a task to a fixed finish date project, Project assigns the constraint that the task is to be scheduled as late as possible before the end of the project. These are two relatively mild constraints, if they can be considered constraints at all. There are other cases, however, when you need to be more restrictive, as shown in the following examples:

- You might have contractual agreements that bind the start or finish of a task to a specific date. If the project involves work for a customer, there could be specific intermediate deadlines defined in the contract. Or, your agreement with a contractor or vendor might stipulate the earliest date you can expect completion of the parts of the project they're responsible for.
- Government regulations could impose date constraints. For instance, income and payroll taxes must be filed no later than designated dates, and environment laws also have compliance dates.
- Your own internal management might impose arbitrary deadlines for individual tasks in the project.

All these special scheduling instructions, including as soon or as late as possible, are entered into Project by defining a *constraint type* for the task and, when appropriate, a *constraint date*.

Understanding the Types of Constraints

The eight constraint types are described in Table 7.1. The order of the listing in the table is not alphabetical (as it will be when you pick a constraint type on the screen), but is arranged to help you understand the constraint types. The abbreviations are occasionally found in Project's Help texts and are included here just for reference.

TABLE 7.1 The Constraint Types in Microsoft Project

Constraint Type	Description
As Soon As Possible (ASAP)	Marks a task as essentially unconstrained. There's no constraint date for the task.
As Late As Possible (ALAP)	Delays the task as long as possible, without holding up the finish of the project. There's no constraint date for the task.
Start No Earlier Than (SNET)	The task can't start before the defined constraint date. It must be scheduled to start on or after that date.
Finish No Earlier Than (FNET)	The task can't finish before the defined constraint date. It can be scheduled to finish on or after that date.
Start No Later Than (SNLT)	The task must be scheduled to start on or before the defined constraint date.
Finish No Later Than (FNLT)	The task can't finish any later than the defined constraint date. It can be scheduled to finish on or before that date.
Must Start On (MSO)	The task must start on the defined constraint date, not earlier or later.
Must Finish On (MFO)	The task must finish exactly on the defined constraint date, not earlier or later.

Summary tasks can only be assigned a few of the possible constraints: As Soon As Possible, Start No Earlier Than (typically used in projects that are scheduled from a fixed finish date), and Finish No Later Than (in the more common case of projects scheduled from a fixed start date, this prevents the summary group from slipping out in time).

Flexible and Inflexible Constraints

When a task has a constraint type other than As Soon As Possible or As Late As Possible, you will see an icon in the Indicators field (see Figure 7.1). These icons resemble little calendars with either a red or a blue dot in the icon. The red dots indicate an *inflexible* constraint, and the blue dots indicate a *flexible* constraint.

7

NEW TERM   *Inflexible constraints* are those that can potentially create scheduling conflicts—
they can present barriers to Project's ability to schedule all your tasks while honoring the constraints. *Flexible constraints* are those that are unlikely to create problems with the schedule.

FIGURE 7.1

All constraints except As Soon As Possible and As Late As Possible display special indicators.

Project scheduled from fixed start date

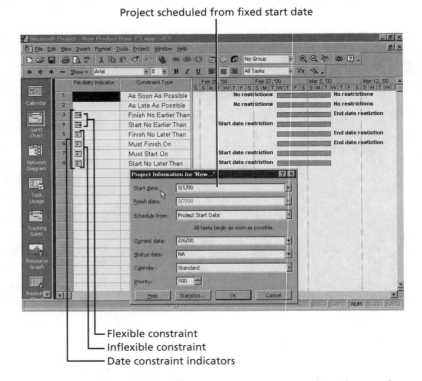

Flexible constraint
Inflexible constraint
Date constraint indicators

NEW TERM   Predecessors other than Start-to-Finish tend to push successor tasks to later and
later dates in projects with a fixed start date. If a successor task has an inflexible constraint, a *scheduling conflict* exists when the predecessors try to push the task past the constraint date.

In projects with fixed finish dates, the predecessors tend to push successor tasks to earlier dates, and a scheduling conflict arises if the predecessors try to push the successor task to a date earlier than the inflexible constraint date.

All constraints restrict Project's freedom to schedule tasks to some degree, but *inflexible* constraints are called that because they can potentially keep Project from scheduling tasks as your linking instructions require. Whether a constraint is inflexible depends on the constraint type and whether the project is scheduled from a fixed start date or a fixed finish date.

- When projects are scheduled from a fixed *start* date, Project generally has to push the schedule toward later and later dates to accommodate all the linked tasks. The inflexible constraint types are those that might keep Project from rescheduling tasks to later dates—they are the Must Start On, Must Finish On, Start No Later Than, and Finish No Later Than types.
- If the project is scheduled from a fixed *finish* date, Project has to push the linked tasks to earlier dates to get everything done by the finish date. For a fixed finish date project, the inflexible constraints are those that might prevent Project from rescheduling tasks to earlier dates—they are Must Start On, Must Finish On, Start No Earlier Than, and Finish No Earlier Than.

Creating Task Constraints

You can enter task constraints in the Task Information dialog box. In Figure 7.2, Task 10, "Develop preliminary investigation plan," is to be constrained to finish no later than 1/31/2000 because any further delay would cause the product to come to market too late.

FIGURE 7.2

Choose the constraint from the type entry list on the Advanced tab of the Task Information dialog box.

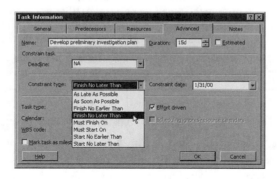

To Do: Entering Task Constraints

To associate a task with a specific date, follow these steps:

1. Select the task you want to constrain.
2. Choose Project, Task Information, or click the Information button on the Standard toolbar to display the Task Information dialog box.
3. Select the Advanced tab.
4. From the drop-down list in the Constrain type field, select the constraint type you want (see Figure 7.2).
5. In the Constrain Date text box, enter the constraint date, if necessary. You can also use the drop-down date picker to set the date. The As Soon As Possible and As Late As Possible constraints do not require a constraint date, but all others require a date entry.

7

▼   6. Click OK to close the dialog box.

> While you have the Task Information dialog box open, it's a good idea to add a note to the task indicating why the constraint was set. This gives you a reminder, and if you are sharing the project file with colleagues, gives them important information, too. To add a note to the task, simply click the Notes tab and type the note in the Notes field.

▲

To remove a constraint, change the constraint type to As Soon As Possible for fixed start date projects or to As Late As Possible for fixed finish date projects. When changing a constraint type like this, any constraint dates that were set will be deleted by Project when you click OK to close the dialog box.

> As tempting as setting date markers may sound, you should avoid placing constraints unless absolutely necessary. Otherwise, you'll find yourself having to help Project find ways to work around them, or you'll find them getting in your way as you try to shorten the duration of the overall project.
>
> Setting task deadlines instead of task constraints may serve your needs better. See the section "Recording Deadlines" later in this hour.

There are several other ways you can set constraints, usually unintentionally.

- If you *enter* a date in the Start or Finish field of the task, Project makes that date a constraint, albeit a flexible constraint. In a fixed start date project, typing a Start (or Finish) date tells Project to set a Start (or Finish) No Earlier Than constraint.

- If you use the mouse to *drag* a task bar to a later date, Project assigns the Start No Earlier Than constraint type and sets the constraint date to be the changed task Start date.

- If you use the mouse to *extend* a task bar to a later finish date, Project also assigns the Start No Earlier Than constraint type and sets the constraint date to be the task Start date.

You should generally avoid entering specific dates for tasks unless they really are required. Let Project calculate the dates for you. Project is generally not free to reschedule constrained tasks to optimize your schedule.

When you attempt to apply an inflexible constraint to a task that has predecessor tasks, Project's Planning Wizard warns you that the constraint could potentially cause a scheduling conflict and asks you to decide whether to continue (see Figure 7.3). The Wizard's dialog box will usually offer you three choices:

- Cancel. No constraint will be set. This is the default selection, and it's the same as clicking the Cancel button. So if you don't change the selection, you will fail to set a constraint whether you click OK or Cancel.

- Continue, but set a flexible constraint, one suggested by Project, instead of the inflexible constraint you requested.

- Continue, forcing Project to set the inflexible constraint, despite any possible scheduling conflicts.

This is one time you don't want to be in a hurry. The Planning Wizard is trying to help you avoid problems. Take the time to thoroughly read and understand these scheduling conflict warnings. (Instead of saying to yourself, "Yeah, yeah" and pressing Escape to make the warning box go away!)

FIGURE 7.3

If an inflexible constraint is entered for a task with predecessors, Project warns you and gives you a chance to change your mind.

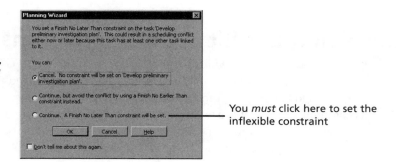

You *must* click here to set the inflexible constraint

If you go ahead and apply the constraint and it does in fact create a scheduling conflict either immediately or later, because of changes in the schedules for predecessor tasks, you will see another Planning Wizard warning that a conflict is about to occur (see Figure 7.4). Your choices now are simply to cancel the action and avoid the conflict, which is the default selection, or to continue and allow the scheduling conflict. You must select the Continue option and then click OK to go ahead with the change you requested.

If you proceed with a change that creates a scheduling conflict, you have to deal with the conflict somehow (see the next section) because it's an indication that your project is not workable as defined.

7

FIGURE 7.4

*When a scheduling
conflict is imminent,
the Planning Wizard
gives you a chance to
cancel the action that
would cause it.*

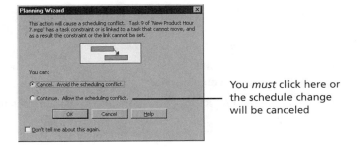

You *must* click here or
the schedule change
will be canceled

You get only one Planning Wizard warning about each scheduling conflict
you create. If you create a conflict and don't deal with it right away, you will
have to find a solution on your own at some later point. The next section
shows you how to find unresolved scheduling conflicts.

Resolving Conflicts Caused by Constraints

If you decide to go ahead with a change that creates a scheduling conflict, you must deal
with the conflict resulting from the constraint. When a scheduling conflict occurs,
Project has to honor the link to the predecessor (and schedule the constrained task past
its constraint date), or it has to honor the constraint and not observe the link to the predecessor. By default, Project honors constraint barriers at all times and ignores the link
instructions because constraints are normally what you call "hard" constraints.

With hard constraints, the screen really doesn't tell you for certain that a scheduling conflict exists. The link arrow doubles back on itself in a tortured S-shape (see Figure 7.5).
However, this could just as well be the link arrow for a Finish-to-Start link with Lead
time. The indicator is just the same as it is for all inflexible constraints, so you can't tell
that there's a scheduling conflict just from looking at the screen. Furthermore, you have
seen the last warning from the Planning Wizard. You're on your own if you want to find
the conflict and fix it.

If you would like Project to honor the predecessor link, it must ignore the constraint.
You can choose that option by instructing Project to make all constraints "soft" constraints.

NEW TERM Microsoft Project must honor tasks' constraint dates (and ignore their predecessor links) if constraints are *hard constraints* in that project; it honors the predecessor links, and not the constraint dates, if the project uses *soft constraints*.

FIGURE 7.5

A scheduling conflict is not really evident on the screen when the constraint is honored.

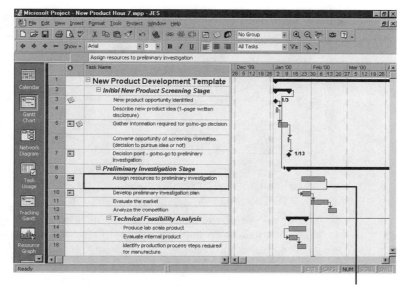

Could *you* tell there's a scheduling conflict here?

You can change the way a project uses constraints, from hard to soft, with the Options dialog box.

To Do: Making Constraints Hard or Soft

To set the default method for handling task constraints, do the following:

1. Choose Tools, Options to display the Options dialog box and select the Schedule tab (see Figure 7.6).

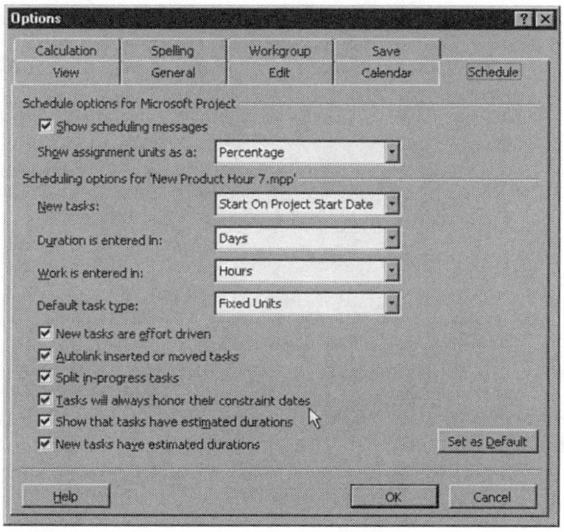

FIGURE 7.6

Make a project's constraints soft in the Options dialog box.

7

▼   2. Clear the check box next to Tasks Will Always Honor Their Constraint Dates to make constraints *soft* constraints. Fill the check box to make them *hard* constraints, and honor constraints over linking relationships.

▲   3. Click OK to close the dialog box.

> Note that the choice of hard or soft constraints is not made task by task: The choice affects the way all constraints are used in the project.

If any task constraint is not honored, Project displays a special indicator next to that task (see Figure 7.7). This indicator is the only easy way to identify scheduling conflicts after the Planning Wizard warnings have ceased being displayed. You can make constraints soft to display the indicator where conflicts exist, find those tasks with conflicts, and figure out what to do about the conflict.

FIGURE **7.7**

The scheduling conflict indicator appears only when you select soft constraints for the project.

Indicator for missed constraint date

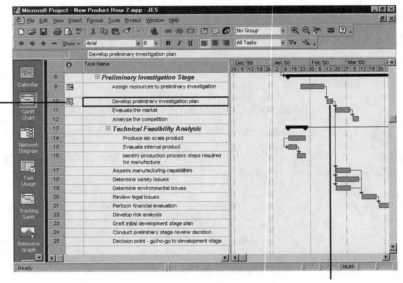

Task link honored instead of constraint

> If soft constraints are in effect, you can still see the Planning Wizard warning when you set inflexible constraints, but you won't see a warning when a scheduling conflict actually occurs.

You can apply the filter named Tasks With Fixed Dates to the task list to filter out all but the tasks with fixed dates. The list includes all tasks with constraints, but it also includes tasks that have already had dates recorded for the beginning of actual work (because dates for actual work are fixed, too, as far as Project is concerned). Nevertheless, the filter can significantly reduce the number of tasks you need to look over to see if the scheduling indicator is showing. And, if you apply the filter before you start tracking actual work, only tasks with constraints are displayed.

To Do: Applying the Tasks with Fixed Dates Filter

To Do ▼

To view only those tasks with fixed dates, do the following:

1. In the Gantt Chart, choose Project, Filtered for, More Filters to display the More Filters dialog box.

2. Scroll down to select the Tasks With Fixed Dates filter.

3. Click the Apply button to close the dialog box and apply the filter.

   The filter restricts the display to only those tasks with constraints or tasks with actual start dates already entered.

4. When finished, you can remove the filter by pressing the F3 function key or by choosing Project, Filtered for, All Tasks from the menu.

▲

After you have identified tasks with conflicting links and constraint settings, you need to decide what, if anything, to do about these scheduling problems. You can correct a scheduling conflict in three ways:

- Change the constraint by changing its type or date or by eliminating it altogether.

- Change the predecessor link or eliminate it altogether.

- Reduce the duration of the predecessor task, or the duration of its predecessors, so that the immediate predecessor to the constrained task finishes in time to allow the constraint to be honored.

Splitting Tasks

Another scheduling trick we will look at in this hour is splitting tasks.

NEW TERM A *task split* is an interruption in the work on a task—work stops at the start of the split and resumes at the end of the split. As far as Project is concerned, you can introduce as many splits in a task as you want.

Usually a task split is introduced because we know that the resources who have to work on the task will be needed elsewhere for the duration of the split, or work has already started on a task and we need to stop it for a while before resuming later. Splits allow us

7

to let a task get started, then be put on hold while attention is on other tasks, and then be completed later.

Until you assign resources to a task, you can create splits only in the Gantt Chart view, using the mouse. With resources assigned, you can also introduce splits in other views (see Hour 14, "Editing Resource Assignments," for more details).

To Do: Splitting a Task

Follow these steps to split a task:

1. With the task displayed in the Gantt Chart view, click the Split Task tool on the Standard toolbar, or choose Edit, Split Task from the menu.

2. Position the mouse pointer over the task bar you would like to split. The Split Task information box will tell you the date when the split will begin (see Figure 7.8). Position the mouse so that the date in the information box is the date you want the split to begin.

Split task
information box

Date split will start
if you click now

FIGURE 7.8

*The Split Task infor-
mation box tells you
where the split will
start if you click the
mouse pointer now.*

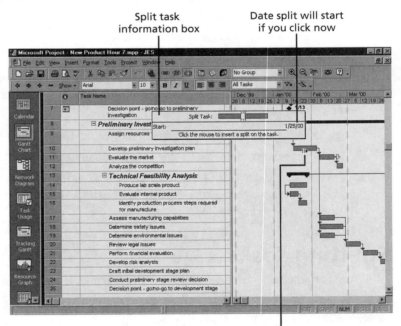

Mouse pointer when
splitting a task

▼ 3. Click the mouse button to start the split on the date in the information box. If you just click and release the mouse button, a 1-day split will appear in the task bar and a new segment will begin after the split.

If you drag the mouse to the right, you can position the new segment on the time period you want the task to resume. A second Split Task information box tells you the dates the segment you are dragging will start and finish (see Figure 7.9).

Task information box   Shadowed segment being moved by the mouse

FIGURE 7.9

If you drag the right-hand segment of the split task, the Task information box tells you when the segment will start and finish if you release the mouse now.

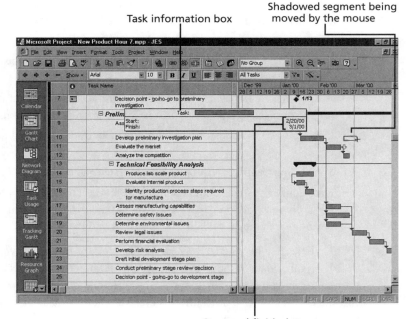

Start and finish dates
for the segment at the
current mouse position

When you position the mouse pointer over a split task segment, the pointer turns into a four-headed arrow and you can drag the segment to the left or right to reposition it. If you drag the first segment of a split task (or if you hold down the Shift key as you drag a later segment), then all the segments move together, maintaining their splits. If you drag any but the first segment, it moves independently of other segments until it touches another segment. If you drag a segment until it touches another segment, the split between them is removed.

7

Be very careful with the mouse in the timeline area of the Gantt Chart. If the mouse cursor is not the right shape when you start dragging, you could create unexpected results—like linking two tasks.

Recording Deadlines

So far in this hour, you have been focusing on setting and managing date constraints for tasks that must meet an important start or finish date. But there have been a few words of caution:

- Date constraints limit Project's ability to freely reschedule tasks as durations and predecessors change.
- A disconnect can occur between a task with a constraint that must be met and any successor tasks that rely on updated information from the constrained task.
- Constraint conflicts can be difficult to detect by just looking at the links on a Gantt chart.
- Scheduling conflicts will bring you frequent visits from the Planning Wizard.
- Date constraints take some control out of your hands as the project manager. It is, after all, your job to keep a close eye on the key tasks in your project and then develop strategies for dealing with delays and interruptions.

NEW FEATURE There may be a better way for you to monitor tasks that would introduce unacceptable risks if they were to slip. Project now lets you set a deadline for each task and warns you if the task moves away from that deadline. The date is not used in schedule calculations, so no conflict is created when the task slips. Project is still free to reschedule the task as conditions change, so no disconnect is created between the task and the rest of the schedule. And no visits from the Planning Wizard, either.

After a deadline is set for a task, the date is represented on the Gantt Chart bar with an arrow (see Figure 7.8). Any changes in the schedule that would cause the task to slip past the deadline causes a warning symbol to be displayed in the task's Indicators column. This warning may be all the information you need from Project to manage the task list effectively.

To Do: Setting or Removing a Task Deadline

▼ To Do

To have Project track a deadline date for a task, follow these steps:

1. Select a task on the Gantt Chart and display the Task Information dialog box by double-clicking on the task or choosing the Task Information button on the Standard toolbar.

▼ 2. Move to the Advanced tab in the dialog box, as shown in Figure 7.8.

3. In the Deadline field, type or choose a date that will mark the end of the selected task as a deadline.

To remove a deadline, select the entry in the Deadline field and press the Delete key.

Current scheduled finish   Advanced tab in Task Information dialog box

FIGURE 7.10

Setting a deadline may be less restrictive than setting a task constraint.

Selected task ——

Deadline date set in dialog box

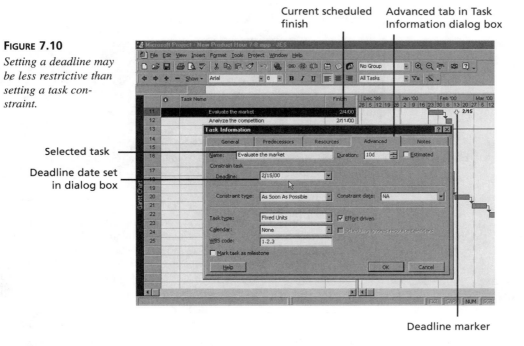

Deadline marker

▲ 4. Click OK to close the dialog box and set the deadline.

> Task deadlines can only be set for the finish date of the task, not the start date, even if the task is part of a Start-to-Start relationship.

Deadlines are not affected by whether the project is scheduled from a fixed start or fixed finish date. The only focus is whether the task is finishing behind schedule. If the schedule changes and the task is rescheduled by Project to now finish later than acceptable, as defined by the deadline, an exclamation mark icon will be displayed in the task's Indicators column, as shown in Figure 7.9. Pausing the mouse over the warning icon causes a warning box to pop up, explaining the problem (also shown in Figure 7.9).

7

Figure 7.11
*Any missed deadlines
cause warning indica-
tors to be displayed.*

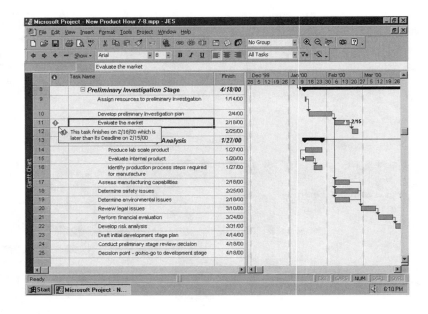

It is possible to set both a task deadline and a task constraint. As you might expect, the constraint takes priority, in that any scheduling conflicts will need to be resolved as discussed earlier in this hour. If you eliminate the conflict by removing the constraint, allowing Project to freely reschedule the task, the deadline date stays in effect and any slippage past the deadline will still cause the warning icon to appear.

To help you quickly identify which tasks have deadlines set, besides scanning through the Gantt Chart bars for deadline markers, Project provides a filter that searches for tasks with deadlines.

To Do: Applying the Tasks with Deadlines Filter

To find tasks that have deadline dates set, follow these steps:

1. In the Gantt Chart, choose Project, Filtered for, More Filters to display the More Filters dialog box.

2. Scroll down to select the Tasks With Deadlines filter.

3. Click the Apply button to close the dialog box and apply the filter.

   The filter restricts the display to only those tasks with deadline dates set.

4. When finished, you can remove the filter by pressing the F3 function key or by choosing Project, Filtered for, All Tasks from the menu.

Summary

By this hour, you have created a task list, applied an outline structure to the list, linked tasks together in a logical sequence, and modified those links as needed to create a project plan. There are probably key tasks and dates that must be met in order for the plan to meet the goals. In this hour, you learned there are two ways to have Project help you keep track of those key dates. By setting task *constraints*, you ask Project to fix tasks to specific dates and warn you, via the Planning Wizard, when those dates cannot be met. By setting task *deadlines* instead, you tell Project it is okay to move tasks around in the schedule as conditions change, but to mark the key dates for you on the Gantt Chart and warn you, via an icon, if the tasks are slipping past the deadline dates.

Q&A

Q My schedule changed and the Planning Wizard warned me that a constraint could not be met. I clicked OK on the dialog box to close the warning so I could fix the problem, but Project deleted my constraint instead of letting me fix it. Why?

A Because of the way the defaults are set in the Planning Wizard dialog boxes. Without making any changes in the box, clicking OK in these schedule conflict boxes is actually the same as clicking Cancel. In both cases, the default selection is accepted by Project, and the default selection is to cancel the activity that caused the problem. To tell Project to allow the conflict, so that you can fix the schedule yourself, you *must* choose another option in the box, typically the option that begins with the word "Continue."

Q One of my tasks has a deadline date set and it is a successor to another task. The predecessor is requiring more time than planned, so I increased its duration. No warning appeared on the task with the deadline. Why not?

A There are a couple of possibilities. If the tasks are linked in a Finish-to-Start relationship, the predecessor duration change was not significant enough to cause the successor task to finish past its deadline. No harm, no foul. But if the tasks are linked in a Start-to-Start relationship, the duration of the first task has no bearing on the successor in any case. The date when an SS predecessor starts is the important date; if it takes longer and finishes later, the second task is not affected.

7

Exercise

Your project includes key tasks that need to be monitored for slippage. In the exercise below, you set both a task constraint and a task deadline and then modify the task list to see the effects on the key tasks. Begin by opening the file, "New Product Hour 7.MPP." The solutions to the exercises can be found on the file, "New Product Hour 7-Exercise.MPP." See the Introduction for instructions to access the sample files and solutions for these exercises on the book's Web page.

1. Which tasks currently have Constraint Dates set? Which tasks have had Deadlines set?

2. If you don't finish identifying the new manufacturing process required for the product by the end of the month, you won't meet your decision date on time. Set a Finish No Later Than constraint of January 31, 2000, for Task 16, "Identify production process steps…." Force Project to set the constraint. Has anything changed on the Gantt Chart?

3. It looks like it will take longer to identify the process steps than you thought. Change the Duration of Task 16 to 10 days. Allow a conflict to be created. Does the Gantt Chart look any different?

4. You will want to be sure the t's are crossed and the i's dotted before proceeding. Put a deadline of 3/15/00 on Task 20, "Review legal issues."

5. The risk analysis on this new product is more complex than originally thought. Change the duration for Task 22, "Develop risk analysis," to 15 days.

6. Is the final milestone still on track to be completed by the deadline date of 5/1/00? How can you tell?

PART III

Displaying and Printing Your Schedule

Hour

HOUR 8

Working with Other Task Views

Besides the Gantt Chart view, several other views in Microsoft Project can be used to work with your task list. The Calendar view displays the task list in a typical monthly calendar format. Some of your project team members might find it easier to monitor their specific tasks using printouts based on the Calendar view. Another useful view is the Network Diagram. The Network Diagram view is often used as a flowchart of the tasks in the entire project. It provides an overview of the project tasks and the sequence of events.

In this hour, you will learn:

- How to navigate and format the Calendar view
- How to apply filters in the Calendar view
- How to modify the task list in the Calendar and Network Diagram views
- How to show and hide outline levels in the Network Diagram
- Options for controlling the layout of the Network Diagram

Exploring the Calendar View

The Calendar view displays project tasks in a familiar monthly calendar format. Each task is represented by a bar or line that includes the task name and duration. The Calendar view is most useful for viewing all the tasks being performed during a specific set of weeks. You can insert, delete, and link tasks from the Calendar view. You can filter the task list to display only specific tasks, such as milestone tasks or tasks performed by a particular resource.

You can display the Calendar view by clicking the Calendar button on the View Bar or by choosing View, Calendar. The standard Calendar view appears (see Figure 8.1).

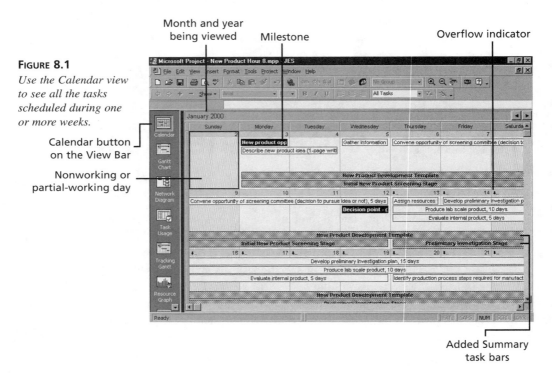

FIGURE 8.1

Use the Calendar view to see all the tasks scheduled during one or more weeks.

The default display shows four weeks at a time. Bars or lines for tasks include the task name and duration. Any nonworking or partial-working days you have identified in the project base calendar appear with a gray background.

The Previous Month and Next Month buttons, along with the scrollbars, are used to display other weeks or months onscreen.

Normal tasks are displayed with task bars outlined in blue. Milestone tasks are represented by black task bars with white text. In Figure 8.1, the "New product opp" milestone task is displayed. Summary tasks, except the Project Summary Task, are not displayed by default. You can include the summary tasks by customizing the Calendar view.

To Do: Displaying Summary Tasks in Calendar View

To display summary tasks in the Calendar view, do the following:

1. Choose Format, Bar Styles to open the Bar Styles dialog box, shown in Figure 8.2.

2. Choose Summary from the list of Task Types.

3. Change the Bar Type from None to either Bar or Line.

List of task types   List of bar types

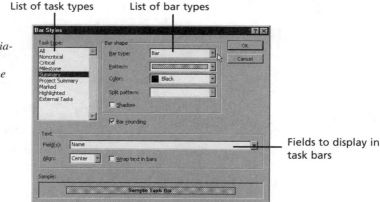

FIGURE 8.2

Use the Bar Styles dialog box to customize the appearance of the task bars in the Calendar view.

Fields to display in task bars

4. Click OK.

5. To update the Calendar view display, choose Format, Layout Now.

In some cases, there isn't enough room in the calendar to display all the tasks whose schedules fall on a particular date. When this happens, you see an overflow indicator in the left-hand corner of the date box (refer to Figure 8.1). The overflow indicator is a black arrow with an ellipsis that indicates additional tasks, which are not being displayed, are scheduled for this date.

You can see all the tasks scheduled for a given date by displaying the Tasks occurring on dialog box for that date (see Figure 8.3). Simply double-click the gray band at the top of the date box.

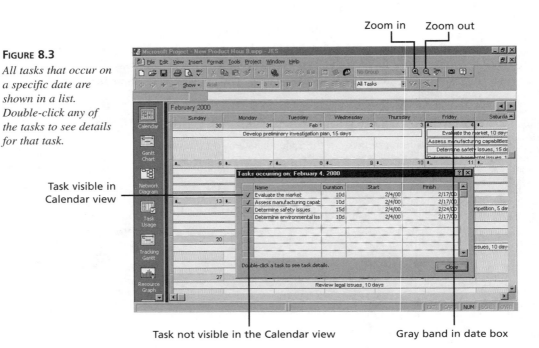

FIGURE 8.3

All tasks that occur on a specific date are shown in a list. Double-click any of the tasks to see details for that task.

Task visible in Calendar view

Zoom in   Zoom out

Task not visible in the Calendar view   Gray band in date box

The Tasks Occurring On dialog box lists all tasks whose schedule dates encompass the date you selected. Tasks visible in Calendar view have a check mark to the left of the listing. Tasks that are not being displayed in the Calendar view do not have a check mark.

To increase the number of tasks that appear in the Calendar view, use the Zoom In button on the Standard toolbar (see Figure 8.3). This action changes the number of weeks visible in the Calendar view. You can display 1, 2, 4, or 6 weeks by clicking the Zoom In and Zoom Out buttons. Changing the zoom in the Calendar view has no effect on the printed Calendar view; it affects only the screen display.

Moving Around in the Calendar View

There are several ways to effectively move around the Calendar view and find the information you want to focus on:

- Use the Previous Month and Next Month arrow buttons to display the week in which the first day of the previous or next month occurs. The beginning of each successive month appears in the first row of the calendar, no matter how many weeks you displayed in the view. Pressing the Page Up and Page Down keys performs the same function as clicking the Previous and Next Month buttons.

- The scrollbars move forward and backward in time on the calendar. When you drag the scroll box on the vertical scrollbar, a date indicator pop-up box helps you locate a specific date (see Figure 8.4).

FIGURE 8.4

Drag the scroll box to move quickly to a specific date.

Previous Month arrow   Next Month arrow

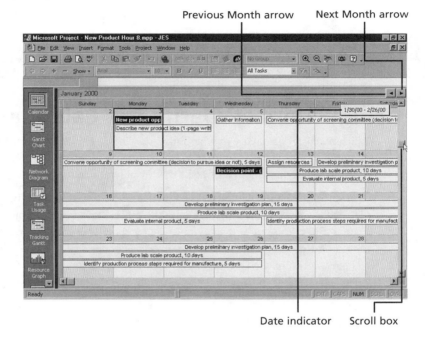

Date indicator   Scroll box

- Press Alt+Home and Alt+End to jump to the beginning and ending dates of the project, respectively.
- The Home and End keys, without adding the Alt key, move you to the beginning or end of a week.
- Left and right arrow keys move the focus one day earlier or later, and the up and down arrow keys move the highlight one week earlier or later.
- Use the Go To command to move directly to a specific task ID or date. Choose Edit, Go To. The Go To dialog box appears (see Figure 8.5). Type in the desired task ID or date and click OK. The selected task will be outlined in gray. If the bar for the task is not visible, try using the Zoom In button to display more task bars for each day.

FIGURE 8.5

Use the Go To dialog box to quickly locate a specific date or task ID.

 The Go To command does not select tasks that don't display task bars in the Calendar view. Therefore, because the default display doesn't display summary tasks, you can't go to a summary task unless you change the task bar styles.

Using Filters to Clarify the Calendar View

When a project has many overlapping tasks, the Calendar view can quickly become very cluttered. As previously discussed, you can zoom in to see more detail, but you can also use filters to reduce the list of tasks that display at one time.

A *filter* limits the display of tasks to just those that match the defined criteria. For example, you can have Project display only the critical tasks in the project by applying the Critical filter. You might display tasks that a specific resource is working on by applying the Using Resource filter. When the project is underway and you want a record of what has been accomplished so far, use the Completed Tasks filter.

All Tasks ▼   To apply a filter to a Calendar view, click the Filter button on the Formatting toolbar and select the list of built-in filters available on the drop-down list.

Viewing Task Details in Calendar View

To display individual task information, you must select the task and open the Task Information dialog box, or you can split the screen displaying the Calendar view in the top part of a dual-pane view, with the task details in the lower pane.

To display the Task Information dialog box (shown in Figure 8.6) while you're in Calendar view, double-click the task bar, or select the task bar and click the Information button on the Standard toolbar. If the task bar is not displayed, you must first select the task by scrolling to it and clicking on it or by using the Go To command.

FIGURE 8.6

The familiar Task Information dialog box offers easy access to most of the data fields for a task.

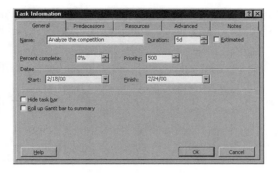

Another way to view task details is to split the screen by choosing Window, Split. The Calendar view appears in the top pane and the Task Form view in the bottom pane.

Editing a Project in the Calendar View

The Calendar view is not designed for creating complex projects. This view is more useful for reviewing and printing tasks and the time frames in which they occur. As you work in the Calendar view, you might need to look up and modify task information. Instead of switching back to the Gantt Chart view, you need to know how to display and edit tasks in this view.

Although the Calendar view is not a good view for creating the details of large projects, it's a great device for sketching out the major components of projects in initial planning sessions, when a group is trying to block out time on a calendar to see how long it will probably take to get it all done.

You can use the mouse to create the tasks quickly by dragging from the estimated start to the estimated finish. Then access the Task Information dialog box to name the task, link the tasks, and adjust task durations as the group debates possible scenarios.

Inserting Tasks in Calendar View

You can create tasks in Calendar view by choosing Insert, New Task or by dragging the mouse to create a new task bar in the calendar. What you select before inserting a new task in the Calendar view makes a big difference:

- If a specific *task* is selected before inserting a new task in the Calendar view, the result is just like adding a task in the Gantt Chart. The new task is inserted before the selected task.

- If a *date box* is selected when you insert a task in the Calendar view, the new task is always given the highest ID number in the project. If you view the new task in Gantt Chart view, the task is at the bottom of the list—even if its dates fall in the middle of the project. Also, the new task is assigned a date constraint of Start No Earlier Than.

- You can click on a date box and drag across days to insert a task in the Calendar view. The effect is similar to selecting a date box before inserting the task. The task created by clicking and dragging is added to the bottom of the task list on the Gantt Chart, and it is attached to the date you started dragging on by a Start No Earlier Than constraint.

> Recall from the previous hour that flexible constraints, such as Start No Earlier Than in forward-scheduled projects, do not generally hinder scheduling. They can, however, make it difficult to reduce the project's overall length.

To Do: Inserting a New Task in the Calendar View

To add new tasks in the Calendar view, do the following:

1. Select a specific task where the new task should be inserted; existing tasks including the one you select will be assigned higher ID numbers in the task list.

   Or, select the date for the start of the task if you want the task constrained to that start date and added to the bottom of the task list.

2. Choose Insert, New Task or press the Insert key on the keyboard.

3. Choose Project, Task Information (or click the Information button on the Standard toolbar) to open the Task Information dialog box.

4. Supply a name and duration for the task.

5. To remove any date constraint automatically given the task, select the Advanced tab and change the entry in the Constraint Type field to As Soon As Possible.

6. Click OK to close the dialog box.

If you prefer to use the mouse to create a task, click on a start date for the new task and drag to the task's finish date. New tasks created by dragging will already have an esti-mated duration value when you open the Task Information box to assign a task name.

Deleting Tasks in Calendar View

To delete a task, simply select it and choose Edit, Delete Task or press the Delete key on the keyboard. If the task bar is not visible onscreen, use the Go To com-mand to select the task. If you accidentally delete a task, choose Edit, Undo or click the Undo button to get it back.

Creating Links between Tasks in Calendar View

Creating task dependency links in Calendar view is similar to creating links in the Gantt Chart view. Select the tasks you want to link and click the Link button on the Standard toolbar. No link line will appear, however, because link lines between tasks are not displayed in the Calendar view.

To change to a different kind of relationship or to add lag or lead time, you must select the dependent (successor) task and display the Task Information dialog box. Use the Predecessors tab to change the dependency link, and add lag or lead time.

Exploring the Network Diagram View

The Network Diagram is a graphical display of tasks in a project; each task is repre-sented by a small box or *node*, and lines connect the nodes to show task dependencies. This view is most useful for getting an overall look at how the process or flow of task details fit together.

The Network Diagram is based on the Program Evaluation and Review Technique (PERT), a project management methodology introduced by the U.S. Navy in 1958. The popular version of the Network Diagram used in Microsoft Project reveals information about the individual task, as well as information about the task's place in the flow of activity.

To display the Network Diagram, click the Network Diagram button in the View Bar or choose View, Network Diagram. Figure 8.7 shows a portion of the Network Diagram view of the New Product project. "New product opportunity identified" is the selected task; its name appears in the Entry Bar. Each node represents a task, which is connected to predecessors and successors by lines. In the diagram, dependent (successor) tasks are placed to the right of, or beneath, predecessors. Different border styles or colors distin-guish summary tasks, critical tasks, and milestones. Summary tasks are above and to the left of subordinate tasks.

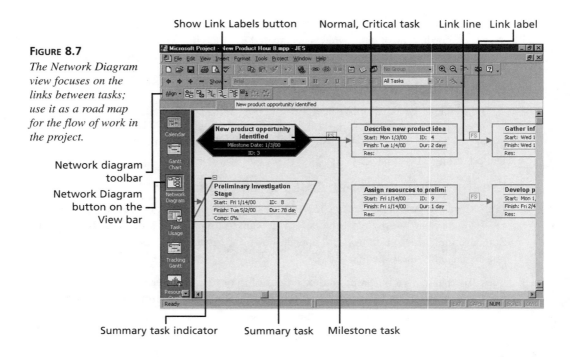

FIGURE **8.7**

The Network Diagram view focuses on the links between tasks; use it as a road map for the flow of work in the project.

Linking relationship types (FS, SS, FF, and SF) are not shown automatically on the Network Diagram, and sometimes the link type is not obvious. Use the Show Link Labels button on the Network Diagram toolbar to identify each link on the diagram by its type.

The display for each type of task defaults to certain Network Diagram settings. The default format for nodes of summary tasks displays six fields for the task: the name, start, finish, ID, duration, and percent complete. Normal tasks, either critical or noncritical, include six fields: name, start, finish, ID, duration, and assigned resources. Milestone tasks display only task name, ID number, and date.

In addition to default field values, task nodes have predefined shapes according to the task type. As shown in Figure 8.7, Milestone tasks have six-sided boxes; Summary tasks are shown in four-sided parallelograms, and normal tasks appear in rectangles. The color of the nodes is also a key; critical tasks are displayed in red and noncritical tasks in blue. Link lines also appear in colors; lines connecting two critical tasks are red, lines leading into or out of noncritical tasks are blue.

Zooming the Network Diagram View

The Network Diagram in Figure 8.7 displays each node enlarged enough to read the field data easily. If you want to get an overview of the links among more tasks, you can zoom the view to show more tasks. Figure 8.8 shows the same task selected, "New product opportunity identified," as in Figure 8.7. When you zoom out, you get a better feel for how that task fits into the overall project.

FIGURE 8.8

Use Zoom settings to get a wider view of the project.

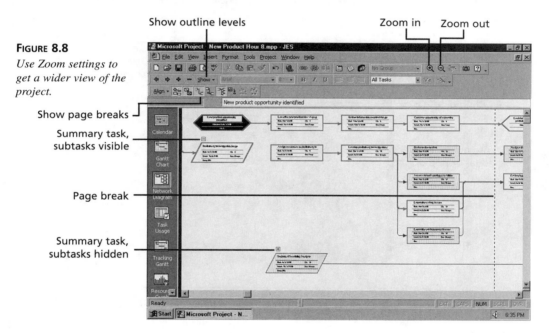

You can zoom to view more tasks by using the Zoom Out button on the Standard toolbar; use the Zoom In button to see the task details. The Zoom In and Zoom Out buttons change the zoom to specific increments each time you click the button, ranging from 25 to 400 percent. Choose View, Zoom to enter a custom zoom percent. In Figure 8.8, the view is shown at a 50 percent zoom setting.

> Using the Zoom command affects only the screen view in the Network Diagram. It does not affect how much of the chart is printed.

For the ultimate "top-level" view of the Network Diagram, you can hide all the task node details and display only the task ID numbers. Click the Hide Fields button on the Network Diagram toolbar. Project displays the task nodes and links but hides all the other field information, as shown in Figure 8.9.

Hide Fields button (toggles)

FIGURE 8.9
Hide all task details to focus only on project flow.

Network Diagram toolbar

All tasks, no details

Pause mouse over node for pop-up details

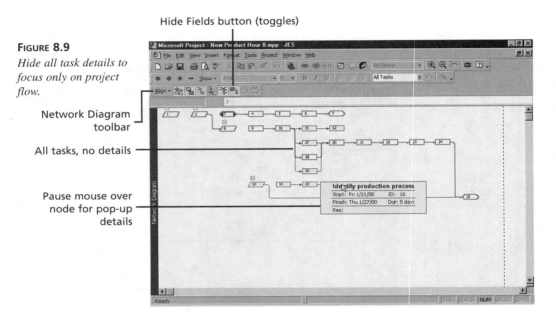

Regardless of the Zoom level, or even if all field details are hidden, you can pause the mouse over any field whose contents are not fully visible and Project will pop-up the entire field entry or all node fields (see Figure 8.9).

Viewing Outline Levels in the Network Diagram

As on the Gantt Chart, summary tasks in a Network Diagram display outline symbols. A plus sign above a node indicates the summary task has been collapsed and its subtasks are hidden. A minus sign above a summary task node means its subtasks are visible. In Figure 8.8, Task 8 is a summary task with its subtasks displayed on screen. Task 13, with a plus sign above it, is a summary task with its subtasks hidden; expanding Task 13 would show additional tasks boxes to its right.

Show ▾   You can also use the Show button on the Formatting toolbar to select the outline level of tasks you want to see.

8

Applying Filters to the Network Diagram

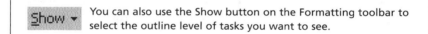 Collapsing the outline is not the only way to reduce the number of boxes visible on the diagram. As with Gantt Chart and Calendar views, you can apply a filter to a Network Diagram. Select Project, Filtered For from the menu and select a filter from the cascading list, or use the filter drop-down list on the Formatting toolbar.

Figure 8.10 shows the Critical filter applied to the project. Note that Tasks 11 through 17 are not displayed; they are noncritical tasks and would appear as blue boxes if all tasks were visible.

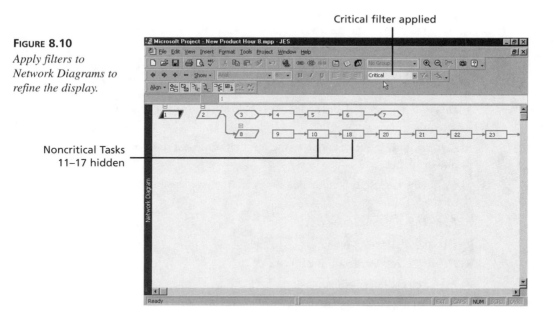

FIGURE 8.10

Apply filters to Network Diagrams to refine the display.

Noncritical Tasks 11–17 hidden

Critical filter applied

Scrolling and Selecting in the Network Diagram

A Network Diagram can spread out quite a bit on the screen, so you need to master scrolling to and selecting tasks in the view to use it effectively. You can use the horizontal and vertical scrollbars or the movement keys (the arrow keys, Page Up, Page Down, Home, and End) to scan through the Network Diagram.

Moving through the project by using scroll bars does not change the currently selected node. After you scroll, you probably can't see the selected node, although the name remains in the Entry Bar. To select one of the visible nodes after scrolling, click anywhere on the node.

> A good habit to develop is to select task nodes by clicking in fields which can be edited. Then you can easily return to the selected node, even though it is not visible. Press the Edit key (F2) as though you plan to edit the selected node. Project will scroll the diagram to display the selected node. Then press the Esc key to cancel the editing. Fields such as the ID number on any task or the Start or Finish dates for Summary tasks cannot be edited.

You can also use the keyboard to move around the Network Diagram. When you use one of the movement keys, the selection changes to another node. The following list defines the rules that the movement keys follow to select the next node:

- *Right-arrow key*. Selects node to the right that is closest to it, on the same horizontal line or lower.
- *Down-arrow key*. Selects node that is below it and at least as far to the right on the screen.
- *Left-arrow key*. Selects node to the left that is closest to it, on the same horizontal line or higher.
- *Up-arrow key*. Selects node that is above it and at least as far to the left on the screen.
- *Page Down*. Down one screen.
- *Page Up*. Up one screen.
- *Home*. Selects earliest project task.
- *End*. Selects latest project task.
- *Ctrl+Page Down*. Moves right one screen.
- *Ctrl+Page Up*. Moves left one screen.

You can also use the F5 key or Edit, Go To menu selection to move to a specific task number or timeframe in the Network diagram.

Editing a Project in the Network Diagram

8

Although the Network Diagram view can be used to create a project, it's more useful for reviewing the sequence of events and the overall flow of the project tasks. As you work in the Network Diagram view, you can change task data, add and delete tasks, and create and modify task links.

To Do: Changing Task Data in the Network Diagram

To edit field values in the Network Diagram, follow these steps:

1. Select the task to edit by clicking the mouse pointer on the node or by using the movement keys.

2. Select the field to edit by pressing the Tab and Shift+Tab keys or by clicking the field.

3. In the Entry Bar, type the new data or edit the existing data.

4. Complete the change by pressing Enter, by selecting the Enter box in the Entry Bar, or by selecting a different field or node.

On the Gantt Chart, you can edit field information directly in the cells on screen. But on the Network Diagram, fields in task nodes are not editable within the boxes; you must use the Entry Bar or open the Task Information dialog box to make changes. Also, if you want to change data in fields that don't appear in the node (such as constraints, task notes, and so on), you can use the Task Information dialog box.

Inserting Tasks in Network Diagram View

You can add tasks directly to the project in the Network Diagram view. You must select the insertion position carefully, however, if you want to control the ID number of the new task. Project inserts a task you add in Network Diagram view just after the currently selected task.

To Do: Adding a New Task via the Network Diagram

To add a new task while working in the Network Diagram, do the following:

1. Select the task you want the new task to *follow*. This step makes sure the new task node will be placed to the right of the selected task and has an ID number that follows that of the selected task.

2. Choose Insert, New Task (or press the Insert key) to insert a blank node to the right of the selected task.

   The ID number for the new task is one greater than the selected task, and all existing tasks with ID numbers higher than the selected task increase by one, just as

▼   they do when you insert a task in the Gantt Chart view. The new task appears
      directly to the right of the selected task.

   3. Type the name for the new task. Tab to the Duration field and estimate the dura-
      tion. Do not enter the start or finish date unless you want the task constrained to
      one of those dates.

   4. The new task will be linked into the task sequence *if* the Autolink feature (dis-
      cussed in Hour 6, "Linking Tasks in the Correct Sequence") is turned on and if you
      insert the new task between two tasks that are connected in a Finish-to-Start rela-
      tionship. Otherwise, you will have to create the links required for the newly
▲   inserted task.

Deleting Tasks in Network Diagram View

You can easily delete normal tasks and milestone tasks while in Network Diagram view.
However, Project will warn you if you are about to delete a summary task (and all of its
subtasks). To delete a task, select the task node and choose Edit, Delete Task or press
Delete.

> If the Autolink option is active (see Tools, Options, Schedule tab), and you
> delete a task in the middle of a chain of tasks linked in simple Finish-to-Start
> relationships, its predecessor and successor will be rejoined to preserve the
> chain.

Linking Tasks in Network Diagram View

You can create and edit task links in Network Diagram view using the same techniques
you used on the Gantt Chart. That is, you can select tasks and click the Link button on
the Standard toolbar, you can click and drag between two tasks (task nodes in this case),
and you can open the Task Information dialog box for the successor task and make
changes on the Predecessors tab.

If linking task nodes by dragging, be sure to drag the mouse from the *middle* of the predecessor task to the *middle* of the successor task. Dragging the border of a task node
merely repositions the node on the screen if Project is set to allow manual positioning of
task boxes (see discussion in the next section). By dragging to link task nodes, the
default Finish-to-Start task relationship is created with no lead or lag time.

Editing task links in a Network Diagram is also the same as in the Gantt Chart view. If
you want to change the relationship type, enter lead or lag time, or delete the task link,

open the Task Dependency dialog by double-clicking the line that links two tasks (as shown in Figure 8.11). Make sure the very tip of the mouse pointer is on the line that links the tasks when you double-click.

Double-click here...

FIGURE 8.11
Edit or delete task links with the Task Dependency dialog box.

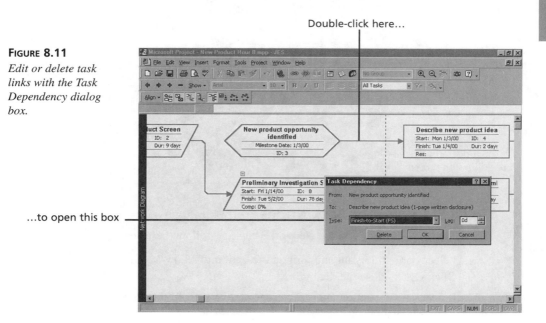

...to open this box

Moving Task Nodes in Network Diagram View

You can change the layout of the Network Diagram by moving individual task nodes or groups of nodes to new positions in the Network Diagram view. But first you must set a Project option to allow the boxes to be moved around on the screen. Select Format, Layout to display the Layout dialog box shown in Figure 8.12. Select the Allow Manual box positioning if you intend to move the Network Diagram boxes around to meet your display and printing needs.

If you select and move a group of nodes together, the nodes retain positions in relation to each other as you move them. The linking lines also follow task nodes to the new locations.

Allow dragging of task nodes

FIGURE 8.12

Project can allow manual the placement of Network Diagram nodes.

Force Layout Now command to move nodes away from page breaks

Show dotted page break lines on screen

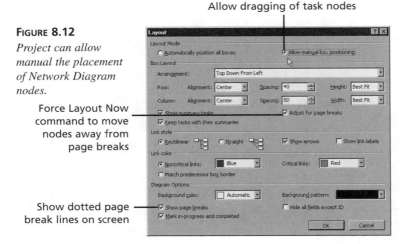

To Do: Moving the Task Nodes

▼ To Do

To manually place nodes on the Network Diagram, follow these steps:

1. Select Format, Layout and turn on the option to Allow Manual box positioning. Click OK to close the dialog box.

2. If necessary, zoom out so you can see an overview of the task layout of the Network Diagram.

3. Click on the task node you want to move.

   To select several nodes, hold the Ctrl key and click on each task to be moved.

   To select a chain of tasks, hold the Shift key and select the first task in the sequence of tasks to be moved.

4. Position the mouse pointer on the border of any selected node. When the pointer shape turns to a four-headed arrow, click and drag the node(s) to the new location (see Figure 8.13).

5. Release the mouse to complete the move. Click in an open space to turn off the selection.

▼

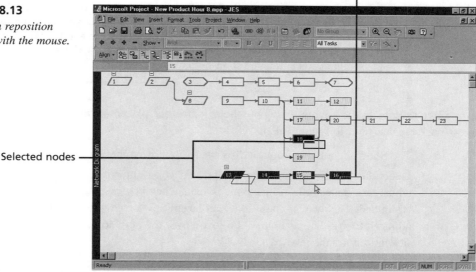

FIGURE 8.13

You can reposition nodes with the mouse.

Drag to new position

Selected nodes

You can quickly select all of a summary task's subtasks by holding down the Shift key as you click the summary task. Drag the border of any task in the selected group to move the entire selected group.

The nodes will stay in the position you place them until you tell Project otherwise. Switching to the Gantt Chart or closing the file (and saving changes), does not put the nodes back in their original positions. To have Project redraw the Network Diagram and place nodes in their default positions, select Format, Layout Now from the menu.

 Layout Now is also available on the Network Diagram toolbar.

Another button on the toolbar, called Layout Selection Now, will reposition only the task boxes you select before clicking the button, leaving all other nodes you may have moved in their changed positions. The Layout Selection Now feature is also available by selecting the task box, right-clicking on the diagram, and choosing Layout Selection Now from the shortcut menu.

When you rearrange the Network Diagram, you want to see the page break lines, so you don't place a task node on a page break. If you place a node on a page break line, part of the node prints on one page and the remainder prints on another page. You will want to make sure the dotted lines representing page breaks are showing onscreen.

Two settings in the Layout dialog box help control the placement of nodes in relation to page breaks (refer to Figure 8.12).

- The Show Page Breaks option displays (or removes) the dotted page break lines.
- Select the Adjust For Page Breaks option if you want Project to automatically adjust task nodes to avoid page break lines when you execute the Layout Now command. This way, no task node can be split by a page break. If a node must be adjusted to avoid a page break, Project moves the node to the right or down until it fits entirely on the next page.

  Use the Show Page Breaks button on the Network Diagram toolbar to toggle the break lines on and off.

Summary

As you've learned in this hour, there are other task views in Microsoft Project that you can use to create or modify your task list. The Calendar view displays the task list in a typical monthly calendar format, enabling you to focus on all the activities of a particular week or group of weeks. The Network Diagram view provides a flowchart of the tasks in the entire project, showing an overview of the project tasks and the sequence of events. Both views can be filtered to help focus on tasks of interest.

Q&A

Q I can't see the summary tasks in the Calendar view. How do I display them?

A By default, the summary tasks don't display in the Calendar view. Choose Format, Bar Styles to display the Bar Styles dialog box. In the dialog box, select Summary from the Task type list. Then change the Bar Type from None to the style of bar you want displayed for summary tasks.

Q How can I see my task link lines in the Calendar view?

A The short answer is, you can't. The Calendar view is primarily intended for viewing and printing the task list ordered by scheduled work days. Use the Gantt Chart or the Network Diagram view to display and print task links.

Q Besides moving the task nodes in the Network Diagram view, is there another way to display more task nodes on each printed page?

A You can use the scaling feature on the Page tab of the Page Setup dialog box to shrink the number of printed pages. When you scale the display, and the Adjust for Page Breaks option under the Layout command on the Format menu is turned on, Project will automatically move nodes to the right and down if the nodes land on a page break. Use the Format, Layout Now command to see the result. Printing views is described in Hour 10, "Finalizing and Printing Your Schedule."

Q When I zoom out to see more nodes in the Network Diagram I can't read any of the field information. Is there another way to see the name of a selected task without having to zoom in and out?

A Position the mouse over any task node and pause. The contents of the node or a particular field in the node will be displayed in an enlarged pop-up box onscreen.

Exercises

Your planning work is well underway and you'd like to look at different presentations of the project tasks. Maybe you're just tired of looking at a Gantt Chart. In the following exercises, you display your project in the Calendar format and in the Network Diagram view. In each view, you will make some changes to the display to see the effects. Begin by opening the file "New Product Hour 8.MPP." The exercise results will be found in the file "New Product Hour 8-Exercise.MPP." See the Introduction for instructions to access the sample files and solutions for these exercises on the book's Web page.

1. Open the file and display the Calendar view.

2. Add the Summary tasks to the Calendar display. Format the summary tasks as bars, with a background pattern in yellow.

3. Reposition the Summary tasks to the show at top of each day.

4. Investigate February 7, 2000, to find out which tasks should be displayed on that date but aren't, because there is not enough room in the date box.

5. Filter the task list to display only critical tasks. Then reset the view to show all tasks again.

6. Switch to the Network Diagram. View the diagram at a 50 percent zoom setting.

7. Task 8, "Preliminary Investigation...," is a summary task. Locate it and hide its subtask details.

8. Reset the diagram to 100 percent size and show all tasks.

9. Use the Network Diagram toolbar to view only the task ID numbers and the linking relationship.

HOUR 9

Formatting Views

As you've already learned in earlier hours, Project offers several different ways to view the various aspects of your projects. These major Project views include the Gantt Chart, which displays information in both a sheet and chart format; the Calendar view, which shows task schedules in a familiar calendar layout; and the Network Diagram, which emphasizes the tasks in your project and their relationships.

Project gives you a great deal of flexibility to enhance and change these available views. You can format selected text, format timescales, and zoom in and out to get a closer or wider look at the view shown. A plain Gantt Chart can be spruced up by adding graphics and text next to task bars. There is even a Gantt Chart Wizard that you can use to have Project do most the work creating enhanced Gantt Charts.

In this hour, you will learn:

- How to change formatting styles for task types
- How to format a Gantt Chart using a supplied wizard
- How to change the appearance of the Calendar view
- How to control Network Diagram formatting
- What options to use when arranging Network Diagram task boxes

Using the General Format Options

Using formatting options to change your Project views can help you emphasize certain information (by changing the font of selected text), change your perspective of the information displayed (by using the Zoom feature), and customize how that information is displayed (by changing features such as colors).

You will find that the different views you work with in Project fall into three categories: sheets, forms, and graphical views. All the sheet views (such as the Task Sheet) share certain characteristics, such as gridlines. Most graphical views, like the Gantt Chart, contain timescales.

These common characteristics mean that after you learn to modify the gridlines for one sheet view, such as the left side of the Gantt view, you will be able to modify them in other sheet views. The same goes for the timescale display for Project's graphical view types, such as the Gantt Chart; after you learn how to modify the timescale for one graphical view, you will know how to do it for the other graphical views.

Form views are the least flexible when it comes to formatting. This makes sense, however, because the various forms you work with are designed more for data entry than for providing a particular view of the information in the project.

Formatting Selected Text

You can easily format the text for a particular resource or task in a particular view to add emphasis. Special formatting can be applied manually to selected tasks or resources, or a style can be modified to format groups of task types. For instance, in the Gantt Chart sheet view, you might want to use bold formatting or a larger point size to emphasize a particular task.

You can manually format selected text in three ways. Use the options at the top of the Format menu, the Formatting toolbar buttons, or the Format Painter tool on the Standard toolbar to apply formatting changes to selected tasks.

To Do: Using Menu Options to Format Selected Text

To format selected text using the Format menu options, do the following:

1. Use the mouse to select the cell or row you want to format.
2. Choose Format, Font to open the Font dialog box, shown in Figure 9.1.

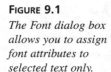

FIGURE **9.1**

The Font dialog box allows you to assign font attributes to selected text only.

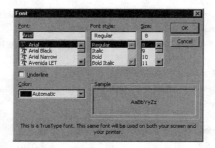

9

3. Select a new font type in the Font box. To change the style of the text to bold or italic (or both), use the Font style box. To change the size of the font, make a new selection in the Size box. Underline selected text and change the color of the text, if desired.

4. After you make your selections in the Font dialog box, click OK to assign the new attributes to the selected text and close the Font dialog box.

Another method for applying manual formatting is by choosing the buttons on the Formatting toolbar to change the format of selected text. Buttons are available for quickly changing the font and font size, and for applying bold, italic, and underline formatting. You can also change the text alignment in a cell (left, center, or right) by clicking a toolbar button. Simply select the text and click the appropriate button or buttons on the toolbar (refer to Figure 9.2).

FIGURE **9.2**

The Formatting toolbar also allows you to assign font attributes to selected text.

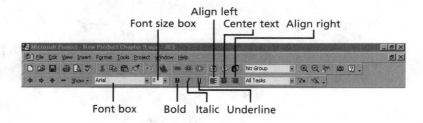

The third method for applying manual formatting is a special form of copy and paste. If you've already assigned formatting to a particular text entry, you can easily copy just that formatting to another text entry by using the Format Painter on the Standard toolbar. Select the text with the desired formatting. Click the Format Painter button; the mouse pointer changes to include a paintbrush. Click the text you want to apply the formatting to, or click and drag to select more than one cell of text. When the mouse button is released the text is displayed in the new format. The cell contents are not changed; only the appearance will be different.

When you apply formatting with any of the three methods discussed previously—menu options, toolbar buttons, or Format Painter— you will find that the Undo feature is not available. To remove the special formatting, you must change each of the font attributes back to the defaults, or you can use the Format Painter to copy the set of normal attributes from an unchanged entry and apply them to the cells you want to reset.

Formatting Text by Category

Instead of manually formatting tasks as discussed previously, applying text *styles* lets you change the text formatting of entire categories of tasks or resources. This allows you to distinguish certain groups of tasks or resources by their font, type size, style, or color. For example, you might want to format your summary tasks in fuchsia (although I'm not sure why!) to make them stand out on the Gantt Chart sheet, or you might want to change the format for the Monthly and Daily titles on the Calendar view.

To Do: Changing Text Styles for Task Categories

To change formatting for groups of task types, follow these steps:

1. Display a view such as the Gantt Chart or the Calendar view. (Text Style formatting is not available on the Network Diagram or any form view.)

2. Choose Format, Text Styles. The Text Styles dialog box appears (see Figure 9.3).

FIGURE 9.3

The Text Styles dialog box allows you to select formatting attributes for an entire category of items.

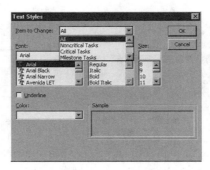

3. Click the Item to Change drop-down box to select a category of items to format. (Categories include Summary Tasks, Critical and Noncritical Tasks, and Milestones, for example).

4. Select the font formats from the appropriate drop-down boxes (Font, Font Style, Size, Color, and Underline).

▼

5. Click OK after you have made your selections. The category of items (or categories of items) that you selected in the Text Styles dialog box will appear in the new format in the current view.

▲

> You can format several categories by only opening the Text Styles box once. Select a category, change the format, and then select another category and do the same.

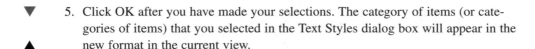

9

Formatting Timescales

The timescale area on a Gantt Chart is the gray area above the chart bars that shows calendar information. Normally, a timescale displays two levels of time units: the major units scale over the minor units scale. For example, the major units scale might use weeks as its unit while the minor units scale displays days. The minor scale units (like days) must be the same as or smaller than the major scale units (like weeks).

You can change the format of the timescales that appear in views such as the Gantt Chart (formatting the Calendar timescales will be covered later in this hour). Several formatting choices are available for timescale elements such as the time units, date formats, and display alignments. In the Format Timescale dialog box, you can choose date labels and timescale units to fit your viewing and printing needs. As you make selections in the dialog box, a preview of the changed timescale is displayed at the bottom of the box for your review.

To Do: Changing Timescale Formatting

To format the Timescale area on a view, follow these steps:

1. Display a view that includes a timescale area, such as a Gantt Chart.
2. Choose Format, Timescale. The Timescale dialog box appears, as shown in Figure 9.4.
3. In the Units drop-down boxes in the Major scale and Minor scale sections, select the units of time you want to use.

> If you don't want to display two levels of time units on the timescale, you can select None in the Minor scale's Units drop-down box.

▼

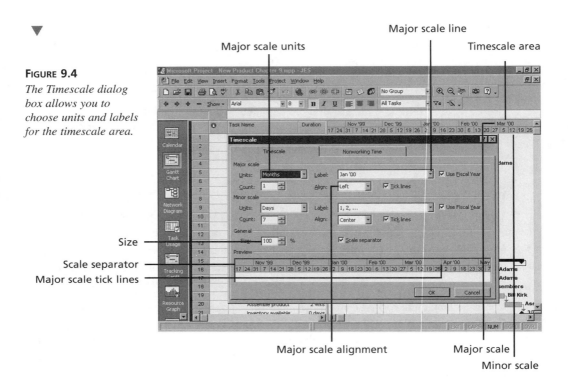

FIGURE 9.4

The Timescale dialog box allows you to choose units and labels for the timescale area.

4. Each set of units (Major and Minor) also has a Label drop-down box. Select the labels you want to use for each scale.

5. Each of the units also has an Align box. Select the display alignment you want to use for each scale.

6. Three other format attributes can be changed in the Timescale dialog box.

   • The *Tick lines* are the vertical lines that separate the labels within each scale. Remove the check mark to turn the tick lines off.

   • The *Scale separator check box* controls the horizontal line that separates the Major and Minor scale (a check mark is "on").

   • The *Size box* allows you to increase or decrease the area needed to display the individual units in both scales. Larger percentages widen the unit display areas for both scales; they cannot be enlarged or reduced separately.

6. After you have finished your selections, click OK. The changes will be applied immediately to the visible timescale.

Formatting Gridlines

Some of the views in Project contain row and column gridlines. You can find them on sheets and tables, on Gantt Charts (such as displaying horizontal lines between the bars), even on timescales (the lines separating the Major and Minor scales).

To Do: Formatting Gridlines

To change the appearance of gridlines on a view, follow these steps:

1. Select Format, Gridlines from the menu. The Gridlines dialog box appears, as shown in Figure 9.5.

FIGURE 9.5

The Gridlines dialog box allows you to format several types of lines in colorful ways.

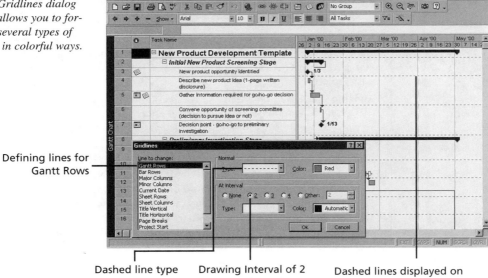

Defining lines for Gantt Rows

Dashed line type   Drawing Interval of 2   Dashed lines displayed on every other Gantt Row

2. In the Line to change list, choose the line type you want to format.

3. In the Normal section, use the Type drop-down box to select a new type for the line and the Color drop-down box to select a new color. Leave the Type area blank to not have any line drawn for the selected type.

4. In the At Interval section, choose None to display all lines of the selected type (None in this case really means "all intervals, none skipped".) Or choose an interval to display lines only at that interval (every other occurrence of the line if the 2 radio button is selected, for example).

5. After you have made your gridline format selections, click OK. The new gridline formats will appear in the current view.

Special Formatting for the Gantt Chart

The Gantt Chart makes it easy to see your project schedule. It gives you both a text view in columns and a bar graph. The Gantt Chart is commonly used as the view to initially build a plan, and it is generally the best view to use when periodically reviewing your plan. A number of formatting options provides flexibility for both building and reporting information in your project.

Using the Gantt Chart Wizard

The quickest way to format the Gantt Chart is to use the Gantt Chart Wizard. It guides you through several formatting options. If you don't like the result, you can run the Wizard again to start over or you can use menu options to tweak the Wizard results.

You can have several different views in your project that are based on a Gantt Chart but formatted differently. For example, the View menu lists the standard Gantt Chart and a Tracking Gantt Chart, which are both provided with Project.

Running the Wizard on a Gantt Chart changes the chart that is currently displayed. If you run the Wizard while the standard Gantt Chart is on the screen, you would have to re-run the Wizard, or make manual changes, to once again see the "normal" blue and black chart.

Avoid this problem of having to re-create Gantt Charts when you need them. Make a copy of the standard Gantt Chart first, and then apply the copy to the screen and run the wizard on the copy. Follow these steps: Select View, More Views, Gantt Chart, and Copy; Rename your copy, click OK; and then click Apply. The View bar will indicate that your copy is now onscreen instead of the original chart. Now run the Wizard; you can't do any damage to your supplied Gantt Chart.

To Do: Using the Gantt Chart Wizard

To format a Gantt Chart using the supplied Wizard, follow these steps:

1. Create a copy of the standard Gantt Chart and display it onscreen (see the previous Caution sidebar).

2. Choose Format, GanttChartWizard from the menu. The first screen welcomes you to the Wizard. Click Next to continue.

▼   3. The next screen asks you to determine the basic type of display for your Gantt
        Chart (see Figure 9.6). Several possibilities are offered:

        • *Standard*   Displays the task bars in the default format.

        • *Critical Path*   Displays tasks on the critical path (which affect the project
          end date) in red, and displays noncritical tasks in blue.

        • *Baseline*   Displays two Gantt bars for each task: a gray baseline bar show-
          ing the original plan and a blue or red bar showing the current schedule for
          each task. (This option creates a Gantt Chart similar to the supplied Tracking
          Gantt.)

        • *Other*   Offers variations of the standard, critical path, and baseline formats.

        • *Custom Gantt Chart*   Select this option to have more control over format-
          ting choices in the next steps of the Wizard.

FIGURE 9.6

*The Gantt Chart
Wizard walks you
through the formatting
steps of your Gantt
Chart.*

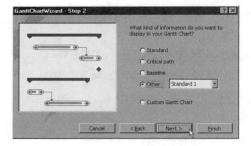

    4. Select the radio button for the format you want to use and then click Next.

    5. If you chose an option on the previous screen other than Custom Gantt Chart, the
       next screen asks you what information you would like displayed with the Gantt
       bars. You can display resources and dates, resources, dates, or none.

    6. Choose the Custom Task Information option to open additional Wizard boxes for
       making your own choices of text to be displayed next to the Gantt bars.

    7. Click Next to continue.

    8. Make one additional choice: whether to show the link lines between task bars.
       Click Next.

    9. On the next screen, click the Format It button. Project will apply your choices to
       the chart.

    10. Finally, click the Exit Wizard button to complete the process and see the finished
▲   product onscreen.

9

If you don't like the appearance of your new chart, you can rerun the Wizard. You might also use these results as a starting point and fine-tune your chart as described in the next sections.

Using the Bar Styles Options

You can change the way the bars are displayed in your Gantt charts without using the Gantt Chart Wizard. Using Bar Styles, you can format the bars for a category of tasks, such as milestones or critical tasks. You can also change which fields of information are displayed with the Gantt bars.

You can also format a bar for a *single* task in the Gantt Chart. Select the task bar, and then select Format, Bar. You can choose shapes, patterns, or colors for the bar on the Bar Shape tab, and choose the text to be displayed on the Bar Text tab.

To Do: Formatting Categories of Gantt Bars

To change the bar formatting for task types, do the following:

1. Display the Gantt Chart view, and select Format, Bar Styles. The Bar Styles dialog box appears.
2. In the table at the top of the dialog box, select the category row (such as Summary) you want to change, as shown in Figure 9.7.

FIGURE 9.7

The Bar Styles dialog box allows you to change the look of the task bars (by category) that appear on the Gantt Chart.

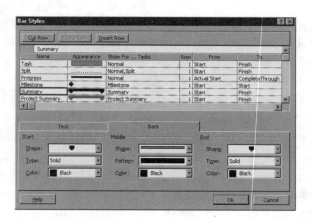

3. With the Bars tab selected in the middle of the dialog box, choose shapes, patterns or types, and colors for the bar under the Start, Middle, and End sections.

▼ Some of the task categories, such as Milestones and Deadlines, logically have only a start shape for their "bar"; these are tasks that occur at a single point in time.

4. Move to the Text tab to make selections for field information to be displayed in up to five areas of a bar: left end, right end, above the bar, below the bar, and inside the bar.

Use the drop-down lists for each area to select the project fields you'd like to see; only one field for each area. (This is a limited list; some fields are not available for display on Gantt Charts).

5. Stay in the dialog box to continue making changes to other categories of task bars.

6. After you have completed your changes, click the OK button to close the dialog box. The bar changes you have made will appear on the Gantt Chart.

▲

The Rollup Views

As you learned in Hour 3, "Starting a New Project and Working With Tasks," project tasks can be grouped into an outline structure of summary tasks and their subtasks. By using the Show Subtasks and Hide Subtasks buttons on the Formatting toolbar, you can collapse the outline and focus on just the task detail of interest to you.

Another formatting option is available for tasks in an outline structure. A task's bar can be rolled up, graphically, into its summary task. The summary task bar will then appear to be divided into segments representing the subtasks beneath it. An additional option lets you show the summary task as a solid line when its subtasks are visible but appear as a segmented line when its subtasks are hidden.

To Do: Rolling Up Subtask Bars

To change the way subtasks are represented on their summary tasks, take these steps:

1. Display the Gantt Chart, and select Format, Layout (see Figure 9.8)

2. Select the check box option to Always Roll Up Gantt Bars.

3. To show summary task bars in rolled up segments *even when* the outline is expanded and the subtask bars are visible, leave the check box option to Hide Rollup Bars When Summary Expanded unchecked.

▼ 4. Finish by clicking OK.

FIGURE 9.8

Subtasks can be rolled up graphically onto their summary tasks.

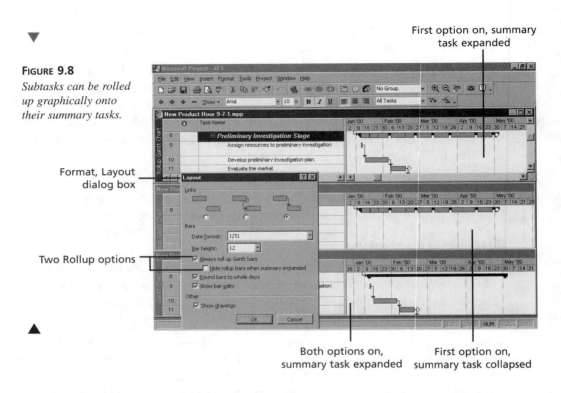

First option on, summary task expanded

Format, Layout dialog box

Two Rollup options

Both options on, summary task expanded

First option on, summary task collapsed

Figure 9.8 shows a combination of Project files with the rollup and outline features set differently in each one. In the top window, the options are set to Always Roll Up the bars, and to show the summary task segments even though the subtasks are visible. The middle window has the same settings and the summary task has been collapsed. This is what you would see for a collapsed summary task with only one rollup setting turned on, instead of the solid black bar to which you've become accustomed. In the bottom window, both options are turned on and the summary task is expanded. With these settings, the summary bar won't appear as segments until its subtasks are hidden.

Adding Graphics and Text to Gantt Charts

Microsoft Project has several drawing tools you can use to enhance your Gantt Charts. You can add graphics, such as arrows and rectangles, to highlight tasks on the chart. You can also add free text to the Gantt Chart that provides additional information or notes for a particular task or group of tasks. This feature is only available on the bar side of a Gantt Chart, not on either the Calendar view or the Network Diagram.

Introducing the Drawing Toolbar

To add the Drawing toolbar to the toolbars currently displayed, select View, Toolbars. Select Drawing from the cascading menu that appears.

To use the buttons on the Drawing toolbar, you select a particular button and move the mouse to the bar area. Then click and drag on the chart to create the object. The Drawing toolbar buttons and their uses are described in Table 9.1.

TABLE 9.1   Drawing Toolbar Features

Icon	Button Name	Object
	Line	Lines without arrows
	Arrow	Lines with arrowheads
	Rectangle	Rectangles
	Oval	Circles and other elliptical graphics
	Arc	Arcs
	Polygon	Many-sided figures
	Text Box	A box containing text
	Cycle Fill Color	Allows you to change the fill color of the selected object
	Attach to Task	Opens the Format Drawing dialog box so you can change how an object is anchored to a bar on the Gantt Chart

Can you draw a perfect circle? You can hold down the Shift key as you drag to draw a perfect object, such as a perfect square or perfect circle.

The very first button on the Drawing toolbar is a drop-down list. It contains tools you can use to arrange and edit the objects that you draw with the other buttons. You must select an object before these options are available:

- *Bring to Front*   Brings the selected object to the forefront if other objects currently overlay it.
- *Send to Back*   Sends an object to the very back of the currently overlaying objects.

- *Bring Forward*   Moves the object forward one object at a time in a group of over-laying items.
- *Send Backward*   Moves an object behind overlaying items, one object at a time.
- *Edit Points*   Allows you to edit the shape of a polygon.

Sometimes the front, back, forward, and backward distinctions are confusing. Think of graphics objects as cards in a deck and a selected object as a single card. Bring to front places the card at the top of the deck; send to back places the card on the bottom of the deck. Bring forward and send backward move the card up or down in the deck, respectively, one card at a time.

Working with Drawing Objects in the Gantt Chart View

Any drawn object—whether it's a line, a shape, or a text box—will be attached to the date on the timescale where you draw it. If you select an item and drag it to another spot on the chart, it will become attached to the date on the timescale at its new position.

To attach an item to a task instead of a date, open the Format, Drawing dialog box by double-clicking on the object or by selecting the object and clicking the Attach to Task toolbar button. Be sure the Size & Position tab is selected on the dialog box (see Figure 9.9).

In the Attach to task section, move to the ID field and type the ID number for the task that you want to attach the object to. Then select whether the object is connected to the beginning or end of the task bar. The Line & Fill tab of this dialog box also allows you to control the line style and color and the fill pattern and color for the object.

You can also easily remove or hide the objects that you place on the Gantt Chart. Select an object and then press the Delete key to remove it. You can hide the objects on the Gantt Chart by choosing Format, Layout. In the Layout dialog box, clear the Show Drawings check box.

Be sure the Show Drawings feature is on if you want your Gantt Chart drawings and text boxes to print!

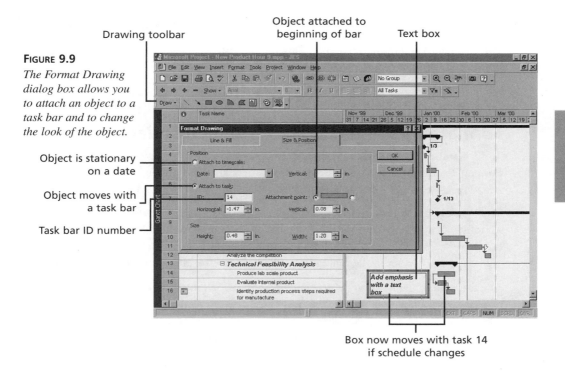

FIGURE 9.9

The Format Drawing dialog box allows you to attach an object to a task bar and to change the look of the object.

Drawing toolbar

Object attached to beginning of bar

Text box

Object is stationary on a date

Object moves with a task bar

Task bar ID number

Box now moves with task 14 if schedule changes

Placing Free Text on the Gantt Chart

You can place extra text near the Gantt Chart bars by using the Text Box button on the Drawing toolbar. When you click and drag to create the text box, an insertion point appears in the box. Type the text that you want to appear in the text box.

Double-click on the text box to edit the settings in the Format Drawing dialog box. As with other drawn objects, you can attach the text box to a particular date on the timeline or to a task bar on the chart.

If you want to edit the text in a box, select the text box and then drag to select the text it contains. Type in new text or edit the current entry. To change the text font, select the text in the box and choose Format, Font to open the Font dialog box. You can change any of the font attributes that are available through the dialog box; toolbar formatting buttons are not available when formatting a drawn text box.

Special Formatting for the Calendar

The Calendar view offers several options for changing the appearance of the calendar itself and for formatting the timescale and bars that appear on the calendar. You can use the mouse for some changes, like making days wider, or you can use dialog boxes opened through the Format menu for more options.

Formatting the Timescale for the Calendar

To format the timescale for the calendar, display the Calendar view, and then select Format, Timescale. The Timescale dialog box appears. This dialog box contains three tabs: Week Headings, Date Boxes, and Date Shading (see Figure 9.10).

The Week Headings tab allows you to change the calendar display by changing the Monthly, Daily, and Weekly titles for the calendar. Each title field has its own drop-down box of selections. You can also choose to show the week with seven or five days. A sample box at the bottom of the dialog box shows you the results of the changes you make.

The Date Boxes tab allows you to include additional elements in the top or bottom row of each of the individual date boxes. You can include Overflow indicators that appear when all the tasks for a given day cannot be displayed in the Calendars date box. Other options include drop-down boxes for the pattern and color of these additional elements.

Format the top and bottom of date boxes

Choose working calendar and shading options

FIGURE 9.10

The Timescale dialog box allows you to change the display settings for the Calendar view, and use shading to indicate nonworking days in the schedule.

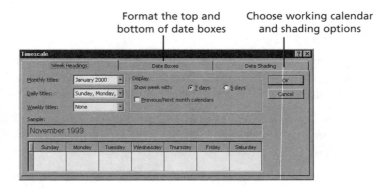

Selecting Calendar Bar Styles Options

You can also control the formatting of the bars on the Calendar. In the Calendar view, select Format, Bar Styles to open the Bar Styles dialog box. This is the same dialog box you used in Hour 8, "Working with the Other Task Views," to turn on the display of Summary tasks in the Calendar view.

A Task type list box allows you to select which category of task bars will have the new formatting applied. In the Bar shape area of the dialog box, drop-down boxes for Bar type, Pattern, Color, and Split pattern give you access to the different formatting options for the bars. Add a shadow on the bottom and right side of task bars by turning on the Shadow option.

A Text Fields(s) area in the Bar Styles dialog box allows you to choose information to be displayed inside the bars. For instance, you might want to include the Duration field in task bars in case the bar is continued on several calendar weeks.

After you have made your bar style formatting selection, click the OK button in the Bar Styles dialog box. The changes you have made to the various bar categories will appear on the Calendar.

Formatting Calendar Layout with the Mouse

Sometimes it is easier to see calendar view bars by making the days of the week wider and the boxes for the weeks deeper. To widen the days, place the mouse over the vertical line separating two day headings, like Monday and Tuesday, as shown in Figure 9.11. Click and drag the line to the right to widen the day. Double-clicking the same line will bring all five (or seven) days back onto the screen.

To deepen the weeks, place the mouse over the top of the week heading. When the pointer changes to a horizontal line with arrows up and down (the same mouse pointer shape used on a Gantt Chart to change table row heights), click and drag to make the week deeper.

FIGURE 9.11

You can widen or deepen the date boxes using the mouse.

Drag here to widen days

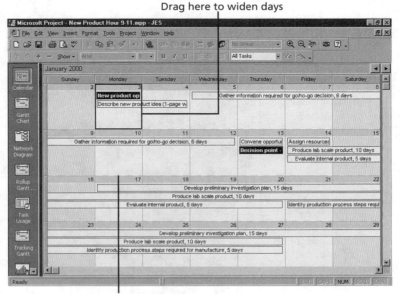

Drag here for deeper weeks

For Project to print deep spaces for the weeks, you must select an option in the Calendar view page setup. With the Calendar displayed, choose File, Page Setup. On the View tab, choose Week Height As On Screen.

Special Formatting for the Network Diagram

There are some special formatting options for the Network Diagram view of your project, too. In Hour 8, you rearranged the diagram task boxes manually, and zoomed in and out to change the perspective on the project. In the following sections, you take a closer look at how task nodes are formatted and at how to control the arrangement of the nodes onscreen.

Reviewing the Format Options for the Network Diagram

The Network Diagram Format menu options allow you to make formatting changes to a single diagram box, to all boxes in a category of tasks, and to the overall appearance of the diagram. You can change the shapes and colors of the boxes as well as control the way the boxes are laid out on the screen to represent the flow of the project.

To Do: Formatting Network Diagram Boxes

To customize the appearance of Network Diagram boxes, follow these steps:

1. Display the Network Diagram. Select Format, Box Styles to display the dialog box shown in Figure 9.12.

To Do

FIGURE 9.12

Change the appearance and formatting of task nodes in the Box Styles dialog box.

Pick task type —

Change box shape and outline color

Add a background color or pattern

Start customizing box contents here

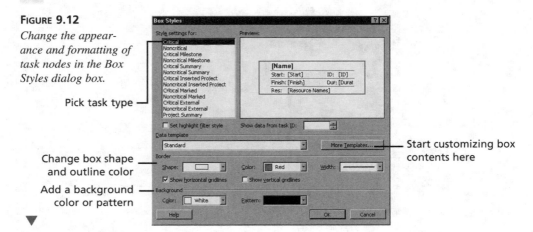

▼ 2. Select a type of task to be formatted in the Style settings for: list.

3. In the Border and Background areas of the dialog box, select the node shape, color, border width, and background appearance.

4. The row and column layout and the contents of each type of task node are determined by box templates. In the Data template area, choose More templates to begin creating custom box types.

> If you choose to experiment with Network Diagram box templates, be sure to make copies of the existing templates and try your hand with the copies. For a detailed discussion of Network Diagram data templates, I recommend *Special Edition Using Project 2000* published by Que.

5. After choosing More Templates, the Data Template dialog box will be displayed. Choose Standard, and then click Copy to begin experimenting. In the Data Template Definition dialog box (shown in Figure 9.13), you can set the Cell Layout (rows and columns) for box types, and choose which fields of Project information to display in those cells.

FIGURE 9.13

The Data Template Definition dialog box offers complete control of Network Diagram node styles.

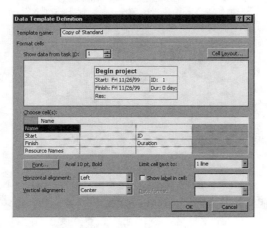

6. Click OK when finished, and then click Close on the Data Templates dialog box.

7. When you have completed the formatting changes, click OK on the Box Styles
▲ dialog box to see the effects on the Network Diagram view.

Selecting Layout Options

The general look of the entire Network Diagram can be changed using layout options. Recall from Hour 8 that boxes are drawn and placed on the diagram automatically, in a predetermined arrangement, unless you choose to allow manual box placement. Positioning and other formatting options for Network Diagrams are available in the layout dialog box.

Select Format, Layout to display the Layout options dialog box (shown in Figure 9.12). The Box Layout area of the dialog box gives you another way to control the order in which the boxes are drawn on the screen. If you are familiar with Network Diagrams, the default arrangement of Top Down From Left will draw the network nodes as you would expect. But because sorting is not allowed in the Network Diagram view, Project provides other arrangement options for the task nodes. As shown in Figure 9.14, box layout arrangements include ordering the nodes by a timeframe or by critical and noncritical tasks.

FIGURE 9.14

Change the appearance of the Network Diagram by choosing box arrangements and link line styles.

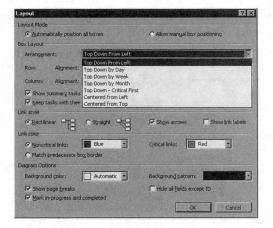

After selecting a box arrangement and closing the Layout dialog box, you must then tell Project to redraw the Network Diagram. Select Format, Layout Now.

If you would like to be able to click and drag the boxes on the Network Diagram to rearrange them, be sure to turn on the feature to Allow Manual Box Positioning in the Layout dialog box. After dragging task nodes on the diagram, reset all task boxes by selecting Format, Layout Now from the menu. To reset the entire diagram, undo any manual movements of the boxes, and prevent dragging of boxes, turn on Automatically Position All Boxes in the same dialog box.

The Link Style area of the Layout dialog box lets you choose between straight or angular lines. You can also turn off the arrowheads on the link lines (which I don't recommend; the flow of the links is an important piece of information). To show the type of linking relationship—FS, SS, FF, or SF—on the link lines, select the Show link labels check box. And, if you must, you can change the default color of critical and noncritical links.

> Many changes to options on the Layout dialog box take effect immediately when OK is clicked and the box is closed. An important exception is choosing an arrangement setting to change the box layout. When you close the Layout dialog box, it will appear that nothing happened. You *must* force Project to redraw the entire diagram. Select Format, Layout Now, or right-click on the diagram and choose Layout Now from the shortcut menu.

9

Summary

This hour has shown you how to format a variety of features on some standard task views. You are now familiar with methods for changing the appearance of the Gantt Chart, Calendar, and the Network Diagram. Experiment! Take a little time to look at different gridline, bar style, and timescale formats. You may be surprised to find that a simple change in appearance can communicate project information much more effectively to your team.

Q&A

Q My project is front-loaded with a lot of tasks. I'd like to make the Calendar view show more tasks per day in the first month and print the rest of the schedule in the default Calendar format. Can I do this?

A You can, but not all in one print command. Set the formatting as you need it for the first month, and then print the first month only. Return to the Calendar view, reset the date boxes to their original size, and print the remaining months. Use the Timescale Dates settings in the Print dialog box to control which months are printed.

Q I dragged some boxes around in the Network Diagram and now I want Project to put some of them, but not all of them, back in their original positions. Choosing Layout Now moves them all. Do I have any other options?

A You need to use the Layout Selection Now feature. This is not a command you can choose from the Format menu. Either display the Network Diagram toolbar and click the last button (pop-up label will indicate Layout Selection Now), or right-mouse click on the Network Diagram and select Layout Selection Now from the shortcut menu. Be sure to select the boxes you want Project to move before issuing the command.

Q I'd like my top-level summary tasks to be a larger point size but all other summary tasks to stay the same size as they are now. If I change the Text Style formatting for Summary tasks, all levels change. Can't I format summary tasks by outline level?

A To Project, a summary task is a summary task is a summary task; there is no distinction between different outline levels. Set the summary task text style to the formatting you'll need the most, probably the lower-level summary tasks, and then manually format the others. Use Format, Font to apply manual formatting.

Exercises

Your creative side has been suppressed long enough. It's time to add some color to your project plan. Begin by opening the file "New Product Hour 9.MPP." The (colorful!) results of the exercises can be found in the file "New Product Hour 9-Exercise.MPP." See the Introduction for instructions to access the sample files and solutions for these exercises on the book's Web page.

1. Make a copy of the Gantt Chart so you can experiment with formatting.

2. Add some emphasis up and down the chart. Display dashed lines, in teal, between every bar on the chart (the Gantt Rows gridlines). Change the tick lines on the Timescale (Title Vertical gridlines) to yellow. And display vertical lines down the chart at the beginning of every week (Major Columns gridlines) in red.

3. On the Calendar view, change critical task bars to be shown in red. Also shade the nonworking days on the base calendar in olive.

4. Now make changes to the Network Diagram. Hide all box fields except the task ID numbers and display the link relationship types on the link lines.

5. Maybe straight lines on the diagram would be easier for people to follow. Straighten the linking lines on the diagram now.

6. Well, that is actually less clear. Reset the lines to be angled. But make the link lines for noncritical tasks aqua so they will stand out.

7. Finally, to give the diagram a time-phased appearance, arrange the boxes top down by week.

HOUR **10**

Finalizing and Printing Your Schedule

Now that you have created the task list, established the dependency links between tasks, and explored the most popular task views, it's a good time to print your schedule. There are several choices when printing the project data. You can print the data as it appears in a view—such as the Gantt Chart, Network Diagram, or Calendar views. On the other hand, you can print one of the 22 predesigned reports in Microsoft Project. These reports often show more detailed information or include calculations, which can help you analyze your schedule.

This hour concentrates on printing views and reports that focus on the project tasks. Hour 17, "Printing Views and Reports with Resources," explains how to print views and reports that focus on your project resources. Customizing standard reports is also discussed in Hour 17.

In this hour, you will learn:

- How to check your task list for spelling errors
- How to set layout and print options for views
- How to include automated information in page headers and footers
- How to view and print standard reports that focus on task information

Checking for Spelling Errors

Before you print a schedule or report, you should spell check the project file. Nothing is more embarrassing than handing a report or printout to a boss or client with misspelled words! The spell checker verifies the spelling of your list of task names and any notes you have added to a task.

Using the Spelling Command

If you have used the spelling feature in other Windows programs, you will be right at home using it in Project. To access the spell check feature, click the Spelling button on the Standard toolbar or choose Tools, Spelling from the menu. The Spelling dialog box (shown in Figure 10.1) appears when Project can't find a word in its internal dictionary.

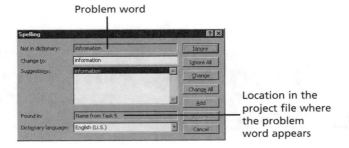

FIGURE 10.1

Use the Spelling dialog box to decide how to treat words not in the internal dictionary.

Problem word

Location in the project file where the problem word appears

The first word not found in the dictionary is listed in the box at the top of the Spelling dialog box. In Figure 10.1, the problem word is *infromation*. The Change To box proposes the most likely correction to the problem word. A list of possible variations on the problem word is displayed in the Suggestions box. You can accept the proposed correction, select one of the alternative words, or type in a correction in the Change To box.

Table 10.1 describes the uses of the buttons on the right side of the Spelling dialog box.

TABLE 10.1   The Spelling Dialog Box Option Buttons

Button	Description
Ignore	Ignores this occurrence of the word.
Ignore All	Ignores all occurrences of the word found in this file.
Change	Replaces only this occurrence of the problem word with the word you select or type in.
Change All	Replaces all occurrences of the problem word found in this file.

Button	Description
Add	Adds the word listed in the Not in Dictionary box to the custom user dictionary. The spell checker will ignore this word if found again in this or any other file.
Suggest	By default, the spell checker is set to always offer spelling suggestions. You can change this setting so that you see a list of suggestions only when you click the Suggest button. To change the default setting, choose Tools, Options from the menu.

Setting the Spelling Options

There are several options you can set for spell checking in Microsoft Project. To access these settings, choose Tools, Options and select the Spelling tab. The Spelling tab, shown in Figure 10.2, lists the fields that are checked when you activate the spell checker.

FIGURE 10.2

You can modify the field and spelling settings from the Spelling tab in the Options dialog box.

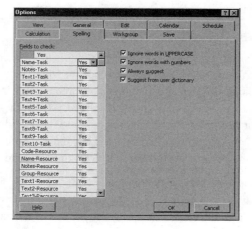

10

In addition to selecting the fields that should be checked for misspelled words, there are four settings you can turn off or on to control the way Project checks the spelling, listed in Table 10.2.

TABLE 10.2   The Spelling Settings in the Options Dialog Box

Setting	Description
Ignore Words in UPPERCASE	Ignores acronyms in all capital letters, such as IBM, AFB, or NYSE. Turn this setting off if you enter all text in capital letters.
Ignore Words with Numbers	Words that contain both letters and numbers are ignored.
Always Suggest	Displays spelling suggestions in the Spelling dialog box.
Suggest from User Dictionary	Checks problem words against words added to the custom user dictionary, as well as the main dictionary.

Printing Views

One way to share your project task list with others is to print a task view, such as the Gantt Chart, Network Diagram, or Calendar. Before you print a view, however, it's important that you prepare the view, set up the print options, and preview what the printout will look like.

As in all Windows applications, the print commands are located on the File menu. The Page Setup command defines page orientation, headers, footers, and so on, for printed views. The Print Preview and Print commands are used to print views. In addition to using the File menu, you can access the Print Preview and Print commands through buttons on the Standard toolbar.

Clicking the Print Preview button allows you to see what the printed copy will look like and also gives you access to the page setup and print commands. You should always preview before you print.

Preparing the View for Printing

The first step in preparing the project view for printing is to select the view you want to print. Choosing which view to print largely depends on which view you think others can easily follow. After the desired view is displayed onscreen, you can modify the project data so that it looks just as you want it to when printed. Although you might be seeing only a portion of your task list onscreen, all the data in your schedule will be printed. In Hour 9, "Formatting Views," you learned how to alter the appearance of the task list by using the buttons on the Formatting toolbar and through commands on the Format menu.

Options in the Format menu vary, depending on which view is displayed. In most task views, you can format the task names and other text to accentuate one or more tasks. In the Gantt Chart and Calendar views, there is a wide range of formatting options for the task bars. In the Timescale dialog box in the Calendar view, you can change the number of days per week displayed and control shading options. The Network Diagram view allows you to select the box and link line styles for the task nodes.

The timescale increments in the Gantt Chart views can be in minutes, hours, days, weeks, months, quarters, half years or years. To quickly adjust the timescale increments, use the Zoom In or Zoom Out buttons on the Standard toolbar.

 Using the Zoom In or Zoom Out buttons in the Calendar view has no impact on what is printed.

If you want the printed view to display only a subset of tasks in the project, or display the tasks grouped together in a special way, you might want to apply a filter or a group to the task list. Refer to Hour 16, "Fine-Tuning the Project Plan," for descriptions and examples of filters and groups available in Microsoft Project.

Page breaks are automatically determined when a view is printed. In the Gantt Chart and Task Usage views, you can set the page breaks manually instead of using the default page breaks. In the Network Diagram view, you can move the task node boxes to place tasks on specific pages. Sections later in this hour describe exactly how to insert your own page breaks.

Changing the Page Setup

In addition to making changes to how the view is displayed onscreen, you need to select options for how the data will appear on the printed page. Page margins, orientation, headers, footers, and the legend can all be modified. Separate print options can be set for each view or report. For example, adding or changing a header for a Gantt Chart does not change the header for the Network Diagram. The next time you print the Gantt Chart view, the print options previously set for it are automatically included. However, the print settings are saved only with the active project file. When you print the Gantt Chart view using another project file, you need to select the print options for the view in the other file. This allows you to establish unique print options in each file.

To change the print settings for the active view, choose File, Page Setup to display the Page Setup dialog box for the active view. Figure 10.3 shows the Page tab of the Page Setup dialog box for the Gantt Chart view.

There are some views that you cannot print. The Task Form is one example. If the File, Page Setup command is not available, the active view can't be printed.

As with other dialog boxes, the Page Setup dialog box has multiple tabs, each one representing a different collection of settings. Table 10.3 describes the print settings on each tab.

10

Name of the active view

FIGURE 10.3

Use the Page tab to set the page orientation and scaling.

Page orientation alternatives

Scaling options

Change paper size (choices depend on printer in use)

Renumber printed pages

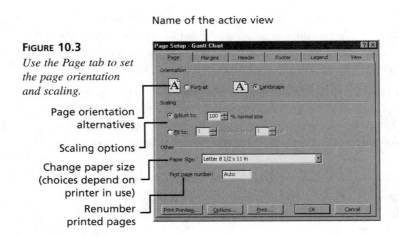

TABLE 10.3   The Page Setup Dialog Box Print Options

Tab	Options
Page	Choose a Portrait or Landscape page orientation. Enlarge or reduce the scale of view by a specified percentage or by a given number of pages. Select paper size and starting number for printed pages.
Margins	Select the Top, Bottom, Left, and Right margins. Microsoft Project prints with a quarter (.25) inch margin, even if you reduce the margin to zero (0). By default, borders surround each page, but can be turned off. The Outer pages option is available only with the Network Diagram view.
Header/Footer	Headers or footers that you want to appear on every printed page can be aligned on the left, center, or right side of the page. Buttons and two drop-down lists are used to insert system codes and project information in the header and footer areas.
Legend	If a printed view can have a legend, you can place text in the lower-left corner of the legend area. There can be up to three lines of text inside this area. Some views contain default legend text. The Width option controls the horizontal size of the legend text area, with the maximum width being five inches (or half the legend area in landscape orientation). The legend can appear at the bottom of every printed page or on its own separate page, or you can choose not to print a legend.
View	This tab displays options specific to the active view being printed. Some options on the View tab might be unavailable (dimmed), depending on the view being printed. Descriptions of the options on the View tab are described later in this hour in sections devoted to printing each view.

Understanding Headers and Footers

On the Header and Footer tabs of the Page Setup dialog box are seven buttons and two drop-down lists that can be used to format text, insert system codes, insert project-wide field values, or insert graphics images into the header or footer. A sample of the header or footer as currently defined is displayed in the top portion of the dialog box. There are no default headers. You can have up to five lines of header text. Most views have a default footer to print the page number on the center alignment tab. You can have three lines of footer text.

Figure 10.4 shows a preview of a header Gantt Chart view. The Project Title, Manager, and Company—as entered in the File, Properties, Summary dialog box fields—are displayed in the upper-left corner of each printed page. The upper-right corner of each page displays the project Percent Complete and Duration values. The Header text has been formatted by using the Font button.

10

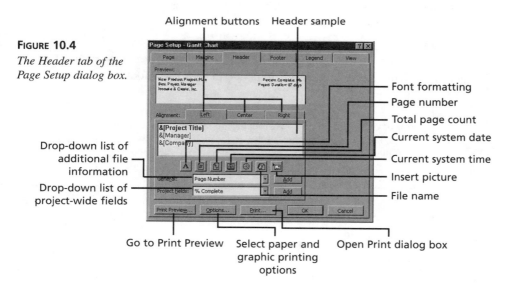

FIGURE 10.4

The Header tab of the Page Setup dialog box.

Headers and footers can be placed on one or more of the Alignment tabs. You can type in text or insert system and field codes using one of the buttons or the drop-down menus. Many of the system codes insert data that appears in the Properties dialog box (File, Properties), some of which you can edit and some are updated automatically by Project.

When printing draft copies, it's extremely useful if you put the filename and view name on your printouts. This will help to remind you exactly what was printed. Additionally, you should place the system date and system time on printouts to record the day and time the draft was printed. This will help ensure you're working with the very latest copy.

To Do: Entering a Header or Footer

To create a header or footer for your printout, follow these steps:

1. Display a view, and then select File, Page Setup.

2. Select either the Header or Footer tab.

3. Choose the desired Alignment tab.

4. Use the box below the Alignment tabs to type the appropriate text you want to appear on the header or footer.

   Or, choose one of the buttons or items from the drop-down lists to insert system codes or project information. If you use one of the items in a drop-down list, click the Add button to insert the information into the header or footer.

You have to type in any descriptive text for the system codes or project fields. For example, to display "Page number - " and the number, you have to type the exact text you want to see, and then add the Page Number code.

5. To format any of the text or codes in the header or footer, highlight the text or code and use the Font button.

After you have established the Page Setup options, the settings become a permanent part of the view in that project file. However, you may change the settings at any time.

Using Print Preview

After you have formatted the view and selected the Page Setup options you want, it's a good idea to preview what the printout will look like before you actually print the view. You can choose File, Print Preview or click the Print Preview button on the Standard toolbar. Figure 10.5 shows the Print Preview screen. Notice that the Header, Footer, and Legend contents are included in the preview of the Gantt Chart. The Header and Footer text has been enlarged by using the Font button. No change has been made to the default Legend setting.

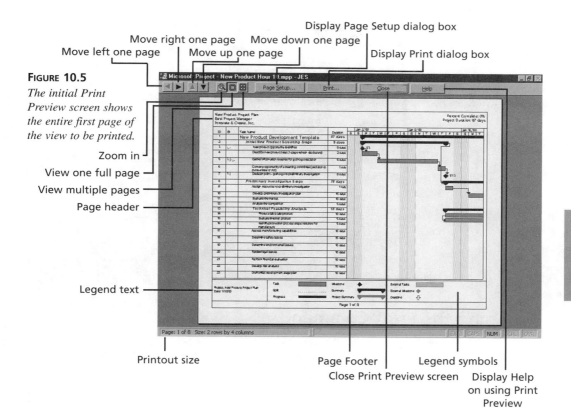

Move left one page
Move right one page
Move up one page
Move down one page
Display Page Setup dialog box
Display Print dialog box

FIGURE 10.5
The initial Print Preview screen shows the entire first page of the view to be printed.

Zoom in
View one full page
View multiple pages
Page header

Legend text

Printout size
Page Footer
Close Print Preview screen
Legend symbols
Display Help on using Print Preview

10

If multiple pages exist, you can use the buttons at the top left of the Print Preview screen to display left, right, up, and down one page at a time. You can zoom in on the details of a page by clicking the Zoom In button or by clicking the mouse pointer on the part of the page you want to see in greater detail. Click again to zoom out. Additionally, you can view multiple pages in the Print Preview screen. Figure 10.6 shows the multipage view of a Gantt Chart.

In this example, the size of the printout is two rows by four columns. Pages are numbered down the columns, starting from the left. Page 2 of the report is the bottom page in the left column in this example of the Print Preview screen.

From the Print Preview screen, click the Page Setup button to open the Page Setup dialog box. The Help button displays information about using the Print Preview screen. When you are ready to print, click the Print button to display the Print dialog box. To make changes to the view or if you decide not to print at this time, click the Close button to display the project view.

FIGURE 10.6

*The multipage view of
a Gantt Chart in the
Print Preview screen
helps you see how your
pages will fit together.*

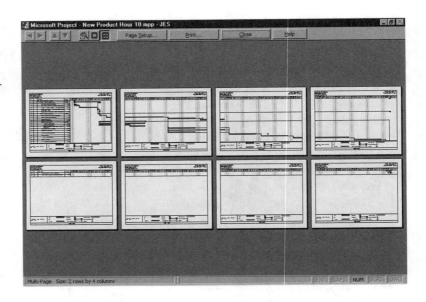

Using the Print Command

When you have formatted the view onscreen and the page setup options are selected, the
final step is to print the view. Choose File, Print and the Print dialog box shows you
choices for printing the current screen view (see Figure 10.7).

 The Print button on the Standard toolbar causes data to be sent to
the printer immediately; you don't get a chance to make selections in
the Print dialog box.

The default printer appears in the Name drop-down list. You can select an alternative
printer if necessary. The printer Properties include selecting legal or letter size paper,
selecting a paper feeder source, and changing the resolution of graphics objects.

 You will not be able to change to a different printer if you enter the Print
dialog box through the Print Preview screen. Go directly to the Print options
from the displayed view (File, Print) to choose another printer.

FIGURE 10.7

Some options in the Print dialog box do not apply to all views and may be dimmed (meaning inactive).

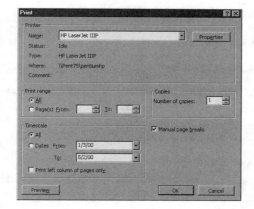

Unless you specify otherwise, all pages shown in the Print Preview screen will print. To print only a few pages, select the Page(s) From and To options in the Print Range area, and type the page numbers you want to print.

Project 2000 allows you to set the starting page number for printouts. For example, you might want to print pages 10 and 11, but have them numbered on the printout as pages 1 and 2. Change the setting in the Page Setup dialog box. Select File, Page Setup, and move to the Page tab. Enter a starting number for your printout in the First Page Number field.

By default, the view prints all the information from the start date of the project through the finish date. You can limit the printed output to a specific time span. In the Timescale area of the Print dialog box, enter From and To Dates to restrict the printout to a "time slice" of the plan.

Another option is to print only the pages on the far-left side of the multipage Print Preview screen; typically these are the pages with ID numbers and task or resource names. This printout is particularly useful for reviewing the task or resource list structure and information when you don't need to focus on graphical information. Use the Preview button to verify which pages are included in the left column.

Even if you select the option to Print left column of pages only in the Print dialog box, Project does not reflect this choice if you return to Preview. All exposed Gantt Chart columns will still be displayed in Preview.

After you have selected the print settings, click OK to start printing the view.

Printing Gantt Charts

When printing the Gantt Chart view, check the following items before you print:

- Are the columns you want to print visible onscreen? Click and drag the vertical divider bar if necessary. The rightmost column that's *completely* visible in the table side of the Gantt Chart is the last column of the table that will be printed, unless you select Print All Sheet Columns on the View tab of the Page Setup dialog box.

- Is the timescale set appropriately, so that the Gantt bars will be "long enough" but not "too long" on the printout. If your project requires several months, don't print the plan down to the hourly level. The increment displayed in the timescale will be the increment printed.

- Will the printout start new pages where you want it to? You can force a page break so that a new page starts at a specific task, even if the automatic page break doesn't occur until farther down the list.

To Do: Setting a Page Break

To force page breaks in a task list, do the following:

1. Select any cell in the row just below the intended page break. This row becomes the first row on a new page.

2. Choose Insert, Page Break. A dashed line appears above the selected row to indicate the presence of a manually inserted page break.

   To remove a page break, select any cell in the row just below the page break dotted line and choose Insert, Remove Page Break.

If the task where a page break was set is hidden because its summary task has been collapsed, Project ignores that page break. The task, and the manual break, must be visible on the screen view to be incorporated into the printout.

Gantt Chart Page Setup Options

The View tab of the Page Setup dialog box includes a set of options specific to the view you're printing. Figure 10.8 shows the View tab in the Page Setup dialog box for a Gantt Chart. To display the Page Setup dialog box choose File, Page Setup, or click the Page Setup button in the Print Preview screen.

FIGURE 10.8

The View tab in the Gantt Chart Page Setup dialog box.

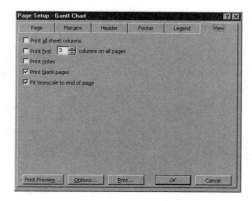

10

These are the View options in the Page Setup dialog box for the Gantt Chart view:

- Print All Sheet Columns—Prints all columns of the Gantt Chart table, regardless of whether they are completely visible on the screen.

- Print First # Columns On All Pages—Prints the specified number of columns on all pages. Figure 10.6 shows a preview of the Gantt Chart view with the default setting, which prints only the visible sheet columns. Printing several columns on all pages makes it easier to determine the task that corresponds to each bar. Remember that the ID number and Indicator columns count as two of the columns.

- Print notes—Prints the task notes on a separate page at the end of the Gantt Chart printout.

- Print blank pages—Uncheck to suppress the printing of blank pages. The default is for all pages to print. In Figure 10.6, the bottom page in the two middle columns do not contain any sheet columns or task bars; they are blank pages. When this setting is unchecked, blank pages appear grayed out in the preview screen.

- Fit timescale to end of page—Leave the box checked to ensure that the timescale extends all the way to the right page margin.

Printing Network Diagrams

A printed copy of the Network Diagram will give you the best look at the logical flow of your project. You can print the diagram on 8 1/2" by 11" paper, but you will get the best result if your printer accepts larger paper sizes or if you have access to a large plotter. As with printing the Gantt Chart, you will need to open the File, Print dialog box to choose another printer. After you are in the Preview screen, the Print button will not allow you to change printers.

When printing the Network Diagram view, you should also check the following items before you print:

- You have a choice on the Margins tab of the Page Setup dialog box as to what type of borders you want to print. The default is to print borders only around the Outer pages. To enclose each page in a lined border, choose Every page. To suppress all borders, choose None. Previewing the Network Diagram and clicking the Multiple Pages button is the best way to see the effect of changing the border options. Figure 10.9 shows the preview of the Network Diagram view, with the Outer pages border option turned on.

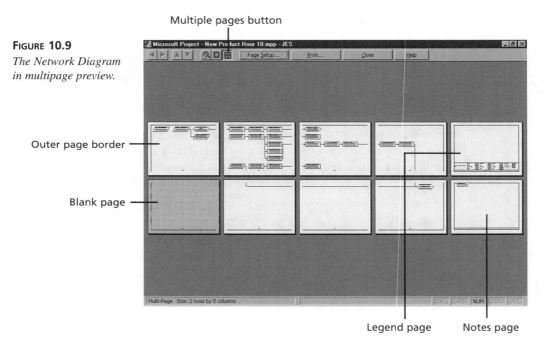

FIGURE 10.9
The Network Diagram in multipage preview.

- When you print the Network Diagram view, you have the option of printing or suppressing the blank pages. In Figure 10.9, the grayed page in the lower-left corner of the diagram is a blank page. The Print blank pages option on the View tab of the Page Setup dialog box has been turned off to suppress the printing of blank pages.
- The way in which the Network Diagram renders the linking lines between tasks can be adjusted through the Format, Layout dialog box before entering Print Preview. The lines can be drawn using just straight horizontal and vertical lines at right angles, or with diagonal lines.

- You can't change the page breaks on the Network Diagram, but you can move the task nodes to either side of the automatic page breaks or use scaling (located on the Page tab of the Page Setup dialog box) to shrink the number of printed pages. When you scale the display, the Adjust for Page Breaks option under the Format, Layout menu automatically moves nodes to the right and down if the nodes land on a page break. Use the Format, Layout Now command to see the result.

If you move a group of nodes simultaneously, the nodes retain positions in relation to each other as you move them. The linking lines also follow task nodes to the new locations. Review the section "Moving Task Nodes in Network Diagram View," in Hour 8, for a complete discussion of manually adjusting task node placement on the diagram.

Printing Calendars

When printing the Calendar view, each month prints on a separate page by default. The View tab in the Page Setup dialog box includes a set of options that control what's printed (see Figure 10.10). You can change the default settings to print two months per page or set the number of weeks to print per page. To open the Page Setup dialog box, choose File, Page Setup or click the Page Setup button in the Print Preview screen.

10

FIGURE 10.10

The View tab of the Page Setup dialog box, for the Calendar view.

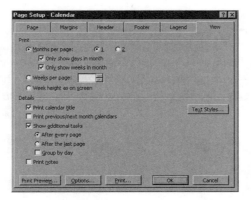

The View options in the Page Setup dialog box for the Calendar view include:

- Months Per Page—Choose to print one or two months on each page. The Only Show Days in Month option doesn't display the dates or tasks in other months on the printed calendar. If the Only Show Weeks in Month option is unchecked, six weeks will print, starting from the first of each month.
- Weeks Per Page—Type the number of weeks to print in the entry box. This option is very useful if you have many tasks and want to print only one or two weeks on a page.

- Week Height as On Screen—Use this option if you have adjusted the height of the weeks on the Calendar view and you want the printed calendar to match the week height from the screen display.

- Print Calendar Title—At the top of each page, the name of the month or the span of weeks is printed.

- Print Previous/Next Month Calendars—The calendar days are a little compressed to make room for miniature calendars of the previous and next months appearing at the top of each page.

- Show Additional Tasks—Use this option when more tasks exist than can be displayed on the calendar. You have the choice of printing these overflow tasks with the After Every Page or After the Last Page options. The Group By Day check box displays the overflow page with the tasks listed underneath every date the task is being worked on. The default grouping is by task.

- Print Notes—Prints the task notes on a separate page.

- The Text Styles button—Allows you to format the font type; font style, size, and color for all printed text; monthly titles; previous/next month miniature calendars; or overflow tasks.

Printing the Overview Reports

Of the 22 predesigned reports in Microsoft Project, the Overview category contains the best set of purely task-oriented reports. To access these reports, choose View, Reports and double-click on Overview to open the Overview Reports dialog box, shown in Figure 10.11.

FIGURE 10.11

The built-in reports in the Overview category.

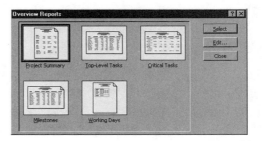

When you double-click a report, it's displayed in the Print Preview screen. From there, you can access the Page Setup and Print dialog boxes. The Print Preview screen, Page Setup dialog box, and Print dialog box options are used the same way for reports as for views, discussed in earlier sections of this hour. Because of the nature of the reports, some of the Page Setup and Print options might not be available.

The Project Summary report is the first report listed in the Overview Reports category. It is slightly different from the rest of the reports in the category in that the Project Summary gives you an overview of the project instead of a list of task categories. As its name implies, much of the Project Summary information pertains to how well the project is progressing. A thorough discussion of this report can be found in Hour 17, particularly the section titled "Customizing Specific Report Types."

The Top-Level Tasks Report

The Top-Level Tasks report shows the highest level summary tasks in a task list. Use this report to focus on the major phases of your project. For each summary task, the ID, Task Name, Duration, Start, Finish, Percent Complete, Cost, and Work are printed. Figure 10.12 shows a sample of this report.

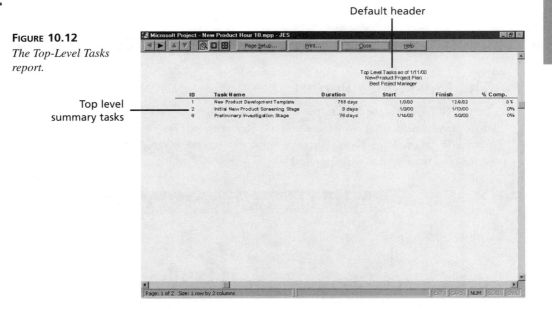

FIGURE 10.12
The Top-Level Tasks report.

The Critical Tasks Report

The Critical Tasks report (see Figure 10.13) displays all the critical tasks, grouped under their summary tasks. For each task, the ID, Indicators, Task Name, Duration, Start, Finish, Predecessors, and Resource Names are listed.

FIGURE 10.13
The Critical Tasks report.

Summary task

Critical task

Successor
(Dependent) task
information

Note

Number of
printed pages

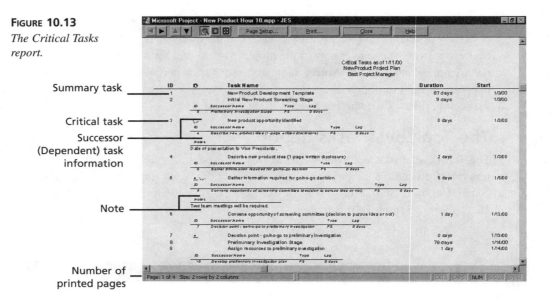

The Milestones Report

Figure 10.14 shows the Milestones report, which offers another way to focus on the major events or turning points in a project. This report shows the ID, Indicators, Task Name, Duration, Start, Finish, Predecessors, and Resource Names for all project milestones and their related summary tasks.

FIGURE 10.14
The Milestones report.

Summary task

Note

Milestone

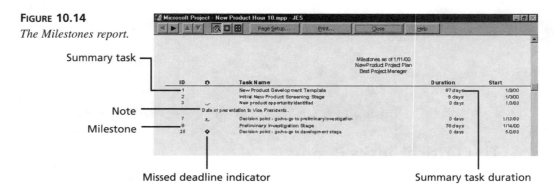

Missed deadline indicator   Summary task duration

The Working Days Report

The Working Days report, shown in Figure 10.15, displays a list of the working and non-working times for each base calendar used in your project. This report provides a good way to verify that the appropriate work hours have been established and that the holidays and other nonworking times are incorporated into your project. The information for each base calendar is printed on a separate page.

Figure 10.15
The Working Days report.

Name of the base calendar

Typical work days and work hours

Nonworking or partial working days

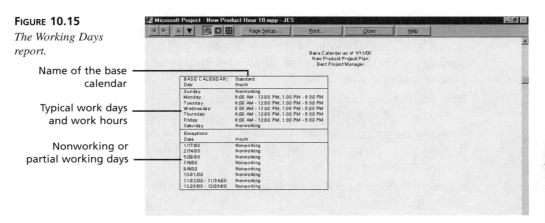

10

Summary

In this hour, you explored the fundamentals of printing views and reports. You learned how to check your task list for spelling errors, prepare the views for printing, explore the options in the Page Setup dialog box, and use the Print Preview screen. You also learned about some specific options available when printing the Gantt Chart, Network Diagram, and Calendar views and became acquainted with the Overview reports.

Q&A

Q **I've moved the divider between the task list table and the timescale bars in the Gantt Chart view so that only the task ID column is visible. When I print the view, however, the ID and Indicator columns continue to be printed. What can I do?**

A To print only the ID, you need to modify the settings for the table displayed on the left side of the Gantt Chart view. Choose View, Table, More Tables; the More Tables dialog box appears with the name of the active table highlighted. Click the Edit button to display the Table Definition dialog box. At the bottom of the dialog box, you need to uncheck the Lock First Column check box. Then click OK to accept the change. In the More Tables dialog box, click Apply. Now when you preview or print the view, only the first column, ID, will print.

Q **Microsoft Project is ignoring the manual page breaks I have set. How can I fix this?**

A Choose File, Print to check the Print dialog box. Make sure the Manual Page Breaks box is checked.

Q **Onscreen, there is some space between the vertical divider bar and my Gantt Chart bars. But when I print the view, the first task bar prints right up against the task list information. How can I keep some space before the bars when I print the Gantt Chart?**

A The only solution to this is to use the Dates settings in the Print dialog box. Enter a starting print date that is actually a little earlier than the project start date. For example, if your project starts on August 1, 2001, and your timescale is set to print in weeks, start the printout at July 15 or so. You'll get the extra space before the bars on the printed copy.

Q **Can I change the legend contents so that only a few key view elements are described?**

A The short answer is no. All the formatting settings defined in the Bar Styles dialog boxes of the various views will be included in the Legend for that view. That can't be changed. *Advanced* users may want to experiment with removing certain task type definitions from the Gantt Chart Bar Styles dialog box, for example, but I don't recommend it. The best options are to turn off the Legend (in the Page Setup dialog box) so that it does not print or to print it on a separate page so that it does not take up valuable print space.

Exercises

The printouts for your project will probably span several pages. In this exercise, you will use view formatting and the Page Setup dialog box to make changes to the Gantt Chart, the Calendar view, and the Network Diagram and fine-tune your printouts. Use the multiple page print preview to see the effects of these changes on the printed output. Begin by opening the file "New Product Hour 10.MPP." The results of the exercise can be found in the file "New Product Hour 10-Exercise.MPP." See the Introduction for instructions to access the sample files and solutions for these exercises on the book's Web page.

1. Display the Gantt Chart and position the vertical divider bar so that only the ID numbers, the Indicators column, and the Task Names are visible. Change the Timescale setting to view Weeks over Days.

2. Change the page setup options so that:

Any task notes in the project will be printed.

Any blank pages will not print.

The legend appears on a page by itself.

Your name will print in the center of the page header.

3. Hard to decipher? Turn the blank page printing back on but don't print the legend.

4. View the calendar and make the weeks (rows) deeper so more tasks can be printed on each day. Preview the results. Does the preview show the bigger date boxes?

5. Change a page setting for this view so that the calendar will print exactly as you have formatted it.

6. Preview the Network Diagram. How many pages will be printed? Will a Legend be printed, and if so, on every page or by itself?

7. Change the setting to print the legend on every page. Now how many pages will be printed?

8. You know that the Network Diagram is particularly handy for viewing the project flow, so you'd like to set up a simple flow diagram. Reduce the nodes on the diagram to view task ID numbers only. Preview the results, and then remove any footer from the printout and put the legend back on its own page.

10

PART IV

Assigning Resources and Costs to the Tasks

Hour

HOUR 11

Defining Resources and Costs

In the previous hours of this book, you created your task list and organized it into a schedule of dates that shows when the project and the individual tasks will start and finish. For the next four hours, Hours 12, "Mastering Resource Scheduling in Microsoft Project," through 15, "Resolving Resource Allocation Problems," you will learn how to incorporate resources and costs into the project plan. But in this hour, you will focus on resources and you will learn:

- How to determine what resources will be needed to complete the project. In other words, who is going to do the actual work, and what equipment, facilities, or materials will they need to do it?

- How to determine when those resources are available for work on this project, and if it is feasible for them to do everything your project calls for in the time you have allotted

- How to determine what your project is going to cost

Improving the Accuracy of the Schedule

You rarely get to work with unlimited resources or funds, and much of project management is concerned with juggling limited resources to produce the project's output at an acceptable cost. Although adding resources and costs to the project plan requires you to devote more time to the care and feeding of the project document, it will return substantial benefits. One of the benefits will be a far more realistic schedule of dates. If you *assign*, or allocate, individual resources to work on specific tasks and have told Project when those resources are available for work, Project will recalculate the schedule to accommodate the working times of the assigned resources. It will schedule work on tasks around the vacations and other nonworking times you have identified for the resources. In Figure 11.1, you can be sure that the scheduled start and finish dates for each task take into account any nonworking days for the resources named next to its task bar.

Resources assigned to the task

FIGURE 11.1

The default format for the Gantt Chart displays assigned resource names next to each task bar.

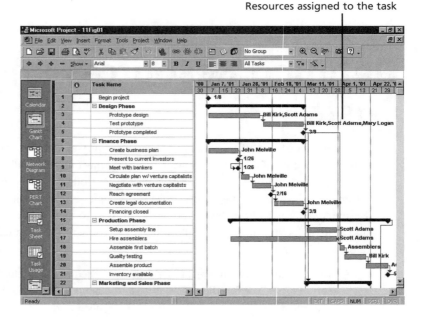

NEW TERM The *resources* for your project include the people who manage and do the work as well as the facilities, equipment, materials, and supplies they use to complete the tasks. The people may be employees, contractors, vendors, or temporary employees. The set of resources available for working on your project is called the *resource pool*.

A *resource assignment* is the result of allocating a resource's time to work on a task. You can assign resources full time, part time, and overtime (beyond their normal working hours). Project calculates the hours of work an assignment involves and the cost of using the resource for that many hours.

Project can help you detect when you have allocated the resource to more tasks than it can complete in the time allowed—in other words, when the resource is *overallocated*. In the resource list shown in Figure 11.2, all the overallocated resources are highlighted, but the seriously overallocated resources have an indicator as a warning. Project can help you reschedule the tasks so that resources are able to complete all the work you have assigned them.

A resource is *overallocated* when it's assigned to do more work than it can complete in that time period. Most often, overallocations result from assigning resources to multiple tasks scheduled during the same time period. Hour 15 addresses the overallocation issue in more detail.

FIGURE 11.2

The resource sheet shows overallocated resources with indicators and highlighting.

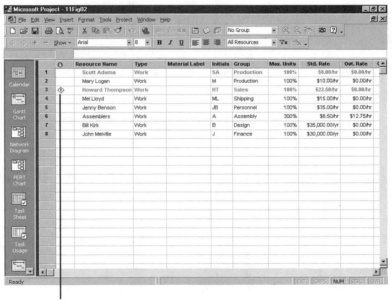

Indicators flag seriously
overallocated resources

Controlling Costs

Another major benefit of adding resources to the project is the added help in cost control it provides. Adding resources and their costs to the project plan will allow Microsoft Project to help you develop a budget for the project and to compare the budget with the actual costs as the work on the project proceeds. You can detect cost overruns while there's still time to take measures to correct them. And, by the time the project is complete, Microsoft Project will have accumulated the data you need to prepare your final reports.

NEW TERM The *costs* of a project usually stem more from the amount of money paid for the resources that work on tasks than from anything else. These are called *resource costs*, but there can also be costs that aren't identified with specific resources. These are called *fixed costs*. Examples of fixed costs might be taxes, licensing fees, or legal fees. *Total cost* for a task is the sum of its resource and fixed costs.

When you're planning the project, of course, the *scheduled costs* and dates for each task are entirely speculative—they're just your best estimates. The scheduled costs can be used as a planning *budget* for the project, which you can use in getting the project approved. Just before you start work on the project, save the details of the entire project plan as a *baseline* (see Figure 11.3), or planned, schedule and budget for comparison later with what actually happens. (See "Setting the Baseline" in Hour 20, "Tracking Work on the Project.")

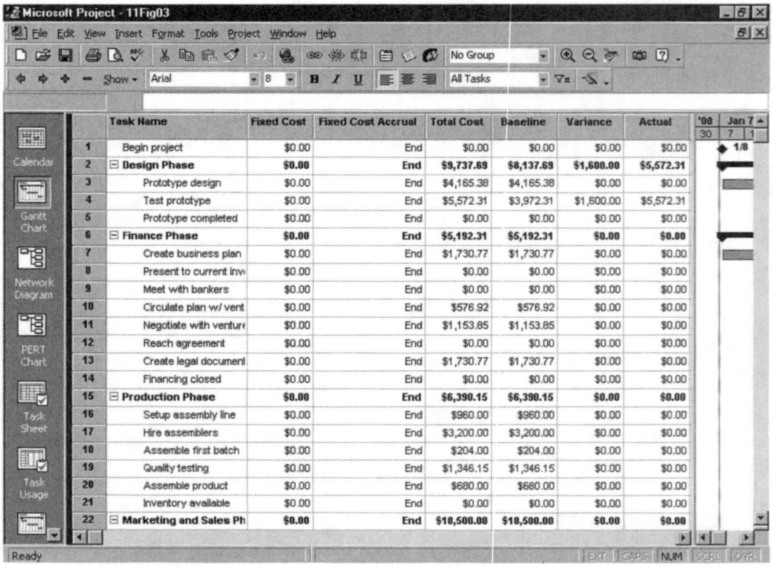

FIGURE 11.3

Project your budget by calcualting task costs: fixed, total, baseline, and actual.

After work starts on the project, you should monitor what actually happens and enter the results in the project document—noting when tasks actually start and finish and letting Project calculate how long they actually took to complete and what the actual costs were. As you enter the actual dates and costs, Project automatically updates the schedule, replacing the speculative dates and costs for completed tasks with the real dates and costs.

If things haven't gone as planned (and they rarely do), Project calculates new schedule dates and estimated costs for the remaining tasks. If the completed tasks are predecessors for tasks not yet started, the dates for the unstarted tasks are recalculated based on the actual dates for their predecessors. Thus, the current schedule now shows the actual dates and cost for completed tasks; although the schedule for tasks not finished is still speculative, it will have better estimates than before.

Sometimes you revise your estimates for unstarted tasks based on your experience thus far in the project. Microsoft Project can incorporate them into the schedule as soon as you enter them, which also improves the accuracy of the current schedule.

Therefore, the project schedule changes from the baseline values as you track actual performance, and you can compare the new estimates with the baseline to gauge how well you are doing. You can detect cost overruns or the possibility of not finishing on time while there's time to take corrective action. When the project is finished, you will have replaced all the estimated dates and costs with actual dates and cost. The baseline values can be compared to the final actual values to see how you did overall and what lessons can be learned for future projects.

11

NEW TERM Project managers generally have to keep costs in line with a budget for the project. *Budgeted* costs are shown as *baseline* costs, and comparing the baseline and *actual* costs as the project progresses is important to cost containment.

In this hour, you learn how to create the pool of resources you will use for the project, how to define when those resources are available for work, and how much the resources cost. In the following hours, you learn how to assign individual resources to work on specific tasks and how Project then schedules the work around the availability of the assigned resources and calculates the cost of each task based on the cost of the resources that do the work.

Defining Your Resources and Costs

This section gives you a general understanding of resource and cost terms. The next section is more specific and actually uses the terms to define your resource pool.

Defining Resources and Their Availability

You can create a list of resources to work on your project, or you can use the resource pool already created in another project. In this hour, you learn how to create a resource pool in the current project. (You can also refer to the section "Sharing Resources Among Projects with a Resource Pool" in Hour 22, "Working with Multiple Projects.")

Many, if not most, of the names in your resource pool may be the names of individual people, machines, and so forth; you have one "unit" of the resource to work with. A resource name can also represent a group of resources, as long as all members of the group have similar skills or job descriptions. For example, you might define a group of nurses in a hospital project as the Nurses resource, or a group of fork-lifts as the Fork-Lifts resource. These are sometimes called *group resources*, but in Microsoft Project 2000, they are called *resource sets*.

NEW TERM   A *resource set* is a resource name that represents a group of people or assets. You can assign several people or units from the set to the same task, but you can't specify which individuals from the group are being assigned. The members of the set all have the same pay rates and work schedules.

Resource sets represent more than one physical resource unit, and you need to let Project know how many of the units are available for assignments. A resource that represents an individual person or piece of equipment is a single unit.

NEW TERM   In defining the resource pool, you enter *resource units* to define the maximum number of units of a resource that are available for assignment. This value sets a limit to the number of units of the resource that can realistically be assigned to various tasks at any one moment. When you assign resources, you specify the units assigned to that task. If you assign more units than the maximum available, Project shows an indicator next to the resource name (see Figure 11.2).

NEW TERM   Microsoft Project 2000 allows you to distinguish between what it calls "work" resources and "material" resources. *Work resources* contribute part of their total time and effort (that is, their work) to a task; but when the task is completed they have not been consumed by the task and they have time that they can devote to other tasks. People, facilities, and equipment are examples of work resources. *Material resources*, on the other hand, are consumed or "used up" when they are assigned to a task and are no longer available to be assigned to other tasks. Gasoline, lumber, and camera film are examples of material resources.

> The default format for work resource units is the percentage format, which is covered later in this hour.

NEW TERM In addition to selecting the maximum units of a resource available for assignment, you may also need to customize a *resource calendar*. A separate calendar for each resource is linked to a base calendar, so it has the same normal work days, hours, and holidays found in the base calendar. However, the resource calendar is the place for you to make changes to reflect exceptions to the base calendar that apply to this one resource —vacation time, leave of absence, special hours, and so fourth. When you assign a resource to a task, Project uses the resource calendar to schedule the task, not the project's base calendar. You looked at base calendars in Hour 5, "Defining When Project Can Schedule Tasks."

Defining Costs

The most common resource cost is the cost of the time a work resource spends during normal working hours on a task. Project multiplies the hours of work by the hourly cost rate (the *standard rate*) you have defined for the resource to get the cost of that resource for that task. You can also define an *overtime rate* for work performed outside the normal working hours, and Project will use that rate when you assign a work resource to overtime work. For material resources, like parts or supplies, you want the cost to reflect the number of resource units used up, not how many hours are needed to complete the task. If you assign multiple resource names to a task, the sum of all the individual resource costs totals the task's resource cost.

For example, when pouring a foundation in construction, there are labor costs as well as the cost of the truckloads of mixed concrete. The labor costs are determined by the wage rate (the standard rate in Project) and the hours the task takes to be completed. The concrete cost depends only on the number of loads delivered and the cost of each load. The duration of the task has no direct correlation with the materials cost.

NEW TERM The *standard rate* is the rate charged per hour of work during normal working hours for a work resource, or the cost per unit of a material resource. The *overtime rate* for a work resource is the rate charged per hour of work outside the normal working hours.

NEW TERM Project can let you view the day-by-day details of resource costs for each resource and each task, or these costs can be summarized by task, by resource, or by project. When summing costs by task, Project adds the fixed costs to the resource costs and calls it *total cost* (or just *cost*).

Controlling How Costs Are Accrued

Suppose you want to print a report to show how far along the project will be as of a certain date and how much it will have cost up to that date. The estimated cost for the project as of that date includes all the costs of tasks that should have been finished by that

11

date and none of the costs for tasks that haven't started by that date. But what about tasks that should be started but not completed by the report date? The way the resource costs are *accrued* determines how the costs are handled in interim reports:

- Normally, Project will *prorate* the estimated costs for tasks that are only partially completed as of a given report date. If the task is 60 percent completed, Project reports 60 percent of the expected cost of the task as the estimated actual cost up to that date.

- If you have to pay a resource in full before it starts work, you tell Project to count the entire cost of that resource in any report printed on or after the *start* date of the task.

- If the resource is paid nothing until the job is finished, tell Project not to count any of the cost of that resource in reports printed before the *end* of the task.

These methods of calculating cost are called "accrual methods," and you can select *prorated*, *start*, or *end* as the accrual method for each resource. The accrual method doesn't affect the final cost of the project. It's important only for interim reports, when tasks might be partially complete.

Creating the Resource Pool

As you can guess from this overview, several fields in Microsoft Project define resources and costs. How many of them you use depends on what you want Project to do for you when you assign resources to tasks:

- If you just want to associate people's names with tasks to assign responsibility, you have to at least enter the resource names in the resource pool and assign them to individual tasks.

- If you want Project to schedule work around the availability of the resources, you have to also define the maximum units available and the working times for the resources.

- If you want Project to assign the cost of the resources to the tasks they work on, and thereby calculate the cost of each task and the cost of the project, you have to define cost rates for the resources.

If you just want to use resource names without all the other information, you can enter those in the Assign Resources dialog box as you assign them to tasks, or you can prepare the list ahead of time with the Assign Resources dialog box or with the Resource Sheet. Then you can pick the names from a list as you assign them.

Using the Assign Resources Dialog Box to List Resources

You will use the Assign Resources dialog box (see Figure 11.4) a great deal in subsequent hours, but for now, let's see how you can use it to create the list of names in the resource pool. You can open this dialog box in any task view and leave it on the workspace as you work with the other views.

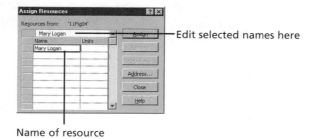

Edit selected names here

Name of resource

To Do: Entering Resources in the Assign Resources Dialog Box

To enter resources in the Assign Resources dialog box, follow these steps:

1. Click the Assign Resources button on the Standard toolbar or choose Tools, Resources, Assign Resources from the menu.

2. Select a cell in the Name column.

3. Type a resource name and press Enter. Project then moves the selection to the cell below and you can type the next name.

4. Repeat step 3 until you're finished entering the names.

5. Click the Close button to put to put the dialog box away.

> Resource names can be very long if you choose, but they cannot contain the slash (/), brackets ([ ]), or the list separator character—usually the comma (,).

If you want to enter more information about each resource, you can double-click a resource name in the Assign Resources dialog box to display the Resource Information dialog box for that resource (see the following section), where you have access to almost all fields that define resources.

11

Using the Resource Sheet

If you plan to define your resources more fully, you might want to start with the Resource Sheet view (see Figure 11.5). This view displays an entry table with columns for many of the major resource fields.

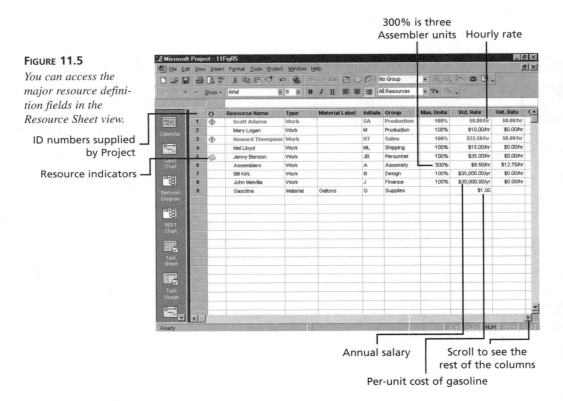

FIGURE **11.5**

You can access the major resource definition fields in the Resource Sheet view.

ID numbers supplied by Project

Resource indicators

300% is three Assembler units   Hourly rate

Annual salary

Scroll to see the rest of the columns

Per-unit cost of gasoline

To Do: Entering Resources in the Resource Sheet

To enter resources in the Resource Sheet, follow these steps:

1. Display the Resource Sheet by choosing View, Resource Sheet or by clicking the Resource Sheet icon on the View Bar.

2. Enter the resource information in the columns provided. You need to use the scrollbar to view additional columns off to the right.

Each column in the Resource Sheet is described in the following sections.

▶ To Do ▼

ID Value

This is a display-only field that Project calculates for you. You can't enter an ID value, although you can change the order of the resources in the list by sorting the list and applying new ID numbers to the new sort order. (See "Sorting the Task and Resource Lists" later in Hour 16, "Fine-Tuning the Project Plan.")

Indicators

Indicators alert you to additional information about a resource. In Figure 11.5, there is a Notes indicator next to Jenny Benson. Resource indicators are covered in greater detail in later hours.

Name

Always identify the resource with a unique name. The name can contain any characters except the slash, the comma, and square brackets ([]). Resource names can be much longer than the space you see on the screen, but short names are easier to deal with in reports and onscreen.

Type

NEW FEATURE   In Project 2000, for the first time you can distinguish between *work resources*, those that contribute their work to tasks but are not thereby consumed in the process, and *material resources*, those resources that in fact are consumed in the process. The cost of the work resources will be based on the number of hours they work on a task and the hourly cost for the resource. The cost of material resources will be based on the cost of a unit of the resource and how many units are consumed.

> The default resource type on the Resource Sheet is Work, but you can use the drop-down arrow in the Type column to select either Work or Material.

Material Label

NEW FEATURE   Use the new Project 2000 *Material Label* field to define the unit of measure that you will use for material resources (gallons, bushels, tons, liters, and so on). You will use this unit when you assign the resource to tasks and when you define the unit cost of the resource.

Initials

Supply initials to use as a shorter display than the full resource name. For example, you can use the initials instead of the full name next to the task bars in the Gantt Chart.

Group

You can identify the resource as a member of a group (such as a department or type of cost). You can use the group label for sorting or filtering the list. You can also calculate cost subtotals for all members of the group. If the resource belongs to several groups, separate them with spaces or commas. See Hour 16 for more information on sorting and filters.

Max Units

Use this field to tell Microsoft Project the maximum number of units of the resource that are available for assignment to tasks. Project uses the Max Units field to determine when a resource has been overallocated. Because you can assign resources to multiple tasks, it's possible to assign the same resource to tasks that wind up being scheduled at the same or overlapping times. If the sum of a resource's assignments to all tasks at a given moment exceeds the entry in the Max Units field, Project alerts you that the resource is overallocated.

You will see in the next hour that when assigning work resources to tasks, the default format for the units assigned is the percentage format. Consequently, the default format for the Max Units field is also a percentage. For example, when you assign an individual person to a task, the default assignment units are 100 percent, which means the person will put 100 percent of his or her working hours into that task for the duration of the task. If that person were assigned to work only half-time on the task, the assignment units would be 50 percent. The maximum percentage that could be allocated for a single person would be 100 percent, so the entry in the Max Units field for that resource would be 100 percent.

If the same resource is assigned full time (100 percent) to one task and half-time (50 percent) to another task during the same time period, the combined assignments call for 150 percent of the person's time. Because the maximum available is only 100 percent, the resource would be overallocated.

Although using the percentage format for a resource that represents an individual person or piece of equipment is easy enough to understand, when the percentage format is applied to resource sets, it's a bit strained. For example, if a resource set represents five nurses or five machines, the maximum units available in percentage format is 500 percent, instead of the simple decimal value 5.

You can change the default format for resource units to decimal, if you prefer, but this change will affect all resources—it can't be limited just to resource sets. I'll continue to use the percentage format because it's the default and will have its advantages in the hours that follow.

> There is no Max Units value for material resources. Project assumes that you will acquire as many units as you have assigned.

To Do: Setting the Default Format for Resource Units

To set the default format for resource units, follow these steps:

1. Choose Tools, Options from the menu to display the Options dialog box and select the Schedule tab (see Figure 11.6).

2. Select the field labeled Show Assignment Units as A, and choose either Percentage or Decimal.

FIGURE 11.6

The default format for displaying resource units applies immediately to all projects, not just the one you are currently working on.

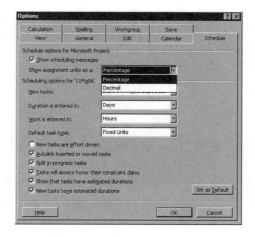

3. Click OK to close the dialog box.

   Note that this choice will remain the display format for all projects until you change it again.

The default value for Max Units is 100 percent in the percentage form; in the decimal format, the default value is simply 1. The largest value you can enter in the Max Units field is 60,000,000 units (in decimal format) or 6,000,000,000 percent (in percentage format).

Standard Rate

The standard rate for a work resource is the cost rate to be charged for the resource's work during normal working hours. Type the standard rate as a number, followed by a *forward* slash, and one of the following time unit abbreviations: m (minute), h (hour), d (day), w (week), mo (month), or y (year). For example, if a worker is paid $12.50 per hour, you would enter 12.5/h. You can use the year as a time unit if the resource is paid an annual salary. If you type just a number (without a time unit), Project assumes it's an hourly rate. For example, type 600/w for $600 per week, 3000/mo for $3,000 per month, 35000/y for $35,000 per year, and 15.5/h for $15.50 per hour. The standard rate for month is new in Project 2000.

For material resources the standard rate is the amount to charge tasks per unit of the resource consumed. For material resources the Standard Rate is entered just as an amount, with no time unit. It is understood to be the amount per unit of the resource, where the unit to use is defined in the Material Label field. For example, if you include Diesel Fuel as a material resource for the bulldozer, its Material Label might be Gallons and the Standard Rate might be 1 (which means $1 per gallon).

You can change the default currency unit, the placement of the currency symbol, and the number of decimal points to display in the Options dialog box on the View tab. However, you must use the Regional Settings application in the Windows Control Panel to change the default settings for all projects.

To Do: Changing the Default Currency Format for the Current Project

To change the default currency format for the current project, follow these steps:

1. Choose Tools, Options to display the Options dialog box and choose the View tab (see Figure 11.7).
2. Type the currency symbol to use in the Symbol field.
3. Select the Placement: before or after the value, with or without a separating space.
4. Enter the number of Decimal Digits to display.
5. Choose OK to close the dialog box. Note that these settings affect only the current project.

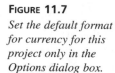

FIGURE 11.7

Set the default format for currency for this project only in the Options dialog box.

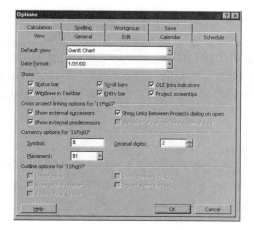

To Do: Changing the Default Currency Format for Windows

To change the default currency format for Windows, follow these steps:

1. Choose Settings, Control Panel from the Windows Start menu to display the Control Panel dialog box.

2. Choose the Regional Settings application and select the Currency tab.

3. Enter the currency symbol in the Currency Symbol field.

4. Select the placement in the Position of Currency Symbol field.

5. Use the Decimal Symbol field to change the decimal character to a comma or other character.

6. Change the number of decimal digits to display in the No. of Digits After Decimal field.

7. Use the Digit Grouping Symbol field to change the grouping character to a period or other character.

8. Use the Number of Digits In Group to enter a value from 0 to 9.

Overtime Rate

The overtime rate field only applies to work resources and is the amount charged for work outside the normal working hours. If the rate for overtime work is the same as the regular rate, you must enter this amount again in the Overtime Rate text box, or overtime hours will be charged at the zero default rate. For salaried employees, you can leave the overtime rate zero, or you can repeat the standard rate if overtime is compensated with comp-time (compensatory time-off during regular working hours).

11

Cost/Use

Use this field for costs that are charged once for each unit assigned, but that are *not* applied for each hour of work. This used to be the way to enter the cost per unit for material resources; but if you identify the resource as a material resource, enter the cost per unit in the Standard Rate field.

Accrue At

The default accrual method is *prorated*. If you must pay a resource in full before work starts, change the entry to Start. If you will not pay the resource until the work is complete, change it to End.

Base Calendar

Select the base calendar that the calendar for this resource will be linked to. The in-cell drop-down list displays all base calendars already defined for the project. You will edit the calendar for the resource in the following section on using the Resource Information dialog box.

Code

Use this field for any accounting or other codes that you want to associate with the cost of using the resource. You can also use this field as another Group field.

Using the Resource Information Dialog Box

All the resource definition fields displayed on the Resource Sheet are also displayed in the Resource Information dialog box. Plus, there are additional fields that are important to the full definition of a resource that aren't accessible on the Resource Sheet. You can display the Resource Information dialog box from any resource view. You can also display it if you have the Assign Resources dialog box displayed in a task view.

To Do: Displaying the Resource Information Dialog Box

Follow these steps to display the Resource Information dialog box:

1. Display a resource view, such as the Resource Sheet or Resource Form.
2. Select the resource name and click the Resource Information tool on the Standard toolbar to display its Resource Information dialog box.

   With some resource views (like the Resource Sheet), you can also just double-click the resource name to display the Resource Information dialog box.

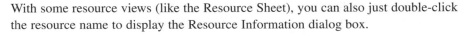

▼ Or, from a task view, you can follow these steps:

    1. Display the Assign Resources dialog box in any task view with the Assign Resources tool (or by choosing Tools, Resources, Assign Resources from the menu.

▲   2. Double-click a resource name to display its Resource Information dialog box.

The Resource Information dialog box (see Figure 11.8) contains four tabs: General, Working Time, Costs, and Notes. The following sections describe those fields on the tabs that have not already been covered.

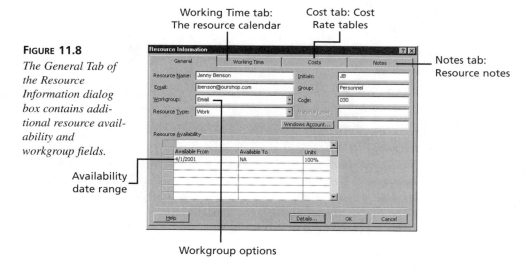

FIGURE 11.8

The General Tab of the Resource Information dialog box contains additional resource availability and workgroup fields.

The General Tab

The General tab contains the following information:

- Resource Availability Table. If the maximum units for the resource will be unchanging for the life of the project, you don't have to make any entries in this table. However, if the maximum units will change during the life of the project, enter each time period with a different value for maximum units on a separate row of the table in chronological order. Enter the beginning date for each period in the Available From field, the ending date in the Available To field, and the maximum units in the Units field.

Setting the availability dates doesn't keep Project from scheduling the resource's assigned tasks outside that range of dates, but if it does happen, Project shows you that the resource is overallocated so that *you* can deal with it. (See Hour 15 for a full explanation).

- Email. Use this field to supply the resource's email address for use in the project's workgroup (see the next paragraph).

- Workgroup. If the members of the project team have communication links via email or a Web site on the Internet or the organization's intranet, you can define one of those links on the Workgroup tab of the Options dialog box. This field is used to specify which link this resource has access to. See Hour 21, "Analyzing Progress and Revising the Schedule," for a complete explanation of workgroup features.

- Resource Type. The default resource type for this field is Work, but you can use the drop-down arrow to select either Work or Material.

- Material Label. Define the unit to use to describe a material resource in this field, for example, Gallons, Lumber, or Camera Film.

- Details. The Details button is used to identify additional details about the workgroup connection. See Hour 23, "Using Microsoft Project in Workgroups," for more information.

The Working Time Tab

The Working Time tab lets you edit the calendar for the resource. You can change the base calendar to which the resource calendar is linked in the Base Calendar field. Initially, the working days and times will be identical to those on the base calendar, but you can use this dialog box to enter exceptions to the base calendar that apply to this resource:

- If the resource is scheduled for vacation days, sick leave, or a leave of absence, make those days nonworking days on the resource calendar, even though they are working days on the base calendar.

- If the resource has special assignments, answering the phone on a day that is a nonworking day for the rest of the organization, make that day a working day on the resource calendar, even though it has been made a nonworking day on the base calendar.

- If the resource has unique hours on any days, enter those in the resource calendar.

Suppose that Jenny Benson has asked to leave work at midday on the Tuesday before Thanksgiving in November, 2001, because she has asked her family and her new husband's family to come to her house for Thanksgiving dinner, and she's never cooked a turkey before. She has offered to work a day and a half on the weekend before Thanksgiving to make up the hours. Every date in her calendar that differs from the base calendar has the date underlined in Figure 11.9:

- November 17 (Saturday) is a nonworking day on the base calendar but it's a work day with the normal working hours for Jenny. The date is underlined to show that it's an exception to the base calendar, and clear to show that it's regular hours.

- November 18 (Sunday) is a nonworking day on the base calendar, but Jenny will work half a day (not the normal working hours). The date is clear with diagonal stripes to indicate a working day, but one with different hours.

- November 20 (Tuesday) is Jenny's half-day off. The diagonal stripes show that she has special hours that differ from the base calendar.

- November 21 (Wednesday) is Jenny's special full day off work, as indicated by the shading and the date underline.

- November 22 and 23 (Thursday and Friday) are company holidays on the base calendar, so they are shaded but have no underline.

11

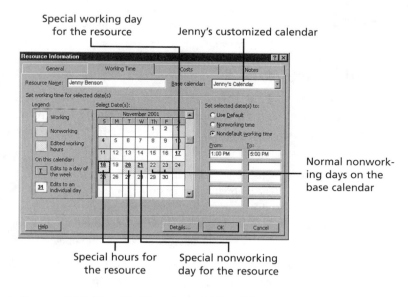

Special working day
for the resource   Jenny's customized calendar

FIGURE 11.9

Enter the resource's special working and nonworking days and times on the resource calendar.

Normal nonworking days on the base calendar

Special hours for   Special nonworking
the resource   day for the resource

Use the same techniques you used in the "Creating and Applying Base Calendars for Special Scheduling Needs" section in Hour 5 to edit the resource calendar.

If you create several customized base calendars for use by resources, remember to make companywide changes in working days and hours on them as well as the standard base calendars. If your company decides to make December 24 a holiday, for example, you need to edit each base calendar used by resources to apply the holiday to all resources.

You can also access the resource calendar from the Change Working Time dialog box. If you want to work on several calendars at once—base calendars and resource calendars—it's easier to work from this dialog box.

To Do: Editing All Calendars

To edit all calendars, follow these steps:

1. Select the top pane. You can't access the calendars from the bottom pane.
2. Choose Tools, Change Working Time to display the Change Working Time dialog box.

Material resources do not have a calendar because they are assumed to be always available. The Working Time tab in the Resource Information dialogue box will be unavailable for a material resource.

The Costs Tab

The Costs tab of the Resource Information dialog box (see Figure 11.10) lets you expand the cost rate data for the resource in two significant ways: You can create different cost rates for different types of tasks, and you can define when and how cost rates will change in the future because of raises, labor contracts, or other influences.

This tab has five Cost Rate tables, labeled A–E, that you can use to define cost rates for different types of assignments. For example, an electrician might have higher rates for tasks involving high-voltage lines. A software engineer might have one set of rates for in-house development projects, several other rates for development or consulting for clients, and another set of rates for the hated chore of writing documentation.

The first row on rate table A contains the rates you define on the Resource Sheet. The rates on rate table A are the default rates Microsoft Project uses for all task assignments. You can select a different rate table for specific assignments. (See "Using the Task Usage View" in Hour 13, "Assigning Resources and Costs to Tasks.")

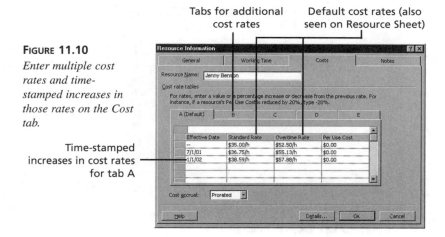

Tabs for additional   Default cost rates (also
cost rates   seen on Resource Sheet)

FIGURE 11.10
Enter multiple cost rates and time-stamped increases in those rates on the Cost tab.

Time-stamped increases in cost rates for tab A

The first row on each rate table has dashes in the Effective Date column to show that those rates are effective from whenever the beginning date of the project might be. You can record future increases (or decreases) in the rates by entering the effect date for the change on the rows below, along with the rates that will go into effect on that date. For example, in Figure 11.10, you see that Jenny Benson's standard rate will go up to $36.75 an hour on 7/1/01. You can enter up to 24 rate changes beneath the initial rates. If a task assignment extends past one of these dates, the new rates will be used for the cost of work done after that date.

11

When entering the rate changes, you can either enter the new amount or you can indicate a percentage increase or decrease and Project will calculate the new rate for you. For example, the increase from $35.00/h to $36.75/h for Jenny Benson in Figure 11.10 was actually created by entering +5% for the new rate—Project calculated the $36.75/h and replaced the percent increase with the new rate.

The Notes Tab

The Notes tab of the Resource Information dialog box lets you record notes about the resource (see Figure 11.11). The Notes indicator will appear next to the resource name on the Resource Sheet so that you know there's a note to be read.

FIGURE **11.11**

Record reminders and other information about a resource in the Notes field.

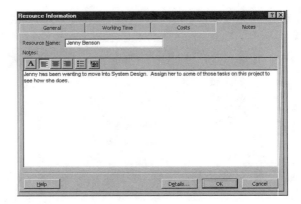

Printing the Resource Pool

As you just learned in Hour 10, "Finalizing and Printing Your Schedule," you can display a view such as the Resource Sheet and then use the File, Print command to get a paper copy. Printing the Resource Sheet view gives you a listing of the project's resources with the basic resource fields.

Summary

This hour was designed to acquaint you with resources, explain how to create a resource pool, and show how costs are calculated in Project. With this foundation, you are ready to assign resources to tasks, modify those assignments, and resolve conflicts that arise with overallocated resources.

Q&A

Q Is there any way to print out the special calendars and Cost Rate tables I've defined?

A Yes, there is a custom report that can be printed with details for the resource calendar, Cost Rate tables, and resource notes.

1. Choose View, Reports from the menu.

2. In the Reports dialog box, double-click the Custom reports group.

3. In the Custom Reports dialog box, scroll the Reports list and select the Resource report.

4. Click the Edit button to display the Resource Report dialog box.

5. Select the Details tab and fill the check box for one of more of the Resource details: Notes, Calendar, Cost Rates. You might have to print separate reports for each of these details.

6. Click OK to close the Resource Report dialog box.

7. Choose Print in the Custom Reports dialog box to start the print job.

Q I want to start a project document for a new project, but I sure don't relish having to retype all the resources, their calendar exceptions, and their different cost rates and cost rate changes. Is there any way to copy the resources and all their information from one project to another?

A Yes, although you'll have to jump ahead a little to Hour 22. Using the techniques in that Hour, tell Project that the new project will use the resources in the document where you've entered all the resource information. Project copies all the resource data into the new document and establishes a link to the original document. Then, using the same resource sharing command again, tell Project you want the new document to use its own resources. Project breaks the link between the two files, but leaves all the resource data it copied into the new document.

If you'll be creating several projects that use the same resources, you should consider making a copy of the project file that has all the resources already in it (call the copy Resources or something like that) and then deleting the tasks. When you want to start a new project, open the file Resources, immediately use the File, Save As command, and save a copy to use for the new project.

11

Exercises

Try these exercises to further build your proficiency in working with resources and costs:

1. Define some of the resources for your project on the Assign Resources dialog box.

2. Go to the Resource Sheet and fill in more details for those resources.

3. Create a couple of material resources in the Resource Sheet.

4. Use the Resource Information dialog box to show that one of your resources will not be available during the first month of your project.

5. Go to the Cost Tab of the Resource Information Dialogue Box and show a 5% increase in the standard rate and overtime rate for a resource starting one year from now.

HOUR 12

Mastering Resource Scheduling in Microsoft Project

In this hour, you learn how Microsoft Project handles resource assignments, and how it then schedules work for those resources. The main thrust of the hour is to explain how the assignment of work resources and task duration are interdependent—duration can affect an assignment, and work resource assignments can also lead to changes in the duration. Material resource assignments, on the other hand, are passively affected by task duration and do not normally induce changes in duration. This hour talks about the relationships among task duration, the number of units assigned, and the amount of work assigned to a resource. You will learn how to use Project's views to assign resources in Hour 13, "Assigning Resources and Costs to Tasks." In this hour, you will learn:

- The fields used to define resources and work
- How to use the work formula for scheduling both work and material resources
- How to control the calculation of work with the task Type setting

- How Project processes your entries when you assign resources or change resource assignments
- How the Effort Driven setting for a task affects assignments when you add multiple resources

Choosing to Enter Resource Assignments

Although it takes more time to add resource assignments to your project, there are many benefits to be gained. Resource assignments allow you to do the following:

- Plan work around the vacations and other downtime periods for individual resources
- Examine the workload your project will require of individual resources
- Identify those resources whose workloads in the project are unrealistically high
- Identify resources that are not fully utilized and might, therefore, substitute for overworked resources on some tasks
- Calculate the effect that changing resource assignments can have on the duration of a task
- Calculate costs for tasks based on the amount of work and the value of the individual resource's time

These benefits have a price tag attached, however. When you introduce resource scheduling into your project, you add a considerable amount of complexity to the project document. A number of settings and rules govern how Project calculates the schedule for a resource assignment. Don't worry, though—you will understand what's going on in those calculations after this hour.

Microsoft Project offers you the flexibility of assigning resources in a fairly simplistic way or of getting really sophisticated. If all you want to do is get Microsoft Project to print resource names next to the tasks on the reports you want to hand out, you can use a fairly simple process that will not require you to master all the information in this hour. You can use this hour to catch up on your email or whatever.

Simply Associating People with Tasks

If all you want to do with resource names is to have people associated with tasks so that they can appear on reports, you do not need to fill in the details about a resource such as a calendar of nonworking days or the various cost rates. You also do not need to be concerned with most of the detail covered in this hour. You can achieve your purpose by making all your tasks Fixed Duration tasks that are not Effort Driven and by leaving the resource calendars unchanged after assignments have been made. You should at least

> review the sections on those topics later in this hour. See Hour 13 for the actual steps you need to take for the minimalist approach to resource assignments. Of course, you are invited to read on in this hour so you will understand *why*...as you're undoubtedly blessed with an inquiring mind.

You're not going to look at the step-by-step process of assigning resources until the next hour. There, you'll learn how to use the views and dialog boxes that give you access to the features I explain in this hour. There are so many combinations of choices for resource assignments that there is no single or simple step-by-step list of things to do. You will have to make your own choices for which you need to understand how Project interprets the fields that you will use. Understanding the process is more than half the battle in this endeavor, and understanding needs to come first.

Defining the Resource Assignment Fields

When you assign a resource to a task in the project, Microsoft Project keeps track of the assignment by filling in values for several fields. The essential fields that define an assignment are the following:

- The name or ID number of the task to be completed
- The duration of the task
- The name or ID number of the resource being assigned to the task
- The number of units of the resource to be assigned to the task
- The hours of work that the resource is expected to complete on the task

Project will fill in default values and calculations for these fields if you don't fill them in yourself. The calculations are controlled by still other settings that characterize the task. Two of the most important of these other settings are the Task Type and whether the task is Effort Driven or not. You'll learn how those two settings govern calculations later in this hour.

The split-window view in Figure 12.1 shows three linked tasks that I'll use this hour to illustrate resource assignment concepts. The view in the bottom pane is the Task Form, and it shows details about the task Install Computers that is selected in the top pane. You'll use this combination view in Hour 13 to assign resources. The bottom pane shows all the fields mentioned in the previous list.

In Figure 12.1, the Install Computers task is selected in the top pane. Pat and Mary are both assigned to that task, and the units and work for their assignments appear in the Resource Details at the bottom of the screen as well as in a label next to the task bar. As you can see in this illustration, the task bar label omits the units display if the assigned units is the default value of 100 percent.

12

Figure 12.1

Resource assignments in the Task Form show the essential fields.

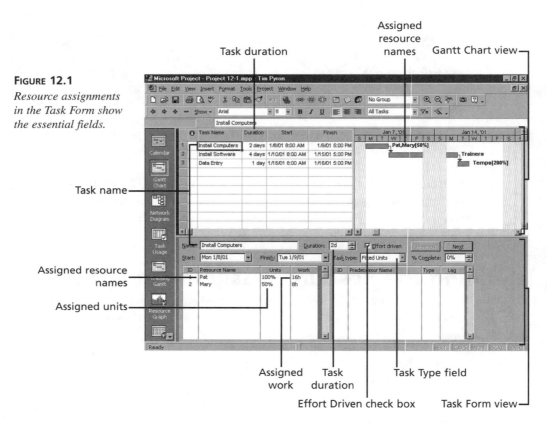

When you make an assignment, you must supply at least the name of the task and the name of the resource. If you don't specify anything more, Project supplies a default value for the number of units of the resource assigned to the task and calculates the amount of work the resource will do. The units assigned and the hours of work require additional explanation.

Defining Resource Units

When you add a work resource name to the resource pool, you also define the maximum number of *units* of the resource that will be available for use in the project and you edit the resource calendar to show the number of hours each day that Project can schedule work for the resource. When you assign the resource to a task, Project will schedule the resource to work on the task only during the times the calendar shows that the resource is available.

When you assign a work resource to a task and specify the number of units of the resource that will work on that task, Project uses the units value in two ways:

1. First, at the moment that you enter the assignment, Project calculates the total amount of work or effort the resource will expend on the task. Project does this by multiplying the duration of the task (the length of time that work will continue) by the assignment units value (how many resource units will work on the task during each hour of the task duration).

   For example, in Figure 12.1 Pat is assigned to work 100 percent on the Install Computers task. The task duration is two days, or 16 hours, so the total work for Pat is 100 percent of 16, or 16 hours. Mary is only assigned to work half the time, or 50 percent, and her work is 50 percent of 16, or eight hours. The total work on the task will be 16 plus 8—24 hours. Thus the assigned units are used by Project as a multiplier that shows how many hours of work will be done for every hour of the task duration.

2. Then, Project uses the units assignment to schedule work for the resource on specific days. The assignment's daily details are shown in Figure 12.2, which replaces the Task Form in the bottom pane with the Task Usage view. This view shows the number of hours of work scheduled each day for each resource on the task that is selected in the top pane.

   For example, in Figure 12.2 both Pat's and Mary's calendars happen to have the standard eight hours available each day during the period shown. For Pat, Project multiplies the number of available hours for each day (eight) by the number of assigned units (100 percent) to calculate the total hours assigned to him on each day. For Mary, Project assigns four hours each day (50 percent of the eight hours available).

   Mary has four hours assigned each day and four hours available for other assignments. Pat has no time for other assignments on these two days.

NEW FEATURE

> In Project 2000 you can attach a task calendar to a task to govern when work will be performed on the task. If there are resources assigned to the task, work will only be scheduled when both the task calendar and the resource calendar show working time available. However, you also have the option to ignore the resource calendar, in which case Project schedules the resource during the working times on the task calendar and ignores the nonworking restrictions in the resource calendar.

12

When a work resource is actually a group resource, for example, a set of similar employees, the resource units will be greater than 100 percent. Suppose that five Nurses work on a 10-hour task. The total work will be 50 hours: five people work 10 hours each for a total of 50 hours. If you express resource units in percentage format (which is the default format in Project), you are recognizing the multiplier aspect of the units value:

the work for the resource will be some percentage multiple of the hours in the task's duration (500 percent of 10 hours for the Nurses). If the nurses' calendar showed that they work only half a day, Project would schedule work equal to 500 percent of those four hours, or 20 hours for the task on that day.

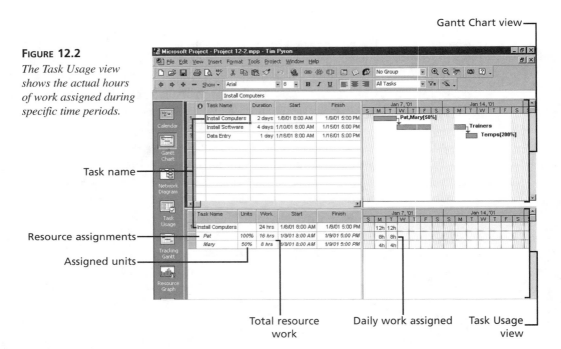

FIGURE 12.2
The Task Usage view shows the actual hours of work assigned during specific time periods.

NEW FEATURE For material resources the units field is used to define how the consumption of the resource is to be calculated. Either a fixed number of resource units will be consumed in completing the task or the number of units consumed will depend on the duration of the task. In the first case, the case of a *fixed consumption rate*, the Units field shows the total number of units that will be consumed. You might estimate that 20 gallons of diesel fuel will be consumed in completing the task. If the number of units depends on the duration of the task, the *variable consumption rate* case, the units field shows the rate of consumption per unit time. For example, you might estimate that diesel fuel will be consumed at the rate of five gallons per hour for the duration of the task.

NEW TERM For work resources, *resource units* is a measure of resource effort or working time per unit of task duration. Units are normally expressed as a percentage—that is, "100%" means the resource can deliver one hour of effort or work for every hour of working time on the calendar. A units assignment of "500%" means the resource can deliver five hours of work for every hour of working time on the calendar. And, a units assignment of "50%" means the resource can devote a half hour of work to a task for every hour of working time on the calendar.

For material resources, *resource units* shows how the consumption of the resource is to be calculated. It is either a fixed amount (a fixed consumption rate) or an amount per unit of time (a variable consumption rate).

If you prefer, you can format units for work resources as decimal numbers instead of percentages. Decimal numbers are more intuitive for group resources, like five nurses or two fork lifts, but they can be misleading because the physical units might not be engaged 100 percent on the task. If all five Nurses work on a task, but only half-time, the decimal units would need to be 2.5—even though five people are working. I think the percentage format is better because it forces you to think of units as the work multiplier: five nurses working half-time contribute work equal to 250 percent of the duration of the task.

For material resources, the units field is always expressed in decimal format plus a label defining the units: five gallons, 20 tons, 10 kilo.

To Do: Viewing Work Resource Units in Decimals Instead of Percents

To view units in decimals instead of percents for a work resource, follow these steps:

1. Choose Tools, Options from the menu to display the Options dialog box.

2. Select the Schedule tab.

3. In the field labeled Show Assignment Units As A, select the Decimal setting. A 100 percent full-time assignment would be the simple digit one (1) in decimal format.

4. Click OK to close the dialog box.

> You can enter fractions of a percent in the Units assignment, but they will display as rounded whole percent numbers. So if you want to specify that a worker spends one hour per eight-hour day on a task (one-eighth or 12.5 percent of a day), you will see 13% displayed after you enter **12.5%**. Project will actually use fractional percents in its calculations (down to tenths of a percent)—it just doesn't display them.

Defining Work

For work resources the Work field measures the amount of time or effort expended by the resource during the assignment. Work is usually measured in hours in Microsoft Project. Work can be entered by the user or automatically calculated by Project.

For material resources, the Work field doesn't show "work" at all. Instead it is used to display the total number of units consumed in the assignment. For fixed rate consumption assignments, the Work field value will equal the Units field value. But for variable rate consumption assignments, the Units field shows the consumption per unit of time and the Work field shows the total consumption for the total duration of the task.

NEW TERM *Work* defines the amount of time or effort that a work resource is actually engaged on a task. Project displays work in hours by default. Alternatively, for material resources, the Work field displays the total number of resource units consumed during the work on the task.

If a resource works full-time on a task that lasts two days (16 hours), the resource will do 16 hours of work. But, if the resource is assigned half-time to the task, it will do only eight hours of work on the task (see Mary in Figure 12.2).

The amount of work that is scheduled depends on the duration of the task and the number of units assigned to the task. The next section defines this relationship more precisely.

Understanding the Work Formula

The work formula ties together the quantitative fields of an assignment: task duration, resource units, and resource work.

This is the formula for calculating work:

```
Task Duration × Resource Units = Resource Work
```

In symbols, the formula looks like this:

```
D × U = W
```

In words, work is calculated by multiplying the task duration by the assigned units. For a given duration, the more units, the more work on the task. For a given number of units, the longer the duration, the more work.

> What follows in this section, showing how resource units or work can affect task duration, and in the following sections on task type, applies only to work resources.

For work resources, simple algebra can be used to reformulate this equation to calculate duration when work and units are given, or units when work and duration are given:

```
Duration = Work/Units     Units = Work/Duration
```

In symbols, the formula looks like this:

```
D = W/U     U = W/D
```

The duration variant of the formula shows that if you increase the units and keep the work the same, duration will be reduced. The units variant of the formula shows that if you increase the duration and keep work unchanged, you can get by with fewer units of the resource.

Although duration can be displayed in minutes, hours, days, weeks, or months, Project converts duration to hours when calculating work. Therefore, if a one-day (eight-hour) task has 200 percent units assigned to it (two full-time units of the resource per hour of duration), the work would be calculated this way:

```
D × U = W
8hrs × 200% = 16hrs
```

According to the work equation, when you change one of the three variables, one of the other two variables must also change, but how do you know which of the remaining variables Project will change and which it will leave fixed? The answer to that question is important because if Project changes duration, for example, it affects the length of time it will take to complete your project.

Project was originally conceived as a date calculator, to evaluate work and units and calculate duration and the schedule of dates for the project. It was assumed that the user would enter an estimated task duration and the number of units of the resource he or she wanted to work on the task. Project was designed to calculate the work from these two values supplied by the user. Then it was assumed that users might adjust the units assigned to change the duration of the task (and the project), but would want the work amount to remain unchanged.

Because of this heritage, Project tends to recalculate duration when it has to choose between changing duration or work or units. In addition, Project is generally programmed to respect the number of units you enter for an assignment as holy writ. So, when Project has to choose which variable to change in a calculation, its bias is to recalculate duration before work and work before units. The following are other considerations:

- Given the choice between duration and either of the other two variables, Project will choose to change duration.
- If duration is fixed (or you have just entered a new duration), Project will choose to change work before it changes units.
- Project changes units only when it can't change duration or work.

You can assert greater control over Project's calculations by defining the task type, as you will see in the next section.

12

Using the Task Type to Control Calculations

To give you more control over calculations involving work resources, Project defines every task as one of three *task types*, and the type determines which variable Project must keep fixed when you force it to recalculate the work formula. The three types are

- Fixed Units (the default for all new tasks)
- Fixed Duration
- Fixed Work

Fixed Units Tasks

The Fixed Units task type is appropriate when you want to control the number of resource units assigned to the task, and there is no particular reason why you need to keep the duration or the work constant. As you can see in the following recap of the work formula (the brackets indicate that the units variable is fixed), if you reduce duration, Project must reduce total work (because units is fixed):

```
Duration × [Units] = Work
```

If you change work, Project must leave units fixed and change duration (with more work requiring a longer duration and less work allowing a shorter duration). Of course, *you* can change the units, in which case Project's bias will dictate that it changes the duration and leaves work unchanged. Note that with work unchanged, increasing the units results in a decrease in duration, and reducing the units leads to an increase in duration.

> Once you assign work resources to a task Project associates an amount of working time with the task. From that point on the duration of the task will equal the number of time periods when work resources have assigned work. The one exception is when the task is a Fixed Duration task. For Fixed Duration tasks the duration is simply the difference between the start and finish of the task.

Fixed Duration Tasks

For some tasks, it makes sense to lock in the duration and keep Project from changing it. For example, if you schedule meetings as part of a project, you should generally make them Fixed Duration. Otherwise, the duration of the meeting would get shorter and shorter as you assign more and more people to attend - a phenomenon that, in my experience, could only be found in *Alice in Wonderland*.

If duration is fixed and you change the units assigned, Project must change work. The more units, the greater the amount of work, and vice versa. If you change work with a Fixed Duration task, Project will *have* to change the units (with more work requiring more units). As you can see, when you define a task as Fixed Duration, you can force Project to overcome its bias against changing the assigned units:

```
[Duration] × Units = Work
```

If you change duration yourself for a Fixed Duration task, Project's bias causes it to recalculate work, not units. The longer the duration, the more work included in the assignment.

Fixed Work Tasks

If your project includes tasks that have a fixed or contracted number of hours of work to be delivered, you should make those tasks Fixed Work. Then Project will leave the work undisturbed and adjust units or duration in its calculations.

If the task is the Fixed Work type, *increasing* units allows Project to *decrease* duration because work is fixed and can't be changed. If you decrease the duration, Project is forced to increase the units because of the fixed work:

```
Duration × Units = [Work]
```

If you change the work yourself for a Fixed Work task, Project recalculates duration and keeps its hands off the units.

Changing the Task Type

You need to change the Task Type field for those tasks for which the default Fixed Units is inappropriate. You can also temporarily change the task type to control how Project adjusts to a change you want to enter, and then return the task to the original type.

You can change the task type for the currently selected task in the Task Form (refer to Figure 12.1) or in the Task Information dialog box (see Figure 12.3). As you saw in earlier hours, you can display the Task Information dialog box by selecting any field in a task view (like the Gantt Chart, for instance) and then clicking the Task Information tool.

As stated previously, the default task type for new tasks is *Fixed Units*, so all new tasks are Fixed Units type until you change them. If you think that most of your tasks in this project will be Fixed Duration or Fixed Work, you can change the default task type so that new tasks are automatically the right type. If you think that most of your projects will consist of Fixed Duration or Fixed Work tasks, you can also change the default task type for all new project documents.

To Do: Changing the Default Task Type

To change the default task type, follow these steps:

1. Choose Tools, Options from the menu to display the Options dialog box.
2. Select the Schedule tab.

12

▼   3. Select the type you want to be the default in the Default Task Type field (see Figure 12.4). This change affects only the current document unless you use the Set as Default button.

4. If you want this task type to be the default for all future project documents, click the Set as Default button.

▲   5. Click the OK button to close the Options dialog box.

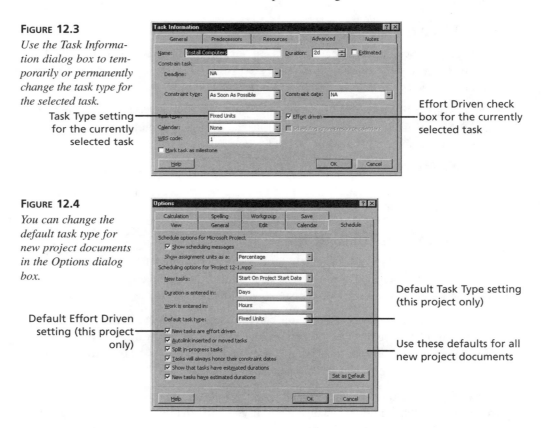

FIGURE 12.3
Use the Task Information dialog box to temporarily or permanently change the task type for the selected task.

Task Type setting for the currently selected task

Effort Driven check box for the currently selected task

FIGURE 12.4
You can change the default task type for new project documents in the Options dialog box.

Default Effort Driven setting (this project only)

Default Task Type setting (this project only)

Use these defaults for all new project documents

Applying the Work Formula in a Work Resource Assignment

NEW FEATURE   When you assign a resource, you must define at least the task and the resource, but you can also define one or both of the units to be assigned and the work to be completed. In this section, I'll show you what happens in each of these cases for work resources. I'll also show you what happens with material resources in the next section.

The task duration will already be defined in all cases because Project sets it to a default value (one day) even if you don't define it yourself, so the duration part of the work formula will already be filled in.

Enter the Resource Name Only

If you enter just the resource name, but don't enter the units or the work, Project assigns a default value of 100 percent to units and calculates the work from the default units and the duration. This is the case for all three task types. For example, if you assign Pat to a two-day task without entering the units, Project first assigns 100 percent in the units field and then calculates the work as 100 percent of the duration (16 hours). This case is illustrated by Pat's assignment to the Install Computers task in Figure 12.5.

In this figure, and in those that follow, I will show the task twice—once before the assignment and then again after the assignment has been added to the task. The two versions of the task are labeled Before and After. In later examples, these two versions will be useful for illustrating the impact of assignments on the schedule and on other assignments.

When Pat is assigned to the task Install Computers (After) without specifying the units or the work, Project supplies 100 percent as the default units and calculates the work of 16 hours.

FIGURE 12.5

You can assign a resource without specifying the units or the work, and Project will supply default values.

Task duration already set to two days

Default units (100 percent) filled in by Project

Work calculated by Project

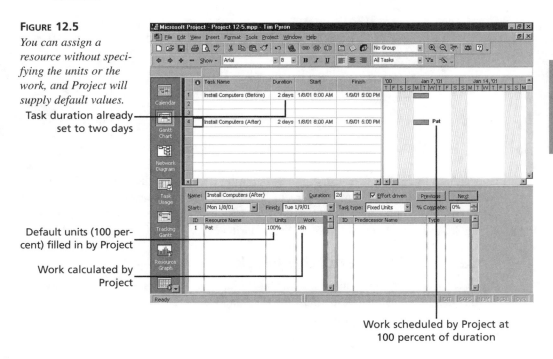

Work scheduled by Project at 100 percent of duration

Enter the Name and the Units

If you enter the units in an assignment, but not the work, Project uses your units entry and the existing duration to calculate the work, and it does this for all three task types. For example, if you assign a resource to a two-day task and enter **50%** in the Units field, Project calculates the work as 50 percent of 16 hours, or eight hours. Project then goes to the calendar and schedules 50 percent of each available working time period during the duration of the task. Figure 12.6 illustrates this case with Mary's 50 percent assignment to the Install Computers task.

FIGURE 12.6

If you define the units, Project calculates and schedules the Work based on your units and the duration.

Task duration before assignment

Units entered as 50 percent

Work calculated as 50 percent of two days (16 hours)

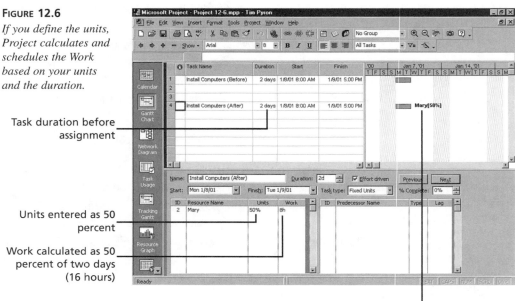

Work scheduled each day of task duration

Notice that Project scheduled Mary for work during each day of the task duration, but has scheduled only four hours (50 percent of her available hours) each day. When Project calculates the assignment schedule, it always schedules the resource for the same percentage of available hours (here, 50 percent) during every period of the task duration.

Enter the Name and the Work

If you enter the work value in an assignment Project will, of course, keep the work value as you entered it and attempt to adjust the task duration to provide enough time to do that amount of work. However, if it's not free to change duration (that is, if the task is a Fixed Duration task), Project will adjust the assigned units instead, keeping the work value you entered.

When you enter the work value, but do not supply the units for Fixed Units or Fixed Work tasks, Project assumes you want the units to be set at the default (100 percent) and calculates a new value for the duration based on the specified work and the assumed value of 100 percent for units.

For example, in Figure 12.7 the resource Trainers is assigned to Install Software, which is originally a two-day task (16 hours). As part of the assignment, 32 hours was entered for the work value but nothing was entered for the units. Project has filled the units field with the default 100 percent and calculated a new duration (32 hours or four days) using this variation of the work formula:

```
Duration = Work/Units
Duration = 32 hours/100% = 32 hours (4 days)
```

FIGURE 12.7

If you enter the name and the work, Project assigns the default units of 100 percent and recalculates duration for the work you entered.

Task duration recalculated to four days

Default units supplied by Project

Work entered as 32 hours

Task duration before assignment

Work scheduled

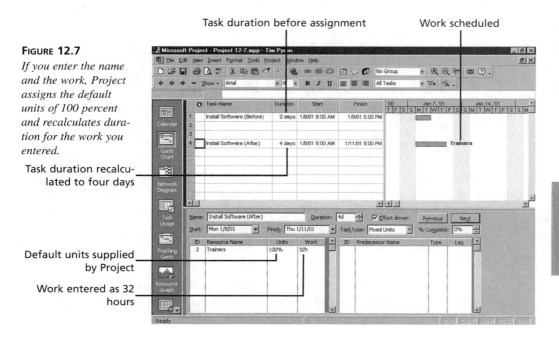

If the task in Figure 12.7 had been a Fixed Duration task, the duration is fixed and can't be changed (note the brackets around duration in the following formula), so the units is the only variable left for Project to adjust to keep the formula valid. Therefore, Project would have abandoned the default units of 100 percent and calculated 200 percent for the Units field.

12

```
[Duration] = Work/Units
16 hours = 32 hours/Units
Units = 200%
```

This example shows how you can get Project to calculate how many units you need to assign if you know the work that has to be done and how long you want the task to take. A number of organizations have tables that define the standard hours of work associated with specific tasks. Auto mechanics, for example, consult manuals published by the auto manufacturers for the standard amount of labor needed to replace a part.

> If you have a task with a known amount of work that you want completed in a specific amount of time, you can change the task type to Fixed Duration task and assign the resource and the known amount of work without entering the units. Project will calculate the units for you. Then you can reset the task type if needed.

Enter the Name, Units, and Work

As described just previously, unless the task is a Fixed Duration task, Project will adjust duration when you enter a specific work amount in an assignment. So, if you enter both the units and the work for a task with either Fixed Units or Fixed Work, Project recalculates the task duration using the values you entered. For example, Figure 12.8 illustrates an assignment to a two-day task named Data Entry; the required work is assumed to be 16 hours. I assigned two temps to the task, entering 200 percent in the Units field and 16 hours in the Work field. Project calculated a new task duration, using this variation of the work formula:

```
Duration = Work/Units
Duration = 16 hours/200% = 8 hours (or 1 day)
```

If the task were a Fixed Duration task, Project would recalculate the units as described in the previous section. In this case, that means that the units value you entered will be changed to match the existing duration and the work you entered.

FIGURE 12.8

If you enter the units and the work, Project recalculates the duration.

Task duration before the assignment

Units entered as 200 percent

Work entered as 16 hours

New Task Duration calculated by Project

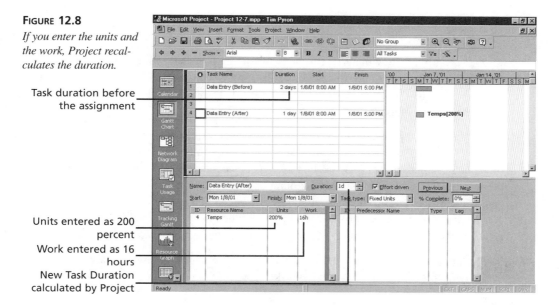

Applying the Work Formula in a Material Resource Assignment

Project treats material resources somewhat differently from the way it treats work resources. The following list shows some of these differences:

- There is no calendar of working and nonworking times for material resources; so, assigning material resources to a task will not alter the schedule due to nonworking time for the resource.

- When you assign material resource units to a task you are defining physical units that will be consumed during work on the task. The Work field for a work resource defines the amount of *time* that the resource will spend on the task. The Work field for a material resource defines the number of physical units that will be consumed.

- Material resource units are entered in decimal format, not percentage format.

- Project will append the material resource label that you defined in the Resource Information dialog box to the values in the Units and Work fields.

- The work formula, wherein Project multiples task duration by the assigned units to calculate work, is optional for material resources. You can define a fixed amount of the resource that will be consumed by the task, or you can define a variable amount that will be calculated by Project by multiplying the value of the Units field by the value of the Duration field to calculate the entry for the Work field.

12

- If there are both work and material resources assigned to a task, the task duration will be determined solely by the work resource assignments.
- Project may allow material resource units to be assigned to the task for dates after the work resources are finished. The duration of the task will reflect the work time period when the work resources are assigned. The finish date for the task will be the date when both types of resources are finished.

As mentioned in this list, the work formula is optional for material resource assignments. You can define a fixed number of units that will be consumed, no matter what the duration of the task happens to be. This is called a *fixed consumption rate*. In such a case, Project doesn't multiply assigned units by task duration to calculate the units for the Work field—it simply copies the units to the Work field. Alternatively, you can define a variable number of units that, like the units for work resources, will be multiplied by the task duration to calculate the total units for the Work field. This is known as a *variable consumption rate*.

 A *fixed consumption rate* for a material resource is a value in the assigned units field that doesn't depend on the task duration.

 A *variable consumption rate* is a units entry with a time unit appended; for example, 2/d means 2-per-day. The total units consumed (the Work field value) would be calculated by Project by multiplying duration by the units value.

For example, if you estimate that a task will require 20 gallons of diesel fuel (which you have given the material label "gal") you could enter **20** in the Units field and Project would respond by displaying 20 gal in both the Units and Work fields.

Alternatively, suppose that the diesel fuel is used by a bulldozer that is assigned to the task and that you estimate that the bulldozer consumes five gallons per hour while in use. You could enter **5/h** in the Units field and Project would multiply that by the task duration to calculate the total gallons consumed. If the duration estimate is 20 hours (or 2.5 days) Project would calculate 20×5 or 100 gallons. It would append the material label and display 5 gal/h in the Units field and 100 gal in the Work field.

Enter the Resource Name Only

If you enter just the material resource name, Project will supply the default units, which is one (1), and display that value, with material label appended, in both the Units and Work fields.

Enter the Name and the Units

If you also place a value in the Units field, Project will calculate the entry for the Work field. If you enter a fixed consumption rate (a simple numeral) Project will place the same value in the Work field. If you enter a variable consumption rate Project will multiply that by duration and place the result in the Work field.

Enter the Name and the Work

If you do not enter a value in the Units field, Project will assume a fixed consumption rate and place the value you put in the Work field in the Units field.

Enter the Name, Units, and Work

For a fixed consumption rate you would never bother to enter both the units and work values—they should be the same. For a variable consumption rate the reaction by Project varies depending on the circumstances:

- If you are only assigning material resources to the task, or if this is the first assignment to the task, and if the task is not a fixed duration task, Project will adjust the duration of the task to accommodate the combination of units and work that you entered. If the task is fixed duration, Project will recalculate the units to be a variable rate that is consistent with the work value and the task duration.

- If you have already assigned one or more work resources to the task then the task duration will be tied to the work assigned to those resources and adding the material resource will have no effect on duration.

  Project will assign the material units at the rate you enter in the Units field for enough time periods to add up to the total units you entered in the Work field. If that takes the same amount of time, or less, than the work resources are scheduled for work then the task finish date and duration will be unchanged. However, if that takes more time than the work resources are scheduled for work, then the task finish date will be increased to allow the total amount of material resources you entered to be consumed. The task duration, however, will remain unchanged because it is based on the time spent by the work resources. Thus you will see a task finish date that is greater than would normally be required for the task duration.

  There is one exception to this peculiar calculation. If the task is a fixed duration task, then project will not extend the finish date to allow all the material units to be consumed. Instead, it will recalculate the variable rate so that the total units will be consumed within the fixed duration.

Assigning Multiple Resources To a Task

Assigning multiple resources to a task means listing multiple resource names in the task assignment. It is similar to increasing the assigned units for a resource. In the previous discussion, when you increased the units assigned for one resource, you saw that unless it's a fixed duration task, Project adjusts the task duration and keeps the work the same: increasing the units allows Project to shorten the duration. That is also the default behavior when you increase the units by adding another resource name and its associated units to the assignment: Project keeps the work, or *effort*, for the task constant and

12

adjusts the task duration. In essence, some of the work is shouldered by the new resource, allowing the previously assigned resource(s) to do less work. You say that the calculation is driven by (determined by) the constant work or effort, and you call such tasks effort-driven.

NEW TERM An *effort-driven task* is assumed to have a fixed amount of work to be done, and changing the number of resources assigned to the task causes the scheduled work for all resources to be reapportioned—usually with an impact on task duration.

For example, if one person is assigned to an effort-driven task with a duration of one week, the work will be 40 hours. If you want the task to be finished sooner, you can assign additional people to work on the task. They will each do less than 40 hours of work, but together they can finish all the work in less than one week.

The Effort Driven task field is used to define a task as effort-driven or not effort-driven (Yes or No). This field appears on the Task Form (refer to Figure 12.1) and in the Task Information dialog box (refer to Figure 12.3). It is simply a check box; if the check box is filled, the task is effort-driven, and if it's not, the task is not effort-driven. By default, all new tasks in Microsoft Project are Effort Driven.

The default status for new tasks in Project is Effort Driven, but if you think that most of your tasks will not be effort-driven, you can change the default in the Options dialog box, right next to where you change the default Task Type (see Figure 12.4). Choose Tools, Options from the menu and select the Schedule tab on the Options dialog box. Clear the New Tasks Are Effort Driven check box to change the default setting. Remember that you must also click the Set as Default button if you want to make this change effective for all new project documents you start.

The Effort Driven setting does not come into play until *after* the first resource assignment has been made. It has no effect on the task if you list several resource names in the Task Form when you make the initial resource assignment to the task. Each resource assignment will be calculated separately. The Effort Driven setting comes into play only when you change the number of resource names on an existing list.

Understanding How Project Calculates Effort-Driven Tasks

To illustrate the effect of the Effort Driven setting, I'm going to use the Install Computers task from Figure 12.1. Recall that both Pat and Mary were assigned to the task. Pat was scheduled for 16 hours of work and Mary was scheduled for eight hours of work; that is, 24 hours of total work was scheduled. Figure 12.9 shows that same task and assignments as Install Computers (Before).

In the task Install Computers (After) I've assigned Todd to work part-time (50 percent) on the task to help Pat and Mary. As a result, the 24 hours of work can now be completed more quickly (in one and a half days instead of two days) and the reduced task duration shows that.

FIGURE 12.9

Adding resources to a task will change the existing resource assignments if the task is effort-driven.

Task duration reduced

Work for Pat and Mary reduced

Effort Driven field is Yes

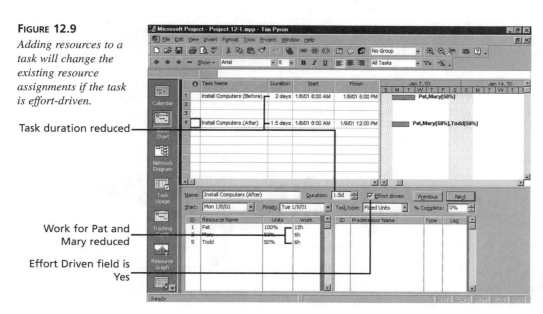

12

Notice in Figure 12.9 in the bottom pane that the work has been redistributed now that Todd is assigned to the task. The hours Pat has been assigned fall from 16 to 12, and Mary's hours fall from eight to six. Also notice that if you add up the total units assigned (100%+50%+50%) the total is 200 percent, with Pat contributing half of that total and Mary and Todd each contributing one-fourth of the total. That's exactly how the work is divided up among the resources: half is assigned to Pat now and one-fourth is assigned to both Mary and Todd. When you change the number of resources assigned to an effort-driven task, Project assigns the work among the resources in direct proportion to their new share of the total resource units assigned.

Sometimes you might need to change the Effort Driven field for a task temporarily. For example, suppose that when initially creating the Install Computers task you had assumed that two days was enough if Pat, Mary, and Todd all worked on the task (with Mary and Todd only part-time), but when the initial resource assignment was made, you forgot to include Todd's assignment. If the task is effort-driven and you later try to add Todd (as you did in Figure 12.9), the task duration will be changed to 1.5 days (which was not what you intended). To add Todd to the task without changing the duration, clear the Effort Driven check box first, add Todd (see Figure 12.10), and then change the task back to effort-driven. As you can see in this figure, adding Todd does not change the task duration or the work loads for the other resources if the Effort Driven field is not checked. The total work for the task increases by the amount of work in Todd's new assignment.

FIGURE 12.10

You can make a task not be effort driven temporarily if you forgot to include a needed resource in the initial assignment.

Task duration
unchanged

Work for Pat and
Mary unchanged

Effort Driven setting is
No

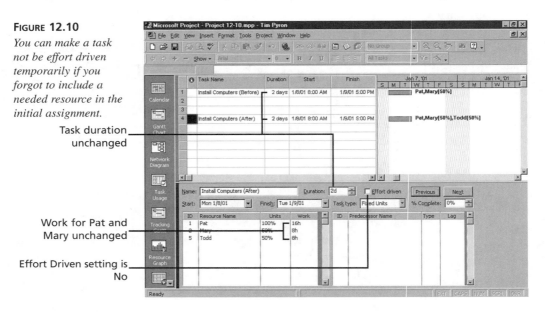

 The Effort Driven status of a task is ignored by Project when you assign additional material resources to a task—the work resource assignments should not be affected.

Summary

Congratulations on staying with this hour! It's a tough one. You've examined the basics of Project's scheduling engine in some detail, although there is still more to come when you look at changing resource assignments in Hour 14, "Editing Resource Assignments." You've reviewed some of the benefits, and burdens, of assigning resources in Microsoft Project. You've seen how to use the resource assignment fields for Units and Work and how to predict the result when Project applies the Work formula to calculate resource assignments and task duration. You've seen that two task settings, task type and effort-driven, give you control over how Project applies the work formula in individual instances. In the next hour, you'll actually work with views and dialog boxes to assign resources.

Q&A

Q **I just changed a resource assignment and it has thrown everything off. How do I fix it?**

A You can probably undo the change and try again after adjusting the task settings to localize the change you've just made. Before making the resource change the second time, try changing the task to Fixed Duration and turning off the Effort Driven setting. This should isolate the change and keep Project from updating the task duration.

Q **When I originally estimated the duration for one of my tasks and assigned resources to it, I forgot to add one of the resources I planned to use. When I added the resource to the task, Project shifted the workload among the other resources and changed the task duration. How can I add the resource without this happening?**

A As in the preceding question, turn off the Effort Driven setting for the task, add the resource, and then turn Effort Driven back on.

Q **I just want to attach a resource to a task for reporting purposes, so Project will show the resource name with the task on reports. I tried assigning the resource to tasks with zero units, but Project turned my tasks into milestones. What can I do?**

A If you make a task a Fixed Duration task first, you can assign a resource at zero percent units and Project will not turn it into a milestone.

Q **Can I assign resources to summary tasks?**

A Yes you can. Usually this is done simply to associate someone with management oversight with the group of tasks. However, Project calculates work for the assignment and the work amount will be virtually meaningless. I suggest you assign resources to summary tasks using zero percent in the Units field. This will allow Project to show the resource name in reports but will avoid calculating work and costs for the resource.

12

Exercises

Begin to think about the tasks and resources in your project in light of the terms introduced in this hour:

- Do you have any tasks that will have a fixed duration and should have the task type Fixed Duration?

- Are there any tasks that have a fixed amount of work and should be changed to Fixed Work?

- Do you have tasks that should *not* be effort-driven? That is, assigning additional resource names to the task will not affect the task duration.

HOUR 13

Assigning Resources and Costs to Tasks

This hour shows you how to use Microsoft Project's views and tools to assign resources and costs. In this hour, you will learn:

- How to change the task settings that affect resource assignments
- How to assign resources using the Task Form
- How to assign resources using the Assign Resources dialog box
- How to assign fixed costs and fixed resource fees

An Overview of Creating Assignments

In the next hour, you see more about editing and fine-tuning resource assignments. To benefit the most from this hour, you should understand the contents of Hour 11, "Defining Resources and Costs," and Hour 12, "Mastering Resource Scheduling in Microsoft Project." There are intricate relationships among task and resource fields covered in those hours.

When first assigning resources to tasks, there are a number of data fields you can use to give Microsoft Project the information it needs to calculate schedules and costs as you intend:

- You can choose the settings for Task Type and Effort Driven that control how Project will calculate changes in the schedule when you change assignments to the task.
- You can, and *must*, provide the resource name when you assign it to a task.
- You can define the units assigned or let Project assign the default number of units.
- You can define the amount of work the resource will perform or let Project calculate that from the task duration and number of units assigned.
- You can choose the cost rates for the resource that will be charged to the task for the resource's time.

This hour shows you how to enter all the preceding information listed. You will also learn how to use pop-up tools to record just the minimum amount of information needed to get the job done. There are a number of different views and tools you can use to assign resources, and you will see how to use the best of them. Each offers its own advantages.

You can also modify Project's calculations by assigning overtime, by introducing delays and splits in an assignment, by applying one of the predefined assignment contours, or by editing the day-to-day work assignments. These refinements will be covered in Hour 14, "Editing Resource Assignments."

As you can see, Project gives you the opportunity to fine-tune resource assignments so that schedule and cost calculations can be precise. You can also get by with just the minimum amount of definition if you don't need all that sophistication.

Choosing the Task Settings for Assignments

As pointed out in the previous hour, the first thing you should do when planning to assign a resource to a task is check the task's Task Type setting. This setting governs whether Project recalculates the task duration after you assign a resource. Specifically, for Fixed Units and Fixed Work tasks the initial assignment may cause Project to recalculate the task duration. However, if the task type is Fixed Duration, Project can't change Duration and it recalculates the Units instead.

To Do: Verifying or Changing the Task Type Setting

▼ To Do

To verify or change the Task Type, follow these steps:

1. Select the task. If the Task Form is displayed in the bottom pane you can view the Task Type field there. If not, use the next two steps to display the Task Information dialog box where you can also view the field.

2. Click the Task Information tool to display the Task Information dialog box.

3. Select the Advanced tab.

4. Check the Task Type setting and change it, if necessary, by clicking the list arrow and selecting Fixed Duration, Fixed Units, or Fixed Work (see Figure 13.1).

5. Click OK.

FIGURE 13.1

Check the Task Type setting for a task before assigning resources to it.

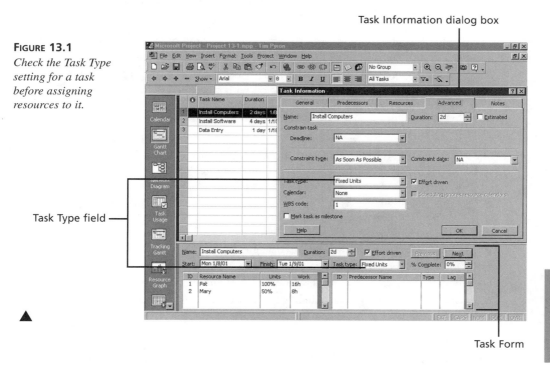

Task Information dialog box

Task Type field

Task Form

13

▲

Assigning Resources to Tasks

You can use a variety of views and dialog boxes, with different methods and techniques, to assign resources to tasks. The most useful of these are

- The Task Entry view, which displays the Gantt Chart in the top pane and Task Form in the bottom pane, provides the most complete control over the variables in an assignment.
- The Assign Resources dialog box, where drag and drop is available, can be kept on the workspace to expedite simple assignments.
- The Task Usage view, which replaces the Gantt Chart task bars in the timescale with a grid of cells that show work details for the assignment during each period in the timescale. You can edit the cells to change the work assignments in individual time periods. This is the best view for fine-tuning assigned work.

The Assign Resources dialog box offers pop-up accessibility from any task view, but it accepts and displays a limited amount of assignment data. The Task Entry and Task Usage views are not pop-up objects, but they display a great deal of information at a glance, especially when used in combination with other views.

After an assignment has been made, the Assignment Information dialog box offers still more details about the assignment. There are no regular views that show you many of the assignment fields found in the Assignment Information dialog box, so it must be used if you want to know those assignment details.

Even though pop-up forms are easy to use, and you will find yourself using them a lot once you get to know Project, I'm going to use the Task Entry view initially to create assignments. This view combines the Gantt Chart and the Task Form, and you will learn more about the process because it shows you what's going on much better than any other view.

Assigning Resources with the Task Form

The Task Form (see Figure 13.2) can display resource assignment details in a minitable at the bottom of the form. The most commonly displayed details are the resource ID, Name, Units, and Work for each assigned resource. This table is a convenient place for assigning resources because

- It allows you to enter either resource Units or Work, or both, for each resource assignment

- It shows you the values for those variables for each assignment
- You still have access to the Task Type list box and Effort Driven check box for the task

FIGURE 13.2

The Gantt Chart with a split window (the Task Entry view) is generally the best view to use for assigning resources.

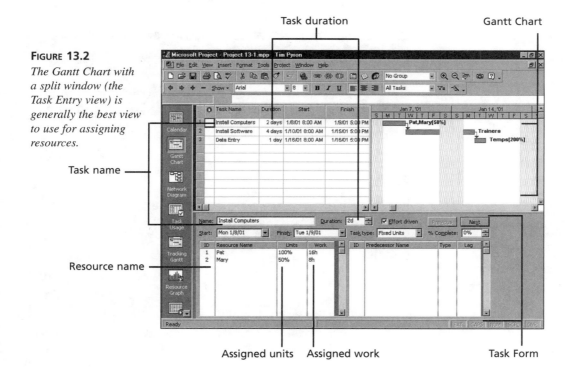

With a combination view like this, you can see how a task relates to other tasks in the Gantt Chart in the top pane, along with a lot of detail about the task in the Task Form in the bottom pane.

To Do: Displaying the Task Form with the Gantt Chart

To display the Task Form with the Gantt Chart for assigning resources, follow these steps:

1. Use the View menu or the View bar to select the Gantt Chart.
2. Split the view by choosing Window, Split. When you split a task view, the Task Form is automatically displayed in the lower pane.
3. Right-click anywhere in the bottom pane to display the Task Form's shortcut menu so that you can choose the details displayed at the bottom of the form.

13

▼   4. From the Details shortcut menu, choose Resources & Predecessors. You could also
          choose Resources & Successors, or Resource Work (see Figure 13.3). All three of
          these choices include the assignment Units field along with Name and Work. You'll
          use the Resource Work details later to assign overtime work.

FIGURE 13.3

The Details shortcut menu for the Task Form shows a check mark next to the current display and lets you select a new display.

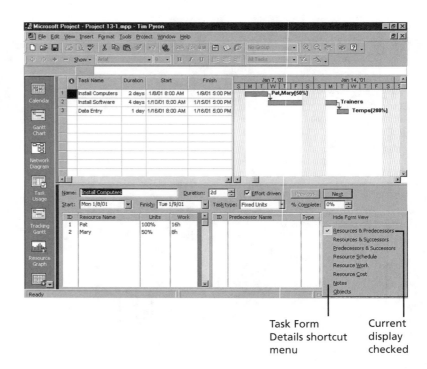

Task Form
Details shortcut
menu

Current
display
checked

▲

To Do: Assigning Work Resources in the Task Form

To assign work resources in the Task Form, follow these steps:

1. Select the task in the top pane. At this point, the task duration is already defined,
   even if it's only the default value of one day. This duration value will be used in
   the work formula when you assign a resource.

> If the bottom pane is active, you can change the task selection in the top
> pane with the Previous and Next buttons in the lower pane. If the task you
> want to select is near the currently selected task, this method will be faster
> than activating the top pane, selecting the task, and then activating the bot-
> tom pane again.

▼

▼ 2. Select the Resource Name field in the Details table.

3. Identify the resource by selecting the resource name from the drop-down list available in the Resource Name field. You can also type in the resource name, but be sure you type it correctly.

If the resource name you want is not on the pull-down list, you can type in the name of a new resource and Project will add the name to the resource pool. After you complete the assignment, you can double-click the resource name in the Task Form to display the Resource Information dialog box and fill in the resource definition details.

If you mistype the resource name, it will be treated as a new resource and added to the resource pool.

4. If you leave the Units field blank, Project will assign the default value, which is 100 percent for work resources. If you want to specify some other units value for the assignment, select the Units field and enter the units you want to assign in percentage format. For example, you could enter 50 percent for a half-time assignment, or 300 percent for three units of a group resource.

5. If you want to specify the amount of work for the assignment, remember that the Task Type setting determines whether the task duration will be affected or not. If you do not want the duration to change, make the task a Fixed Duration task before making the assignment and Project will calculate the number of units necessary to complete your work entry within the existing duration. You can change the task type after the assignment is completed. The following discussion assumes that the task is not a Fixed Duration task.

To enter the work amount, select the Work field and type in the time period. If your entry is for any time unit other than hours, you must add the unit of measure (minutes, days, weeks, or months). Project's default display for work, however, is hours, and your entry will be converted to hours when you click OK.

If you leave the Work field blank for a work resource, Project will calculate the amount of working time for the assignment by multiplying the task duration by the assigned units, and it will display the result in hours. If you have also left the Units
▼ field blank, Project will use the default units of 100 percent in the calculation.

13

▼   6. If you are assigning multiple resources, you can enter them in the next rows of the Resource Name column.

▲   7. After all resource assignments are made for the task, click the OK button.

When you click OK, Project will calculate the values for those fields you did not fill in, in accordance with the principles discussed in the previous hour. If you assigned several resources at once, Project will calculate the assignment for each independently. The assignment that takes the longest time to complete will determine the task duration.

To Do: Assigning Material Resources in the Task Form

To assign material resources in the Task Form, you follow essentially the same steps outlined previously, with the differences that are elaborated as follows:

1. Select the task in the top pane.

2. Select the Resource Name field in the table at the bottom left of the Task Form.

3. Select the resource name from the drop-down list.

4. If you leave the Units field blank for a material resource, Project will assign the default value which is one (decimal one) with the material label appended (for example, 1 gallon). If you want to specify some other units value for the assignment, select the Units field and enter the units you want to assign. For material resources, you always enter units in decimal format. Project will append the material label to your decimal entry.

   • For a fixed consumption rate assignment (where the total units consumed is not affected by changes in the duration of the task) enter the decimal number by itself. For example, if you enter **20** for the material resource Diesel Fuel, which has the label gal, Project will place 20 gal in both the Units field and Work field when you click OK. This is the amount that will be consumed by the task no matter what the duration of the task turns out to be.

   • For a variable consumption rate, (where the total units consumed increases if the task duration increases) enter the units as a decimal number, followed by a slash, followed by a time unit or time unit abbreviation. For example, if diesel fuel is consumed by a bulldozer that's assigned to the task and the dozer consumes fuel at the rate of five gallons per hour, you could enter **5/h** as the units for the Diesel Fuel resource. Project will convert the Units entry to 5 gal/h and will calculate the total units consumed and display that amount in the assignment Work field (discussed next).

▼ 5. If you want to specify the total number of units that will be consumed, select the Work field and type in the number of units in decimal format.

If you leave the Work field blank for a material resource, Project will calculate the total number of units consumed and place that value in the Work field with the material label appended. If the assignment is a fixed consumption rate, the Work field value will be the same as the Units field value.

If the assignment is a variable consumption rate, the Work field value will be calculated by Project by multiplying the Units field value (for example, 5/h or five gallons per hour) by the task duration (for example, one day). The result in this example would be 40 gallons (assuming eight hours per day).

6. If you are assigning multiple resources, you can enter them in the next rows of the Resource Name column.

▲ 7. After all resource assignments are made for the task, click the OK button.

You can also remove a resource assignment easily with the Task Form.

To Do: Removing an Assignment from a Task

To Do

To remove an assignment from a task, follow these steps:

1. Select the task in the top pane.

2. Select the resource name you want to remove in the Task Form.

▲ 3. Press the Delete key and click OK.

Using the Assign Resources Dialog Box

The Assign Resources dialog box is a handy, versatile tool for basic assignment management. In addition, you can use this dialog box to add resources to the resource pool.

 Display the Resource Assignment dialog box by choosing Tools, Resources, Assign Resources or by clicking the Assign Resources tool. Figure 13.4 shows the Assign Resources dialog box over the Task Entry view in the background so you can see how the same field values are displayed differently.

In Figure 13.4, the selected task is Install Computers. If you didn't have the Task Form at the bottom of the screen, you could still tell which resources are assigned to the task by the check marks next to their names in the Assign Resources dialog box. You can see more detail about the assignments (the work) in the Task Form in the bottom pane.

13

FIGURE 13.4

Use the Assign Resources dialog box to create task assignments on-the-fly.

Assign Resources tool   Assign Resources dialog box

Resource Name

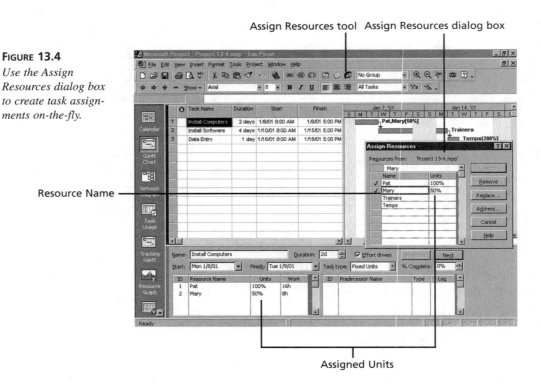

Assigned Units

Adding Resources

You can add resources to the resource pool with the Assign Resources dialog box.

To Do: Creating a Resource with the Assign Resources Dialog Box

To add a resource to the resource pool with the Assign Resources dialog box, follow these steps:

1. Select a blank cell in the Name column of the Assign Resources dialog box.

2. Type in the resource and press Enter.

3. Double-click the new resource name to view the Resource Information dialog box.

4. Use the tabs of the Resource Information dialog box to define the values for the resource.

5. Click OK to close the Resource Information dialog box.

You can add resources directly from your email address book. Click the Address tool on the Assign Resources dialog box to open your email address list and select a name. When you close the address list, Project will add the name to the resource pool.

Assigning Resources

You can assign resources with the Assign Resources dialog box in a couple of ways. You can use the Assign tool or you can drag a resource to a task in the underlying task view.

The underlying view must be a task view and it can't be a form. For instance, you can use the dialog box to assign resources with the Gantt Chart or the Calendar view active, but you can't use it to assign resources if the Task Form in the bottom pane is active.

To Do: Assigning Resources with the Assign Resources Dialog Box

To add a resource assignment to a task or group of selected tasks using the Assign tool, follow these steps:

1. Select the task or tasks to which you want the resource assigned. You can use the Ctrl or Shift keys to add additional tasks to the selection. The task Data Entry is selected in Figure 13.5.

2. If it's not already displayed, display the Assign Resource dialog box.

3. Select a cell in the row for the resource you want to assign, or select a blank row and type in the name if you are creating a new resource as you assign it. The row for Temps is selected in the figure.

4. Select the Units field and enter the units if you don't want Project to supply the default 100 percent. In the figure, the units will be 200 percent (two temporary employees).

   For material resources, enter the units in decimal format. If it's to be a variable consumption rate assignment, remember to append a slash and a time unit.

5. Click the Assign tool or press Enter to assign the resource and unit information to the selected tasks.

   If multiple tasks were selected for this assignment, they will all receive the same units assignment.

13

▼   6. If you are adding more resources to the same tasks, select the next resource name
        to be assigned, type the number of units in the Units field, and select Assign to
        assign this resource to the selected tasks.

     7. You can click the Close button to close the Assign Resources dialog box if you
        want to hide it; or you can leave it open on the workspace while you work in the
▲   underlying views.

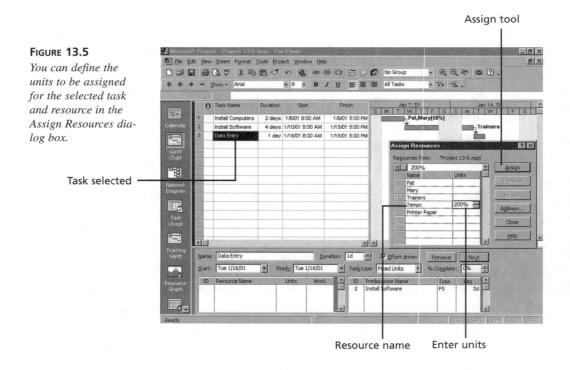

FIGURE 13.5

You can define the units to be assigned for the selected task and resource in the Assign Resources dialog box.

Assign tool

Task selected

Resource name   Enter units

When you click the Assign tool on the Assign Resource dialog box, a check mark appears to the left of the resource assigned, as shown previously in Figure 13.4. This check mark will appear only when the assigned task is selected in the underlying view.

With the Assign Resources dialog box, you can also use drag-and-drop to assign resources to tasks. You don't have to pre-select the task to which the resource will be assigned. This option gives you a quick, efficient way of assigning different resources to one task at a time.

When you drag-and-drop with the Assign Resources dialog box to assign resources to tasks, Project gives you no choice but to use a unit value of 100 percent for the resource assignment you create with this technique. Of course, you can change the units assignment later, but that will lead to other automatic calculations that might not be intended, such as a change in duration.

To Do: Assigning Resources to a Task by Using Drag and Drop

To assign resources to a task by using the drag-and-drop feature, perform the following steps:

1. Display a task view such as the Gantt Chart.

2. Display the Assign Resources dialog box by clicking the Assign Resources tool.

3. Select the resource by clicking in the Name field.

4. Position the mouse pointer in the gray rectangle just to the left of the resource name. The mouse pointer changes to display the Assign Resources graphic (see Figure 13.6).

FIGURE 13.6

When you point to the gray area to the left of the resource name, the pointer appears as a selection arrow with the Assign Resource graphic attached.

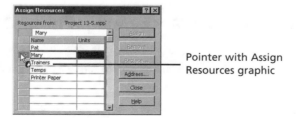

Pointer with Assign Resources graphic

5. Hold down the mouse button. A plus sign will appear next to the pointer graphic.

6. Now drag the mouse pointer over the task to which the resource should be assigned. Project will highlight the entire task row (see Figure 13.7).

7. When the task is highlighted, release the mouse button to assign the resource.

13

To assign multiple resources to a task by using the drag-and-drop feature, select multiple resource names in the Assign Resources dialog box. When you drag the mouse pointer to the task, all the selected resources are assigned at once.

Targeted task

FIGURE 13.7

Drag the pointer over the task to be assigned.

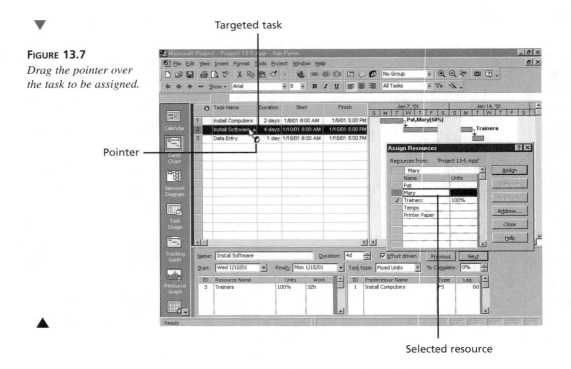

Pointer

Selected resource

Removing Resource Assignments from One or More Tasks

You can use the Assign Resources dialog box to remove assignments as well as add them.

To Do: Removing a Resource Assignment from a Task

To remove a resource assignment from one or more selected tasks, follow these steps:

1. Select the task or tasks in the view that have resource assignments you want to remove.

2. Display the Assign Resources dialog box by clicking the Assign Resources tool.

3. Select the resource or resources you want to remove from assignments by clicking the check mark or the resource name.

Resources assigned to the selected task are identified by check marks to the left of the resource name. If a check mark is gray instead of black, your task selection in the view includes some tasks that have that resource assigned to them and some that do not.

4. Choose the Remove tool. The resource (or resources) selected in the Assign Resources dialog box are removed from any assignments they might have with the task or tasks selected in the view.

You can remove a group of resources in one step if you select all of them before clicking the Remove tool.

Changing Resource Names and Unit Assignments

Use the Assign Resources dialog box to change the resource name or unit assignment for tasks. Each resource name and unit assignment must be replaced individually.

To change units assigned for a resource, select the task and then edit the unit assignment in the Assign Resources dialog box. When the new unit assignment is entered, click the Replace tool. Remember, however, that changing the units usually changes either the task duration or the assigned work. So, check what happened to the task if you use this procedure.

To substitute one resource for another resource in an assignment, select the currently assigned resource and then choose Replace. Then, in the Replace Resource dialog box, select the new resource name.

To Do: Replacing an Assigned Resource with Another

To replace an assigned resource with another resource, follow these steps:

1. Select the task or tasks for which you want to substitute resources in an underlying task view.

2. Display the Assign Resources dialog box by clicking the Assign Resources tool.

3. Select the resource name to be replaced. (It will have a check mark next to it.)

4. Click the Replace tool. Project will display the Replace Resource dialog box over the Assign Resources dialog box (see Figure 13.8). I moved the new dialog box aside in Figure 13.8 so you can see both.

To Do

13

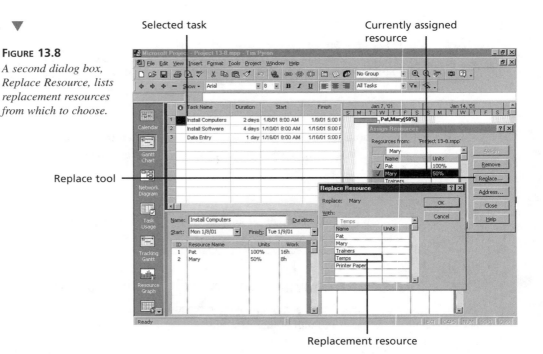

Selected task

Currently assigned resource

FIGURE 13.8
*A second dialog box,
Replace Resource, lists
replacement resources
from which to choose.*

Replace tool

Replacement resource

5. Select the new resource name.

6. Select the Units field for the selected resource and enter the value, if you want it to be changed. Otherwise, the new resource will have the same assigned units as the original resource.

 7. Click OK.

 You can't add a new resource in the Replace dialog box; if you're going to substitute a new resource you must define it before clicking the Replace tool.

 ## To Do: Replacing the Number of Units in a Resource Assignment

To replace the number of units in a resource assignment, follow these steps:

1. Select the task in the view. You can select multiple tasks if you plan to make an identical assignment change in all of them.

▼ Remember to adjust the task type if you want to change how Project will recalculate duration or work when you complete this procedure.

2. Display the Assign Resources dialog box by clicking the Assign Resources tool.

3. Select the Units field for the resource whose assignment is to be changed.

4. Type the new unit assignment for the resource.

▲ 5. Click Close or press Enter.

Assigning Fixed Costs and Fixed Resource Fees

In some cases you might have costs that will not change as the duration or work on a task changes, or they may not be associated with any specific resource. For that matter, they may not even be associated with any one task. These are called *fixed costs* (see Hour 11) because the cost amount does not change as the work on a task changes.

To Do: Displaying the Cost Table

To display the Cost table in a task view, follow these steps:

1. Activate the view where you want to display the table.

2. Choose View, Table to display the Table submenu.

3. Select the Cost table from the submenu.

For an even faster method, right-click over the blank gray title area above the column of row numbers and select Cost Table from the shortcut menu.

In Figure 13.9 I've applied the Cost table to the Gantt Chart. The Cost table includes columns for Fixed Cost, Fixed Cost Accrual, and Total Cost. The Total Cost column sums the cost of the resources and the fixed costs. The Fixed Cost Accrual column lets you control when the Fixed Cost will be considered to have been spent once work on a task starts (see "Controlling How Costs are Accrued" in Hour 11).

As an example of a fixed cost, suppose that you want to record $100 for power strips that you must use in the installation of the computers. You could create a resource called Power Strips, but if you don't want to do that you can simply attach the cost to the task as a fixed cost. In Figure 13.9 the $100 is entered in the Fixed Cost column next to the task Install Computers. I've displayed the Resource Cost details in the bottom pane so you can see that Pat and Mary's resource costs for the task are $800 ($480 + $320). The Total Cost for the task in the top pane sums the resource cost and the fixed cost and is $900.

13

Fixed Cost of power strips Total Cost = Fixed Cost ($100) +
Resource Costs ($800)

FIGURE 13.9

*Use the Cost Table in a
task view to record
Fixed Costs. Total Cost
is Fixed Cost plus the
Resource Costs.*

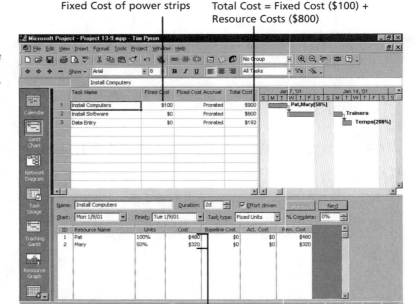

Resource Cost details total $800

To Do: Enter a Task Fixed Cost

The following steps would record the fixed cost.

1. Choose a task view that has a table (like the Gantt Chart) and apply the Cost table.

2. Select the Fixed Cost field for the task.

3. Enter the Fixed Cost amount and press Enter. Project will include the Fixed
   Cost in the value in the Total Cost column.

4. Because the cost is not associated with any obvious resource I strongly suggest you
   also enter a Note for the task explaining what the cost is for. You or your cowork-
   ers will appreciate knowing the source of the added cost later.

> If you enter an amount directly into the Total Cost field, Project will calcu-
> late the difference between what you entered and the sum of any resource
> costs and place that difference in the Fixed Cost field.

If a resource that is assigned to a task is working for a fixed fee (like a contractor or vendor), you will want that cost to remain fixed no matter what happens to the task duration. In this case you would not need Project to track the hours of work for the resource because the contractor or vendor needs to manage those hours; you only require that they finish on time. Your cost won't be affected if the work takes more time or money than the contractor estimated.

If the contractor is the only resource assigned to the task, you must make the task type Fixed Duration. Otherwise Project will treat the task as a milestone.

You use the following process to record fixed resource costs:

1. Assign the contractor or vendor as a resource to the desired task.
2. Enter a zero in the Units field so that the work amount will be calculated as zero. With zero hours of work, the hourly resource cost for this resource will also be zero.
3. Click OK to complete the assignment.

After you complete the assignment, Microsoft Project will allow you to enter a fixed amount in the resource Cost field and this amount will not be overwritten by Project as it calculates other resource costs.

To continue our illustration of fixed resource cost, suppose that Alamo PC will install the computers for $300 (far less than the cost of Pat and Mary's time on this task), and they promise to finish the task within the same two-day duration you had scheduled for Pat and Mary. You will still supply the power strips, however.

To Do: Enter a Fixed Resource Cost

1. In a task view, like the Gantt Chart, split the view with the Window, Split command.
2. Activate the bottom pane and choose Format, Details, Resource Cost to display the resource Cost details (see Figure 13.10).
3. Select the task and set its Task Type to Fixed Duration. Also adjust the duration if needed.
4. Enter the Resource Name and enter **0%** in the Units field. The zero units keeps Project from calculating Work and the rate-based cost associated with work.
5. Click OK to let Project recognize that work will not be calculated. You must click OK before you can enter values in the Cost field.
6. Enter the contract fee in the Cost field. In Figure 13.10, the Cost amount is $300.

▼ To Do

▼

13

▼   7. Click OK again to record the cost amount.

Project adds the $300 resource cost to the $100 fixed cost and returns $400 in the
Total Cost field.

If you have cleared the Actual Costs Are Always Calculated By Microsoft
Project check box on the Calculation tab of the Options dialog box, you will
have to enter the fixed resource cost in the Actual Cost field instead of the
Cost field. See Hour 20, "Tracking Work on the Project," for more information about entering and calculating actual costs.

FIGURE 13.10
*Enter fixed fees or
contract amounts in
the Cost field for the
resource.*

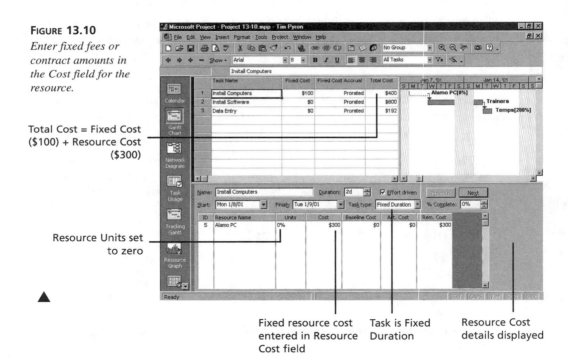

Total Cost = Fixed Cost
($100) + Resource Cost
($300)

Resource Units set
to zero

Fixed resource cost   Task is Fixed   Resource Cost
entered in Resource   Duration   details displayed
Cost field

Summary

In this hour you've seen how you actually enter the task assignments into your project,
using either the Task Form or the Assign Resources dialog box. You have also seen how
to handle fixed costs and the special case of an assignment that has a flat fee or contracted cost.

Q&A

Q I just want to assign names to the tasks so they will show up on reports; I don't want to be bothered by all this schedule calculation stuff. How can I do this?

A I hear you. You have to make sure that task durations won't be affected by the resource assignments because you obviously are going to set durations and dates yourself.

To safely assign names to the tasks without getting into the fine details, follow these steps:

1. Make all the tasks Fixed Duration tasks.
2. Turn off the Effort Driven check box on all the tasks.
3. Use the Assign Resources dialog box to assign resources and let Project assign resources at 100 percent.
4. Make sure that you do not add nonworking time to resource calendars after assignments are made.

The last step is necessary because of the way Project reacts if you introduce non-working time during the period when a resource is assigned to a Fixed Duration task: Project extends the duration of the task to allow the resource to complete the work already assigned.

Q I know how much work is involved in my tasks (from past experience) and I know how long I want to allow tasks to last. How can I get Project to tell me how many units I have to assign?

A You need to make the tasks Fixed Duration tasks. When you assign a resource, enter the hours of work and let Project calculate the Units. After that you can make the tasks Fixed Units for future changes in the schedule if you like.

Q Some of my resources have new pay increases that are scheduled to go into effect during my project. But now Project uses the new rates even for work on tasks that are scheduled before the new rates become effective. What can I do to fix this?

A If you enter resource rates on the Resource Sheet, they will not be given a date stamp to indicate when they are to go into effect and Project will use them for assignments in all time periods. You should add new rates as a new row, with an effective date, on the resource's Cost Rate tables in the Resource Information dialog box.

13

Q **When assigning a resource I typed in the name incorrectly. Now the task is assigned to a new (misnamed) resource instead of the resource I want it assigned to. What do I do?**

A Substitute the correct resource name for the incorrect one and then delete the incorrect resource name in the Resource Sheet.

Exercises

Start a new project document to experiment with and create three tasks named Fixed Units Task, Fixed Work Task, and Fixed Duration Task. Create two resources named Work Resource and Material Resource.

Then conduct a series of experiments by assigning a resource to one of the tasks. After each assignment, review how Project reacted to the assignment and then undo the assignment before making the next assignment.

For each resource and task combination do four assignments:

1. Assign the name only and see how Project uses default values.
2. Assign the name and a units value other than 100 percent.
3. Assign the name and a work value.
4. Assign the name, the units, and the work.

This exercise will solidify your understanding of task types and assignment values.

HOUR 14

Editing Resource Assignments

In this hour, you look at techniques you can use to fine-tune the resource assignments you've made and the schedule that Project calculates for those assignments. You also review the effects that changes in the assignments could have on the overall task schedule. I will save dealing with the problem of overallocated resources and how to adjust the schedule to resolve the overallocation problem until Hour 15, "Resolving Resource Allocation Problems."

The scheduling adjustments you will examine in this hour are:

- Selecting the cost rate table to use for pricing a resource's work
- Arranging for one resource to start later (or finish earlier) than other resources assigned to the same task
- Interrupting or splitting assignments that are in progress to allow for work on other tasks
- Applying a predefined work *contour* to an assignment
- Manually changing or contouring daily work levels for a task
- Assigning overtime work

Working with the Task Usage View

Before you begin editing resource assignments, it will be a good investment of your time to get acquainted with the views that allow you to fine-tune assignments. These include the Task Usage view (covered in this section), as well as the Resource Usage view and the Assignment Information dialog box, which will be discussed in subsequent sections. You will use the Task Usage view and Assignment Information dialog box in this hour to view and edit several aspects of assignments. You'll use the Resource Usage view more in the next hour.

You will get the most out of this hour if you are comfortable with the material presented in Hour 12, "Mastering Resource Scheduling in Microsoft Project," and Hour 13, "Assigning Resources and Costs to Tasks."

After an assignment is created, you can modify additional aspects of the assignment in the Assignment Information dialog box and you can fine-tune the work schedule in either the Task Usage or Resource Usage view. You can only access the Assignment Information dialog box from one of the two usage views; you'll begin by learning how to use the Task Usage view. These techniques also apply to the Resource Usage view.

The Task Usage view displays a list of the project's tasks in a table (the Usage table) on the left side of the screen (see the top pane in Figure 14.1) with each task's resource assignments indented under that task row. The rows for assignments are italicized as well as indented to help you identify the assignment records. In Figure 14.1 the Windows, Split command has displayed the Task Form in the bottom pane so that you can see the connection between the assignment information in both views. The tasks are the same computer installation tasks used in the last two hours.

Note that though the assignment names in the top pane look just like resource names, these are assignment records, not resource records. Double-clicking an assignment row displays the Assignment Information dialog box instead of the Resource Information dialog box.

Double-click here to
display the Assignment
Information dialog box

Double-click here to
display the Task
Information dialog box

Work total for
this task for all
assignments

Cell with
timephased work
detail for Monday

Task Usage view

Work total for
this task for
this Monday

FIGURE 14.1

*You can examine a
wealth of detail about
a task, its assignments,
and the resources
involved in the assign-
ments in this combina-
tion of Task Usage and
Task Form views.*

Double-click here to
display the Resource
Information dialog box

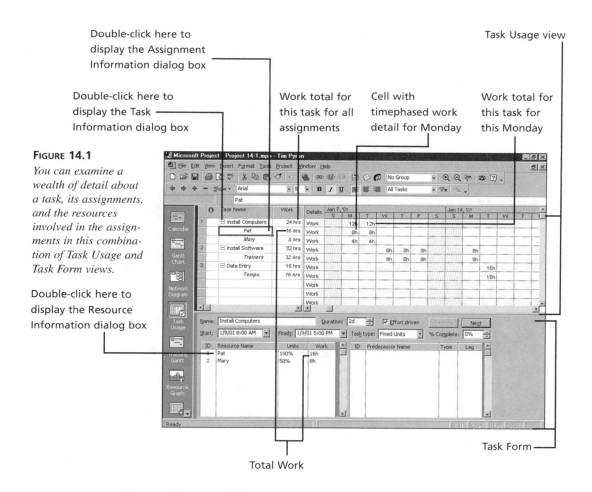

Total Work

Task Form

To display the combination view shown in Figure 14.1, click the Task
Usage icon on the View Bar or choose View, Task Usage from the
menu. Use the Windows, Split command to display the Task Form in the bottom pane.

The table's columns are task fields, assignment fields, or both in some cases. If the column is an assignment field only, the cell in a task row will be blank (and vice versa).

14

The Resource Usage view is similar to the Task Usage view, except that the table displays a list of the resources in the resource pool with task assignments indented under each resource.

The right side of the view is a timeline with a grid of cells that show assignment details on a period-by-period basis. The information in this grid is called *timephased data* in Microsoft Project. In Figure 14.1, the grid displays the default Work details, but you can display other details like Cost, Overtime Work, and so on, if you prefer. For instructions on changing the timephased data that is displayed, see the section "Assigning Overtime Work" later in this hour.

NEW TERM   *Timephased data* is task, resource, or assignment information (primarily work and cost data) that is distributed over specific time periods during the assignment duration. You can view timephased data in the Task Usage and Resource Usage views in the grid under the timeline or in a few reports. Microsoft Project calculates the timephased values for any time period granularity (in hours, days, weeks, or months) that you choose to display.

> For both the Task and Resource Usage views, use the Go To Selected Task tool to scroll the timeline to the grid data for the selected row in the table.
>
> To jump to the start or end of the project timeline, first click anywhere in the grid, and then press the Home or End key.

In Figure 14.1, Pat's assignment to Install Computers is selected in the table in the top pane. The usage grid shows his scheduled work on Monday and Tuesday. The usage grid also shows that the sum of the work for all assignments (Pat and Mary) on each day is 12 hours. The Work column in the table shows that the total work for this assignment for Pat is 16 hours and that the total work for the task (for all assignments—for Pat and Mary) is 24 hours.

Editing Assignments with the Task Usage View

With the Task Usage view (or the Resource Usage view) you can adjust the amount of work scheduled during any time period shown on the grid. When you make a change in the timephased data, Project will recalculate the total work for the assignment, the resource, and the task.

To Do: Editing Timephased Data

You can edit timephased data in the Resource Usage or Task Usage view to fine-tune the scheduled assignment.

1. Adjust the timescale to display the time period you want to change.
2. Select the cell for the time period you want to change.
3. Type in a new value, with a time unit appended unless it is the default "h".
4. Either press Enter or select another cell to complete the change.

As soon as you finish a cell entry, Project immediately recalculates the following:

- The total work for the task for that period (in the task row above the selected cell)
- The Work field entry for the resource in the table on the left
- The total work for the task in the table on the left
- The duration for the task

Editing Assignments with the Assignment Information Dialog Box

The Assignment Information dialog box gives you additional information about an assignment—and it's the only way to modify some assignment fields.

To Do: Displaying the Assignment Information Dialog Box

Displaying the Assignment Information dialog box provides the most comprehensive venue for modifying an assignment.

1. Display either the Task Usage view or the Resource Usage view.
2. Select the row for the assignment whose information you want to display.
3. Click the Assignment Information tool on the Standard toolbar or double-click the assignment.

Figure 14.2 shows the Assignment Information dialog box for Pat's assignment to Install Computers. As you can see, the dialog box has several familiar fields you have already worked with, including the assigned work, the assigned units, and the start and finish dates for the assignment. You can also change the name of the assigned resource here, but there's no list to select from, and you must know how to spell the name correctly.

14

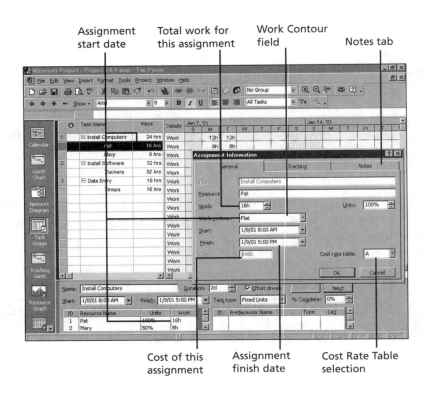

FIGURE 14.2

*The Assignment
Information dialog
box contains several
assignment fields not
normally displayed
anywhere else in
Microsoft Project.*

The assignment fields on the Assignment Information dialog box include:

- The Work Contour field lets you choose from a set of predefined work contours.
  See the section "Contouring Resource Assignments" later in this hour for detailed
  instructions.

- The Start and Finish fields let you frame the time period during which the resource
  will do its work.

- The Cost Rate Table field lets you choose one of the five different Cost Rate tables
  for the resource to be applied to this assignment. The default assignment is table A.

- The Cost field is usually a display-only field that shows you the total calculated
  cost of this resource for this assignment. If the resource has been assigned with
  zero units, the Cost field becomes available for you to enter a fixed cost for the
  assignment.

- On the Notes tab, the Notes field lets you record notes about an assignment. Use
  the Notes field liberally to explain any unique features of an assignment. You can
  even include these notes on printouts that you distribute to the resource to explain
  your expectations.

▲ You will use the Assignment Information dialog box in the next section to change the cost rate table to use for an assignment.

Changing the Cost Rate Table for an Assignment

When you assign a resource to a task Project uses the Cost Rate Table A by default for pricing the hours of work. If you have defined additional cost rate tables for different types of work, use the Assignment Information dialog box to apply a different table to the assignment.

To Do: Applying a Different Cost Rate Table to an Assignment

When an assignment is to use cost rates other than the standard rates, use the Assignment Information dialog box to select the rate to be used.

1. Display the Task Usage or Resource Usage view.

2. Select the row for the assignment.

3. Either double-click the assignment or click the Assignment Information tool on the Standard toolbar to display the Assignment Information dialog box.

4. Choose one of the lettered tables in the Cost Rate Table field to assign the standard rate and overtime rate from that table to the work for this assignment.

5. Click OK to complete the transaction.

> You can edit the Cost Rate tables only in the Resource Information dialog box. To display it, first display the Assign Resources dialog box or a view with fields for resources and double-click the resource name to display its Resource Information dialog box. Click the Costs tab to display the five Cost Rate tables, A to E, and enter the cost rates to be used for that table.

▲

Introducing Delay in an Assignment

Now, let's get back to fine-tuning the scheduled work for an assignment. You may remember from Hour 11, "Defining Resources and Costs," that when a project is scheduled from a fixed start date, Microsoft Project automatically schedules all assignments to begin as soon as the task begins. However, you can delay the start of one or more assignments so that they start later than the other assignments for that task.

14

Conversely, if the project is scheduled from a fixed finish date, Project automatically schedules all assignments to finish just as the task finishes. You can override the default assignments by allowing one or more assignments to finish before the task and the other assignments finish. Although this change causes the assigned work to finish earlier, and therefore also start earlier, it is recorded as a *negative* delay by Project's scheduling engine.

NEW TERM An *assignment delay* for a fixed start date project is the difference between the start of a task and the delayed start of the assignment to that task. The start date of the task, plus the amount of delay, yields the start date for the assignment.

For projects with a fixed finish date, an assignment delay is the amount of time between the finish of the task and the finish of the resource's work on the task. It measures how much earlier the resource's work on the task is finished compared to the rest of the work. The finish of the task, minus the amount of the delay, yields the finish of the assignment.

In this discussion, it will be easier if you begin by examining projects with fixed start dates and then show how the principles apply to projects with fixed finish dates. You learned how to set the fixed start or finish date in Hour 3, "Starting a New Project and Working with Tasks."

Delaying Assignments in Fixed Start Date Projects

Why would you want to delay an assignment in the first place? Well, many of the tasks you create for your projects will undoubtedly encompass more than one action. You don't want to create separate tasks for every little step that has to be taken; that leads to projects that are too finely detailed to be practical. Consequently, some of your tasks might require work from different resources at different times.

For example, in the Install Computers task, one of the last steps in the installation process is configuring Windows to recognize the printers available on the network. Suppose Todd is assigned to the Install Computers task force to configure the network printers. His work needs to come toward the end of the task, but Project schedules all assignments at the beginning of the task by default. You need to be able to tell Project to *delay* the start of Todd's assignment.

This simple equation explains what you want to achieve:

```
Task start date + Assignment delay  =  Assignment start date
```

An easy way to create delays is to display the Task Form in the bottom pane below a task view and apply the Resource Schedule details. Figure 14.3 shows the Task Usage view in the top pane and the Task Form with Resource Schedule details in the bottom pane. You could as easily have used the Gantt Chart in the top pane; I used the Task Usage view so you can see the details of the resource's work schedule with the delay.

FIGURE 14.3

An entry in the Delay field shifts the assignment start and its scheduled work to a later period in the life of the task.

Zero work scheduled
on Monday

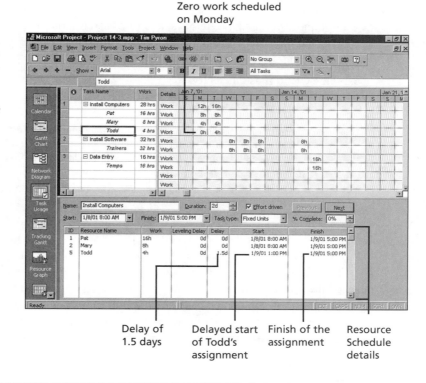

Delay of
1.5 days

Delayed start
of Todd's
assignment

Finish of the
assignment

Resource
Schedule
details

Note that there are two delay fields on the Task Form: Delay and Leveling Delay. Leveling Delay records a delay in an assignment that's designed to let the resource finish another assignment that's scheduled for the same time period. That process is called "leveling" and it's covered in the next hour.

To Do: Viewing or Editing Assignment Delays

Use an assignment delay to delay the start of one resource assignment without delaying other assignments to the same task.

1. Display a task view, such as the Gantt Chart or the Task Usage view.

2. Split the window with the Window, Split command.

3. Activate the Task Form by pressing F6 or by clicking anywhere in the bottom pane.

4. Right-click anywhere in the Task Form to display the Details shortcut menu and select Resource Schedule.

▼ To Do

14

5. Enter an amount of time in the Delay column, using a number and a time unit (for example, h for hours, d for days, and so forth). Alternatively, you can enter a later date and time in the assignment's Start field instead of making an entry in the Delay field. Either method leads to the same results.

6. Click OK to finish the entry.

> Although changing the assignment start date is an alternative way of creating a delay, changing the assignment finish date has a different effect—it is interpreted to mean you are changing the length of the assignment and, therefore, the amount of work to be done.

Figure 14.3 shows Todd's assignment to the Install Computers task. The original schedule had Todd starting at the same time Pat and Mary start—on Monday at 8:00 a.m. In this case, however, a delay has been added to shift his assignment to a day and a half later. The bottom pane shows the 1.5d entry in the Delay field. After that entry, Project changed the start date for his assignment. The delay is apparent from the zero-work entry for Todd on Monday in the top pane and from the entry in the Start field in the bottom pane. Instead of entering the delay amount, you could have entered **1/9/01 1:00 PM** in the assignment Start field and Project would have calculated the delay value.

> The Delay field is never empty or blank; if there is no delay it contains a zero. To remove a delay, you must enter zero in the Delay field.

"Delaying" Assignments in Fixed Finish Date Projects

The preceding discussion is based on a project with a fixed start date, in which the delay field is used to schedule one assignment to start later than other assignments. If your project has a fixed finish date, by default Project schedules assignments to finish when the task finishes, not to start when the task starts. The Delay field is used to cause one assignment to *finish earlier* than other assignments.

In the example used in the previous figures, Todd's assignment to configure the printers would automatically be scheduled at the end of the task if the project had been a fixed finish date project. There would have been no need for a delay. However, suppose Todd's assignment was to help unpack all the computer boxes at the beginning of the task. In that case his work should come at the beginning of the task. If the project is a fixed finish date project, Microsoft Project would schedule his four hours to finish when the task finishes, and you would need to be able to force Project to schedule his assignment to finish earlier.

Delays in fixed finish date projects must be entered as *negative numbers* in the Delay field because they move the finish date to an earlier date.

Substituting "finish date" for "start date" in the formula used earlier, you have this formula:

```
Task finish date + Assignment delay  =  Assignment finish date
```

In the case of fixed finish date projects, the delay value must be a negative number because the assignment finish must come before the task finish in projects with fixed finish dates.

In Figure 14.4, the Install Computers task is scheduled in a fixed finish date project, and Todd's assignment is initially scheduled by Project at the end of the task. To schedule his hours at the beginning, you would need to introduce a negative delay in his assignment. I have already entered the delay (-1.5d) in the bottom pane, but have not yet clicked the OK button to add it to the calculations.

FIGURE 14.4

In a fixed finish date project, schedules are calculated backward from the defined finish date for the project.

Work initially scheduled on last day of task

A negative delay entered (but not yet calculated)

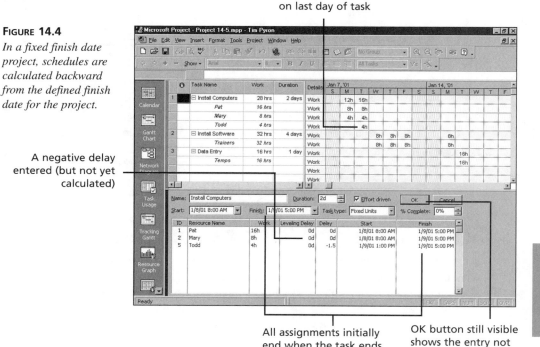

All assignments initially end when the task ends

OK button still visible shows the entry not calculated yet

14

Figure 14.5 shows the result after the OK button is clicked. Notice that Todd's work now starts at the beginning of the task on Friday.

Work is now scheduled for first day of task

FIGURE 14.5

After the (negative) delay is added, Todd's assignment is scheduled to finish and start earlier.

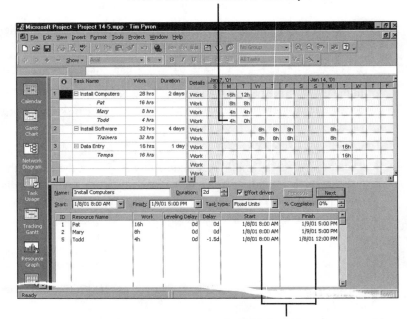

Early finish for this assignment also means rescheduled start

 The assignment Start field has no effect on the delay in a fixed finish date project. Instead, its changes are interpreted by Project to signal a change in the length of the assignment and therefore in the amount of work to be done.

Splitting Tasks and Task Assignments

You might have noticed that you hardly ever get to work on a task from start to finish without having to stop and work on something else; you're putting out fires or you're diverted temporarily to another task with a higher priority. If you know in advance that you will have to interrupt your work on a task, you can build in a *split* in the task work schedule. Project can show that the work stops at the point of the split and then resumes at a later time.

NEW TERM   A *split* in a task or in a task assignment is an interruption in the schedule, so that work stops at the point of the split and then resumes later at the end of the split.

If you split a task, Project also splits all the assignments to that task. In this case, the task's duration is not affected (the number of working time periods has not changed), although the time span between the start and finish of the task is now longer because of the non-working interruption introduced by the split.

If you split just one assignment on a task, however, the other assignment schedules continue unchanged and the task itself won't be split. The resource whose assignment was split will likely have to work beyond the original dates for the task to make up the time lost to the split. If that happens, the task duration will increase because of the split.

> In a fixed start date project, the resource whose assignment is split would finish later than the originally scheduled finish. In a fixed finish date project, the resource would have to start earlier than the originally scheduled start to get all the work done.

You saw back in Hour 7, "Working with Deadlines and Constraints," in the section "Splitting Tasks" how to split a task with the Split Task tool on the Standard toolbar. Assignment splits have to be created in either the Task Usage view or the Resource Usage view. In both cases, you activate the grid on the right side of the view, select the time period during which the interruption should occur, and press the Insert key. Project will insert zero-work cells in the cells you selected while pushing the scheduled work cells out of the way to the right to make room.

> For a fixed start date project, inserting cells in a Usage view pushes selected cell(s) to the right—shifting that work to later dates. For a fixed finish date project, inserting cells in a Usage view pushes work cell(s) to the left—rescheduling that work to start earlier.

14

To Do: Splitting a Task Assignment

Use a split in an assignment to build in an interruption of work without interrupting other assigned resources.

1. Display either the Task Usage view or the Resource Usage view. This view needs to be either full-screen or the top pane of a combination view.

2. If necessary, adjust the timescale so that the grid shows time periods that let you select the exact period during which work will be interrupted. For example, if you are going to split a task for a number of days, the minor units in the timescale should be days.

   Use the Zoom In and Zoom Out tools on the Standard toolbar to quickly change the time units displayed. See "Formatting the Timescale for the Calendar" in Hour 9, "Formatting Views," for more details.

3. On the row for the task to be split, select the period or periods the interruption will occupy in the timescale grid. (See the following Warning for an exception.) To select multiple time periods you can drag with the mouse or use the Shift key with the left or right arrow keys.

4. Choose Insert, Cells or press the Insert key. Project pushes the selected cells out of the way to the right or left (depending on the type of project) and replaces them with cells having zero work (0h) assigned. For projects with fixed start dates, Project pushes the selected cells to the right to later dates, thus pushing the assignment finish to a later date. For projects with a fixed finish date, Project pushes the selected cells to the left to earlier dates, thus pushing the assignment start to an earlier date.

> Project behaves differently when performing this operation in projects scheduled from a fixed finish date. Instead of starting the split in the cell you select, Project starts the split in the cell *to the left* of your selected cell. With fixed finish date projects you need to select the cell to the right of the point where you want the split to start.

 The Contoured indicator will appear in the Indicator column to signal that the work on this assignment has been edited.

To remove a split, or to shorten the period of the interruption, select one or more cells with zero work and press the Delete key. This action shifts leftward all cells that are to the right of the deleted cell.

▼ To illustrate splitting an assignment, I'll introduce a new task for Pat: He needs to attend a project meeting at one of the company's other sites on Tuesday, but that's during the second day of the Install Computers task. You can split Pat's assignment for the Install Computers task, rescheduling his work from Tuesday to Wednesday. In Figure 14.6, Task 2, Project meeting, is also assigned to Pat and scheduled for Tuesday. Pat's Tuesday work schedule for the Install Computers task is selected. Pressing the Insert key inserts a zero-work cell in place of the selection and shifts the selection to the right (the project is a fixed start date project again).

FIGURE 14.6

Pat and Mary are scheduled to finish installing the computers on Tuesday, but Pat needs to attend a meeting on that day. You can split the installation task so he can attend the meeting.

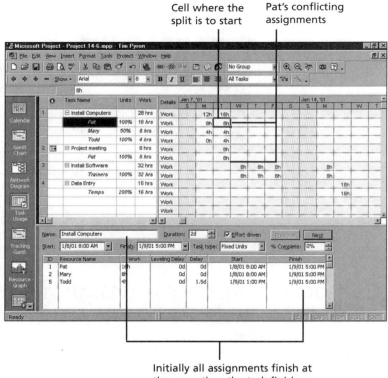

Cell where the split is to start

Pat's conflicting assignments

Initially all assignments finish at the same time the task finishes

Figure 14.7 shows the split in place. Pat has zero hours (0h) scheduled on the Install Computers task on Monday and eight hours scheduled on Tuesday. Notice that because the Install Computers task now finishes later, the tasks that follow it have been pushed out to the right also, and the finish of the Data Entry task is now delayed until the fol-
▼ lowing Monday.

14

▼ Contour indicator shows   No work scheduled for this   Work shifted to this
   schedule has been edited   assignment in this period now   period

FIGURE 14.7

*Pat's assignment is
split, with his last eight
hours of work on the
Install Computers task
scheduled now for
Tuesday.*

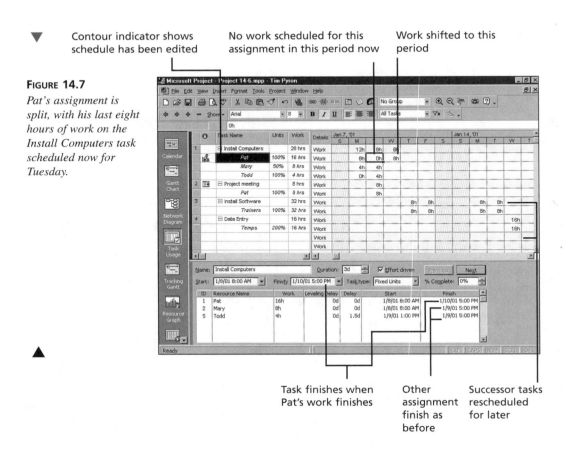

Task finishes when   Other   Successor tasks
Pat's work finishes   assignment   rescheduled
                             finish as   for later
                             before

Contouring Resource Assignments

When Project creates an assignment schedule, it takes the value in the assignment Units
field and uses that same value with the resource calendar to schedule work each day until
the task is completed. As long as the resource calendar has the same number of available
hours each time period, this produces a level or *flat* amount of work for each period. This
is called a *flat assignment profile*, with the assigned units neither rising nor falling over
time. In reality, many tasks require varying amounts of work throughout their duration.
For some assignments, most of the work comes up front and then tapers off (sometimes
called a *front loaded profile*). To create this schedule you would need to schedule more
units each day during the early part of the schedule and then smaller units later in the
schedule. Other assignments start out with light work loads that build as the task nears
completion (called a *back loaded profile*). Here you need to schedule small units early on
and then larger units later in the assignment.

If the actual work profile needs to vary from period to period, with peaks and valleys of activity, or a rising (or falling) trend of activity, you can use one of Project's predefined assignment profiles, called *contours*, to schedule different numbers of units at different times during the assignment. You can also create your own contour by manipulating the scheduled work for each period.

NEW TERM An assignment *contour* is a work profile or pattern that describes how scheduled work is distributed over time. Project has built in algorithms that generate varying numbers of assigned units per period during the work on the task in order to create varying amounts of work per period.

If the work assignment has been changed from the default Flat schedule, an icon appears next to that assignment in the Indicator column in the Task Usage or Resource Usage view (see the indicators in Figure 14.8). In either of those views, you can also manually adjust the assigned hours over the course of the task duration. If you make manual changes, the icon in the Indicator column shows a pencil imposed on the Scheduling Pattern icon (see row 9 in Figure 14.8).

Identifying the Predefined Contours

Microsoft Project provides eight predefined work contour profiles that you can apply to a resource assignment. One of them is the default assignment profile, called *flat*, that is used by Project when it initially calculates an assignment. Examples of the different contour profiles are illustrated in Figure 14.8.

Figure 14.8 compares the schedules that Project calculates for each contour. The original task had a duration of five days and the resource was assigned 40 hours with units of 100 percent. The first row, labeled "Flat," shows how the default assignment looked initially. The 100 percent units were assigned each period until the 40 hours of work was completed.

Each of the other contours reduces the unit assignment during selected days in the assignment; the choice of which days are reduced is what distinguishes the different profiles and gives rise to the contour names. Because less work is scheduled in some days, the total assignment takes longer to complete; for some contours, Figure 14.8 shows that the duration is doubled to 10 days.

The Resource Graph view in the bottom pane of Figure 14.8 has been formatted to show the units assigned in each period for the contour that is selected in the top pane (in this case, the Double Peak contour). Notice how the graph profile is the inspiration for the contour's indicator graphic. The assigned units appear beneath the graph bars (labeled % Work Allocated) to illustrate that this is the real mechanism at work in contours. Project assigns different units each time period when you apply a contour, and that's what leads to different amounts of work each period.

14

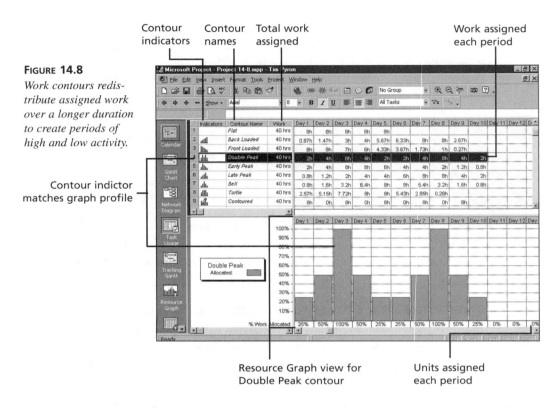

FIGURE 14.8
Work contours redistribute assigned work over a longer duration to create periods of high and low activity.

Contour indictor matches graph profile

Contour indicators   Contour names   Total work assigned   Work assigned each period

Resource Graph view for Double Peak contour   Units assigned each period

Row 9 in Figure 14.8 is labeled Contoured, and it indicates that the user has manually edited the schedule to create a unique contour, in this case by scheduling the work every other day for nine days instead of every day for five days.

Applying a Predefined Contour

To apply one of the predefined contours you must display either the Resource Usage or Task Usage view. Then you must select the assignment, and use its Assignment Information dialog box to select the contour.

To Do: Selecting a Contour for an Assignment

To select a contour for an assignment, follow these steps:

1. Select the assignment in the Task Usage view or the Resource Usage view.

2. Display the Assignment Information dialog box by double-clicking the assignment row or by clicking the Assignment Information tool.

3. On the General tab, use the list arrow in the Work Contour field to select one of the predefined contours.

▼   4. Click OK to have Project calculate the new assignment pattern.

When you assign a contour, Project keeps the total work of the assignment constant (see the following Caution for an exception). However, the duration of the assignment is usually longer because work in some periods is reduced. Therefore, the total work must be spread out over a longer time period.

> If you assign a contour to a Fixed Duration task, the task duration cannot change. Therefore, when the contour reduces work in some periods the total work for the task will be reduced.

> If you want to restore the assignment contour to the default pattern, or if you have edited the assignment and want to restore the original assignment, choose the predefined contour named Flat.

▲

Assigning Overtime Work

You can reduce the duration for a task by allowing some of a resource's work to be scheduled as overtime work. The total work to be done on the assignment remains the same, but the amount of work scheduled during regular working hours is reduced. Project calculates the cost for overtime work by applying the resource's overtime rate.

 Overtime work is work that is scheduled to take place outside the working hours of the resource calendar.

Understanding How Overtime Affects the Schedule

When you assign a resource to a task for the duration of the task, Project schedules work for the resource only during the regular working times (those times defined in the resource calendar). If you assign overtime work, you are telling Project that part of the task will be completed outside the regular working times (for example, in evenings or on weekends) and that Project doesn't have to use regular hours to schedule that part of the work.

To Project, if part of the work on a task is to be done in overtime, that reduces the amount of work that needs to be scheduled during the regular working times. To handle the calculations, Project divides Work (which is the same as total work) into Regular Work and Overtime Work. When you assign overtime to a resource, Project subtracts

14

Overtime Work from Work to get Regular Work and schedules that amount of work in regular hours. Because it's work during regular time that Project counts in calculating duration, reducing Regular Work effectively reduces the task duration.

 Regular work is work that is scheduled during the working times defined on the resource calendar.

When you assign overtime work, this is how Project recalculates the schedule:

- Your entry in the Overtime Work field is subtracted from the assignment's total work, and the difference is called *Regular Work*.

- The new, reduced Regular Work is scheduled during the hours available on the resource calendar. If you have selected a work contour for the assignment, the new work Regular schedule is apportioned over time in the same pattern as the contour.

- The Overtime Work is then scheduled over the same period of time as the Regular Work, and with the same contour.

> If you assign all the work to be done in overtime, Project reduces the Regular Work, and consequently the duration of the task, to zero and automatically flags the task as a milestone. You can remove the milestone flag by opening the Task Information dialog box and clearing the Mark Task as Milestone check box on the Advanced tab. The milestone symbol will no longer appear in the Gantt Chart for the task, although its duration will still be zero.

Entering Overtime Work

You can view the assigned overtime work in the Task and Resource Usage views, but you can't assign overtime in those views. You can enter the amount of Overtime on the Task Form if you apply the Resource Work details at the bottom of the form.

To Do: Displaying Overtime in the Task Usage View

To change the timephased details displayed in the Task Usage view, follow these steps:

1. Click anywhere in the grid and choose Format, Detail Styles (or double-click in any work-day cell in the grid) to open the Detail Styles dialog box (see Figure 14.9).

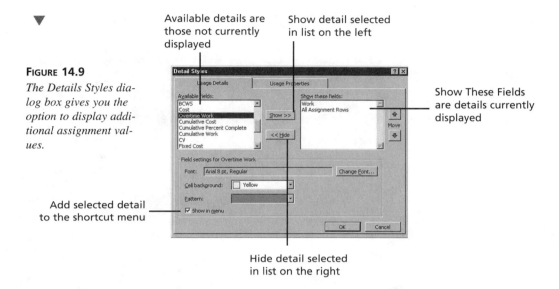

Available details are those not currently displayed

Show detail selected in list on the left

FIGURE 14.9
The Details Styles dialog box gives you the option to display additional assignment values.

Show These Fields are details currently displayed

Add selected detail to the shortcut menu

Hide detail selected in list on the right

2. Select Overtime Work from the Available Fields list box on the left. These are the details that are not currently displayed.

3. Click the Show button to move the item to the Show These Fields list box. This action displays the item for the time being, but doesn't permanently add the item to the shortcut menu for easy access. If you think you will frequently want to work with this detail, you should execute the next step.

4. Select the Show in Menu check box to add this item to the Details shortcut menu permanently (see Figure 14.10).

5. Click the OK button.

Figure 14.10 shows the Overtime Work details added to the display. It also shows the shortcut menu you can access by clicking the right mouse button over the grid. Details that are currently displayed are checked on the shortcut menu. Click a checked item to hide it; click an unchecked item to display it.

14

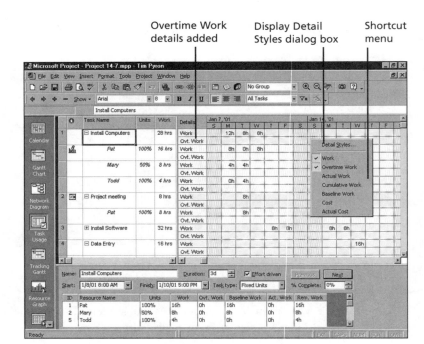

FIGURE 14.10
The Details shortcut menu lets you change the displayed details quickly.

Overtime Work details added · Display Detail Styles dialog box · Shortcut menu

Using the Task Form to Enter Overtime

You can use any of the task-oriented views like the Gantt Chart in the top pane to display and select the task for which you want to record overtime. The Task Form in the bottom pane can then be used to enter the amount of overtime.

To Do: Entering Overtime in the Task Form

Assign overtime work to a resource to reduce the amount of regular working time used for an assignment.

1. Choose a task-oriented view for the top pane.

2. Select the task for which you want to schedule overtime.

3. Display a combination view by choosing Window, Split.

4. Press F6 to activate the Task Form in the bottom pane.

5. In the bottom pane, right-click anywhere and choose Resource Work from the shortcut menu to display the Resource Work details (see Figure 14.11).

Task and
assignment
costs

Overtime work
timephased
details

Assignment
split

Finish of
successor
task

FIGURE 14.11

*You can enter overtime
hours and reduce task
duration in a combina-
tion view.*

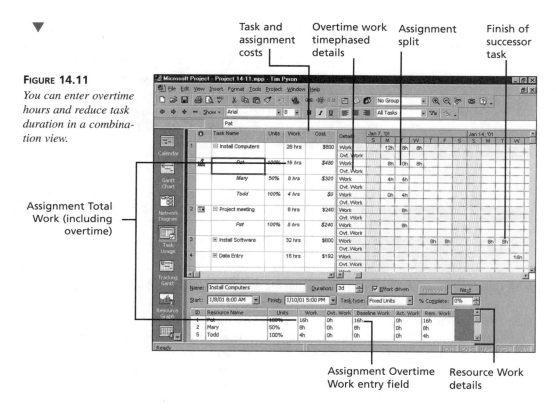

Assignment Total
Work (including
overtime)

Assignment Overtime
Work entry field

Resource Work
details

6. Select the Ovt. Work field and enter the amount of work you are scheduling in
overtime. Enter a number followed by a time unit abbreviation (h, hr, or hour for
hours, and so on), and then press Enter or click the Enter box on the Edit bar.

Do **not** reduce the entry in the Work field. That field's entry shows the *total*
amount of work to be done, including both the regular work and the overtime
work.

7. Click OK to complete the overtime assignment.

If you want to clear an overtime entry, you must enter a *0*. You can't leave
the field empty; it must have a value.

14

For example, in the computer installation example earlier in this lesson, Pat was scheduled for 16 hours of work on the Install Computers task. Remember that this schedule caused a conflict with a meeting on Tuesday, which was resolved by splitting his assignment and letting him complete the installation task after the meeting. However, another option would be to let Pat do the eight hours originally scheduled for Tuesday over the weekend or after hours on Friday (assuming he's a good-natured fellow and is willing). This time would be overtime hours, and Pat's assignment would be finished by the time of the meeting.

 Although you can't edit scheduled overtime hours in Project to put them in the exact time periods when you really plan for them to take place, you can record when they took place after the fact when you're tracking actual progress on the project. See Hour 20, "Tracking Work on the Project."

Figure 14.11 shows the same information that was in Figure 14.7 (where Pat's assignment was split), but with a slightly different display to get ready for adding overtime. I've added a column for Cost, and I've added Overtime Work to the details in the timescale. In the bottom pane, I've changed the details from Resource Schedule to Resource Work because that's where I will schedule the Overtime. In the Cost column, you can see that Pat's assignment costs the project $480 (because Pat's standard rate is $30 per hour). The total cost for the task is $800, which includes the costs for all three assigned resources.

Figure 14.12 shows Pat's assignment changed to include eight hours of overtime. The overtime was entered in the bottom pane in the Ovt. Work field. Notice that the total Work for the assignment is still shown as 16 hours. Total Work includes regular work and overtime work.

Project displays the overtime hours in the timescale on Monday, although Pat can do the work whenever he wants—evenings or on the weekend. Had this assignment still spanned several days, even with the overtime, Project would have distributed the overtime hours over all the days in the duration.

Higher assignment cost   Overtime hours scheduled   Split removed

FIGURE 14.12

By scheduling part of an assignment in overtime, the duration of the task is usually reduced.

Total Work unchanged

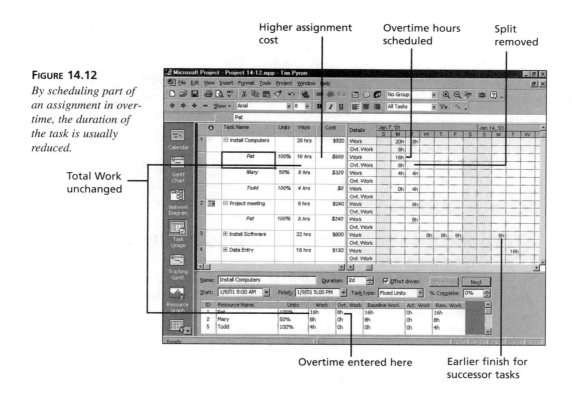

Overtime entered here   Earlier finish for successor tasks

Notice these changes in the schedule as a result of the overtime assignment:

- The cost for Pat's assignment has risen from $480 to $600 because Pat gets more for overtime work than for regular work (see his cost rate table in Figure 14.13).

- The overtime hours enable Pat to complete his assignment before Tuesday. The split that started on Tuesday is no longer needed (there's no more work for Pat to do), so Project has removed the split.

- The successor tasks are now scheduled earlier, and this little project finishes a day earlier than before.

14

FIGURE 14.13

*The Overtime rate for
resources is entered on
the Costs tab of the
Resource Information
form.*

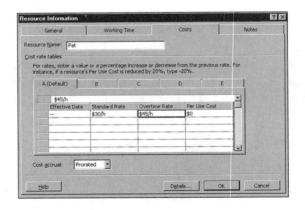

An Alternative to Overtime: Changing the Calendar

Another way of scheduling extra time is to change the resource calendar and increase the
working time that is available for scheduling the resource. You edit the resource calendar
and make these days and hours working times rather than nonworking times. Be aware,
however, that Microsoft Project charges no overtime rate for work done during the regular calendar hours. If you don't pay premium overtime rates, editing the calendar is a
viable option for scheduling overtime. Indeed, by editing the calendar, you can state
explicitly when the extra work time takes place. If you pay premium overtime rates,
however, you should enter overtime hours in the Overtime field so that costing is done at
the overtime rate.

Project will only schedule overtime work for those assignments where you
assigned overtime hours. However, if you attempt to simulate overtime by
changing the resource calendar, Project will use the extra time for any and
all assignments that are due for work when the extra hours become available.

Thus, you can't rely on Project to use the extra working time for a particular
task. You will have to manually edit the timephased data in the Task Usage
or Resource Usage view to assure that only particular assignments are scheduled during the extra time you've created. You will see how to examine a
resource's schedule and reschedule work among competing assignments in
Hour 15.

Understanding the Effects of Changing Task Duration

Recall from Hour 12 that the duration of a task is determined by how long it takes the *driver resources* to complete their assignments. Therefore, the task's finish is tied to the finish of the driver resource assignments. Any resource whose assigned work equals the task duration is a driver resource. When you increase the duration for a task, Project increases the assigned work for all the driver resources, but leaves unchanged the assignments for non-driver resources (those that don't need the full duration of the task to complete their work). When you reduce task duration, Project reduces the assigned work for the driver resources and only reduces the work for non-driver resources if you reduce duration to the point where they can't finish their assigned work.

Summary

This hour has explored the techniques you can use to fine-tune resource assignments to better fit the reality of work in your project. You've learned how to use the Task Usage view to review and edit task assignments. You've dealt with the general case of changing the Flat assignment, the "work straight through at a steady rate until it's finished" type of schedule. You've looked at the special cases of delaying and splitting assignments, as well as the facilities for contouring assignments to meet different work patterns. Finally, you've seen how to use overtime to shorten the regular schedule, thereby shortening the duration of the task.

Q&A

Q I've been playing around with the assigned work in the Task Usage view, but I've returned the schedule to the original values. Yet, the contour indicator is still in the indicator column. How do I get rid of it?

A Apply the Flat contour to the assignment to remove the indicator.

Q I assigned overtime work to a resource and it reduced the duration of the task—but the cost of the task went down! What gives?

A The regular work was charged at the resource's standard rate. The overtime rate was charged at the resource's overtime rate, but you've left the overtime rate zero. Many people do this, especially for salaried employees who aren't paid for overtime. It's certainly misleading as an indicator of how much of the organization's resources are used up by the project. I recommend putting at least the standard rate amount into the overtime rate field for salaried employees; it gives you a better measure of opportunity cost.

14

Q Does Project still consider the non-working days on the resource calendar when calculating a contour?

A Absolutely. The contour is extended around vacation days and holidays.

Exercises

Create a task and assign two resources to it. Then experiment with the following:

1. Use the Task Usage view to modify the assigned hours by editing the timephased data.

2. In the same view introduce a split in one of the assignments.

3. Use the Assignment Information dialog box to change the cost rate table to be used for one of the assignments.

4. With the Task Usage view use the Window, Split command to display the Task Form in the bottom pane. Insert a delay in one of the assignments.

5. Apply one of the predefined contours to one of the assignments.

6. Return both assignments to the flat contour.

HOUR 15

Resolving Resource Allocation Problems

You undoubtedly know what it means to be assigned more work than you can possibly get done in the time allowed. When that happens Microsoft Project would call you an "overallocated resource." When the resources in your project are overallocated you will need to make changes in their assignments or else they won't finish tasks as planned.

In this hour, you will learn:

- How overallocations happen in the schedule
- How to identify which resources are overallocated and when the overallocations occur
- Techniques for eliminating overallocations
- How to use resource leveling

How Do Resource Overallocations Happen?

When you schedule resources to work on tasks in your project, you almost inevitably create some "impossible" resource workloads. Microsoft Project calls it an *overallocation* when a resource is assigned to more work than can be realistically completed.

NEW TERM *Overallocation* is a term that's used to refer to the situation where a resource's assignments for a given time period call for more hours of work than the resource has available to deliver. The resource is said to be *overallocated* during that time period. The situation is created when the sum of the resource units assigned to all tasks during that time period is more than the maximum number of units available for the resource for that time period. The maximum units available for a resource during any time period is defined in the Resource Information dialog box.

How do overallocations occur? Actually, they can happen very easily. When Project schedules assignments, it doesn't normally look to see whether the resource is already assigned to other tasks during the same time period; therefore, Project's default scheduling process can easily double-book or overallocate a resource.

> You can change Project's default to have it check for other assignments each time it schedules a resource and, if necessary, delay a new assignment until the resource is free to work on it. Before you decide to change this default, however, you should read the rest of this hour, especially the last section, "Understanding the Pitfalls of Automatic Leveling."

Because Project normally ignores existing scheduling conflicts when scheduling resources, you can unwittingly (maybe even wittingly) create overallocations as you assign resources:

- You can create multiple assignments that are scheduled during the same time period; if the combined assignments require more work than the resource can possibly do in that time period, the resource is then overallocated. This is by far the most common source of overallocations.

- You can accidentally (or intentionally) assign more than the maximum available units of a resource to a task. Project will let you do that, but it immediately highlights that resource as overallocated.

- You can assign a resource to a task scheduled outside the dates when the resource is available. Again, Project will let you do that, but it highlights the resource as overallocated.

If your project has overallocated resources, it can't realistically unfold as planned. Either some tasks will not finish on time—and the project itself might not meet its deadlines—or some of the tasks will be rushed or not as well executed as expected.

You need to identify overallocations and modify the project plan to eliminate them (in a process called *leveling*). The following sections show you how to identify resource over-allocation problems and how to correct them.

NEW TERM *Leveling* is the process of adjusting the assignments for a resource so as to "level out" the demands for that resource's time. Leveling is necessary when assignments are bunched up and too much work falls in too short a time period, thus creating a "peak" of work that needs to be spread out more evenly (leveled) over a longer period.

Identifying Overallocated Resources

Project uses highlighting to help you identify not only which resources are overallocated, but also to pinpoint the time periods during which overallocations occur. Furthermore, Project displays a special leveling indicator to distinguish serious overallocations that need rescheduling from those that are less serious and that can be resolved by the people doing the work without having to change the project schedule.

A resource is technically overallocated if for even one minute anywhere in the project there are more units assigned than are available for assignment. Some overallocations, however, do not put the project at risk, so it's not worth taking the time to adjust the "official" schedule. In those cases, you can let the people assigned to the task make minor adjustments to the schedule.

For example, suppose Pat is assigned to only two tasks on a particular day, and each task should take about an hour to complete. If, however, both tasks were scheduled for the same time period, say 8:00 a.m., Microsoft Project would highlight Pat's name in red because Pat is technically overallocated. The only way Pat can finish both tasks is to delay one until the other is finished. Whether you consider this delay a serious problem is a judgment call, based largely on the nature of the project and how sensitive you think the success of the project is to delays like this.

If the project is very sensitive to delays and needs to be on schedule hour by hour, you would take Pat's conflicting assignments very seriously and make changes in the schedule to resolve the conflict so that both tasks can be completed on time. On the other hand, if you feel secure so long as the project is on schedule on a day-by-day basis, you could save the effort of tinkering with the project schedule and leave it to Pat to figure out exactly how he will get both tasks finished by the end of the day.

You can define how sensitive your project is to overallocations, whether it must be on schedule minute by minute, hour by hour, day by day, week by week, or month by month. I call this the *leveling sensitivity setting* (although Project refers to it onscreen as the "basis" for leveling calculations and Project's programmers like to call it the leveling "granularity"). Project will alert you when an overallocation exceeds the leveling sensitivity setting you've chosen by displaying an indicator next to the resource name. For example, if you select day by day and a resource is assigned more work than it can finish in a day, Project will flag that resource with the indicator.

To Do: Changing the Leveling Sensitivity Setting

Use the leveling sensitivity setting to control which overallocations are flagged for your attention.

1. Choose Tools, Resource Leveling from the menu to display the Resource Leveling dialog box (see Figure 15.1). We'll spend more time with this dialog box shortly.

FIGURE **15.1**

Select the setting for how sensitive your project is to delays by using the Resource Leveling dialog box.

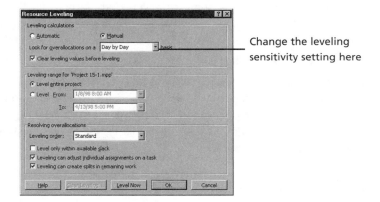

Change the leveling sensitivity setting here

2. Click the Look For Overallocations On A list arrow in the box to the right of the label and select the time period sensitivity.
3. Click the OK button.

If you select the setting Day by Day, for instance, Project will display the leveling indicator next to any resource name that has more work assigned during any one day than can be completed in that amount of time (see Mary in Figure 15.2).

All overallocated resources are highlighted in red; however, only those that exceed the sensitivity setting have the leveling indicator displayed next to the resource name.

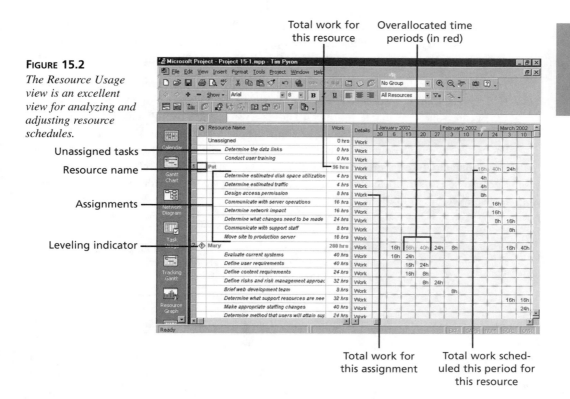

Total work for this resource

Overallocated time periods (in red)

15

FIGURE 15.2
The Resource Usage view is an excellent view for analyzing and adjusting resource schedules.

Unassigned tasks

Resource name

Assignments

Leveling indicator

Total work for this assignment

Total work scheduled this period for this resource

Viewing Overallocated Resources

The Resource Usage view shown in Figure 15.2 is one of the most useful views for finding and assessing resource overallocations. This view displays all the resource names, with each resource's assignments indented under its name. A grid of timephased data under the timescale on the right shows the amount of work scheduled during each time period. In Figure 15.2, the timescale is divided into weeks, and the numbers in the grid represent the total work that is assigned for each week.

  To display the Resource Usage view click the Resource Usage icon on the View Bar or choose View, Resource Usage from the menu.

You can easily identify a resource that is overallocated during one or more time periods because its name will be highlighted in red text. With just a small effort you can also identify the time period(s) when overallocation(s) occur—the number in the grid cell on the row for that resource will also appear in red if the resource is overallocated during the time period spanned by that cell. Although you can't tell it easily in the black-and-white figure, the names for both Pat and Mary in Figure 15.2 are highlighted in red.

The numbers for the work amounts annotated as "Overallocated time periods" in Figure 15.2 are also highlighted in red. Mary is scheduled for 56 hours in the week of January 13. Because she is available for only 40 hours a week, she's overallocated. Pat is scheduled for only 16 hours in the week of February 17, yet that value is also in red. Although Pat can easily do 16 hours of work in a week, it turns out that all 16 hours are scheduled in just one day (see Figure 15.3), and that is too much work to be scheduled in one day. Because he is overallocated at some point during that week, the work value for that week is displayed in red in Figure 15.3

If there's an overallocation at any time during the period spanned by a cell, Project highlights that period's values in red, no matter how far you zoom out to include larger time periods within the cell.

FIGURE 15.3

Pat's daily detail for the week of February 15 shows that all the work falls on one day.

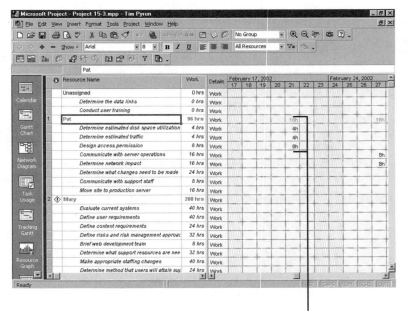

All Pat's work for the week of February 17 is scheduled on one day, February 21

In Figure 15.3, you see the leveling indicator next to Mary's name but not next to Pat's. That's because the leveling sensitivity setting for this project is week by week. Mary has 56 hours scheduled the week of January 13, which is excessive for the leveling sensitivity setting. Pat has no more than 40 hours scheduled in any week, so even though Pat is overallocated on a single day, it's not too much for a week. In that case, the indicator is not displayed.

> You can pause the mouse pointer over a leveling indicator to see a ScreenTip that identifies the leveling sensitivity setting. This is quicker than opening the Leveling dialog box to see how the leveling sensitivity setting is defined.

Finding Overallocations

Use the Go To Next Overallocation tool on the Resource Management toolbar to search through the project for the next date when an overallocation occurs. When an overallocation is found, Project selects the resource name or task name, depending on the type of view you are using. If you're in the Resource Usage view or Task Usage view, then after Project selects the row for the resource or the task, it also selects the cell in the timeline grid on that row for the date when the next overallocation occurs.

In Figure 15.4 I have just used the Go To Next Overallocation tool and Project selected the row for Mary's name on the left and selected her total resource work for January 17 in the grid. The grid entries below identify the conflicting assignments that contribute to the workload on that date and that must be adjusted to resolve the overallocation.

When you use the Go To Next Overallocation tool again, Project selects the next overallocated resource on the currently selected date before moving on to find the next date with an overallocation and selecting each of its overallocated resources in turn. You must scroll the timescale to the start of the project if you want to find all overallocations. I'd suggest you drag the timescale's horizontal scrollbar button all the way to the left to move to the start of the project.

FIGURE 15.4

Identifying the period when an overallocation occurs helps you analyze the source of the problem.

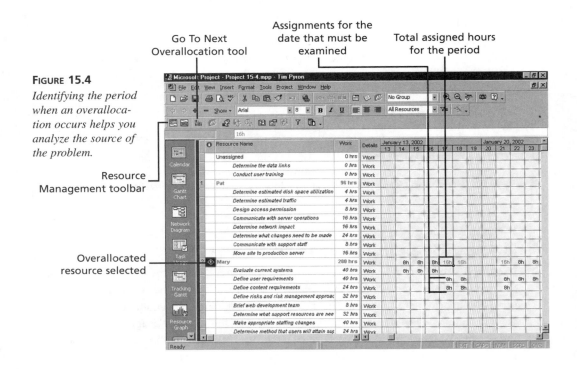

Go To Next Overallocation tool

Assignments for the date that must be examined

Total assigned hours for the period

Resource Management toolbar

Overallocated resource selected

If you want to force Project to stop only at the overallocations for a particular resource, you must put the Resource Usage view in the bottom pane of a split screen with another resource view in the top pane. (You could have the Resource Usage view in both panes.) Select the resource you want to examine in the top pane and that resource and its assignments will be the only rows in the bottom pane. Then activate the bottom pane and use the Go To Next Overallocation tool. Project will select only the dates when that resource is overallocated. However, it selects any overallocation for the resource, not just those that exceed the leveling sensitivity setting.

Eliminating Resource Overallocations

Now that you know how to find overallocations in your project, let's look at ways to correct them. If you want to eliminate an overallocation, you have to edit the project schedule to do either of the following:

- Increase the amount of the resource that's available in the time period when the overallocation occurs

- Reduce the demands for the resource during the time period when the overallocation occurs

You have to identify when the overallocations occur and then either increase the availability of the resource or reduce the assignments for the resource during the period of the overallocation. The next sections offer suggestions for strategies to resolve the overallocations.

Increasing the Resource Availability

If you decide to increase the availability of the resource, you have to negotiate the change with the resource supplier and then enter the changes in the Resource Information dialog box, as you did in Hour 11, "Defining Resources and Costs." I won't repeat those steps here, but let me give you some pointers for gaining access to the Resource Information dialog box while finding overallocations.

To display the Resource Information dialog box, you must be in a view that allows you to display resource data. Of course, any of the resource views (such as the Resource Usage view and the Resource Sheet) offer this access. After selecting a resource name, you can use the Resource Information tool to display the Resource Information dialog box.

If you're in a task view (such as the Gantt Chart or the Task Usage view), you can use the Assign Resources tool to display the Assign Resources dialog box. The resources assigned to the selected task have check marks next to them. You can double-click a resource name to display the Resource Information dialog box for that resource.

Consider the suggestions in the following list for increasing the resource availability:

- The overallocation could be caused by an assignment that is scheduled outside the dates when the resource is available. Note the dates for the assignment and check the General tab of the Resource Information dialog box to see if any part of the assignment falls outside the available dates. If that is the case you can consider negotiating a change in the availability of the resource.
- Also consider the Units available in each time period in the Resource Information dialog box. You may be able to negotiate an increase in units.
- You can increase the hours of work the resource can deliver during the period of the overallocation by changing the working hours on the resource calendar—assuming the resource is willing to work longer hours.

You can also schedule overtime hours if the resource is willing to work more hours during the period of overallocation. However, you can't handle overtime on the Resource Information dialog box. You must display the Task Form with the Work details, as you did in Hour 14, "Editing Resource Assignments," to schedule overtime.

Reducing the Workload of the Overallocated Resource

You can reduce the workload for a resource in an overallocated period in a number of ways. This list summarizes the possibilities:

- You can reduce the total work defined for one or more task assignments during the overallocated period. There could be non-essential work or "frills" included in the task definition that can be removed, or you might have to reluctantly downgrade the quality of the finished task to resolve the overallocation. However, you must consider the effect this "downscaling" will have on the ability to meet the deliverables expected for the project.

- You can reduce the number of tasks assigned to the resource during the period by canceling unnecessary tasks or by reassigning tasks to other resources. Sometimes it helps to break a large task up into several smaller tasks that can be reassigned more easily than one conglomerate task.

- You can shift the workload for one or more assignments to other periods by delaying the start of one or more tasks or by changing the assignment's contour to shift work to later time periods for those tasks. Of course, delaying any of the assigned work in the project schedule naturally extends the duration for the task and could compromise finishing the project on time.

Reducing Workload with the Resource Allocation View

The Resource Allocation view was specially designed for reassigning and delaying tasks. You can display the Resource Allocation view by displaying the Resource Management toolbar and clicking the Resource Allocation tool. You can also display the view from the menu by choosing View, More Views, selecting Resource Allocation from the Views list, and clicking the Apply button to display the view.

This composite view shows the names and task assignments of all resources in the top pane (see Figure 15.5), highlights overallocated resources in red, and displays the leveling indicator for those resources that need your attention. When you select a resource in the top pane, all the tasks assigned to that resource appear in the Leveling Gantt in the bottom pane. The Leveling Gantt has a specially formatted Gantt Chart that will be particularly helpful when we discuss delaying resource assignments.

Selected resource   Resource Usage view

FIGURE 15.5

The Resource Allocation view is designed specifically for dealing with resource allocation problems.

Assignments

Tasks assigned to selected resource

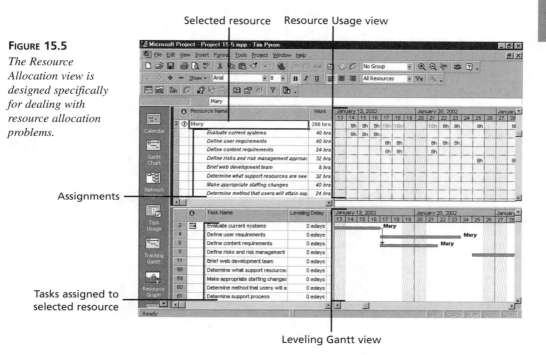

Leveling Gantt view

You can use the Go To Next Overallocation tool in either pane of this view to pinpoint overallocated resource assignments. In the top pane, a resource view, the Go To Next Overallocation tool identifies *resources* that are overallocated. If you activate the lower pane, a task view, the tool is limited to finding overallocations for the resource you have selected in the top pane, and it selects successive *tasks* associated with an overallocation.

If you want to remove an assignment from a resource without assigning another resource in its place, you can simply select the assignment and choose Edit, Delete Assignment (or press the Delete key). The assignment will disappear from under the resource and reappear in the Unassigned category at the top of the Resource Usage view. You can assign the task to another resource later.

If you want to redefine aspects of a task, select the overallocated resource in the top pane, and then select the task in the bottom pane. Either double-click the task or use the Task Information tool to display the Task Information dialog box, where you can adjust variables such as the task duration, task type, constraints, and so on.

Reassigning Tasks

 One of the most successful methods for dealing with the problem of overallocated resources is to reassign tasks to other, underutilized resources. In Figure 15.6, Mary is the overallocated resource selected in the top pane of the Resource Allocation view. I used the Hide Subtasks tool to hide the assignment rows for the other resources so I could see at a glance the time periods in which each of them are available for additional assignments.

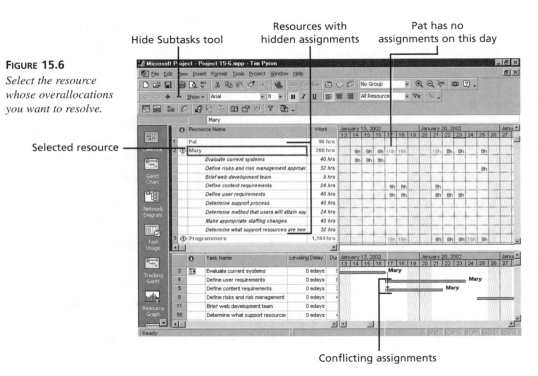

FIGURE 15.6

Select the resource whose overallocations you want to resolve.

To Do: Reassigning Tasks for Overallocated Resources

Use the Resource Allocation view to substitute underutilized resources for overallocated resources.

1. Display the Resource Allocation view and select the overallocated resource in the top pane.

2. Activate the bottom pane by clicking anywhere in the pane.

3. Go to the start of the project by clicking anywhere in the grid and pressing the Home key.

▼ 4. Use the Go To Next Overallocation tool (with the bottom pane activated) to find the next time period when the selected resource is overallocated.

5. Decide which task will be reassigned to another resource and select that task in the lower pane.

6. Click the Assign Resources tool to display the Assign Resources dialog box (see Figure 15.7).

15

Assign Resources dialog box with assigned resource selected

FIGURE 15.7

Use the Assign Resources dialog box to change the resource assignments.

Replace button

Task to be reassigned

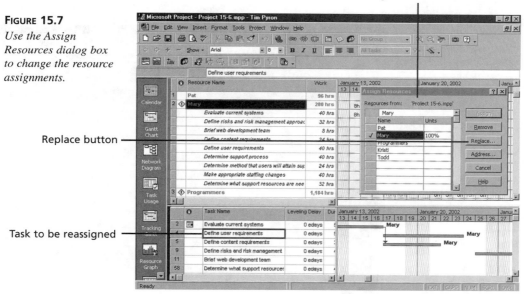

7. Select the resource you want to replace (the assigned resources are checked), and click the Replace button to display the Replace Resource dialog box (see Figure 15.8).

FIGURE 15.8

Select the replacement resource in the Replace Resource dialog box.

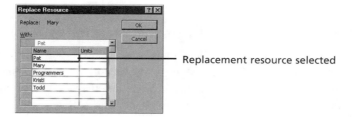

Replacement resource selected

▼   8. Select the name of the resource that you want to assign as a substitute.

9. Change the Units assigned for the new resource, if desired.

▲   10. Click OK to complete the substitution.

In this example, I reassigned the task Determine User Requirements to Pat, which reduces Mary's assignments for the day of January 17 to just eight hours (see Figure 15.9). After changing the assignment, the task disappears from Mary's list of assignments and can be seen in Pat's list.

Mary's workload down to eight hours for the day

FIGURE 15.9

The reassigned task now appears in Pat's list of things to do.

Task now assigned to Pat

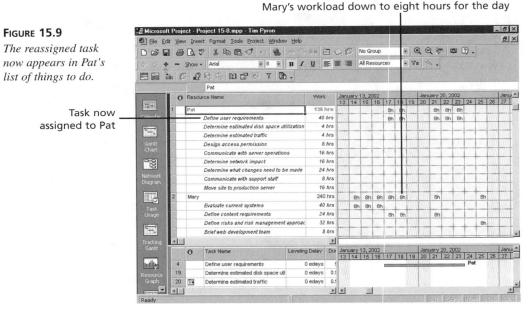

Substituting resource assignments is often the most effective solution for resolving resource overallocations. The drawback is the time it takes to analyze the situation and reach a decision.

Using Delays to Level Out the Workload

If you can't resolve an overallocation by increasing resource availability or removing assignments, you need to spread the assigned work out over a longer period so that the resource can finish its assigned tasks. Spreading the work out requires that some of the bunched-up assignments be shifted to later or earlier dates.

In a project that is scheduled from a fixed start date, all tasks are scheduled as close to the start date as possible. When you attempt to level out the workload in these projects, you can shift assignments only by delaying them to later time periods. A special task field, called the Leveling Delay field, is used to record the amount of the delay for leveling purposes.

NEW TERM Delaying some assignments to later dates could mean that successor tasks are also delayed—indeed, it might mean you can't finish the project when originally planned. The amount of time you can delay a task without affecting the project finish date is called *total slack time* (or sometimes just *slack time*). The amount of time you can delay a task without affecting any other task's schedule is called *free slack*. If there is free slack, there has to be total slack. If you want to resolve an overallocation by delaying assignments, you cause the least disturbance to the schedules of other tasks (and to the finish date of the project) if you delay tasks that have free slack. If you can't find tasks with free slack to delay, you can at least avoid delaying the project's finish if you choose tasks that have total slack.

The Resource Allocation view includes the Leveling Delay field as a column in the table of the Leveling Gantt chart in the bottom pane (see Figure 15.10). The bars in the timeline area are customized to show the amount of free slack as a thin line extending to the right of the task bar and the amount of the leveling delay as a thin line on the left of the task bar (drawn from the original start date for the task to the delayed start date).

Red highlight shows overallocation

FIGURE 15.10

The Leveling Gantt is designed to help manage task delays when leveling assignments.

Three overlapping tasks

Leveling Delay field

Free slack task bar

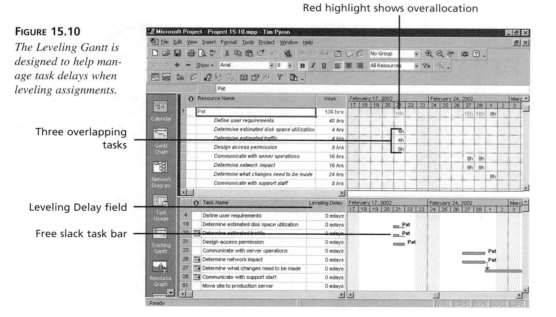

If you let the tip of the pointer rest over the free slack bar or the delay bar, a ScreenTip will identify the name of the bar for you.

The Leveling Delay field uses time amounts the way people use them in everyday conversation: a day is 24 hours and a week is seven days. This measurement is called *elapsed duration* in Microsoft Project. Elapsed duration time is continuous time; unlike the standard measure of *duration*, it makes no distinction between working and non-working time, nor is it governed by your definition of "day" and "week" in the Tools, Options dialog box.

NEW TERM   *Elapsed duration* is Project's name for the standard measures of time used by people in normal conversation: One day is 24 hours and one week is 7 days. Elapsed duration is entered with an *e* before the time unit. For example, "2 edays" is two elapsed days, which is equivalent to 48 hours..

In Figure 15.10, Pat has three tasks scheduled at the same time on February 21 that produce an overallocation on that date. The first two tasks have some free slack as evidenced by the slack bar to the right of their task bars. If the second task is delayed until the first is finished (a four-hour delay), and the third is delayed by one day, the overallocation will be resolved. The delays are shown in Figure 15.11, where the second conflicting task is delayed by four elapsed hours (4 ehrs) and the third by one elapsed day (1 eday). The task bars are shifted to the right for the delayed tasks, as shown by the delay bar that replaces the original task bar. The free slack is now gone for the first two tasks.

FIGURE 15.11

Delaying the Determine Estimated Traffic and Design Access Permission tasks removes the overallocation for Pat on February 21.

Red highlight gone

Delay value (in elapsed duration)

Delay bar

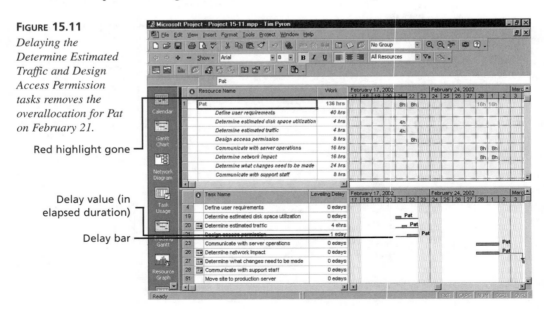

To Do: Entering Leveling Delays for Tasks

If a resource is overallocated, you can delay one or more of its assigned tasks to relieve the overallocation.

1. Display the Resource Allocation view by clicking the Resource Allocation tool on the Resource Management toolbar.

2. Select the overallocated resource in the top pane. Its assignments will appear in the bottom pane.

3. Activate the bottom pane use the Go To Next Overallocation tool to find the next overallocation. Project will select the first of the conflicting assignments and will scroll the timescale to the period of the overallocation.

4. Determine which of the conflicting assignments will be delayed. Estimate the length of time for the delay by examining the duration of the task that is not to be delayed. The task Duration field is to the right of the Leveling Delay field in the table. Scroll to the right to see the duration of the task that must finish before the task to be delayed can start.

5. Enter the duration of the delay in the Leveling Delay field. If you do not use an "e" in the time unit, Project will supply one for you. For example, to enter a delay of 2 days you could enter **2d**; Project would display 2 edays when you press Enter. If the overallocation persists, you might have to experiment with the length of the delay.

You can use Undo (Ctrl+Z) immediately after entering a delay amount to restore the previous value to the delay field, and you can remove a delay by entering a zero in the delay field. Note that you can't delete a delay value and then leave the entry blank.

When tasks have multiple resources assigned to them, and only one of the resources is overallocated, it might be better to resolve the overallocation by delaying the assignment for just that resource, leaving the other resources unchanged. This would be especially helpful when the task has no slack but the overallocated resource's assignment is shorter than the task duration. The assignment would then have some slack even though the task does not.

To add a leveling delay for an assignment, you would need to add the Leveling Delay field to the table in the Resource Usage view in the top pane. (The Leveling Delay field in the bottom pane only affects tasks because that view only displays tasks.) Then you can enter leveling delays for individual assignments in the top pane. Strangely, although Project uses elapsed duration for task leveling delays it does *not* use elapsed duration for *assignment* leveling delays.

15

▼ To Do

▲

To Do: Adding the Leveling Delay Field to the Resource Usage View

▼ To Do

Add the Leveling Delay field to the Usage table in the Resource Usage view if you want to delay individual assignments instead of tasks and all their assignments.

1. Display the Resource Usage view.
2. Right-click the Work title cell above the Work column.
3. Choose Insert Column to display the Column Definition dialog box.
4. Select the Leveling Delay field.

▲ 5. Click the Best Fit tool to adjust the column width to the title.

In Figure 15.12 you can see the Leveling Delay field added to the Usage table in the top pane. I've removed the delays for the tasks in the bottom pane and entered delays for the assignments in the top pane instead.

FIGURE 15.12

Use the Leveling Delay field in the Resource Usage view if you want to delay individual assignments instead of tasks.

Leveling Delay for Pat's assignments

Task delays are zero

Leveling Delay field

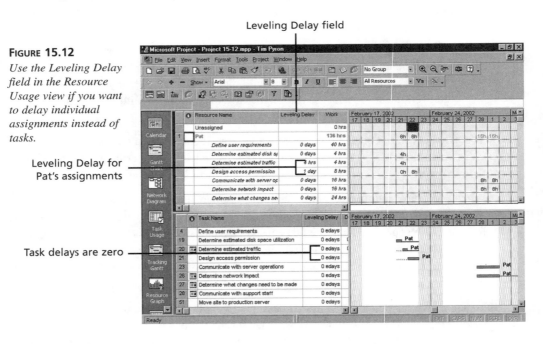

Using a Delay in Projects With Fixed Finish Dates

15

In a project that is scheduled from a fixed finish date, the tasks are already scheduled as late as possible. The only way to shift assignments to level out the workload is to schedule some assignments earlier than originally planned (because finishing any later would run into the fixed finish date). Idle time is inserted at the end of a task or assignment and has the effect of forcing the task to start and finish earlier than originally scheduled.

You use the same Leveling Delay field to record the idle time, or delay amount, as you do for projects with fixed start dates. However, you can enter only negative numbers in the field when the project is scheduled from a fixed finish date. When added to the original finish date, the negative numbers cause the dates to become earlier dates.

In a fixed finish date project, delaying tasks (moving them to earlier dates) forces predecessors to start earlier and could force the project start date to be moved to an earlier date. Slack, in these projects, is the amount of time a task can be shifted to earlier dates without changing the project *start* date (total slack). Project does not calculate free slack in projects with fixed finish dates.

> Although you can use the Resource Allocation view with projects that have fixed finish dates, the custom bars that show the amount of the leveling delay and free slack in the Leveling Gantt are incorrect. They were designed for projects with fixed start dates, so they aren't accurate for fixed finish date projects. You could design new bar styles for a project with a fixed finish date, but that's beyond the scope of this book.

Splitting Tasks and Assignments to Resolve Overallocations

Recall from Hour 4, "Starting the Scheduling Process," that you can split a task into disconnected time periods, which is sometimes a helpful technique for resolving overallocations. You could split a long task around a shorter task that has a date constraint or a higher priority for being completed as scheduled. If some of the work has already been finished on a task that is competing for an overallocated resource, you can split the task to reschedule the remaining work at a later time.

You can split assignments in the top pane of the Resource Allocation view by inserting zero work cells in the timephased data. You can split tasks in the bottom pane by using the Split Task tool on the Standard toolbar to split the task bar.

Letting Project Level Overallocated Assignments

Instead of manually leveling overallocations as described in the previous sections, you can take the easy route and let Project do the work for you. However, Project can resolve overallocations only by calculating delays—it can't increase resource availability on its own, or adjust the work content of tasks, or substitute one resource for another. It can simply do a mathematical trick and calculate delays in tasks or assignments as a substitute for the more intelligent methods. You will almost always produce a better schedule if you level assignments manually.

> For more of my prejudicial opinions about the Level Now command, see "Understanding the Pitfalls of Automatic Leveling" later in this hour.

If you want to use the automated leveling feature you must use the Tools, Resource Leveling command to display the Resource Leveling dialog box where you can set options that affect how the command works and also execute the command with the Level Now tool.

If the project is scheduled from a fixed start date, Project adds *positive delays* to tasks to remove overallocations. If the project is scheduled from a fixed finish date, Project adds *negative delays* to tasks to remove overallocations.

Using the Level Now Command

Use the Tools, Resource Leveling menu command to display the Resource Leveling dialog box, shown in Figure 15.13. The Level Now tool executes the command that causes Project to calculate delays and splits that may be able to resolve the resource overallocations in your project. The Level Now command can also calculate delays and splits at the individual assignment level instead of at the task level, if you so choose.

> The Level Now command changes only those assignments that have triggered the leveling indicator.

FIGURE 15.13

The Resource Leveling dialog box governs leveling operations.

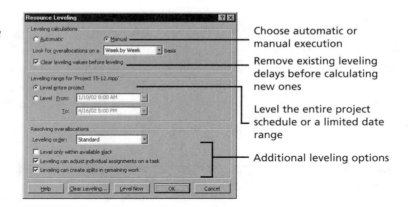

Choose automatic or manual execution

Remove existing leveling delays before calculating new ones

Level the entire project schedule or a limited date range

Additional leveling options

The settings in this dialog box govern how Project proceeds in calculating resource leveling delays:

- Select the Automatic option if you want Project to level tasks the moment one or more overallocated resources are detected. Automatic leveling takes place as you enter the tasks into the project. See the section "Understanding the Pitfalls of Automatic Leveling" before choosing this option.

  Select Manual if you want leveling to be executed only when you use the Level Now command. Manual is the default status for leveling.

- As you've already seen, the entry in the Look For Overallocations On A box determines the sensitivity of leveling calculations. If the setting is Month by Month and a resource is overallocated only on a Day by Day basis, Project doesn't level that resource's assignments or display the leveling indicator for it.

- Select the Level Entire Project option to have Microsoft Project search for overallocations from the beginning to the end of the project.

  Fill in dates in the Level From and To boxes if you want to limit the date range that Project scans for overallocations to be corrected.

- The Leveling Order option lets you vary the way Project chooses among conflicting tasks to decide which tasks will be delayed and which will remain with its original schedule. We don't have time to explore those options in detail in this book, however.

For more complete coverage of the topic, refer to my more comprehensive book, *Special Edition Using Microsoft Project 2000*, published by Que Corporation.

NEW FEATURE If you would like to control the priority of tasks to keep high priority task from being delayed in a leveling operation, change this setting to Priority, Standard. You can assign a high priority for individual tasks in the Priority field on the Task Information dialog box to keep them from being delayed during leveling (see Figure 15.14). Enter a value in this field from 1 (making the task most likely to be delayed) to 999 (making the task the last choice for being delayed). To keep the task from ever being delayed by the Level Now command, enter a priority of 1000 (the highest possible value).

FIGURE 15.14

Use the Task Information dialog box to assign tasks a high priority so they are not delayed in leveling operations.

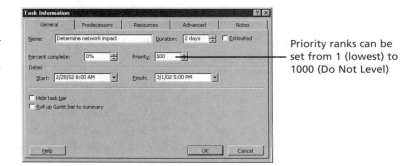

Priority ranks can be set from 1 (lowest) to 1000 (Do Not Level)

- Fill the Level Only Within Available Slack check box if you want Project to avoid delaying any task that would delay the project's finish date (or move the project's start to an earlier date for fixed finish date projects). With this constraint, the leveling operation might not resolve the overallocation problem. If you clear this box, and no task constraints exist to serve as impediments, Project can resolve the resource overallocation through leveling, although usually with a delay in the project's finish date.

- Fill the Leveling Can Adjust Individual Assignments on a Task check box so that Project can delay individual assignments instead of entire tasks, thus allowing some assignments to start on time even though one or more have to be delayed for leveling purposes.

- Fill the Leveling Can Create Splits in Remaining Work check box so that Project can split tasks and assignments around other tasks that have constraints or higher priorities.

- Click the Level Now button to manually start Project's leveling calculations.

- Click the Clear Leveling button to have Project reset to zero the delays it added to tasks and assignments in the last leveling calculations. This tool is only active if the active view is a task view; in other words, you must be in a task view to execute the Clear Leveling command.

15

If you select the Level Now command when a task view is active the leveling occurs immediately, without any prompts. If you select the command when a resource view is active, you will get the Level Now dialog box (see Figure 15.15), where you can restrict the changes to delaying only those tasks that are assigned to the resources you have selected.

FIGURE 15.15

You can level assignments for all overallocated resources or for just those you have selected.

If you choose the Selected Resources option, only the overallocations for the resources in the selection are reviewed for leveling operations. If you select Entire Pool, all resources and all tasks are reviewed.

When you click OK, Project tries to resolve the resource overallocations by delaying tasks or assignments. Before any delays are calculated, however, Project captures a copy of the originally scheduled start and finish for all tasks. These "preleveling" dates are used to display the Preleveled Task Bar in the Leveling Gantt Chart (see Figure 15.16). Then the delay values are calculated and applied.

FIGURE 15.16

After the Level Now command has changed the schedule, the Leveling Gantt displays preleveled task bars for comparing the original schedule with the delayed schedule.

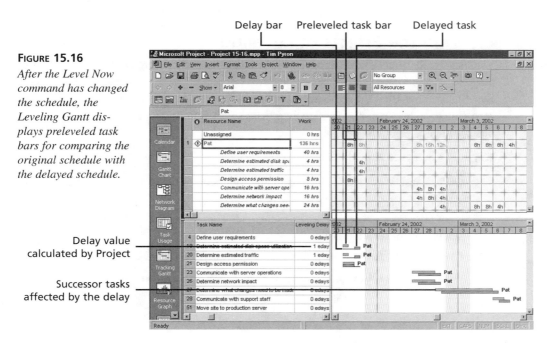

In Figure 15.16, you see the result of the automatic leveling operation for the resource Pat. Two delayed tasks are seen in this time frame. Note the new *preleveled bars* above the newly calculated *scheduled bars* for all tasks. Comparing preleveled bars with the new task bars shows which tasks were affected by the leveling operation.

If Project finds that it can't resolve one or more overallocations when you execute the Level Now command, you will see an alert similar to the one shown in Figure 15.17.

FIGURE 15.17

Sometimes Project can't resolve all over-allocations and displays this alert.

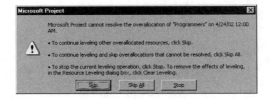

To respond to this alert, do one of the following:

- Click Skip to have Microsoft Project skip this overallocation and continue looking for other overallocations.
- Click Skip All to have Project skip this overallocation and all others that can't be resolved without displaying any more alert messages.
- Click Stop to stop the leveling process. Any delays already calculated will be left in place. See the next section for ways to clear the calculated delays.

Clearing the Effects of Leveling

You can use the Edit, Undo command immediately after executing the Level Now command to undo all delay entries created by the command. You can also use the Clear Leveling command on the Resource Leveling dialog box to reset leveling delay values to zero. You can choose to reset all leveling delays or just those from selected tasks. To use this command, you must be in a task view.

To remove delays, follow these steps:

1. Make a task view active, such as the bottom pane of the Resource Allocation view.
2. Select the task(s) for which you want to reset the delay to zero (unless you want to reset all tasks). Click and drag to select adjacent tasks. Press Ctrl while clicking to select nonconsecutive tasks.
3. Choose Tools, Resource Leveling to display the Resource Leveling dialog box.
4. Click Clear Leveling. The Clear Leveling dialog box appears (see Figure 15.18).

15

FIGURE 15.18

You can quickly remove all leveling delays from the entire project or from selected tasks with the Clear Leveling command.

5. Select Selected Tasks to change the values for only the tasks you selected. If you want to remove all delay values for all tasks, select Entire Project.

6. Click OK. The delay values will be reset to zero.

Understanding the Pitfalls of Automatic Leveling

The first option on the Resource Leveling dialog box is Automatic Leveling (see Figure 15.13). If you select this option, Microsoft Project watches for resource overallocations *as* you assign resources and as the project schedule changes. The moment Project detects an overallocation, it quietly attempts to resolve it by delaying tasks in the background as you go on building the schedule. This seems like a powerful and useful option, but it has definite drawbacks.

If you use Automatic Leveling, you won't be aware of the leveling decisions going on in the background. Had you seen a leveling indicator, you might well have chosen an alternative (such as substituting resources or increasing resource availability) that doesn't require delaying tasks—which usually also delays the finish of the project. It's not uncommon to wind up with a bloated schedule that has lots of unproductive time because of all the leveling delays.

Most important, *you* are a far better judge of the best choices for changing your schedule. You can't give Microsoft Project all the information you bring to the decision-making process as you make scheduling choices.

You should also note that Project doesn't optimize the leveling strategy. The program doesn't examine all possible combinations of task delays to choose the best solution in terms of lowest cost, earliest project finish date, or any other consideration. So listen to Uncle Tim and Just Say No to automatic leveling.

Summary

In this hour, you've seen how to identify and correct overallocated resources. You've been introduced to the Resource Allocation view and the Go To Next Overallocation tool. You now know techniques for resolving resource overallocations manually as well as how to let Microsoft Project do the work through delaying tasks and assignments.

Q&A

Q In the Resource Allocation view, the list of assignments in the top pane under a resource name is not in the same order as the list in the bottom pane, and it makes it hard to find the task in the bottom pane. How can I get them in the same order?

A Activate the top pane and choose Project, Sort, By ID to have Project sort the top pane by ID number. The lists should then be in sync. If not, activate the bottom pane and sort it by ID also.

Q I used the Level Now command, but there are still overallocated resources, even though Project didn't give me any alerts saying it was unable to resolve an overallocation.

A The Level Now command tackles only overallocations that trigger the leveling indicator. So if your project has the leveling sensitivity setting Week by Week, for example, there might still be resources that are overallocated on an Hour by Hour or Day by Day basis.

Q I entered a leveling delay for a task in the Leveling Gantt view, but Project doesn't show the preleveled task bar for the task.

A The preleveled task bar is based on the fields Preleveled Start and Preleveled Finish. These fields are calculated only when you use the Level Now command.

Q I tried to increase a resource's availability by changing working hours with the Tools, Change Working Time command. I found the Change Working Time command grayed out. What gives?

A The Change Working Time command is unavailable if the bottom pane of a combination view is active. As an alternative, display the Assign Resources dialog box and double-click on the resource name you want to work with. The Resource Information dialog box will appear, and you can use the Working Time tab to adjust the hours.

Exercises

1. Find one of your projects that has overallocated resources by viewing the Resource Sheet or Resource Allocation view.

2. Use the Resource Allocation view with that project and search for the overallocations with the Go To Next Overallocation tool.

3. Reassign conflicting assignments to other resources using the Assign Resources dialog box.

4. Manually enter Leveling Delays in the bottom pane to resolve an overallocation.

5. Use the Level Now command on the entire project.

6. Clear all leveling delays with the Clear Leveling command.

15

PART V

Finalizing and Publishing Your Plan

Hour

Hour 16

Fine-Tuning the Project Plan

After you have defined and entered your tasks and resources into a project plan, you might start to feel overwhelmed by all the details displayed in Project's different views. Project is certainly a tool for dealing with minutiae. However, Project also gives you the ability to step back from the project and view the information so that you can see the big picture and evaluate the plan's effectiveness.

In this hour, you learn to display a summary of the important statistics of a project, such as the start and finish dates. You also learn to use filters that allow you to view a selected subset of the project's tasks or resources and how to apply a new grouping feature that lets you organize and summarize information in certain views. You will look at identifying the critical path for your project and working with strategies that help you reduce the project's duration. Finally, you learn how to review the cost schedule and find ways to reduce the project costs.

In this hour, you will learn techniques that help you focus on the overall quality of your project, including:

- Displaying a summary of important project statistics
- Applying filters and concentrating on specific tasks or resources
- Creating and applying a group structure to summarize task and resource information
- Reviewing the cost schedule for the project
- Revising your plan to meet established goals by applying accepted Project Management strategies

Looking at the Big Picture

As you have worked through the previous hours in this book, you probably realize that one of Project's greatest strengths is its capability to provide every detail of your project plan. The different views of Project allow you to focus on the project's details in different formats.

Sometimes, however, after you've defined your tasks, determined durations and constraints, created dependency relationships, and assigned your resources, you might want to broaden your view of the plan to see how all the parts fit together. Several tools are available that can help you take a look at the plan's big picture. These tools include compressing the timescale, collapsing the task list, filtering, grouping, and reviewing the cost schedule. You will work with each of these tools this hour.

Recall from earlier hours some important Project definitions:

- *Duration* is the calendar time period required to complete a particular task.
- *Tasks* are linked by dependencies. For instance, one task must be completed for the next task to begin. The second task is dependent on the first.
- A *constraint* is a restriction on the start or finish date of a task. You can specify that a task start on a particular date or finish no later than a certain date, for example. The task is said to be *constrained*.

You can view an overall statistical summary of the Project by opening the Project Statistics dialog box. The information in this dialog box is calculated from the values found in your Project. This summary will only be as up-to-date as the information found in your plan.

To Do: Opening the Project Statistics Dialog Box

To view overall project statistics in a single dialog box, follow these steps:

1. Right-click on any of the currently displayed toolbars. On the toolbar menu, select the Tracking toolbar.

2. On the Tracking toolbar, click the Project Statistics button.

3. The Project Statistics dialog box opens and gives you a statistical summary of the current project, as shown in Figure 16.1.

16

FIGURE 16.1

The Project Statistics dialog box gives you a summary of your project's schedule, work, and cost information.

Project Statistics for 'New Product Hour 16.MPP'		

	Start	Finish
Current	11/26/00	4/16/01
Baseline	11/26/00	4/18/01
Actual	11/26/00	NA
Variance	0d	-2d

	Duration	Work	Cost
Current	101d	2,772h	$48,553.38
Baseline	103d	2,612h	$0.00
Actual	25.51d	844h	$11,368.46
Remaining	75.49d	1,928h	$37,184.92

Percent complete:
Duration: 25%   Work: 30%

[Close]

> The Project Statistics dialog box is also available by selecting Project, Project Information and clicking the Statistics button.

The Project Statistics dialog box provides several different summary details. The following list describes the information given in this dialog box:

- The top of the Project Statistics dialog box shows the current start and finish dates. A row is also provided for baseline dates if a baseline was set when the project plan was first designed. The Actual row gives you a start and finish date if the project has started and has been completed (this would be calculated from tracking information you enter). A Variance row is also provided for the start and finish dates to display the variance between the baseline dates and the scheduled dates.

- **NEW TERM** The *baseline* for a project represents your expectations for the project and the completion of its tasks. *Baseline dates* include projected start and finish dates for tasks and the project itself. See Hour 20, "Tracking Work on the Project," for information on how to set a baseline for the various aspects of the project.

- A second area in the dialog box lists summary information on the duration of the project, the work (in hours) completed on the project, and the cost of the project. A row is devoted to the Current data (duration, work, cost), Baseline data, Actual data, and Remaining data.

- A third area in the dialog box is reserved for information about the percentage of the project that has been completed. The Percent Complete section displays both the percentage of the duration and the work that has been completed.

Obviously, the statistics in the Project Statistics dialog box are dynamic in nature, meaning that the information given (except for the baseline information) changes each time you update the data in the Project file. You will find that it makes sense to periodically view the project summary statistics in this dialog box to get an overall feel for how your project is progressing.

> There is no direct way to print the Project Statistics dialog box contents. But you can print a supplied report containing the same information and more. Select View, Reports, and choose the Overview category. Select the Project Summary report, preview it, and then print it. This report, and other Overview category reports, are discussed in more detail in Hour 10, "Finalizing and Printing Your Schedule."

Compressing the Timescale

Another strategy for broadening your view of the project details is to compress the timescale on the Gantt Chart, which gives you a good overview of the project's workflow. The default Major timescale for the Gantt Chart is weeks and the Minor timescale is days. By compressing the timescales, you can effectively zoom out from the project details. For instance, you might want to change the Major scale to months and the Minor scale to weeks to get a much broader view of the bars and other information in the Gantt Chart. The simplest way to change the timescales is to use the Zoom Out and Zoom In buttons on the Standard toolbar.

To Do: Compressing the Timescale for the Gantt Chart

To change the timescale units on the Gantt Chart, do the following:

1. In the Gantt Chart view, click the Zoom Out button on the Standard toolbar.
2. Each click of the Zoom Out button selects a larger set of time units for both the Major and Minor scales.

3. To decrease the time units on the scales, click the Zoom In button on the Standard toolbar.

Using the Zoom Out and Zoom In buttons can vary the detail (and scope) of your view of the task bars in the Gantt Chart. Project also gives you a way to zoom out and view the entire project. Choose View, Zoom to open the Zoom dialog box (see Figure 16.2).

FIGURE 16.2

Zoom out to see the entire project with the Zoom dialog box.

16

The Zoom dialog box has a number of standard timescale zoom settings and a custom setting drop-down box. To zoom out to see the entire project, select the Entire Project radio button, and then click OK. You can then see your entire project in the Gantt Chart.

After you have finished viewing your project at a particular zoom setting, you can reset the view (return to the default timescale settings) by reopening the Zoom dialog box with the View, Zoom menu choice. In the Zoom dialog box, click Reset and then OK to return to the Gantt Chart.

> You can make additional changes to the timescale by choosing Format, Timescale. The Timescale dialog box is discussed in Hour 9, "Formatting Views."

Collapsing the Task List Outline

Another way to step back from the project details and get an overview of the items in your project is to collapse the task list outline. This can be done in any view that displays your tasks in a list table, and it's an excellent way to hide the subtasks in a project and just view the first few levels of summary tasks in the outline.

To Do: Collapsing the Task List Outline

▲ To Do

To quickly collapse a task list down to specific outline levels, do the following:

1. Display a view containing a task list, such as the Gantt Chart.

2. Click the Show drop-down arrow on the Formatting toolbar (see Figure 16.3).

3. Select an outline level to view.

   The Outline Level 1 option will show the tasks that are leftmost in the outline. Outline Level 2 will show the Level 1 tasks plus all tasks indented one position. Level 3 will show the Level 1 tasks plus 2 indentation positions, and so on.

4. To display all subtasks again, click the Show drop-down arrow and choose All Subtasks.

FIGURE 16.3

The Show button on the Formatting toolbar allows you to collapse the tasks outline.

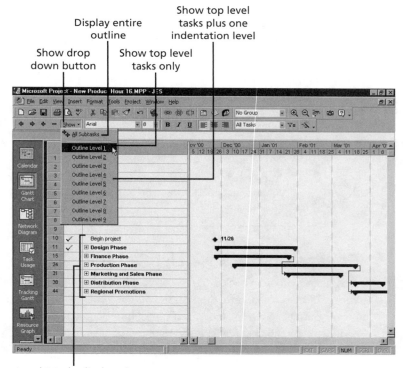

▼ As you've been learning, an obvious overall strategy for obtaining overview information in your project is to move from very specific information to a more general view by, for example, zooming out on the Gantt Chart or collapsing the task list outline. Another approach to reducing the clutter on your screen is to look at specific portions of the information displayed by the different views of your project. The next section deals with filtering tasks and resources, which gives you a subset of the information in a particular view.

16

> Collapsing the task list outline and zooming out on the Gantt Chart timescale provide you with two overviews, text and graphics, of the same information.

▲

Filtering Tasks or Resources

You can cut down on information overload by temporarily hiding tasks or resources you're not interested in at the moment. By applying filters to a list, only the rows that meet certain criteria will be displayed. So, another strategy for focusing your attention, and fine-tuning your plan more efficiently, is to filter the information so that you can view a subset of the tasks or resources in a list.

New Term *Filtering* simply means that you set certain conditions so that only those tasks or resources meeting those conditions are displayed. For example, to reduce the tasks shown in a list, you could create a filter that shows only the milestone tasks.

You can also create filters that *highlight*, with special formatting, the items meeting the conditions in the filter, but which still display the entire list of tasks or resources. You have two options for using filters: You can use Project's predefined filters or create your own custom filters. The fastest way to filter information is through Project's AutoFilters.

Using AutoFilters

AutoFilters are the quickest way to view subsets of your tasks or resources. You can apply an AutoFilter to any Microsoft Project view that contains a list of tasks or resources. The AutoFilter feature is not available for views such as the Network Diagram and the Calendar view, but regular filters can be applied to views such as these that do not contain columns or lists.

To Do: Filtering a List Using an AutoFilter

To quickly filter a task or resource list on-screen, do the following:

1. Display a view containing a list, such as the Gantt Chart or the Resource Sheet view.

2. Choose Project, Filtered For, AutoFilter. A drop-down arrow will appear next to each column heading (as shown in Figure 16.4).

 You can also invoke the AutoFilter command by clicking the AutoFilter button on the Formatting toolbar.

3. Click on one of the AutoFilter drop-down arrows to view the criteria options for that column. The drop-down list contains an entry for every value in that column.

   Lists for certain field types will also contain special filter conditions that are appropriate for the field type. For example, a date field may contain filter tests for dates within the next week or month. A Duration field may include a test for tasks with durations longer than one week.

4. Click the drop-down arrow for a heading and select a filter condition. As soon as you select the filter condition, the table is filtered, showing you only a subset of the information in the list. The column heading and filter drop-down arrow will turn blue in the column that now has a filter applied.

5. You can filter by more than one condition. To include additional conditions in the filter, use the drop-down lists for other column headings. For example, you might want to filter the list by start date (tasks that start within the next month) and Resource Names (tasks assigned to a resource on the list). Both column conditions must be met for a list item to still appear on the screen.

6. To move a filter from a single column, click the AutoFilter drop-down arrow for the column and choose (All).

7. To turn off AutoFiltering and once again see all items on the list, select Project, Filtered For, and click AutoFilter to turn the feature off.

AutoFiltering gives you a fast and fairly flexible method for filtering list data. Another possibility for filtering the information in your list is to use the predefined, standard filters that Project provides.

Duration filtered
for tasks lasting
more than a week

Filter drop down
list arrow

AutoFilter
toolbar button

FIGURE 16.4

*AutoFilter allows you
to quickly choose a
condition or set of con-
ditions by which to fil-
ter your list.*

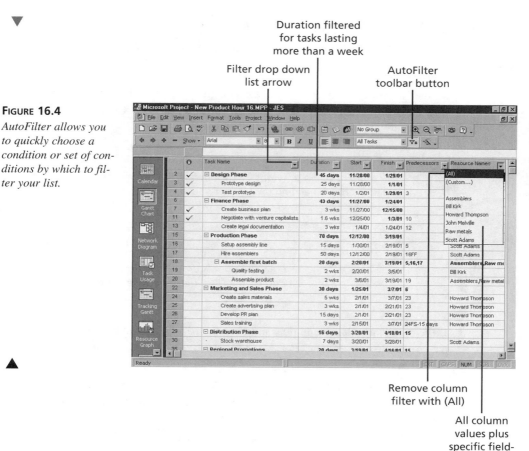

16

Remove column
filter with (All)

All column
values plus
specific field-
type choices

Using the Standard Filters

Project has several standard filters you can use to show only a few items in your list. You can, for example, filter by critical tasks, milestone tasks, summary tasks, incomplete tasks, and tasks that use a particular resource.

The More Filters dialog box shows a complete list of supplied filters. In this dialog box, you can examine how the supplied filters are defined, you can create your own filters, or you can make copies of the supplied filters and try your hand at making modifications. If you create new filters, you can use the Organizer feature to make the filter definitions available to other files. See Hour 17, " Printing Resource Details and Customizing Reports," for a discussion of the Organizer, particularly the section titled "Customizing the Standard Reports."

To Do: Using a Standard Filter

To apply an existing filter to a task or resource list, do the following:

1. Select Project, Filtered For.

2. On the cascading menu, select the standard filter you want to apply (Completed Tasks, Critical, Incomplete Tasks, and so on for a task list). The filter will be immediately applied to your list.

> You will find that a different list of standard filters appears on the filter cascading menu, depending on whether you are currently viewing a task-related view or a resource-related view.

>  You can also open a drop-down list of standard filters by clicking on the Filter button on the Formatting toolbar.

3. If the cascading filter menu does not have the particular standard filter you want to use, select Project, Filtered For, More Filters to open the More Filters dialog box (see Figure 16.5).

    Two radio buttons appear at the top of the More Filters dialog box: one for Tasks and the other for Resources. If you are filtering a task list, the Tasks button will be selected.

5. Select the Filter you want to use from the filter name scroll box.

6. Click the Apply button to activate the filter. The results of the filter will appear in your task or resource list.

7. To remove a filter that you have applied to your list, choose Project, Filtered For, All Tasks (or All Resources).

Typically you will apply a filter to a view containing a list of tasks or resources. It is possible, though, to apply filters to other types of views. On a Network Diagram, an applied filter will hide the diagram boxes for tasks that do not meet the filter criteria. If you have displayed a form view, such as the Task Form, as a full-screen view, an applied filter controls which tasks will be shown as you chose the Next and Previous buttons on the form. These buttons will no longer step you through the entire list of tasks or resources; only the items matching the filter criteria will appear, one at a time, as you step through the list with these buttons.

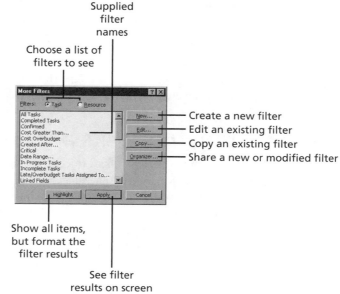

Choose a list of
filters to see

Supplied
filter
names

FIGURE 16.5

See the complete list of supplied filters in the More Filters dialog box.

Create a new filter
Edit an existing filter
Copy an existing filter
Share a new or modified filter

Show all items,
but format the
filter results

See filter
results on screen

You can examine or make changes to an existing filter by selecting the filter name from the list in the More Filters dialog box and clicking the Edit button. You can also create your own filters by clicking the New button in the dialog box. But, particularly for new Project users, it's a good idea to copy an existing filter and experiment with the copy. That way, your existing, predefined filters will not be changed. You can then use the Organizer button to begin sharing your new or copied filter with other Project files.

Changes are made to filters in the Filter Definition dialog box (see Figure 16.6). This box will open if you choose New, Edit, or Copy from the More Filters box.

FIGURE 16.6

Create or modify filters in the Filter Definition dialog box.

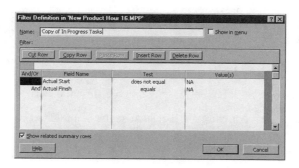

Take some time to explore the standard filters before you attempt to create your own. Creating filters requires a good understanding of the Project database fields and the values they can contain. Using the standard filters guarantees you that the filter is performing correctly.

If you do create a new filter, its name will appear in the More Filters dialog box. Select it as you would any other filter and click Apply to filter the displayed list.

Sorting and Grouping Tasks and Resources

In addition to applying filters, there are two other Project features that let you view your lists differently: sorting and grouping. Filters (other than Highlight filters) have the effect of reducing the number of tasks or resources seen onscreen; those that do not match the criteria are temporarily hidden. On the other hand, sorting a list or grouping list items leaves all task or resource rows onscreen, but arranges the rows in a different order. In the case of grouping, rows are actually added to the screen to show where groups begin and end.

Sorting the Task and Resource Lists

Another way to focus your view of task and resource lists is to use the sort feature. This allows you to view the task or resource rows in an order that you define. You can sort tasks or resources by criteria such as task name, deadline, or start date. Sorting these items does not alter the ID numbers for the items or change the project schedule.

For instance, you might want to sort a list of tasks by their start date. After you have finished viewing your list in the new order dictated by the sort, you can easily return the items to their original order.

> Sorting order from your last sort is maintained when you switch views and is saved when you close a project file.

To Do: Sorting a List

To display a task or resource list onscreen in a different order, do the following:

1. Display a view containing a list, such as the Gantt Chart or the Resource Sheet view.

2. Choose Project, Sort. A cascading list of supplied sort options appears for the type of list you are currently viewing. For the task list, standard sorts are available for Start Date, Finish Date, Priority, Cost, and ID. For the resource list, standard sorts are available for Cost, Name, and ID.

▼ 3. Select a standard sort option from the list. For instance, to sort a task list by task start date, select Start Date.

   4. To return the list to its original order, sort by ID (this works for both tasks and resources).

   5. If you want to sort by more than one field, choose Project, Sort, Sort By to open the Sort dialog box (see Figure 16.7).

16

FIGURE 16.7

The Sort dialog box allows you to sort a list by more than one field.

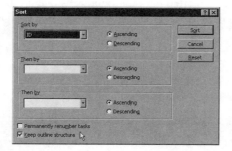

   6. The Sort dialog box allows you to sort by up to three fields. For instance, you could sort tasks by start date, duration, and then cost. In the Sort By box, use the drop-down list to select the field you want to sort by first, and then place additional fields in the Then By boxes provided. Select Ascending or Descending sort order for each field you select.

▲ 7. After you have selected the fields you want to sort by, click the Sort button. The list will be sorted by the fields that you chose (and in the direction you selected).

There are two check boxes included at the bottom of the Sort dialog box: Permanently Renumber Tasks and Keep Outline Structure.

The default selection is to Keep Outline Structure on, meaning subtasks are sorted within their own groups, and then summary tasks are sorted. This way, subtasks will remain tied to their summary tasks. If the feature is turned off, summary tasks can—and do—float away from their subtasks.

You can also renumber your items according to the new sort by turning on the Permanently Renumber Tasks option. But if you then decide you want to restore the original ID sequence, your only solution is to undo the sort. As your very next step, select Edit, Undo Sort. Otherwise, there is no easy way to return a list to its original numbering sequence.

Grouping the Task and Resource Lists

NEW FEATURE

What if you could not only sort your lists, but also hide some details and show subtotals for numeric values at each sort level? That's what grouping is all about.

Applying a Group definition to a list reorders the list by field values, just as sorting does. But with groups, you can then hide the list rows in a group, like having a second outline structure. Also, you can define the intervals for the groups. You might, for example, want to display tasks that have not started in one group, tasks that are finished in another group, and tasks that are in progress in a third group onscreen. Figure 16.8 shows tasks in exactly these groups.

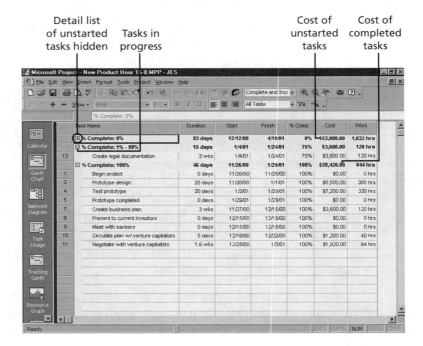

FIGURE 16.8
Lists can be collapsed, summarized, and displayed in intervals by defining field Groups.

Project supplies nine predefined task group definitions and five resource groups. As with other Project elements, you can create your own groups or make copies of existing definitions and modify the copies.

To Do: Grouping a Task or Resource List

To group items in a task or resource list, and create subtotals for numerical fields, do the following:

1. Display a view with a list, such as the Gantt Chart or the Resource Sheet.

▼ 2. Select View, Table to display the data fields you're interested in.

3. Select Project, Group By.

4. To apply an existing group definition, choose from the cascading menu.

5. You could also choose More Groups to display the More Groups dialog box (see Figure 16.9). From this dialog box you can create a new group definition, modify an existing group, or create a copy of an existing group and modify the copy.

6. To remove the grouping and return the displayed list to its original structure, select Project, Group by, No Group.

16

| No Group ▼ | Apply or remove grouping quickly by choosing from the Group By drop-down list on the Standard toolbar. |

FIGURE 16.9

Use the More Groups dialog box to modify or create group definitions.

In Figure 16.8, the Summary Table was applied to the Gantt Chart view, and then the Complete and Incomplete Tasks group definition was applied. The top group was then collapsed to hide detail rows in the same way you have been collapsing the task outline: by clicking on the minus sign next to the group heading—% Complete:0%. Notice that each group has its own heading row, with background color formatting. These header rows contain rolled up numerical values where appropriate. In this example, the Cost and Work values are subtotaled for the tasks within each group and displayed on the header rows. This is a simple, but useful, application of the grouping feature.

You are not limited to a single level of grouping. Create groups within groups to summarize your plan at different levels of detail. The task list in Figure 16.10 is grouped on two levels: Critical and noncritical tasks (in descending order) and then by % Complete (unstarted, in progress, and complete).

First group   Second   Second group
level   group level   level interval

FIGURE 16.10

*Lists can be grouped
into multiple levels.*

Task Name	Duration	Start	Finish	% Comp.	Cost	Work
⊟ **Critical: Yes**	83 days	12/12/00	4/19/01	0%	$23,080.00	864 hrs
⊞ **% Complete: 0%**	83 days	12/12/00	4/19/01	0%	$23,080.00	864 hrs
⊟ **Critical: No**	100 days	11/26/00	4/13/01	46%	$54,020.00	1,732 hrs
⊞ **% Complete: 0%**	72 days	1/3/01	4/13/01	0%	$30,000.00	768 hrs
⊟ **% Complete: 1% - 99%**	15 days	1/4/01	1/24/01	75%	$3,600.00	120 hrs
13 Create legal documentation	3 wks	1/4/01	1/24/01	75%	$3,600.00	120 hrs
⊟ **% Complete: 100%**	46 days	11/26/00	1/29/01	100%	$20,420.00	844 hrs
1 Begin project	0 days	11/26/00	11/26/00	100%	$0.00	0 hrs
3 Prototype design	25 days	11/28/00	1/1/01	100%	$6,500.00	300 hrs
4 Test prototype	20 days	1/2/01	1/29/01	100%	$7,200.00	320 hrs
5 Prototype completed	0 days	1/29/01	1/29/01	100%	$0.00	0 hrs
7 Create business plan	3 wks	11/27/00	12/15/00	100%	$3,600.00	120 hrs
8 Present to current investors	0 days	12/15/00	12/15/00	100%	$0.00	0 hrs
9 Meet with bankers	0 days	12/15/00	12/15/00	100%	$0.00	0 hrs
10 Circulate plan w/ venture capitalists	5 days	12/18/00	12/22/00	100%	$1,200.00	40 hrs
11 Negotiate with venture capitalists	1.6 wks	12/25/00	1/3/01	100%	$1,920.00	64 hrs

To Do: Creating a Multi-Level Group Definition

▲ To Do

To create a more sophisticated, multiple-level group structure, do the following:

1. Select Project, Group by, More Groups to display the More Groups dialog box
   (refer to Figure 16.9).

2. Select a group definition name from the list.

3. Click Copy to make a working copy of the definition. The Group Definition dialog
   box will open, as shown in Figure 16.11.

FIGURE 16.11

*Create a multi-level
grouping in the Group
Definition dialog box.*

▼

▼   4. Click in the next available row in the Field Name column.

      5. Select a field to group by from the in-cell drop-down list.

      6. Choose a sort order for the group field: ascending or descending.

      7. To control how Project organizes the groups for the field selected in the Field
         Name area, click Define Group Intervals. The Define Group Interval dialog box
         will be displayed, as shown in Figure 16.12

16

FIGURE 16.12

*Create your own
group intervals or use
Project's suggestions.*

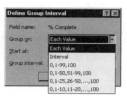

      8. Open the Group On drop-down list to see the choices available for the type of field
         you have selected.

         Most Project fields will be grouped by Each Value by default. Some fields may
         lend themselves to certain obvious groups; for example, a Duration field might be
         logically grouped into duration values in days, values in weeks, and so on.

      9. To use one of Project's suggested group settings, choose it from the drop-down list.
         Or choose Interval to create your own definition. If you choose Interval, you will
         need to fill in the Start At and the Group interval fields.

     10. Click OK to close the Define Group Interval dialog box.

     11. Click OK to close the Group Definition dialog box.

▲   12. Click Apply in the More Groups dialog box to see the effects onscreen.

Viewing the Costs

The strategies discussed so far help you get a good general overview of how your plan is
laid out. But project managers often want to see the numbers; how much is this project
costing? Another view that you might find helpful as you optimize your plan is the
Summary table. In the case of a task list, the Summary table lists information that
focuses on the costs of the events in your project and the duration of these tasks. For a
resource list, the Summary table gives you information on the cost of the resource and
the hours that the resource will be employed.

To Do: Viewing the Summary Table for a List

To display current Work and Cost information in a list format, view the Summary Table by following these steps:

1. Display the Gantt Chart or other list views.
2. Choose View, Table, Summary. A different set of columns will appear for the list, as shown in Figure 16.13. In the case of tasks, the summary columns are Duration, Start, Finish, % Complete, Cost, and Work.

FIGURE 16.13

Applying the Summary Table gives you a quick look at cost and duration information.

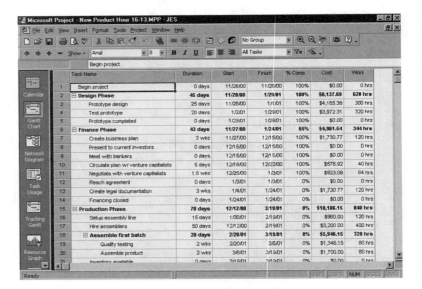

3. Use the Summary Table view of your tasks and resources along with filters, sorts, and grouping to order the summary information to suit your particular needs.

4. To return to the original set of table columns, choose View, Table, Entry.

When you use the Summary Table view on the Gantt Chart view, you may have to resize the chart area so that you can see all the columns in the Summary Table list. Place the mouse pointer on the vertical divider bar between the table and the chart, and click and drag to the right.

Shortening the Critical Path

Using the strategies for reviewing the various aspects of your project that have been covered so far in this hour, you might conclude that you need to make some adjustments in your plan. In most cases these changes revolve around time and money; there is seldom enough of both. For instance, you might need to reduce the time frame for your project. One way to do this is add more resources to get the job done; however, adding resources greatly affects the project's final cost.

The most straightforward method of reducing the time it takes to complete the project is to determine which tasks are truly driving the project completion; that is, which tasks are on the critical path. Recall that tasks that cannot be rescheduled without affecting the end date of the project are critical, and the sequence of those tasks is the critical path through the project. After you identify the critical tasks, you may be able to shorten their duration, or use other strategies, to compress the time frame for the project; this is called "shortening the critical path."

Identifying the Critical Path

`All Tasks ▾` You can use any of the task views to identify the critical tasks in your project. One of the best ways to view the critical tasks is to filter the task list for critical tasks when you are in the Gantt Chart view. Choose Project, Filtered For, Critical from the menu or use the Filter list on the Formatting toolbar.

> As you rework your project and its tasks, you will find that noncritical tasks can become critical and critical tasks can become noncritical. Make sure you rerun the critical task filter after you make changes to your schedule so that you are looking at the critical path's most recent version. Press Ctrl+F3 to quickly rerun the filter.

You might want to see all the tasks on the list and just highlight the critical tasks with special formatting. Use the More Filters dialog box to do this. Select Project, Filtered For, More Filters. In the dialog box, select Critical from the list of filter names, and then click Highlight. All tasks in the list will be visible onscreen, but the names of critical tasks will be a different color (blue by default). Figure 16.14 shows a task list where the critical tasks are highlighted.

Noncritical task
names still black

Critical Filters applied
as highlight filter

Figure 16.14

The critical task filter can be used to highlight matching tasks.

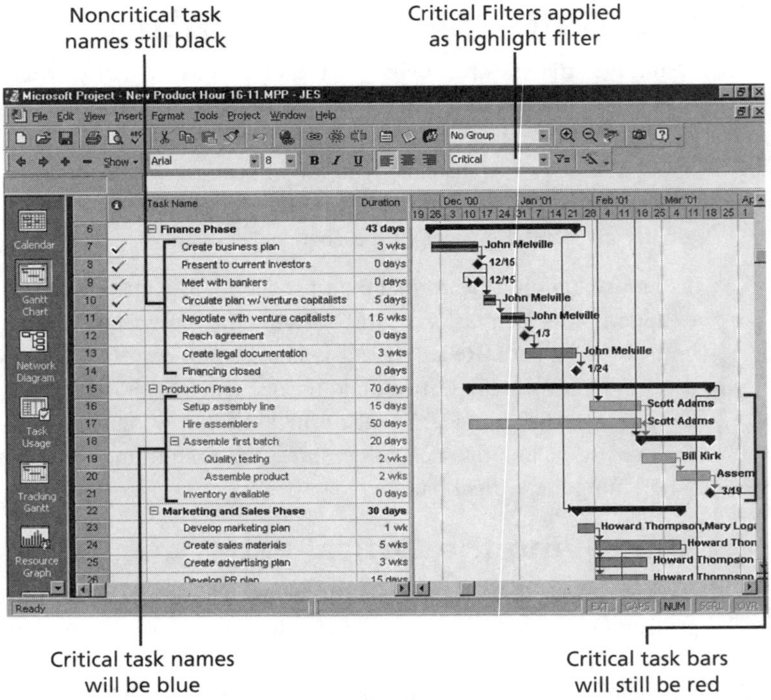

Critical task names
will be blue

Critical task bars
will still be red

After you have the critical tasks displayed (or highlighted) on the Gantt task list, it makes sense to split the Gantt Chart view and display the Task Form on the bottom of the screen. This allows you to select a critical task in the Gantt task list and view all of its vital statistics in the form. With this screen arrangement, you can edit task details quickly while keeping your eye on the big picture with the Gantt Chart.

To split the Gantt Chart view, select the Window menu, and then choose Split. The window will be divided into the Gantt Chart (on the top) and the Task Form on the bottom (see Figure 16.15).

With the Task Form displayed, you can choose which task details you want to see or edit. Right-click on the form, and choose a layout from the pop-up shortcut menu. You might, for example, be interested in seeing both Predecessors and Successors for a critical task to better understand the effects of changing the task's schedule or duration. In that case, choose the Predecessors & Successors option from the pop-up details list.

Gantt Chart shows
the big picture

FIGURE 16.15

*Split the Gantt Chart
view to see the task list
and the Task Form in
the same window.*

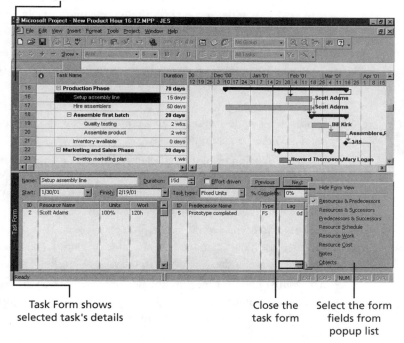

16

Task Form shows
selected task's details

Close the
task form

Select the form
fields from
popup list

To remove the Task Form from the screen, select Window, Remove Split. You can also
choose Hide Form View from the same pop-up shortcut menu used for selecting which
form fields to view.

Strategies for Crashing the Schedule

After you have the critical tasks identified, you can move from critical task to critical
task on the task list, looking for possible ways to reduce the duration of each task.

 Crashing the schedule is a strategy for reducing the overall length the critical
path for your project.

If you identify a task that can be compressed, you can quickly edit it in the Task Form.
Keep in mind the strategies in the following list as you attempt to crash your schedule:

- The name of the game is to reduce the duration of the project by, primarily, reducing the duration of the critical tasks. Assign more resources, if available, to a task
  to shorten the time frame for it (the task must be Effort Driven for this strategy to
  have the desired effect).

- Examine the predecessor and successor of each task and see if tasks can be made to overlap. In some cases, tasks involved in a finish-to-start relationship can be realigned so that the second task (in the relationship) can be started before the first one is completed. Create some lead time in the linking relationship (a negative value in the Lag field for the link).

- You can always schedule overtime for your labor resources (budget permitting) to reduce the regular work hours for a particular task.

- Break large tasks into smaller tasks. Although it might require more resources, this approach may allow you to take a critical task and break it down into subtasks that can be worked on simultaneously.

- Use your existing resources efficiently. You don't want to have resources sitting around on their hands. Make sure you are getting the appropriate amount of output from each resource. If you find you have resources with downtime, you might be able to use them on a critical task to shorten that segment of the schedule.

- Identify and correct errors in the project. If you have inadvertently scheduled a resource for more than one task at a time or placed a task at the wrong point in the schedule, correct these errors before trying to crash the schedule.

- Your only option for meeting the project deadline may be reducing the scope of the project. Completing all planned tasks within a timeframe just may not be possible. Consult with your team, management, or customers to identify which tasks or phases could be cut from this project.

The most obvious suggestion for successfully optimizing a plan is to gain as much project management experience as you can. Managing small projects with Microsoft Project will give you the background you need to tackle those large, complex project plans.

Reducing Costs

The most significant portion of your project budget is related to the cost of your resources. It is very important that you keep tabs on the project's tasks and their current and projected costs. Having tasks exceed the budget because of neglect will never do.

Reviewing the Cost Schedule

An excellent way to review project costs is to periodically examine information in either the Cost or Summary table. When viewing your costs for tasks, it also makes sense to view the Task Form, which gives you information on the resources allocated to the particular task.

To Do: Viewing Cost Information

To display task and resource costs for tasks, do the following:

1. In the Gantt Chart view, choose View, Table, Summary (or Table, Cost).
2. Show the Task Form by selecting Window, Split.
3. Select a task in the Gantt Chart.

   The Task Form will give you information on the resources involved in the selected task.

4. To see a different set of fields on the Task Form, right-click on the form and choose from the pop-up shortcut menu. The Resource Cost settings give the most complete set of costing fields.

▲

16

Strategies for Reducing Costs

Project automatically tracks two types of costs in a plan: resource cost (both labor and materials) and fixed costs. You may be able to lower your task (and project) costs by negotiating better contracts with your vendors. High material or fixed costs can make the best plan economically unfeasible.

The largest cost component in a project is usually resource costs. To reduce project costs, your best option is to find ways to lower the resource price tag on your various tasks. One way to reduce costs is to use less-expensive resources. However, you should keep in mind the old adage "you get what you pay for" as you seek to reduce the cost of the resources you use. Substituting less expensive labor may mean that your task duration needs to be increased, if the labor is also less experienced or less productive.

Another significant way to reduce your final costs is to keep a close eye on tasks that are threatening to go over budget. If the task is becoming too costly because of overtime pay (let's say you decided to use overtime to reduce the time frame for the task), you may want to reallocate resources to the project so that the particular task is still completed on time but only during regular working hours. With overtime pay-rates out of the picture, you might be able to bring the task in on budget.

It also makes sense to take a hard look at the tasks in the project and see if any of them can be completely deleted. If other tasks do not depend on a particular task, you may find that it was an unnecessary step in the project. For example, having four quality control checks for a particular product might be a little redundant, especially if the first two quality control tasks are catching all of the faulty product.

Reduce project scope by deleting tasks that do not add to the plan's overall productivity. Redefining deliverables or modifying quality requirements can help bring in a project on schedule and at a lower cost. However, this could also lower the "quality" of the final outcome, which certainly should be considered carefully.

Summary

In this hour, you had the opportunity to review your project plan and explore some of the strategies for optimizing the plan. The strategies range from tools that allow you to gain an overview of the project, such as the Zoom Out feature in the Gantt Chart view, to tools that allow you to focus on certain aspects of your plan, such as the task and resources filters.

You also learned about strategies that can help you crash your project schedule and reduce costs. Hour 21, "Analyzing Progress and Revising the Schedule," discusses reviewing your project progress in detail and additional strategies for modifying the plan once it is underway.

Q&A

Q **My company uses a specific timescale setting and labeling scheme on our Gantt Charts. After I apply a Zoom setting or click the Zoom In or Zoom Out toolbar buttons, how can I return to my custom settings?**

A There is no way to create custom timescale settings and then quickly re-apply them in one step. Once you choose Zoom, Reset or click the Zoom toolbar buttons, your manual settings are lost. You will have to recreate them via the Format, Timescale dialog box. However, you can create a new Gantt Chart (View, More Views) and then view this copy onscreen anytime you want to experiment with zooming. This way, the original Gantt Chart will retain your manual settings and formatting changes in the copy won't affect the original.

Q **Does the Grouping feature have any kind of onscreen counterpart to AutoFiltering? I'd like to be able to experiment with groups without having to return repeatedly to the More Groups and Group Definition dialog boxes.**

A You can experiment with creating groups in an interactive way using the Customize Group By option. It's best to start by applying an existing group definition that you think might be close to what you'd like to see. Then choose Project, Group by, Customize Group By to display the Group Definition dialog box. Change the group settings as described in this hour, and then click OK in the dialog box. Your results will be applied immediately to the onscreen list. When you have just the display you want, open the Customize Group By dialog box again and click Save to name and save the definition for later use.

Q Can I apply a filter to a task list I've already filtered? I'd like to see only the critical tasks in a certain date range.

A You won't get the result you want if you apply the Critical filter and then the Date Range filter. Only the results of the second applied filter will be displayed. To see the list as you describe it, you will need to create a new, custom filter that combines and applies both sets of criteria at one time.

Q Can I create a very narrow focus on my list by applying a group definition to a filtered list?

A Yes, you can filter a grouped list, or filter first and then apply a grouping. Either way, the effect is to eliminate one or more headings from the grouped list. (The exercises below include this use of filters and groups.)

Exercises

At this point in managing your project, you should focus some attention on specific information in the plan to be sure you are meeting your deadline and budget goals. In the following exercises, you will view the statistics for the project and consider alternatives for reducing the project length. Also, you will display your plan in different ways to see cost values. Begin by opening the file "New Product Hour 16.MPP." The solutions to the exercises can be found in the file "New Product Hour 16-Exercise.MPP." See the Introduction for instructions to access the sample files and solutions for these exercises on the book's Web page.

1. View the Project Statistics dialog box and note the following values:

   Current (scheduled) Start

   Current (scheduled) Finish

   Current (scheduled) Cost

2. The plan is not meeting its planned finish date of 4/18/01. Examine the critical tasks to see which phases of the project are controlling the finish date.

3. It might be helpful to see the critical tasks in a different order, longest to shortest, to see which tasks on the critical path are good candidates for having their durations adjusted.

4. You notice that the Promo Weeks late in the plan are each requiring two weeks of time. Reduce each one to five days (one week). Then return to the Statistics box and see the results on the project Finish date. Have you met your finish goal?

5. You'd like to see the cost contribution to the project of the critical tasks. Remove the Critical filter and return the task list to task ID order. Then view the Summary table on the Gantt Chart and apply the Critical Group.

6. Hide the details for the noncritical tasks.

7. Remove the noncritical task group from the screen completely by applying the Critical filter to the grouped list.

HOUR 17

Printing Resource Details and Customizing Reports

This hour shows you how to format and print views and reports that contain resource information. Project 2000 can list your resources with detailed information about their task schedules, their assigned work, and their cost to a task or to the project. The Usage views can display and print several lines of detailed resource information.

A number of predefined reports that focus on resource information are supplied with Project. This hour includes instructions for customizing the standard reports—both resource and task type reports. I also discuss creating new reports by copying a supplied report or by starting a report from scratch.

In this hour, you will learn:

- How to display detailed information in the usage views
- Which built-in reports focus on resource costing

- How to print resource assignments, schedules, and workloads
- How to customize standard reports to fit your needs
- How to create and save new reports based on three standard report types

Formatting and Printing the Usage Views

Both the Task Usage and Resource Usage views let you see who is assigned to which tasks throughout the project. The assignment information is broken down by task. The Task Usage view groups the resource assignments with the task names; the Resource Usage view groups the assignments with each resource name. With either view, the right side of the screen presents a time-phased breakdown of detailed resource information.

When you create a new project file, the usage views display assigned work for each resource and each task on the right side of the screen (see Figure 17.1). However, you're not limited to seeing only the assigned work information. The following section "Choosing the Details" teaches you how to change the information displayed on the right side of a usage view. Also, you might want to adjust the timescale for the grid columns with Zoom In and Zoom Out buttons on the Standard toolbar.

FIGURE 17.1

The standard Task Usage view shows detailed resource information for each task.

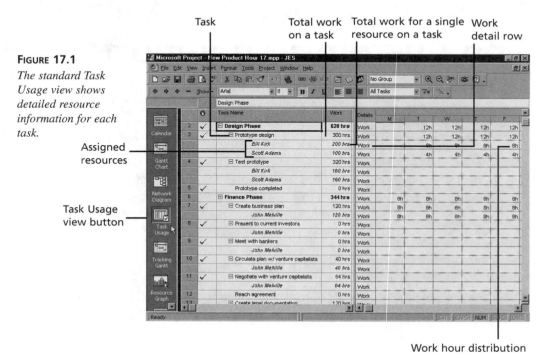

The Resource Usage view is similar to the Task Usage view, but is organized by resource instead of by task. The following notes and steps apply to both usage views.

Choosing the Details

A *detail* in a Project Usage view is a row associated with each resource in the view. The work detail row is shown by default. There are five other commonly used detail rows that can be displayed easily. Digging a little deeper reveals that any resource-related numeric field can be displayed as a detail row.

To Do: Displaying Detail Rows in Task Usage View

To display or hide commonly-used detail rows in a Task Usage view, follow these steps:

1. Choose View, Task Usage or choose Task Usage from the View Bar.

2. Choose Format, Details and select the detail row you would like to display. Items with check marks will be displayed; items without check marks will be hidden from view (see Figure 17.2).

17

FIGURE 17.2

The most common usage detail fields are available from a cascading menu.

3. Return to Format, Details as many times as necessary to display or hide the common resource detail rows to fit your needs.

For faster access to the common detail options, right-click the right-side grid on a usage view.

You might want to display a detail row that is not among the common details list. For example, the amount of actual work completed per person on a task could be of interest.

To Do: Displaying Additional Resource Rows in Task Usage View

To view the complete list of available resource details and add them to the Task Usage view, do the following:

1. Choose View, Task Usage or choose Task Usage from the View Bar.

2. Choose Format, Detail Styles, Usage Details. All available detail row fields are listed on the left side of the dialog box; all fields currently marked to be shown are listed on the right side (see Figure 17.3). Customize the usage view by showing or hiding fields and by ordering the rows with the Move buttons.

FIGURE 17.3

Many Project fields are available for displaying on a Usage view.

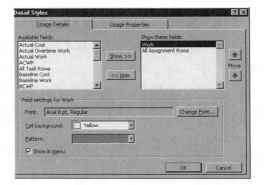

3. Click OK to close the Detail Styles dialog box and see the row changes on the view.

You can customize the pop-up details list by selecting the Show in Menu check box for each field at the bottom of the Usage Details tab.

Formatting the Detail Styles

You can change the emphasis of each displayed detail row by changing the formatting. A different color or background pattern for more important rows can make the grid easier to interpret.

To Do: Choosing Colors and Patterns for Detail Rows

To change the formatting of detail rows in a Usage view, follow these steps:

1. Choose Format, Detail Styles.

2. Highlight the field to be formatted from the Show These Fields list.

3. Make any necessary changes to the font, point size, and text color, as well as cell background color and pattern, for each detail field.

4. Click OK when finished. Note that the special formatting is not applied to *each* detail row, but only to the first row of the *group*. That is, the formatting changes show on the Task Name lines in the Task Usage view, but not on each individual resource's line.

> The assignment rows in the Task Name or Resource Name column can be formatted to stand out, too. Choose Format, Text Styles, Assignment Row to make the change.

17

> Undo is not available for removing the formatting changes in Detail Styles or Text Styles.

Working with Cost Reports

In addition to the Task and Resource Usage views, there are several predefined reports in Project 2000 that print resource-related information. One group of reports is focused on cost and the budget breakdowns for the project (see Figure 17.4). Tracking project costs over time, and budgeting accordingly, is usually a key management concern. Also, Project 2000 computes and prints cost totals in the cost reports. The Cash Flow report, for example, shows total costs allocated in a time period, as well as the total cost of each task over the entire project.

> All reports supplied with Project 2000 contain certain default settings. To make changes to the default settings for a report, see the section "Customizing the Standard Reports" later in this hour.

FIGURE 17.4

Reports that focus on project costing are in the Costs report category.

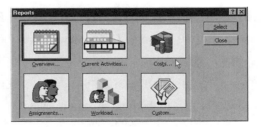

To Do: Previewing the Cost Reports

To preview the supplied cost reports onscreen, do the following:

1. Choose View, Reports.
2. Double-click on the Costs category, or choose the Costs category and click Select.
3. Double-click on a report option, or choose the report option and then click Select.

Cash Flow Report

For a printout of expected cash flow over time, throughout the project, choose the Cash Flow report. Expenses are displayed in time increments. The default time increment is weekly. The dollar amounts in each time period are calculated by Project based on assigned resources and their pay rates, material resources and their cost rates, fixed costs, and the accrual methods chosen for each. By default, resource costs are payable when the resource does the work or the material resource is consumed, and fixed costs are payable at the end of a task. Per-use costs for resources are always payable at the beginning of the task. In the Cash Flow report, totals are computed and displayed at the bottom of the report for each time period and at the far right side of the report for each task.

Budget Report

The Budget report prints a list of tasks with their associated fixed and total costs, remaining funds available for each task, and the current cost variance from the original baseline cost values. This is the same information available by applying and printing the Cost table on the Gantt Chart, with one important difference: The Budget report also computes and prints totals for each column of numbers.

To see project totals for fixed costs, resource costs, and variances from the original project budget, print the supplied Budget report.

Working with the Assignment Reports

The key to managing a project team efficiently is knowing what the resources are responsible for over the life of the project. Important questions to review include who is supposed to be doing what work, when the work is due, and whether any resources are assigned more work than they can complete, based on their working calendars. The Assignment Reports are designed to answer these questions and more.

The four standard reports in the Assignment reports group print resource assignment lists for your review and for distribution to project team members. The focus of each report is slightly different (see Figure 17.5). Preview these reports the same way you previewed the Cost reports: select View, Reports; double-click on the Assignments button, and then double-click on an individual report button.

FIGURE 17.5

The supplied reports in the Assignment group help track resources and their workloads.

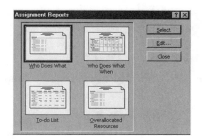

Who Does What Report

The Who Does What report is good for getting a detailed view of your team and its efforts. This report lists every labor resource from the resource list, whether any work has been assigned to him or her, but does not include material resource information. For each resource in the report, the total amount of work on the project is given, along with a breakdown by task of the units per task (in % effort), work per task, and start and finish dates per task.

Who Does What When Report

As the name implies, the Who Does What When report lists people and equipment on the project resource list, which tasks each resource is assigned to, and when those work assignments occur. The time period for the report is a daily list by default. Totals for work per time period and work per resource are *not* printed on this report by default, but, as with other reports, Who Does What When can be edited directly, or a copy can be edited, to include totals.

The Who Does What When report could produce long multi-page printouts because of its daily timescale setting. You might want to change the timescale (see the section "Customizing Crosstab Type Reports" later in this hour) or print only a portion of the report (type in dates for the Timescale setting in the Print dialog box.)

To-Do List Report

The To-do List is a filtered report designed to focus on one resource at a time. Each time you preview the report, you must choose a resource, either work or materials type, from the drop-down list of all resources that appears on the screen. The report lists all task assignments for the resource, including task details such as duration and start and finish dates. The assignments are listed in task ID order within calendar groups; by default, the grouping is weekly.

Overallocated Resources Report

The Overallocated Resources report is the result of taking the Who Does What report and filtering it to show only those resources that are overallocated sometime, in one or more time periods, in the life of the project. For these resources only, the same task assignment details, as in the Who Does What report, are listed.

Using the Workload Reports

The two supplied Workload reports are named Task Usage and Resource Usage (see Figure 17.6). Don't let the names fool you, however; they are not simply printouts of the Task or Resource Usage views. Presented in a table format, known as a *crosstab*, the Workload reports list only one detail line of tasks and resource assignment information over time. The default time period for each report is weekly. The option to add detail rows, as with the Usage views, is not available in the usage reports. You can, however, define and print multiple usage reports with different detail information in each report. Also, Project calculates and prints totals by task, or by resource, and by time period in the usage reports but not in the usage views.

FIGURE 17.6

Workload reports focus on resources and their assigned work by time periods.

The new grouping feature in Project 2000 lets you define and display groups of related tasks or resources and display them onscreen. Any numerical values included in the display can be rolled up to the group levels.

 Reports are not the only way the view summarized values in Project. Review Hour 16, "Fine-Tuning the Project Plan," for more information about Grouping tasks or resources.

Task Usage Report

The supplied Task Usage report lists all tasks in the project with the accompanying resource assignments. For each resource, the assigned hours within the time period are given. For each task, the total of the assigned resource hours is also given on the rightmost page of the report. For each time period, total assigned resource hours are printed at the bottom of the table.

17

Resource Usage Report

In an orientation different from the Task Usage report, the supplied Resource Usage report provides a list of resources and their task assignments. Assigned hours per task per time period and total hours for the resource in each time period are given. Project calculates and displays the total work hours per time period for all resources and total work per resource over the life of the project. The default time period for this report is weekly.

Customizing the Standard Reports

As comprehensive as the supplied reports are, they might not meet your needs exactly. You might want to change some text formatting or the sort order in a report, for example. Because reports are a combination of table information, filters, and detail settings, this section shows you how to change these features in the supplied reports.

 If you follow these procedures and customize the supplied reports, the original settings are lost. To return to the original report, you must either re-edit the settings or use the Organizer feature to copy the report definition from the global.mpt.

If you prefer to keep the original report and create one that's similar to it, see the section "Creating a New Report Based on an Existing Report," later in this hour.

Common adjustments made to the supplied reports include setting and removing page breaks in the underlying views, modifying the header and footer information, adding emphasis with text formatting, rearranging the report information by sorting a different way, and adding or removing detailed information on a report for enhanced readability.

Controlling Page Breaks in a Report

There's no method for setting or controlling page breaks within a report. However, manual page breaks can be set on views, which will affect some reports. Most reports that are simply lists—that is, they have no time period data—will not be affected by manual page breaks; there's no way to directly control the page breaks in these reports. The resource reports explored in this hour that can be controlled by manual page breaks set on views are the following:

- Cash Flow
- Who Does What When
- Task Usage
- Resource Usage

For a detailed discussion of setting and removing manual page breaks in list views, see Hour 10, "Finalizing and Printing Your Schedule," particularly the section titled "Printing Gantt Charts."

Choosing the Page Setup Options for a Report

After a report is previewed on the screen, the Page Setup options for the report become available. These options include the print orientation (portrait or landscape), printed page margins, and header and footer settings.

To Do: Accessing Page Setup Options for a Report

To set report printing options, do the following:

1. Choose View, Reports.
2. Double-click on a report category, or click the category and choose Select.
3. Double-click on the report option, or click the report option and then choose Select.

▼   4. At the top of the Preview screen, click the Page Setup button. The Page Setup dialog box appears, as shown in Figure 17.7.

Report name   Legend and View not
                       available for reports

FIGURE 17.7
Change print settings in the Page Setup dialog box.

Paper settings depend
on selected printer

Set starting page
number if needed

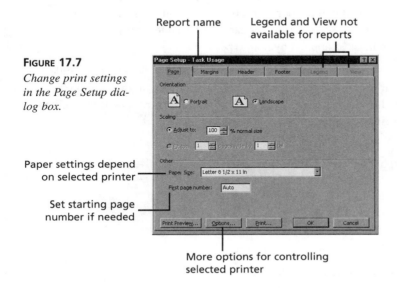

More options for controlling
selected printer

5. Make your selections on the Page, Margins, Header, and Footer tabs. The Legend and View tabs will not be available because they do not contain settings pertaining to the reports.

Initially, the default page settings for the specific report will be chosen, but after they're changed, the new settings stay with the report. You don't need to change the Page Setup options every time you run a report.

▲   6. Click Print Preview to display and review the new settings.

Two new features in Project 2000 give you more printing flexibility. You can choose any paper size permitted by your printer directly on the Page tab of the Page Setup dialog box. Also on the Page tab, you can set a starting number for printed pages if you intend to print only a few pages of the report.

Formatting Text in a Report

Manual or text style formatting applied to a view is not carried over to reports. Text formatting for reports is changed in the report definition itself. Within a report, text formatting is done by type of item. Tasks or resources can't be formatted individually in reports; text formatting must be applied by item types only.

Task items that can be formatted could include summary tasks, critical tasks, or milestones, for example. In resource reports, items to format might be all overallocated resources, all allocated resources, or resource cost or work totals. Several different items can be formatted in distinctly different ways within the same report, and each report can have its own combination of text formatting applied to items.

To Do: Changing the Text Formatting in a Supplied Report

To modify formatting of text items in a report, do the following:

1. Choose View, Reports.
2. Double-click on a report category, or click once on a category and choose Select.
3. Click once on the report you want to modify.
4. Click the Edit button to open the report definition dialog box.
5. Select the Definition tab. Click the Text button, and the Text Styles dialog box appears, as shown in Figure 17.8.

FIGURE **17.8**

*Formatting in reports
is applied to item
types.*

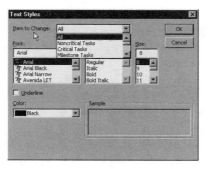

6. Use the Item to Change drop-down list to select the items of interest, making your changes to one item type at a time.
7. When all items have been formatted, click OK on the Text Styles dialog box, and click OK again on the Report Definition dialog box.
8. Now preview the revised report by double-clicking its name or by clicking once and choosing Select.

Changing the Sort Order for a Report

The order in which tasks and resources are printed is predefined in each report. You can change the report sort and print orders by using Project's three-level sort capabilities.

To Do: Changing the Sort Order of a Report

To sort report information into a different order for printing, follow these steps:

1. Choose View, Reports.
2. Double-click on a report category, or click once on a category and choose Select.
3. Click once on the report you want to modify.
4. Click the Edit button to open the Report Definition dialog box.
5. Select the Sort tab in the dialog box (see Figure 17.9).

FIGURE 17.9

Apply up to three levels of sorting to the reported information.

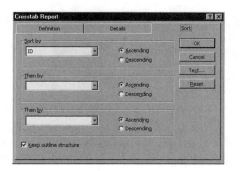

6. Use the drop-down lists to choose the field to Sort By and select Ascending or Descending order for the list. Make choices for the second and third sort levels, if you like. For task reports, these lists will include only task fields; for resource reports, they will be resource field lists.
7. Click OK on the Sort tab.
8. Now preview the revised report by double-clicking its name or by clicking once and choosing Select.

Displaying or Hiding Task Detail in a Report

Some supplied reports might give you more data than you need, resulting in information overload. Unfortunately, some reports might not give you all the detailed information you want. The type and amount of supporting information supplied in each report can be changed by displaying or hiding detail options in the report definition.

To Do: Displaying or Hiding Report Details

To include or remove printed details on a report, do the following:

1. Choose View, Reports.

2. Double-click on a report category, or click once on a category and choose Select.

3. Click once on the report you want to modify.

4. Click the Edit button. The Report Definition dialog box appears.

5. Select the Details tab in the dialog box, as shown in Figure 17.10.

FIGURE 17.10

The Details tab allows you to show or not show several types of supporting information per task or resource.

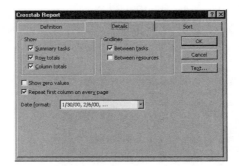

6. A check box next to a detail option indicates that the option can be set to be displayed (a check mark in the box) or to be hidden (no check mark in the box), independently of any other options. Turn on the details you would like to see; leave the other check boxes blank.

   The available details vary by report type. Timescaled reports let you choose the date formatting for that report only, for instance. Other options include whether to include summary tasks in the report, which could duplicate some information on the report, or whether to show numeric totals on the report.

7. Click OK on the Details dialog box.

8. Now preview the revised report by double-clicking its name or by clicking once and choosing Select.

Customizing Specific Report Types

Despite the quantity of supplied reports in Project 2000, most reports are based on one of three report types:

- Task reports
- Resource reports
- Crosstab reports

Task and Resource reports are simply lists of project data focused on either task or resource information. The Crosstab report adds a time period dimension to reports and can be focused on either task or resource information.

The remaining report types (not listed previously) are the Project Summary report and a few calendar-based reports.

> Before you begin to either customize the existing reports or make copies of them to experiment with, it will be worth your time to take a look at each of the supplied reports. You may find that somewhere in those 22 supplied reports is just the printout you need.

Creating a New Report Based on an Existing Report

In the previous section, you made simple formatting changes to the supplied reports. But what if a report doesn't contain exactly the information you'd like to see? For example, the To-do List report might be more informative if the resources' tasks were broken into time periods so they could see which tasks they should be working on within, say, a two-week period. You could edit the supplied To-do List report to include a time period breakdown. But then if you needed to print the original To-do List report, it would no longer exist because you made changes by adding the timing element.

The best move to make in a case like this is to copy the To-do List report and make your changes to the copy. That way you will retain the original report in case you need it later, but you will also have a customized report that suits your other needs.

The following sections discuss customizing the various types of reports in Project. I recommend you make copies of existing reports before following along in the next sections.

To Do: Creating a New Report

To create a new report in this Project file, do the following:

1. Select View, Reports.
2. Double-click the Custom category. The Custom Reports dialog box will be displayed (see Figure 17.11).

▼

FIGURE 17.11
Copy reports or create new ones in the Custom Reports dialog box.

Select a report to copy

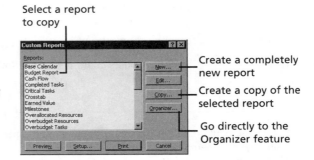

Create a completely new report

Create a copy of the selected report

Go directly to the Organizer feature

3. Copy or create a report:

- To make a copy of a supplied report, select a report name in the Reports list. Then click Copy. A report definition box—either Task Report, Resource Report, or Crosstab Report—will open.

- To create a new report from scratch, click New. Select a basic type of report in the Define New Report dialog box (see Figure 17.12), and then click OK.

FIGURE 17.12
New reports are based on one of four report types.

4. Type a descriptive name for this report in the Name field.

▲ 5. Customize the new report as described in the following sections.

The report you created, either by copying an existing report or by creating a totally new report, is only saved in the current Project file until you take an additional step. Recall from the "Managing Your Calendars" section of Hour 5, "Defining When Project Can Schedule Tasks," the Organizer feature is the key to sharing customized Project elements such as reports. The Organizer is also useful for deleting new reports that don't quite fit your needs.

To Do: Sharing Custom Reports with Other Projects

To make your new or customized reports available to other Project files, follow these steps:

1. Select View, Reports.

▼ 2. Open the Custom group.

▼ 3. Click the Organizer button on the Custom Reports dialog box (refer to Figure 17.11).

4. To work with customized reports, be sure the Reports tab is selected. (To share other Project elements, move to the appropriate tab.)

The Reports created or used in this session of Project will be listed on the right side of the Organizer dialog box.

5. Make the desired changes in the Organizer dialog box:

- To make a report available to all other files based on your underlying Project template (called `global.mpt`), select a report in the current file list, and then click Copy in the middle of the dialog box.

- To permanently erase a report, select its name from the active file list and click Delete.

- To give a report a different name (or in case you let Project name your report for you, something like Report 1), select its name from the active file list and click Rename. Enter the new name and click OK.

6. To leave the Organizer, click the button labeled Close (if you have made any
▲ changes) or Cancel (if no changes were made).

Customizing Task Reports

All Task reports list task names or IDs first on a report line, and include columns of project data from task tables in the project file. Task reports can include information on all tasks or only a group of tasks, if a filter is specified in the report definition. A Task type report discussed in this hour is the Budget report. In the Overview report group, discussed in Hour 10, the Top-level Tasks, Critical Tasks, and Milestones reports are all task type reports.

In addition to the text formatting and sort order changes discussed previously, the report definition dialog box, shown in Figure 17.13, allows you to do the following:

- Change the report name. This is not recommended for the supplied reports but is highly recommended for new reports you create.

- Break up the report into periods of calendar time, such as printing by quarters. This is not the same as creating a crosstab report type; it merely breaks the report into calendar segments.

- Apply and print data from a different task table. Any custom tables you create will be among your table choices.

• Apply any filter to the list, including custom filters you might have created. Filters can also be applied as highlighting filters; that is, instead of temporarily hiding the tasks that do not match the filter, all tasks appear, but the tasks that *do* match the filter are highlighted, or displayed differently.

FIGURE 17.13

The Definition tab in the Task Report dialog box allows you to customize some parts of the Task report.

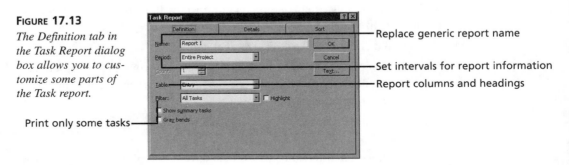

Replace generic report name

Set intervals for report information

Report columns and headings

Print only some tasks

To Do: Customizing a Task Type Report

To customize a report for your specific needs, follow these steps:

1. Follow the To Do instructions earlier in this hour to copy an existing report or create a new report.

   After creating a new or copied report, the report's Definition tab will be displayed (see Figure 17.13).

2. On the Details tab, show or hide supporting information and make changes to text formatting.

3. Change the order of printed information on the Sort tab.

4. Select the Definition tab in the dialog box.

5. Replace the generic report name with something more descriptive.

6. Set the calendar period for the report. The Period and Count fields work together. Count sets the increment for the period. That is, with a Period of weeks and a Count of 1, a *weekly* report will be produced. With a Period of weeks and a Count of 2, a *biweekly* report will be produced.

7. Select a Table of field information for the report. The table column titles will appear as column headings across the top of the report.

8. Apply a Filter to restrict the tasks reported, if desired.

9. Click OK on the Report Definition dialog box.

10. Now preview the revised report by double-clicking its name or by clicking once and choosing Select.

Customizing Resource Reports

Resource reports are very similar to task reports. The emphasis has just been shifted to resource information. In fact, the customization choices are the same for the two report types: Name, Period (and Count), Table, and Filter. Follow the procedures given for customizing task type reports to customize resource reports instead.

Resource type reports discussed in this hour are the Who Does What, To-do List, and Overallocated Resources. Now the differences between these reports should be clear:

- The Who Does What report, filtered for resources that are overcommitted in some timeframe in the project, becomes the Overallocated Resources report.
- The To-do List is simply the Who Does What report, filtered for a single resource with information grouped by a period of weeks, count 1. Changing the count to 2 on this report would produce a biweekly listing instead.

Customizing Crosstab Type Reports

The third report type that's most commonly used is the Crosstab report, which breaks project information into time periods and prints it out in a grid instead of a list format. As with Task and Resource report types, a Crosstab report can be sorted by up to three levels and the amount of detail displayed in the report can be controlled. The Sort and Detail tabs in the Report Definition dialog box control those options. However, a Crosstab report can be either task or resource oriented. This focus and the time period settings are controlled on the Definition tab of the Crosstab Report dialog box.

The Cash Flow report, the Who Does What When report, and the Task Usage and Resource Usage reports are all Crosstab type reports.

To Do: Customizing a Crosstab Report

To customize a crosstab-type report, do the following:

1. Follow the To Do instructions earlier in this hour to copy an existing report or create a new report.

   After creating a new or copied report, the report's Definition dialog box will be displayed. Figure 17.14 shows a Crosstab Report definition dialog box.

2. On the Details tab, show or hide supporting information and make changes to text formatting.

3. Change the order of printed information on the Sort tab.

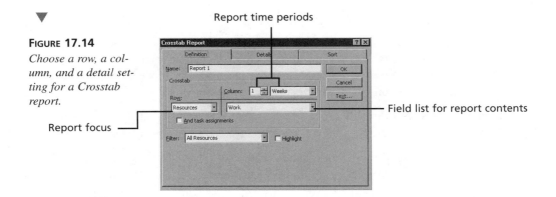

FIGURE 17.14
Choose a row, a column, and a detail setting for a Crosstab report.

Report focus

Field list for report contents

4. Select the Definition tab in the dialog box.

- The Row setting will be either Task or Resource—the focus of the report.
- The Column settings define the time periods in the report columns.
- The intersection of a row and a column can be any of the fields in the drop-down list on the Definition tab. The choice of fields varies, depending on whether Row is set to Task or to Resource.
- Do you also want to print assignments for the tasks or the resources? Turn on the And task (or resource) assignments box.
- Apply a filter to restrict the task (or resource) report.

6. Select the Details tab to display or hide row and column totals and to choose a date format for this report only.

7. Select the Sort tab to alter the printed order of the report.

8. When finished, click OK on any tab in the Report Definition dialog box.

9. Now preview the revised report by double-clicking its name or by clicking once and choosing Select.

Customizing the Project Summary Report

The Project Summary report prints the "big picture" of the project. It provides information similar to the project Statistics display. The contents of this report, found in the Overview report category, can't be changed, and there are only four items on the Summary Report that can even be reformatted:

- Project Name
- Company Name
- Manager Name
- Details

Project uses the Project Name, Company Name, and Manager Name you entered on the File, Properties, Summary tab. If you did not supply this information, Project simply leaves the spaces for them on the Summary Report blank. The fourth item, Details, contains all the other project information summarized on the report.

Formatting the Details information on the Summary Report with a larger point size could cause the numbers in certain fields to be too large to print in the allotted space. In that case, all you will see are pound signs (###) where numbers should be. Experiment and preview before printing the report.

To Do: Editing the Formatting for the Project Summary Report

To change the look of the Project Summary report, follow these steps:

1. Choose View, Reports.
2. Double-click on the Overview report category, or choose the category and click on Select.
3. Select the Project Summary Report option.
4. Click the Edit button.
5. Use the Item to Change drop-down list to modify the formatting for the four possible items discussed previously.
6. Click OK.
7. Now preview the revised report by double-clicking its name or by clicking once and choosing Select.

To get the "big picture" of your project at any time, display the project statistics. Choose Project, Project Information and select the Statistics tab. To print this information, use the Project Summary report.

Customizing the Calendar Type Reports

As with the Project Summary report, the editing options for the Calendar reports are limited to formatting changes—and not very many of those. Only two items can be modified: the calendar name itself and the calendar details taken as a whole group.

17

Summary

This hour provided an overview of the views and reports you will be most likely to use when exploring resource assignments in a project. The Task and Resource Usage views allow great flexibility in which fields can be displayed. For example, you might want to focus a Resource Usage view on work and show several work-related field rows: scheduled work, actual work, baseline work, overtime work, and cumulative work. Working with Detail Styles makes this possible.

Reports, on the other hand, offer a different look at your project. The many predefined reports are designed to answer commonly asked questions, such as: Are any resources overallocated, and if so, on what tasks? How are the current costs comparing to the original budget? What will the engineers be working on each month in this project? You aren't limited to the questions addressed by Project 2000 reports. Working with tables, filters, time periods, and formatting enhancements, you can create an almost endless variety of reports.

Q&A

Q Should I print views or reports, and how do I know which one to print?

A A view prints the information currently displayed on your screen, including displayed columns. The formatting for any task or group of tasks, as well as Gantt Chart bars and some Usage rows, can be changed in a view. Reports are the better choice for more detailed information that can answer a specific question about your project plan. For example, which resources are overcommitted and what tasks are they assigned to? The Overallocated Resources report lists those resources and their assignment lists, as well as each resource's total work, effort, and start and finish dates for each task.

Q I'd like to add the Task ID column to the left side of the Who Does What When report. How can I do that?

A The short answer is: you can't. You can see in any Crosstab report definition dialog box, there is no option to include extra columns on the report or to print a certain table of columns. This feature of the report can't be changed.

Q I changed the sort order on a Crosstab report. Now the page breaks aren't where I want them to be. How can I fix this?

A The setting for a manual page break is associated with the task or resource row where it was set. The break is not associated with, for example, a set number of lines. So, sorting a task or resource view from within a report definition causes the manual page breaks to move with the sorting. It's better to sort the view first, exactly as you intend to sort the report, and then insert manual page breaks on the sorted view.

Exercises

You'd like to see a bit more information on the Resource Usage view, and some of the reports should be modified to meet your needs. Begin by opening the file "New Product Hour 17.MPP." The solutions to the exercises can be found in the file "New Product Hour 17-Exercise.MPP." See the Introduction for instructions to access the sample files and solutions for these exercises on the book's Web page.

1. Add a detail row to the Resource Usage view to show the amount of work actually completed by each resource on each task.

2. Some reports print several pages. Modify the Who Does What When report to include the total number of pages in the footer.

3. Make a copy of the Who Does What report and change it to print resource assignments grouped in two week periods.

4. Make your new Who Does What Biweekly report available to all files which are based on your Global template file.

17

HOUR 18

Creating Custom Views

The *good* news is that Microsoft Project 2000 is a highly customizable product. The *bad* news is that Microsoft Project 2000 is a highly customizable product. There are so many features you can modify to meet your needs within Project that it is common for inexperienced users to feel overwhelmed by the possibilities. There should be a logical order to your experimentation. Most users begin by customizing tables and reports. Many then create custom filters. Some go further and combine custom tables and filters into custom views. Along the way, you might create custom fields for storing additional information about your project, or display your tasks in a different order. Although there are eleven main components of Project that can be customized, this hour focuses on the three most commonly used: custom fields, tables, and views.

In this hour, you will learn:

- How to create custom tables to display columns of interest
- How to modify an existing table onscreen
- How to choose view elements
- How to create a custom view
- How to define new data fields for your project

Creating Custom Tables

Project supplies 15 task-related tables and 10 resource-related tables. Each of these tables was designed with a theme in mind. For example, the Cost tables group task-related and resource-related cost fields in one location. The Work tables group task-related and resource-related work fields together, such as scheduled work, baseline work, actual work, and work variances. The Entry tables are the default tables for the Gantt Chart and the Resource Sheet views and were envisioned as your primary data entry tables.

But the supplied tables may not meet your display or printing needs exactly. Tables are the elements most commonly customized by Project users. There are essentially three methods for creating custom tables in Project:

- Create a new table from scratch
- Copy and modify an existing table
- Modify a supplied table, either using the Table Definition dialog box or directly onscreen

With the exception of onscreen editing, tables are customized by specifying choices in the Table Definition dialog box.

To Do: Creating Additional Tables

To create a new table from scratch, to modify an existing table, or to use an existing table as the starting point for a custom table, you start with these steps:

1. Select View, Table, More Tables. The More Tables dialog box appears as shown in Figure 18.1.

FIGURE 18.1

Get started customizing tables with the More Tables dialog box.

2. In the More Tables dialog box, display the list of interest by choosing a type of table: Task or Resource.

3. To create a new table from scratch, click the New button on the right side of the dialog box. To modify an existing table and keep the same table name, click Edit. To use an existing table as the starting point for a custom table, select the table first, and then click Copy.

▼   4. The Table Definition dialog box opens. Make changes as desired, using the instruc-
        tions in the following sections. Click OK when finished.

     5. To see your new or custom table onscreen, click Apply from the More Tables dia-
▲   log box.

Entering a Table Name

After choosing New, Edit, or Copy from the More Tables dialog box, the Table
Definition dialog box appears as shown in Figure 18.2. You use this dialog box to make
explicit choices to define the custom table. The first step is to type a new Name for the
table, to distinguish it from any existing tables. Project gives a new table the default
name of Table and a number; copies of existing tables are named Copy of *original table
name*. Simply replace these Project defaults with names you choose.

FIGURE 18.2

*Use the Table
Definition dialog box
to choose project fields
for a custom table.*

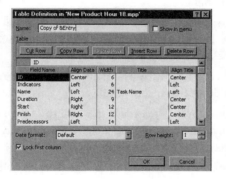

18

Add custom tables to the View, Table cascading menu list by selecting the
Show in Menu check box next to the table name in the Table Definition dialog box.

Adding and Changing the Columns in the Table

After typing a name for the table, the next step is to define the table contents by working
in the Table area of the dialog box. The layout in this area is the reverse of the way the
table is displayed on the screen: *Each row in the table definition defines a column for
onscreen display.* For each box-row/screen-column, you must specify a field from the list
of available Project fields. Other areas in the table definition are given default values by
Project.

To Do: Completing the Table Definition Area

To define the table you began creating in the preceding exercise, follow these steps:

1. Click on a row in the Field Name column.

2. Select a Project Field Name from the in-cell drop-down list. You can type the field name instead, but your typing must match a Project field name *exactly*; you cannot move the cursor away from the cell until it does.

3. Data in table columns is displayed right-justified by default. Move to the Align Data column and use the in-cell drop-down list to choose left or center justification instead.

4. Table columns have a width of 10 characters by default. Move to the Width column and use the in-cell spinner arrows to choose any width between 0 (the column is hidden) and 128 maximum.

5. The title that appears onscreen at the top of the table column is the field name itself. If you want to label the column something else, move to the Title cell and type the desired label.

6. Titles are displayed center-justified by default. Move to the Align Title column and use the in-cell drop-down list to choose left or right justification instead.

7. Use the row-editing features to rearrange the field rows. You can Cut, Copy, Paste, Insert, and Delete rows as you build the table. You can always return to the table definition later to make more row adjustments.

8. Repeat steps 1 through 7 for each row in the Field Name column to finish building and modifying the table.

> Undo is not available in the Table Definition dialog box. Work purposefully, or be prepared to re-do some steps.

Completing the Definition of the Table

Before you finish with the Table Definition dialog box, there are three additional choices you can make from the bottom of the dialog box:

- *Date Format*: Choose how dates will be displayed in this table only.

> Use the Date Format option to create a special table to display the time of day for task start and finish dates, without changing the default display for all dates.

- *Row Height*: How deep the rows of this table will appear, not how many bars will appear on the Gantt chart. Typically, leave this number at the default value of 1.

- *Lock First Column*: Turn this setting on to prevent the first column and only the first column of the table—usually the ID or Name field—from scrolling off the screen to the left as you move around in the table onscreen. Notice that Project differs from what you may be used to in Microsoft Excel: In Project, you can prevent only the first column from scrolling off the screen; you cannot freeze more than the first column. This limitation may influence the field you choose to display first in the table.

When you have finished making selections from the Table Definition dialog box, click OK.

To see your custom table onscreen, click Apply in the More Tables dialog box.

The column headings are always displayed as you scroll down in the project task list. There is no setting to turn this feature on or off, or to modify it in any way.

Changing Table Features from the View Screen

You have an alternative to making changes to a table using the Table Definition dialog box: onscreen editing. You can change the settings for columns that already appear, as well as add and remove columns.

Be aware that onscreen changes made to a table—adding or removing columns or changing column settings—actually edit the underlying table definition and affect all views which use that table. If you want to keep the original settings for a supplied table, you should create a copy of the table and work with the copy onscreen instead of the original.

To Do: Editing Columns in a Table Onscreen

To change column contents or formatting onscreen, follow these steps:

1. Move the vertical divider bar if necessary so that the column you want to modify is visible.

2. Position the mouse pointer over the column title and double-click. The Column Definition dialog box appears as shown in Figure 18.3.

FIGURE 18.3

Column settings can be adjusted onscreen.

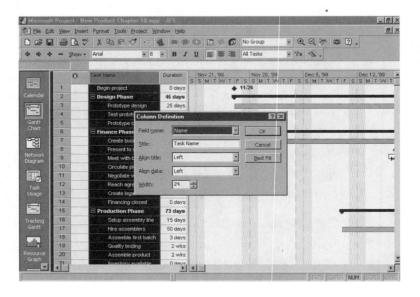

3. The Column Definition dialog box lets you set the same five column characteristics that you can set in the Table Definition dialog box, namely Field Name, Title, Align Title, Align Data, and Width.

4. When finished making changes to the columns, click OK to return to the screen and view the new table settings.

> From the Column Definition dialog box, choose Best Fit if you aren't sure how wide to make the column. But choose Best Fit after making other desired changes; clicking the Best Fit option closes the dialog box and applies all the column settings.

In addition to changing column settings, you can add and remove columns while viewing the table.

To Do: Adding a Column to a Table Onscreen

To add a column to the table currently onscreen; follow these steps:

1. Select any cell in a column where you want the added column to appear. Existing columns to the right of the selected column are moved farther to the right; the new column is inserted to the left of the selected column.

2. Choose Insert, Column. The Column Definition dialog box appears.

▼   3. For the information to be displayed in this column, select a Project field name from the drop-down list box.

   4. For the other fields, you can accept the default settings or make changes as desired.

▲   5. When finished, click OK.

To Do: Removing a Column from a Table Onscreen

To remove a column from the current table, do the following:

   1. Position the mouse pointer over the title for the column you want to remove.

   2. Click the column title so that the entire column is selected.

   3. Select Edit, Hide Column. The selected column is removed and remaining columns to the right of the selected column move back to the left.

▲

The phrasing for removing columns can be misleading. The Edit, Hide Column command implies to most users that the column width is set to zero, and it can be displayed again (as is true in Microsoft Excel). In Microsoft Project, the column is actually removed from the underlying table definition. You must follow the procedures for inserting a column to redisplay the "hidden" column.

18

Creating Custom Views

Although a number of predefined views are supplied with Project, they may not meet your needs exactly. Perhaps you would prefer that the Summary table be displayed with the standard Gantt Chart instead of the Entry table. Or perhaps your boss wants to see a Gantt Chart printout containing only milestone tasks. You can create custom views from scratch, edit existing views, or create a custom view by copying an existing view that is close to what you need but not quite right. All three options are available from the View, More Views command. Project views are comprised of several components:

- The view name, such as My Gantt Chart
- The basic screen type for the view, such as Gantt Chart or Task Usage
- The table of Project fields displayed; either a supplied table or one you have customized
- The group definition to be used, if any, to see the tasks or resources in an order other than strictly by ID number
- The filter in effect; either no filter (to show all tasks or resources), a supplied filter, or a filter you have already customized

All these view components are specified in a single dialog box. The choices you make are stored with the view definition. The next time you apply your custom view, the correct table, group definition, and filter are applied to the basic screen type you chose for this view.

To Do: Creating a Custom View

To begin the process of creating a custom view (whether you want to create a custom view from scratch, edit an existing view, or copy an existing view that is close to what you need), start with these steps:

1. Select View, More Views. The More Views dialog box appears as shown in Figure 18.4.

FIGURE 18.4

Edit or copy an existing view or create a new view in the Move View dialog box.

2. To create a new view from scratch, click the New button on the right side of the dialog box.

   To modify an existing view and keep the same view name, select a view from the list and click Edit.

   To use an existing view as the starting point for a custom view, select a view from the list and click Copy.

3. The View Definition dialog box opens, as shown in Figure 18.5. Make changes as desired, using the instructions in the following sections. Click OK when finished.

FIGURE 18.5

Define components of a custom view in the View Definition dialog box.

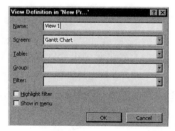

4. To see your new or custom view on the screen, click the Apply button at the bottom of the More Views dialog box.

Entering the Name of the View

The first step in defining a custom view is to give the view a name. Microsoft Project gives the new or copied view a default name, such as View 1. Replace the default name by typing any name that makes logical sense to you, up to a maximum of 50 characters (shorter is better). To create a *keyboard shortcut key* (the underlined character you see on other menu choices), type an ampersand (&) before the letter you want to use as the shortcut key.

Selecting the View Components

After providing a view name, you must select a table, a group definition, and filter for the view. If you created a completely new view instead of copying or editing an existing view, you must also do the following:

- Identify the new view as a full-screen single view or a split-screen combination view; most views are full screen.

- Select a screen type for the view. In the View Definition dialog box shown in Figure 18.6, choose the basic layout from the drop-down list of possible Screen types.

18

FIGURE 18.6
Base a custom view on an existing screen type.

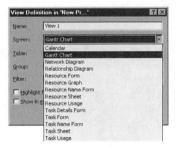

Selecting the Table for the View

Which columns of Project fields should be displayed in your custom view? Choose the appropriate set of fields from the Table drop-down list in the View Definition dialog box. Any custom tables you have created also appear in this list.

> You are not limited to displaying only the table named in the view definition. After any view is displayed, select View, Table to show a different table on the screen. This action changes the definition of the view; the next time it is displayed, the table applied using View, Table will be the table shown onscreen.

Selecting the Filter for the View

Should you display all task (or resource) rows in this view or only some of them? Choose the appropriate rows to be displayed from the Filter drop-down list box in the View Definition dialog box. Any custom filters you have created also appear in this list. If you choose All Tasks or All Resources, you have effectively selected no filter. A filter does not have to hide rows. If you would rather see all rows in the view but have the rows that match the filter appear on the screen in blue (by default), select the Highlight filter check box in the View Definition dialog box.

Displaying the View Name in the Menu

After a custom view has been created, you can apply it by choosing View, More Views and selecting the name from the complete list of views. If this is a view you intend to use often, make it easier to access by placing its name directly on the View menu. To do that, select the Show in menu check box in the View Definition dialog box.

Creating a Combination View

When you create a new view from scratch, the first question to be answered is whether the new view will be a full-screen single display or a split-screen combination display. A split-screen view displays two levels of information:

- The top view is the main focus
- The bottom view provides more specific information about the tasks or resources selected in the top view

Before creating a split view, the individual views to be used for the top and bottom sections must already exist. Split views supplied by Project include Resource Allocation and Task Entry.

To Do: Creating a Split-Screen View

To create a new view, consisting of one view on the top and another view on the bottom, follow these steps:

1. Select View, More Views.
2. Click New on the right side of the More Views dialog box. The Define New View dialog box appears (see Figure 18.7)

▼

FIGURE 18.7

Views can fill the screen or be split into top and bottom portions.

3. Select Combination View and click OK. A variation of the View Definition dialog box appears.

4. As with the single-view View Definition dialog box discussed in the earlier section, "Selecting the View Components," enter a Name for the split view and indicate whether or not it will Show in menu.

5. Select the view to be displayed in the Top of the combination view; select a view to be displayed in the Bottom of the combination view. You have no table, group, or filter choices when creating a combination view; the tables, groups and filters to be used in each half of the combination view are specified in the definitions of those individual views.

6. Click OK when finished.

▲

7. To see your new view on the screen, click the Apply button in the More Views dialog box.

18

To switch the display from a split-screen view back to a full-screen view, press and hold the Shift key and select a view from the View Bar or the View menu.

Saving the View Definition

Custom views, like custom tables, groups, and filters, are automatically saved with the Project file in which they were created. There is no additional "save to file" step to perform. Just be sure to save the file.

Creating Custom Fields

In addition to all of the Project fields you have been using—Start, Finish, Duration, and so on—there are many empty fields in Project with generic names, available for use for your own purposes. Customizing a field in Project can be as simple as renaming a field to something more descriptive, or as sophisticated as entering a list of values for a field to restrict data entry. You can also create a formula in a custom field to calculate values based on other Project fields.

Perhaps you need to track a work order number with tasks. A renamed custom Text field would work well. Maybe you are using Project as an estimating tool and would like to add a markup percentage to the cost figures. A custom Cost field that uses a formula you define would calculate the markup for you.

To Do: Customizing Field Names and Values

To define one of Project's custom fields for your own use, do the following:

1. Choose Tools, Customize, Fields to display the Customize Fields dialog box (see Figure 18.8).

FIGURE 18.8

130 Task fields and 130 Resource fields can be customized to suit your needs.

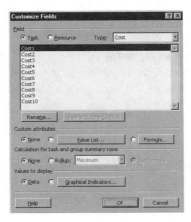

2. In the Field area, focus on Task or Resource fields, and then choose a custom field Type from the drop-down list.

3. Select a generic, numbered field from the list. Fields that have already been given new names will display both the field number and the assigned name.

4. Choose Rename to assign a more descriptive name to the field you've chosen.

5. In the Custom attributes area, you can choose one of the following options:

   Choose None to simply use the field for data entry (common for Text fields).

   Choose Value List to create a drop-down list of acceptable values for the field. (You can Restrict the field to values in the list or Allow additional items to be entered into the list.)

   Choose Formula to create your own calculated field, probably based on other Project fields.

6. For numeric field types, control the summary row values in the Calculation for task and group summary rows area. You may want a summary row to show the field value sums or an average, for example.

▼   7. The Values to Display option allows you to replace actual data on the screen or printout with symbols, which represent possible ranges of values in the field.

▲   8. Click OK when finished.

Now that you have a custom field, what do you do with it? Your field can be added to any table or sheet view, as described previously in the custom tables discussion. Both the generic field name and the new name will be shown in any drop-down list of task fields, such as on the Insert, Column dialog box. Also, using the Organizer feature, custom field definitions can be copied to other Project files—no need to re-create them!

By way of example, let's define the custom cost field, discussed previously, which will calculate cost markup on each task in the project.

Custom Field Example

Follow this example to define a custom field whose values are calculated from another Project field.

1. Choose Tools, Customize, Fields.

2. Choose Task in the Field area and select Cost from the Type drop-down list.

3. Select Cost1 (or any numbered field; they do not have to be used in any order).

4. Click on Rename, and in the Rename Field dialog box type **Markup**. Click OK (see Figure 18.9).

18

FIGURE 18.9
Custom fields can be assigned more descriptive field names.

5. Choose Formula in the Custom attributes area to display the Formula dialog box (as shown in Figure 18.10).

FIGURE 18.10
Custom fields can contain formulas to compute values based on other Project fields.

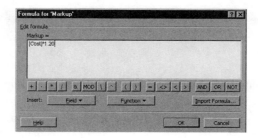

6. In the Edit formula area, notice that Project has started us off with Markup=; you don't need to type an = sign. To compute a 20 percent markup value, click in the open area and type:

   `[Cost] * 1.20`

   You could also choose the [Cost] field from the Insert Field drop-down list, and then click the * for multiplication. Finish the formula by typing in **1.20**.

7. Click OK, and click OK again to accept Project's warning that any existing values in the Markup (Cost1) field will be lost.

8. Notice in the Field list in Customize Fields dialog box, Cost1 is now also known as Markup. Click OK to close the Customize Fields dialog box.

9. Add the custom field to the table onscreen. Figure 18.11 shows the Markup field inserted into a copy of the task cost table.

Total planned costs   Total costs plus 20 percent markup

FIGURE 18.11

View a customized field by modifying a table.

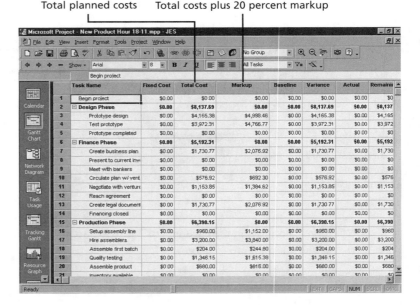

Summary

You can gain full control over what is displayed onscreen, and printed out, by combining customized tables and fields with filters and groups (from Hour 16, "Fine-Tuning the Project Plan"). Tables can be customized the easy way—onscreen—or the more exact way—making copies of existing tables and modifying the copies. In the long run, you will save yourself time by creating and naming custom tables and using the View menu to switch quickly between them. Also, renaming generic fields for your own needs can turn Project into a true information repository for your project plan. Custom views can be the pay-off for taking the time to create customized fields, tables, filters and groups, allowing you to combine them into specialized views for different managers or to meet printing requirements.

Q&A

Q **I named my customized Gantt Chart** *My Gantt Chart*. **An ampersand is in front of the letter** *G* **in the chart Name field in the View Definition dialog box, and the chart name appears on the View menu. But when I open the View menu and press G to display the chart, the menu highlight moves to the original Gantt Chart option and neither chart appears on my screen. Why?**

A The *G* you picked as the hot key for quick access to your customized chart is already in use by the original Gantt Chart. When you open the menu and press G, Project doesn't know which G you mean. You can either look at the menu, choose an access key not already in use, and return to the View Definition dialog box to move the ampersand in front of a different key; or leave the view alone but press G twice and then press Enter to display your customized chart from the View menu.

Q **I'm creating a new Combination view, but it won't let me specify the tables or filters to use. Why not?**

A A Combination view is just that—a combination of two *existing* views. You must first create each of the two halves of the view. When you create the views for the top and bottom of the combination view, specify your table and filter choices in each of those view definitions.

Q **I experimented with creating some custom views before finding one I like and want to keep. How can I get rid of the ones I don't want in my file?**

A Use the Organizer to do some housekeeping. Choose Tools, Organizer to display the dialog box. Select the Views tab at the top of the box. Look for the name of the *open* file at the top of a view list, probably the list on the right side of the box. Select the views to be removed, and then click Delete and confirm your choice. Note that you can also rename your custom views in this dialog box.

Exercises

In the following exercises, identify and name a custom text field to be used for identifying the type of work needed for each task. The data entries for the field will be restricted

18

to certain key words. Then that field is used in a custom table. Finally, the new table is included as an element for a new custom view. Work with the file, "New Product Hour 18.MPP." The completed exercises can be found in "New Product Hour 18-Exercises.MPP." See the Introduction for instructions to access the sample files and solutions for these exercises on the book's Web page.

1. Customize Task field Text1 by renaming it as "Work Type."
2. Restrict the values for this field to Design, Engineering, Sales, and Finance.
3. Make a copy of the entry table and name it Custom Entry.
4. In the new table, insert the Text1 (Work Type) field between the Indicators column and the Name column. Apply the table to the screen.
5. Create a new, full-screen view based on a Gantt Chart. Name the view Entry Gantt. Use the new Custom Entry table, and display all tasks without any grouping.
6. View the Entry Gantt onscreen.

Hour 19

Publishing Projects on the Web or an Intranet

In this hour, you will see how you can save your project file as an HTML document that can be published to the Internet or your corporate intranet. This hour introduces you to all of Microsoft Project 2000's Web features and shows you how to create HTML documents to communicate important information about your project.

In this hour, you will learn:

- How to save your project data to a web page
- How to include a picture of a Gantt Chart in your HTML document
- How to create a hyperlink from a task or resource to navigate to other files or web pages

Overview of Project 2000's Internet Features

Microsoft Project 2000 has many powerful features that take advantage of the Internet's power. As with all the other Microsoft Office applications, Project 2000 gives you the capability to save your project as an HTML document that can be viewed with a Web browser, such as Microsoft Internet Explorer or Netscape Navigator (see Figure 19.1).

FIGURE 19.1

Your project can be saved as an HTML document that can be viewed through a Web browser, such as Microsoft Internet Explorer.

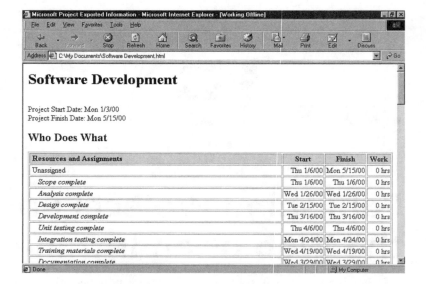

Some other Microsoft Project 2000 Web-related features include the following:

- The capability to navigate to a Web site on the Internet or a document on your network from a hyperlink field on a task or resource.

- The capability to track your project's progress by collecting actual work and remaining work estimates from project team members on your corporate intranet (see Hour 23, "Using Microsoft Project in Workgroups").

- The capability to create an Import/Export map that allows you to select the specific task, resource, and resource assignment information you want to publish in your HTML document.

- The capability to easily include a picture of your project's Gantt Chart in your Web document.

- The capability to customize your HTML document to include a header row (resource assignment rows indented below their associated task) or to be based on a customized HTML template that includes your company logo or other graphics.

Navigating with Hyperlinks

When you are out browsing the Web using Internet Explorer or Netscape Navigator, you become very accustomed to clicking on underlined text or graphics to move to another location on the Internet. Whenever the cursor changes to the familiar "pointing finger," it is an indication that by clicking the Web page with your mouse, you will be navigated to some other Web page. The technical name for the place on a Web page that navigates you to another location is called a *hyperlink*.

A Web browser is designed to display documents formatted using the *Hypertext Markup Language*, or *HTML*. The HTML code contains all the information for how your browser should display the text, graphics, and hyperlinks in a Web page.

Most browsers give you the capability to view the HTML code for the active Web document. For example, to view the HTML code for a Web document in Microsoft Internet Explorer, select View, Source from the menu. Figure 19.2 shows the HTML source code for the Web document displayed in Figure 19.1.

FIGURE 19.2

This figure shows the HTML source code for a Microsoft Project 2000 HTML document. Fortunately, you do not have to write this code yourself, because Project will generate it for you automatically.

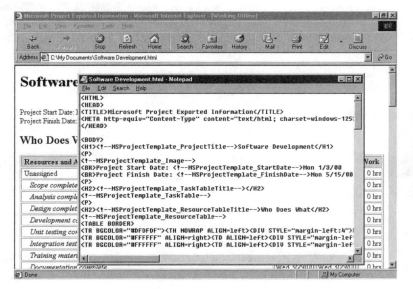

Exporting Project Data to Web Pages

In this section, you will step through the process of saving your project file as an HTML document. Each of the following examples uses the Software Development.mpt project template that comes with Project 2000. You can access this template by choosing New from the File menu and clicking the Project Templates tab in the New dialog box. Or, you can work through the following examples using one of your actual projects.

Saving Your Project as an HTML Document

One of the key benefits of being able to save your project as an HTML document is that you can publish the information *you* want to communicate about your project *without* giving people in your organization access to the project file itself.

> It's a good idea to save your project as a standard .MPP file before saving it as an HTML document.

To Do: Saving Your Project File as an HTML Document

To save your Project file as an HTML document, follow these steps:

1. Open your project file, and from the menu, choose File, Save As Web Page. The Save As dialog box will be displayed (see Figure 19.3).

FIGURE **19.3**

The Save As dialog box allows you to save your project as an HTML document.

2. Click Save, and Project displays the Export Mapping dialog box (see Figure 19.4), where you can select the "map" on which to base your HTML document. A map is essentially a set of instructions that tells Project the type of data you want to save in your Web document. For example, you may choose to export all tasks that are in danger of finishing late, or all resources that are currently over budget. Project comes with 12 predefined map files you can use to create your HTML document, or you can create your own map files.

▼

FIGURE 19.4

The Export Mapping dialog box allows you to select the map file used to determine which data to export to your HTML document.

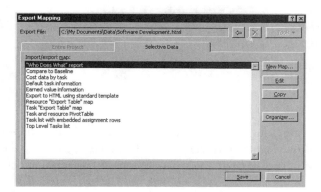

NEW TERM   A *map* is essentially a set of instructions that tells Project the type of data you want to save in your Web document. For example, you might choose to export all tasks in danger of finishing late or all resources currently over budget.

> By default, Microsoft Project 2000 saves your HTML file to the same directory and assigns it the same name as your project file (but with the extension `.html`). You can override these defaults in the Save As dialog box by selecting the directory and filename as you would in any other Windows application.

3. From the Selective Data option on the Export Mapping dialog box, select the Task List With Embedded Assignment Rows map, and click Save. Your project is now saved as an HTML document.

▲

Viewing Your Project as an HTML Document

Now comes the really fun part: You get to view your project file through your Web browser to see how it will look when it's actually published on your intranet or on the Internet. In this section, you view the HTML file created in the previous section, "Saving Your Project as an HTML Document," using Microsoft Internet Explorer 5.0, but most browsers have a similar feature you can use to follow the example.

To Do: Viewing Your Project File with a Web Browser

To view your Project file in a browser, follow these steps:

1. Start Microsoft Internet Explorer, and from the menu, choose File, Open. The Open dialog box will be displayed (see Figure 19.5).

19

▲ To Do

▼

FIGURE **19.5**

The Open dialog box in Microsoft Internet Explorer allows you to select the HTML file you want to view in the browser.

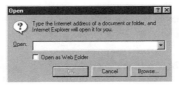

2. Click the Browse button to navigate to the HTML file you want to view, and from the Browse dialog box, click Open. From the Open dialog box, click OK, and your HTML document will be displayed in the browser (see Figure 19.6).

FIGURE **19.6**

Microsoft Internet Explorer enables you to view the HTML document based on the "Who Does What" report map.

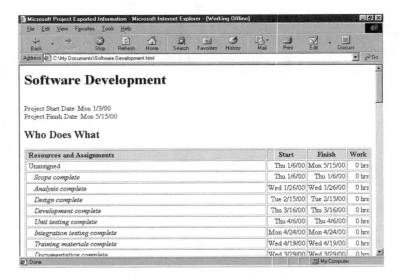

▲

For more information about saving your Project files to the Web, including using Project to create your own import/export maps, see *Special Edition Using Project 2000*, published by Que.

Defining Import/Export Map HTML Options

In addition to using the predefined maps that come with Project 2000, you can create your own map on which to base the HTML document. In this section, you step through the process of creating your own map to export only those tasks that are on the critical path. In addition, you will explore some of the other available options you can use when exporting your project data to an HTML file.

A *critical path* is a series of tasks in your project that must finish on time in order for your project to finish on time. In other words, if any task on your project's critical path ends up finishing later than its planned finish date, your *project's* planned finish date will be directly affected.

To Do: Creating an Export Map for your Project file

To create an export map for your Project file, follow these steps:

1. Open your project file, and from the menu, choose File, Save As Web Page. The Save As dialog box will be displayed.

2. Select the filename and location for your HTML file, and click Save.

   If you have previously saved your HTML file, the following dialog box will be displayed (see Figure 19.7). To overwrite your existing file with the new file, click OK.

FIGURE 19.7
To overwrite your existing HTML file, click OK in this dialog box.

3. From the Export Mapping dialog box, click the New Map button. The Define Import/Export Map dialog box will be displayed (see Figure 19.8).

FIGURE 19.8
The Define Import/Export Map dialog box allows you to choose the project data you want to export to your HTML document.

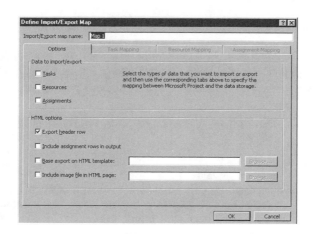

4. In the Import/Export Map Name field, type **Critical Tasks**.

5. In the Data To Import/Export section, select the Tasks check box (because you will be exporting rows of tasks in your HTML document).

Each type of project data you select in this section will create its own table
in your HTML document. For example, because you selected Tasks, your
HTML document will contain a table with rows of tasks from your project
plan. If you had selected Tasks and Resources, your HTML document would
contain a table with rows of tasks *and* a table with rows of resources from
your project.

6. Select the Task Mapping tab, and the Define Import/Export Map dialog box will
    display the mapping options for your project's task data (see Figure 19.9).

FIGURE 19.9

*You can select the task
fields you want to
include in your Web
document on the Task
Mapping tab.*

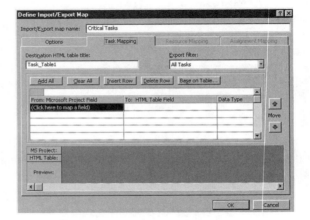

7. In the Destination HTML Table Title field, type the text you would like to appear
    above the task table in your Web document. Because the document you are creat-
    ing will display tasks that are on your project's critical path, type **Critical Tasks** at
    this prompt.
8. From the Export Filter drop-down list, select the Critical filter (see Figure 19.10).

The filters displayed in the Export Filter drop-down list are the same filters
you can choose from a task type view, such as the Gantt Chart in Project
2000. See Hour 18, "Creating Custom Views," for information on how to create your own filters in Microsoft Project.

FIGURE 19.10

Select the Critical filter to display only tasks that are on your project's critical path.

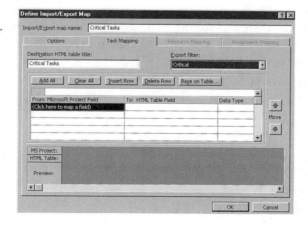

9. Click the Base on Table button, and the Select Base Table for Field Mapping dialog box will be displayed (see Figure 19.11).

FIGURE 19.11

Select the Project table on which you want to base your task table in the HTML document.

19

10. From the Select Base Table for Field Mapping dialog box, select the Schedule table. Click OK, and notice how all the fields from the Schedule table are now listed in the Task Mapping tab (see Figure 19.12).

FIGURE 19.12

The Task Mapping tab displays all the fields in Project 2000's Schedule table.

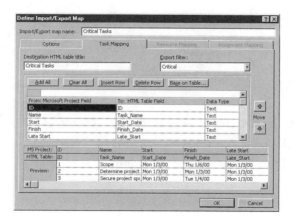

▼　11. Sometimes a table in Project might contain fields that you do not want to display in
your HTML document. For example, suppose you don't want to include the Late
Start, Late Finish, and Free Slack fields in your HTML document. Select the Late
Start row and click the Delete Row button; then delete the Late Finish and Free
Slack fields from the table.

12. In addition to displaying schedule information for the tasks, you decide you want
to display the total work for the task, as well. To do so, select the Total Slack row,
and click the Insert Row button. In the From: Microsoft Project Field column,
select the Work field from the drop-down list.

13. In the To: HTML Table Field column, change the text Scheduled_Work to Task
Work Estimate. This text will become the new column header for the Work field in
the HTML document.

14. Click OK, and the Export Mapping dialog box will be displayed.

15. Click Save, and your project will be saved to an HTML document.

16. Open the Web document in your browser to view the tasks that are on the critical
path in your project (see Figure 19.13).

FIGURE 19.13
*This HTML document
displays the schedule
information for those
tasks on your project's
critical path.*

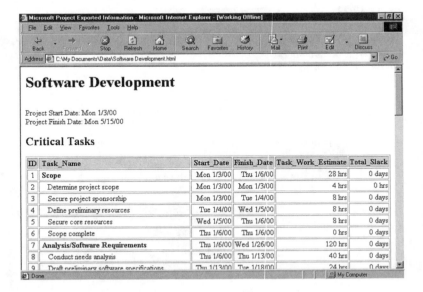

ID	Task_Name	Start_Date	Finish_Date	Task_Work_Estimate	Total_Slack
1	**Scope**	Mon 1/3/00	Thu 1/6/00	28 hrs	0 days
2	Determine project scope	Mon 1/3/00	Mon 1/3/00	4 hrs	0 hrs
3	Secure project sponsorship	Mon 1/3/00	Tue 1/4/00	8 hrs	0 days
4	Define preliminary resources	Tue 1/4/00	Wed 1/5/00	8 hrs	0 days
5	Secure core resources	Wed 1/5/00	Thu 1/6/00	8 hrs	0 days
6	Scope complete	Thu 1/6/00	Thu 1/6/00	0 hrs	0 days
7	**Analysis/Software Requirements**	Thu 1/6/00	Wed 1/26/00	120 hrs	0 days
8	Conduct needs analysis	Thu 1/6/00	Thu 1/13/00	40 hrs	0 days
9	Draft preliminary software specifications	Thu 1/13/00	Tue 1/18/00	24 hrs	0 days

Including Resource Assignments with Tasks

If you would like to include the resources assigned to tasks in your Web document, you
can set an additional option to display this information.

For more information on assigning resources, refer to Hours 11–15.

To Do: Displaying Resource Assignments in your HTML Document

Follow these steps to display resource assignments in your HTML document:

1. Open your project file, and from the menu, choose File, Save As Web Page. The Save As dialog box will be displayed.

2. Select the filename and location for your HTML file, and click Save.

3. In the Export Mapping dialog box, select the map file you want to modify and click the Edit button. In this example, you will continue to use the Critical Tasks map from the previous section.

4. In the Define Import/Export Map dialog box, check the Include Assignment Rows In Output option in the HTML Options section (see Figure 19.14).

FIGURE 19.14

Check the Include Assignment Rows In Output option to display resource assignment information in your HTML document.

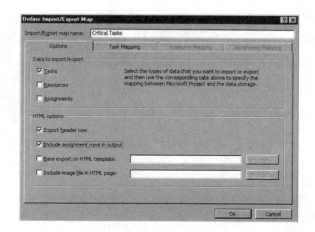

19

5. Click OK, and click Save on the Export Mapping dialog box. Your project will be saved as an HTML document.

6. Open the HTML document in your browser, and you will see the resource assignments indented below each task in your project (see Figure 19.15).

FIGURE 19.15

This HTML document displays the resource assignments for each task in the project.

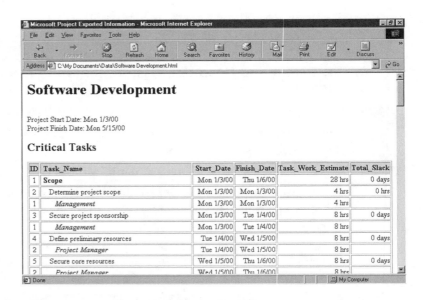

Displaying a Gantt Chart in Your HTML Document

It's often said that a picture is worth a thousand words, and this is very true when it comes to designing your HTML documents in Project. In addition to the Project data, you can easily display an image of your project's Gantt Chart in your Web document to make it more visually interesting and informative.

For more information about Gantt Charts, see Hour 2, "Becoming an Instant Project Guru."

To Do: Adding a Gantt Chart Graphic to your Web Page

To add a Gantt Chart to your Web page, follow these steps:

1. Open your project file, and from the View Bar, select the Gantt Chart view.

2. In the Standard Toolbar, click the Copy Picture button to open the Copy Picture dialog box (see Figure 19.16).

3. In the Copy Picture dialog box, select the To GIF Image File option. By default, Microsoft Project assigns the image file the same name as your project file, but gives it a .GIF extension.

A *GIF file,* which stands for a Graphics Interchange Format, is a type of compressed graphics file format that's very commonly used in Web pages.

FIGURE **19.16**

The Copy Picture dialog box allows you to capture a graphic image of your Gantt Chart that can be included in your HTML document.

4. In the Timescale section, select the date range you want to include in the Gantt Chart image, or select As Shown On Screen to capture the timescale that's currently displayed on the screen.

5. Click OK, and within a few seconds, Project will capture a graphic image of your Gantt Chart (see Figure 19.17)

FIGURE **19.17**

This figure shows Microsoft Project exporting a picture of the Gantt Chart to a GIF file.

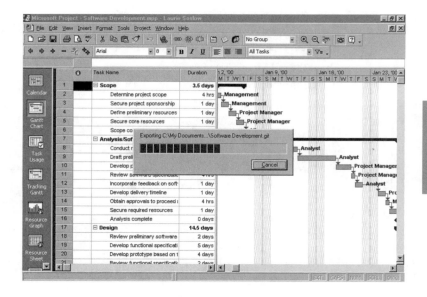

6. From the menu, choose File, Save As HTML. The Save As dialog box will be displayed.

7. Select the filename and location for your HTML file, and click Save.

8. In the Export Mapping dialog box, select the map file you want to modify and click the Edit button. In this example, you will continue to use the Critical Tasks map from the previous section.

▼   9. In the HTML Options section, check the option Include Image File in HTML Page.
       When you check this option, Project automatically displays the information for the
       Gantt Chart GIF image (see Figure 19.18).

FIGURE 19.18

Select the Include Image File in HTML Page option to include the image of your project's Gantt Chart in the HTML document.

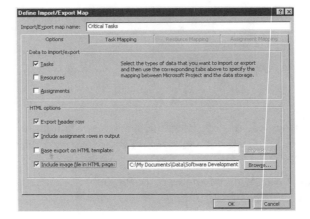

   10. Click OK, and from the Export Mapping dialog box, click Save. Your project will
       be saved as an HTML document.
   11. Open the HTML document in your browser, and you will see the Gantt Chart dis-
       played in your Web page (see Figure 19.19).

FIGURE 19.19

This HTML document displays an image of the project's Gantt Chart.

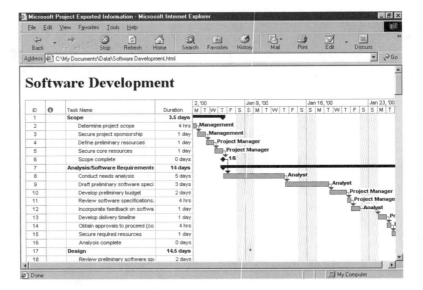

▲

Working with Hyperlinks in Tasks and Resources

In addition to being able to save your project as an HTML document, Microsoft Project 2000 includes several hyperlink fields that allow you to navigate to another document or Web site from a task or resource in your project. For example, suppose you have developed a task checklist in Microsoft Word that includes all the detailed processes for a task in your project. You can add a hyperlink to the task so that when you click on it, you go directly to the task checklist.

Adding a Hyperlink

It's fairly easy to add a hyperlink to a task, resource, or assignment from any view. However, it's easiest to use the hyperlink if you display a view that has an indicator column so you can simply click on the hyperlink indicator icon to jump to the hyperlink target. In this example, I will be adding a hyperlink to a task using the Gantt Chart view.

To Do: Adding a Hyperlink to a Task, Resource, or Assignment

Follow these steps to add a hyperlink:

1. Open a project in any view.

2. Select the task, resource, or assignment to which you want to add a hyperlink, and from the menu, choose Insert, Hyperlink. The Insert Hyperlink dialog box will be displayed (see Figure 19.20).

FIGURE 19.20

The Insert Hyperlink dialog box allows you to add, delete, or modify a hyperlink in your project.

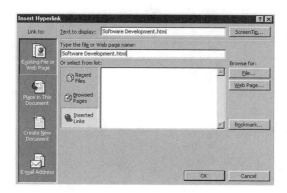

3. In the Type the File or Web Page Name box, enter a Web site URL or a filename. If you prefer, you can browse buttons to browse for a file or web page.

   Project 2000 also includes a feature to navigate the user to a specific section of a

▼ file, such a Microsoft Word bookmark or a named range in an Excel file. To do this, simply append the name of the bookmark or named range to the end of the file or web address, preceded by the # symbol. For example, if the bookmark name in a Word document is SectionOne, you would enter C:\My Documents\Report.doc#SectionOne.

The Insert Hyperlink dialog box also allows you specify the text to display and screen tip to display when you user moves the mouse over the hyperlink indicator for the task or resource. To do so, enter this information in the Text to display and Screen Tip fields on this dialog. Additionally, if you are inserting a hyperlink to another Microsoft Project file, you can navigate the user to a particular task, resource, or View by selecting the Bookmark button and selecting the desired destination.

▲ 4. Click OK, and the hyperlink will be created for the selected task.

You can delete a hyperlink by selecting the task, resource, or assignment and choosing Edit, Clear, Hyperlinks. To jump to the hyperlink reference, simply display the project in a view that has the indicator column displayed and click the hyperlink icon on the row for the task, resource, or assignment.

Editing a Hyperlink

Sometimes it might be necessary to edit an existing hyperlink in your project file. For example, a hyperlink could point to a document that has been moved, or it might reference a Web site on the Internet that has changed its URL address.

To Do: Modifying a Hyperlink for a Task or Resource

To modify a hyperlink for a task or resource, follow these steps:

1. Select a task in your project that you want to modify a hyperlink for, and from the menu, choose Insert, Hyperlink.

2. Enter the new hyperlink information as described in the previous section, "Adding a Hyperlink."

▲ 3. Click OK, and the hyperlink will be modified with the new information.

Deleting a Hyperlink

Sometimes you might need to remove a hyperlink from a task or resource in your project file. For example, you may no longer want to reference a document on your corporate intranet, or a Web site you were pointing to might not exist on the Internet any more. In these cases, you need to delete the hyperlink from the task or resource in your project.

To Do: Deleting a Hyperlink for a Task or Resource

To delete a hyperlink for a task or resource, follow these steps:

1. Select a task in your project that you want to modify a hyperlink for, and from the menu, choose Insert, Hyperlink.

2. Select the hyperlink you want to delete and click the Remove Link button.

Navigating to a Hyperlink

Hyperlinks are commonly used to associate relevant documents or Web sites to tasks and resources in your project. For example, if you have a task in your plan called "Evaluate Project 2000," you might want to create a hyperlink to the 60-day free evaluation copy of Microsoft Project 2000 on Microsoft's Web site at `http://www.microsoft.com/office/project/`. After you have added hyperlinks to your project, it's very easy to navigate to the referenced Web sites or documents.

To Do: Navigating to a Hyperlink from a Task or Resource

Follow these steps to navigate to a hyperlink from a task or resource:

1. Select a task or resource that contains a hyperlink, and from the menu, choose View, Table, Hyperlink. The Hyperlink table will be displayed (see Figure 19.21).

FIGURE 19.21
The Hyperlink table allows you to navigate to a hyperlink associated with a task or resource in your project.

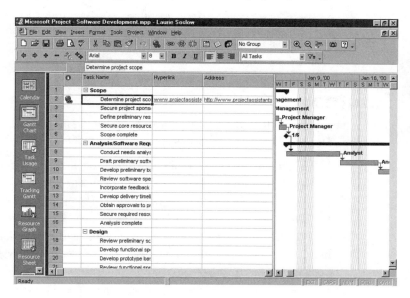

2. Click the blue, underlined hyperlink to navigate to the Web site or document referenced by the hyperlink.

Publishing Your Web Documents

After you have created your HTML documents, you need to publish them on the Internet or your corporate intranet.

If the Web documents will be viewed from your intranet, you need to copy all your HTML files (and related graphics files, if you included an image of your Gantt Chart, for example) to a location on your network server (as specified by your intranet administrator).

If you will be publishing your Web documents to the Internet, a convenient way to do this is with the Web Publishing Wizard included on the Microsoft Office 97 and Microsoft Office 2000 CD-ROMs. The Web Publishing Wizard can walk you through the process of publishing your Web pages in an easy-to-follow, step-by-step fashion.

To see if you have the Web Publishing Wizard installed on your computer, from the Windows taskbar, click the Start button, and choose Programs, Accessories, Internet Tools. The Web Publishing Wizard should appear in the Internet Tools folder. If you don't have it installed on your computer, you can download it for free from Microsoft's Web site at http://www.microsoft.com/windows/software/webpost/.

> For more information about using the Microsoft Office Web Publishing Wizard, see *Teach Yourself Office 2000 in 24 Hours*, also published by Sams Publishing.

Summary

So now you are all ready to become a Web publishing mogul! Let's just review the basic steps for publishing your project as an HTML document:

1. Make sure your plan has been updated to reflect the latest information about your project. You want to make sure the information you're publishing is current.

2. Choose the Save as HTML option from the File menu, and select the Import/Export map you want to use. Remember, the Import/Export map determines the specific project task, resource, and assignment information you will be publishing. It also contains information about the Web template that gives your HTML document its own "look."

3. If you want to include a picture of your Gantt Chart on your Web page, be sure to use the Copy Picture function on the Standard Toolbar, and select the option to Include Image File in HTML Page on the Import/Export map.

4. Use the Web Publishing Wizard to publish your HTML documents to the Internet or your corporate intranet.

Q&A

Q Can my HTML page be updated automatically when my project data changes?

A While Project 2000 does not include this feature "out of the box", you can automate the steps to publish your HTML document by recording a macro in Project as you are manually saving your HTML document for the first time. Then, simply run the macro each time you want to update your web page. You can even assign the macro to a toolbar button or menu item!

For more information about automating Microsoft Project 2000 using macros and Visual Basic for Applications (the programming language that is built into Project 2000), you can refer to *Special Edition Using Microsoft Project 2000*, published by Que.

Q How many hyperlinks can be included with a task or resource?

A Microsoft Project allows you to insert one hyperlink per task, resource, and assignment.

Exercises

Try these exercises to further build your proficiency in publishing Project data online:

1. Consider applying some your new HTML talents to other Microsoft Office applications, such as Word, Excel, and FrontPage. For example, your may want to create a project "home page" using Microsoft Word or FrontPage that contains an overview of all of the active projects in your organization. From the home page, you can create a link to each of the HTML pages you created in Project 2000.

2. Try out the various HTML templates included with Project 2000 to give your web page a new "look and feel". You can select a different template from the "Define Import/Export Map" dialog box, as described in this hour.

3. Consider using the Insert Hyperlink feature to link up all of your organizations project related documentation, such as task procedures, checklists, and sign-off forms.

19

PART VI

Managing and Tracking the Project

Hour

Hour **20**

Tracking Work on the Project

If you have been applying the lessons in this book to your own project, you should have a finalized schedule or plan for completing the project on time and within budget—like an architect's plan for a building that meets all the builder's requirements. Now your role as a project manager shifts from planning the project to managing the plan as conditions change. This hour discusses making the transition from using the Microsoft Project document as a preproduction planning device to a working blueprint that helps you manage the project and meet the project goals on time and within the budget.

In this hour, you will learn:

- The logic behind tracking your plan in Project
- Which Project fields are used for tracking
- What tracking tools are available in Project
- When and how to enter actual progress values
- How to reschedule work for interrupted or delayed tasks

Using Project as a Management Tool

After work on the project is underway, you will find that your plan, like the blueprints, will be consulted constantly, and it will be revised as you discover new information about the tasks and the resources you assigned to them. Sometimes actual events even threaten to make the plan unravel, but having your schedule already entered in Microsoft Project makes it much easier to figure out how to get things back on track, as in the following examples:

- If it appears that a task is going to take longer than you planned, and therefore delay other tasks and maybe even the finish of the project itself, you can enter the new estimated duration in Microsoft Project and see the calculated effects on other tasks and resource assignments. You can use Microsoft Project to try "what if" scenarios to find the best way to minimize the impact on the project's finish date and cost.

- If a resource becomes unavailable or costs more than anticipated, you can quickly evaluate alternatives, including ways to substitute less expensive resources.

- If you have to add a task to the schedule, you can add it, find ways to minimize the impact on the timeline and costs, and alert all those whom are affected by the change.

An orderly approach is required to effectively track progress and change the schedule in Project. The recommended steps are as follows:

- Make a copy of the *current schedule* just before you start work on the project. This copy will serve as a *baseline* to use for comparing with later, revised schedules, especially the final schedule that shows what actually happened. Project calculates *variances* that show the difference between the baseline and scheduled entries.

- Start using the current schedule to tell resources when to start work on specific tasks.

- When work actually starts and finishes on tasks, put those *actual* dates back into the Project file to replace the scheduled dates. If the actual dates differ from the scheduled dates, Project recalculates the schedule for the remainder of the project so you can better predict what is likely to happen. By entering actual data in the document, you improve the accuracy of the current schedule and are in a better position to assess how well the project is going.

- If you want to manage costs carefully, record how much work was actually done on the tasks and what the costs actually were. You can then compare that data with the baseline costs to see if you're staying within budget.

NEW TERM The *current schedule* is the one you have been working with so far—it's made up of the fields you use to enter estimates for tasks and assignments. Microsoft Project uses this schedule to do calculations and changes as you enter new information into the project.

NEW TERM The *baseline schedule* is a set of fields that Project uses to preserve a copy of the current schedule at a specific point, usually the moment just before work actually starts. Baseline fields are not changed by your revisions to the schedule; they are changed only by explicit commands to set aside baseline copies of the current schedule.

NEW TERM The *variances* are calculated by subtracting the baseline field from the corresponding current schedule field. Variances tell you how much the schedule value has changed since the baseline was created.

NEW TERM The *actual fields* are where you enter actual dates, work, and costs to show what actually happens. Project automatically copies these actual values into the corresponding fields of the current schedule to update it.

This process of monitoring progress, updating the schedule, and comparing the new schedule with the baseline schedule helps you assess whether you're likely to meet your goals in a timely fashion. This information can let you know that you need to make changes before it's too late. When the project is finished, your efforts should leave you in the position to gloat over how you finished early and for less cost than originally planned. Even if the project takes longer or costs more than planned, however, the tracking data you have recorded can help you explain where time was lost or why costs went over budget. You have also gathered information that will be useful in planning future projects.

In this hour, you will focus on the mechanics of updating the schedule. The variances and other analysis techniques are covered in the next hour.

Understanding the Tracking Fields

The date, duration, work, and cost fields you have been working with in Microsoft Project are fields in the *current schedule*. These are the fields you use to plan and calculate a schedule. They tell you what your latest and best thinking is and how to complete the project.

Table 20.1 lists the current schedule fields that have tracking counterparts: baseline, variance, and actual fields. There are baseline and actual fields for both tasks and resource assignments. Therefore, the baseline schedule shows not only when a task was scheduled to start and how much work was supposed to be done, but can also show when each resource assignment for the task was scheduled to start and how much work each resource was scheduled to perform.

20

TABLE 20.1   The Fields Used in Tracking

Task Fields			
Current Schedule	*Baseline*	*Variance*	*Actual*
Start	Baseline Start	Start Variance	Actual Start
Finish	Baseline Finish	Finish Variance	Actual Finish
Duration	Baseline	Duration	Actual Duration (and Duration Variance Remaining Duration)
*Work	*Baseline Work	Work Variance	*Actual Work (and Remaining Work)
*Overtime Work			*Actual Overtime Work (and Remaining Overtime Work)
*Cost	*Baseline Cost	Cost Variance	*Actual Cost (and Remaining Cost)
Overtime			Actual Overtime Cost Cost (and Remaining Overtime Cost)

Assignment Fields			
Current Schedule	*Baseline*	*Variance*	*Actual*
Start	Baseline Start	Start Variance	Actual Start
Finish	Baseline Finish	Finish Variance	Actual Finish
*Work	Baseline Work	Work Variance	*Actual Work (and Remaining Work)
*Overtime Work			*Actual Overtime Work (and Remaining Overtime Work)
*Cost	Baseline Cost	Cost Variance	*Actual Cost (and Remaining Cost)
Overtime Cost			Actual Overtime Cost (and Remaining Overtime Cost)

Fields in Table 20.1 marked with an asterisk also have timephased components—the data can be displayed and tracked for specific time periods (hourly, daily, and so on) in the Task Usage or Resource Usage view.

Notice that you can track actual overtime work and overtime costs, but there's no baseline record of how much overtime work or cost was in the schedule when the baseline was captured. Also note that *duration* is a task-level phenomenon—there's no duration measurement at the assignment level.

Project's *variance fields* show the difference between the current value and the baseline value for each task. The formula is *current scheduled value* minus *baseline value*. Positive variances mean the current schedule calls for *more* than the baseline plan called for: You'll be running late or doing more work or spending more on costs than you had planned.

For example, observing Task 11 in Figure 20.1, the currently scheduled finish date is 1/03/01 and the baseline finish date is 1/05/01, so the variance is calculated by Project to be 1/03/01 minus 1/05/01 or -2 days. A negative variance means you'll finish earlier than planned; a positive variance means you'll be finishing later than planned. Therefore, positive variances are bad (it took longer or cost more), and negative variances are good (it took less time or cost less).

The Variance field in Figure 20.1 shows that Task 3 finished one day later than originally planned. Because of that, the next several tasks finished late also. Task 7 finished on time (probably by having a shorter duration) and gets the project back on track (the variance is zero). Starting with Task 11, some time is saved somewhere, and the other tasks in that group are also scheduled to finish two days early (variance is minus two days). By Task 16, you are again one day behind schedule, probably because this phase is linked to an earlier phase that has already slipped.

In Figure 20.1, you can compare the tracking fields for finish dates. The Finish column is the currently scheduled finish date for each task. I've bolded the actual dates that have been entered and the corresponding scheduled dates that are now fixed to those same values. Below the bolded (fixed) dates, the scheduled dates are free to be recalculated as circumstances change, but as new actual dates are entered for those tasks, their scheduled dates will become fixed, too.

When you enter a value in an actual field for a task, Microsoft Project does three essential things (there are even more calculations covered later in this hour):

- The value is entered in the actual field you are editing.
- The actual value is also copied into the current schedule field, replacing the estimated value with the actual value. This replacement could cause Project to recalculate current schedule values for successor tasks.
- Project tags the current schedule field as "fixed" now that an actual value is known and will not recalculate it again. For example, after you enter an actual start date

20

for a task, Project won't recalculate that start date even if a predecessor task changes. Only you can change the field now by entering a new value in it or its actual counterpart.

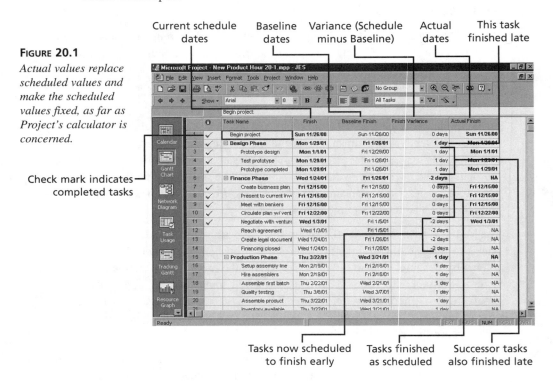

FIGURE 20.1

Actual values replace scheduled values and make the scheduled values fixed, as far as Project's calculator is concerned.

Check mark indicates completed tasks

As you track actual performance, the current schedule changes from its original speculative values to the known actual values. By the end of the project, the current schedule is identical to the actual schedule.

Now that you've surveyed the fields to be used in tracking, let's get on to the mechanics of putting data into those fields.

Setting the Baseline

The Planning Wizard prompts you to create the baseline when you first save a file (see Figure 20.2). Thereafter, it prompts you to update the baseline whenever it detects that the baseline is incomplete. You can also manually update the baseline from the menu at any time or save up to 10 interim versions of the baseline to show how the project plan has changed over time.

FIGURE 20.2

The Planning Wizard stands ready to save baseline information when you first save a project file.

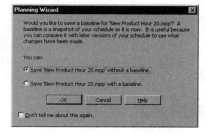

Capturing the Baseline

The first time you save a file, after you have supplied the filename, the Planning Wizard asks if you want to save a baseline as part of the saved file (see Figure 20.2). In a departure from standard Microsoft practices, clicking OK on the default selection does *not* save the baseline: It saves the file *without* creating the baseline. You have to select the second option and then click OK to make Project save the baseline. If you don't want to be bothered with this dialog box, you can click the check box labeled Don't tell me about this again. Doing so makes the Planning Wizard stop checking for the baseline when you close a file. Just remember—it's up to you to remember to capture the baseline before you start recording actual events. If you save the baseline and then subsequently make changes that should be in the baseline, you will again be prompted to update the baseline when you attempt to close the file after making those additions.

> The prompts to save the baseline were added to Project just to remind users about the importance of saving the baseline. You can safely ignore them, and even discontinue displaying them, as long as you can remember to save the baseline before you start entering actual values. On the other hand, it does no harm to continually update the baseline during the planning process.

20

You can use the Save Baseline command on the menu at any time to update the baseline. You should use this command just before you get ready to start tracking actual dates and costs to be certain that the baseline is updated to reflect the final plan. You can also use this command to update the baseline just for selected tasks. For example, if you add a task after the project has started, you could select that task and then use this command to record baseline values for that one task without disturbing the baseline values for any other tasks.

To Do: Saving the Baseline Manually

To save a baseline manually, follow these steps:

1. Choose Tools, Tracking, Save Baseline from the menu to display the Save Baseline dialog box (see Figure 20.3).

FIGURE 20.3

The Save Baseline dialog box allows you to save the baseline at any time, for the entire project or just for selected tasks.

2. Select Save Baseline to copy the task and assignment field values from the current schedule to the baseline fields.

3. At the bottom of this dialog box, you can choose whether to update all tasks and assignments or just the tasks that were selected when you started the command. (If you started from a resource view, this choice is not available.) Select Entire Project to save baseline values for all tasks, or Selected Tasks to save values for just the task(s) you selected beforehand.

4. Click OK to start the save process and close the dialog box.

Saving Interim Schedules

You might want to record multiple baseline dates in some projects. For instance, you might want to see how the project dates change during the planning process. Or, during a project with a long timeline, you are likely to have major revisions in the plan, even after work starts, and it might be useful to save the date schedules that are being replaced as interim plans for later reference. In situations like these, you can record up to 10 sets of interim project plan dates. These interim plans include only the task dates—no work, cost, or assignment data is saved.

To Do: Capturing Interim Plan Dates

To save task start and finish dates at interim set points, do the following:

1. Choose Tools, Tracking, Save Baseline from the menu to display the Save Baseline dialog box (refer to Figure 20.3).

2. Select Save Interim Plan to copy task dates to any of 10 pairs of interim plan date fields (Start1/Finish1, Start2/Finish2, and so forth).

▼ 3. In the Copy field, select what will be copied. The default is Start/Finish, which is the current schedule dates. You can also choose Baseline Start/Finish to copy the baseline dates into an interim plan, or you can copy one of the interim plans (Start1/Finish1, Start2/Finish2, and so forth) into another interim plan.

4. In the Into field, select which interim plan will receive the copy.

▲ 5. Click OK to start the copy process and close the dialog box.

Clearing the Baseline Fields

NEW FEATURE Sometimes it happens. You accidentally say yes to letting the Wizard save the baseline for you while closing a file. Or perhaps you saved the baseline information without understanding that this is a step to be done when the project leaves the planning phase and before any actual values or changes to % Complete are entered in the file. You can clear all of the project Baseline fields at any time. Just remember to save all your planning efforts at some point before beginning to use the plan as a tracking tool.

To Do: Clearing the Baseline Information

To Do To remove all baseline information from your plan, do the following:

1. Choose Tools, Tracking, Clear Baseline.

2. In the Clear Baseline dialog box, select Clear baseline plan (see Figure 20.4).

FIGURE 20.4
All baseline values can be cleared in one step.

3. Make the selection to clear the baseline for the entire project or only the tasks selected before opening the dialog box.

▲ 4. Click OK to start the clearing process and close the dialog box.

20

Tracking Actual Performance

There's a wide range in the level of detail you can choose to record when tracking actual work on your project. Tracking can be simple or sophisticated, depending on your reporting needs and the time you have to do it. The time it takes to keep a project file updated can be a considerable drain on the project manager's schedule. You must choose the level of detail based on the tradeoff between the time it takes you to keep the project updated and the value of the information that results. Here are some guidelines to keep in mind when tracking actual work:

- At the very least, you should record when tasks actually start and finish. If tasks finish late, the rest of the project might be in jeopardy of finishing late. If tasks finish early, resources could be freed that can help out with other tasks.

- For longer tasks that have started but not yet finished, you can record not only when the task started, but also how far along the task is—what percent of the scheduled task duration has been completed. You probably wouldn't want to take the time to do this for shorter tasks.

- Instead of tracking the percent of the task duration completed, and letting Project calculate how much work that involves, you can record the actual work itself for the task. Or, for even greater accuracy, you can record the work completed by each resource assigned to the task.

- By default, actual costs are always calculated by Microsoft Project, and you can't overwrite its calculations until the task is 100 percent complete. You have the option to supplement the cost calculations by entering actual costs for each resource assignment yourself. This option takes more time (unless you use the automated workgroup messaging described in Hour 23, "Using Microsoft Project in Workgroups"), but it can be the most accurate of all tracking methods.

In the following sections, you'll look at how you use Project's tracking facilities for each of the tracking approaches just outlined. Most of this discussion assumes that you will update the task fields and that you want Project to calculate appropriate actual values for the task assignments. The choice between this and the alternative, for you to enter actual work for each resource directly, is governed by a choice on the Calculation tab of the Options dialog box.

Collecting the Tracking Information

Before you get started, just a word about gathering the information you need to track progress. You should decide in advance how you will collect the progress data and then give the human resources a way to supply it to you. You might want to print forms to be completed and sent to you on a regular basis or schedule meetings when the resources can report their progress. If all your resources have access to a computer and share email, you can use Microsoft Project's workgroup feature to automatically send notices of task assignments and changes in assignments and to automatically request progress reports after tasks are scheduled to be in production. Then, after reviewing the progress reports sent by the resources, you can upload them automatically into Project to update the schedule. However you do it, you need to establish the mechanism and level of reporting detail needed in advance.

Another important decision to be made early in your project is who will be responsible for actually updating the Project file. Project does not provide an audit trail for plan changes. Allowing updates by more than one person can cause confusion; team members may wonder how the plan they were working with has suddenly changed without any additional input from them.

Typically, either the project "owner" makes all updates to the file, or else the tracking information is submitted to an administrative staff member for data entry.

Tracking Start and Finish Dates

You can enter the actual start and finish dates for a task in a variety of ways, but I'll show you only the most commonly used methods. One of the most useful views for tracking task dates is to display the Tracking Gantt Chart and apply the Tracking table to that view (see Figure 20.5). The Actual Start and Actual Finish columns are easily accessible next to the Task Name. The Tracking Gantt Chart shows a baseline task bar (in gray) beneath the current task bar (in color). Completed work is shown in a darker color on the current task bar.

FIGURE 20.5

The Tracking Gantt view displays several visual clues to project progress.

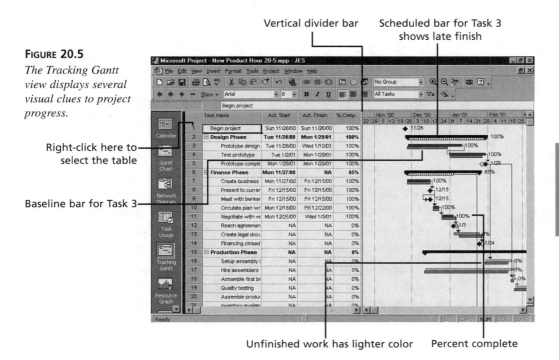

Vertical divider bar — Scheduled bar for Task 3 shows late finish

Right-click here to select the table

Baseline bar for Task 3

20

Unfinished work has lighter color — Percent complete

To Do: Tracking Start and Finish Dates

To enter date values in the Tracking table, do the following:

1. Choose View, Tracking Gantt from the menu or use the Tracking Gantt icon on the View Bar to display the Tracking Gantt view.

2. Right-click in the header row above the task ID numbers to display the shortcut menu for Tables and choose Tracking to display the Tracking table. If necessary, drag the vertical divider bar to the right to see the tracking columns.

3. Enter actual start dates in the Act. Start column and actual finish dates in the Act. Finish column.

> The actual date fields display NA until you take a step that sets an actual date. You can remove the actual date by typing **NA** in an actual date field.

> IIf you enter an actual finish date without having entered an actual start date, Microsoft Project assumes the task started on schedule and puts the scheduled start date in the actual start date field.

When you enter a date in the Actual Finish date field, indicating the task is 100 percent complete, Project performs several calculations, described in the following list, to supply values for all the task's actual fields:

- As described earlier, Project changes the scheduled finish date to match the new actual finish date and tags the Finish field as fixed and not to be rescheduled by changes in other tasks.

- If the actual start date has *not* been manually entered, Project sets it to equal the scheduled start date.

- Project calculates the Actual Duration field, based on the actual start and finish dates, and also enters that duration value into the scheduled Duration field.

- Project sets the Percent Complete (which is the percentage of duration completed) to 100 percent. See the following section for more on the Percent Complete field.

- If resources are assigned to the task, Project sets the actual start and finish dates of all assignments, calculates the actual work for each assignment, and then calculates the actual cost for each assignment.

- With the assignment work and cost calculated, Project then sums those amounts and puts the result in the task's Actual Work and Actual Cost fields.

- Finally, if the task was a "critical" task, Project changes it to noncritical. Recall from Hour 16, "Fine-Tuning the Project Plan," that the purpose of the critical flag is to point out the tasks you could shorten or reschedule if you want to shorten the overall project. Because the task is now finished, it's no longer a candidate for helping you shorten the project, and the critical status is removed.

When the task is finished, Project will have calculated values for all the actual fields you didn't manually place an entry in.

Project doesn't show a summary task as finished until all of its subtasks is finished.

If you want to enter actual work and cost information that differs from the work and cost that Project calculates, see the sections that follow.

Tracking Progress for Unfinished Tasks

After a longer task has started, you might want to keep track of how the work is going while it's still far from being finished. Project has several ways to show partial completion of a task. If a task is partially completed, some of the scheduled duration (calendar periods when work takes place) must have already occurred. You can enter the progress on the task in three ways:

- You can enter Actual Duration as an amount (like two days or 40 hours).

- You can enter the Percent Complete, which is the Actual Duration divided by the scheduled Duration. When nothing has been done on a task, the Percent Complete is zero; when the task is finished, it's 100 percent.

- You can enter the Remaining Duration, which is the scheduled Duration minus the Actual Duration.

20

NEW TERM *Actual Duration* is the amount of calendar time that one or more resources have actually been working on the task.

NEW TERM *Remaining Duration* is the difference between the scheduled Duration field and the Actual Duration field.

NEW TERM *Percent Complete* is calculated by dividing Actual Duration by the scheduled Duration field. It's the percent of scheduled Duration that has been completed.

If you enter any one of these three actual amounts, Project calculates the other two for you, using the value you entered and the scheduled duration. However, if you enter values in both Actual Duration and Remaining Duration, Project assumes you're trying to tell it something like this: "We've spent this much time on the task, and we estimate that we need this much time to finish." By entering both the Actual Duration and the Remaining Duration, you're telling Project to change the Duration in the current schedule; therefore, it adds Actual Duration and Remaining Duration and puts that value in the scheduled Duration field.

Similarly, if you enter an Actual Duration greater than the scheduled Duration, and make no change to the Remaining Duration, Project assumes that the task is finished and took longer than scheduled. Project changes the current scheduled duration to match the new, longer actual duration, and then the Percent Complete and Remaining Duration fields are set to 100 percent and 0 (zero), respectively, to indicate that the task is complete.

You can enter all these values in the same view used earlier and shown in Figure 20.5— the Tracking Gantt with the Tracking table applied. You just need to drag the vertical divider bar to the right or scroll to the right to bring the columns labeled % Comp, Act. Dur, and Rem. Dur. into view.

You can also use the tools on the Tracking toolbar to update tasks if you don't want to change the view you're using at the moment.

To Do: Using the Tracking Toolbar to Update a Task

To update task progress quickly, using the Tracking toolbar, do the following:

1. Choose View, Toolbars, Tracking to display the Tracking toolbar, shown in Figure 20.6.

2. Select the task you want to update.

3. Click one of the Percent Complete buttons if the task is progressing as scheduled and is complete to one of these percentages (25%, 50%, 75%, or 100% only).

4. Otherwise, click the Update Task tool to display the Update Tasks dialog box (see Figure 20.6).

5. Record the Actual Start Date if it is different from the scheduled start date.

6. Record the progress on the task in the % Complete field, the Actual Dur. field, and/or the Remaining Dur. field.

7. If the task is complete, enter the Actual Finish date.

8. Click OK to close the Update Tasks dialog box.

Percent Complete
buttons

Scheduled Duration
(display only)

Tracking toolbar

Selected task name

% Complete field

Actual Start

Actual Finish

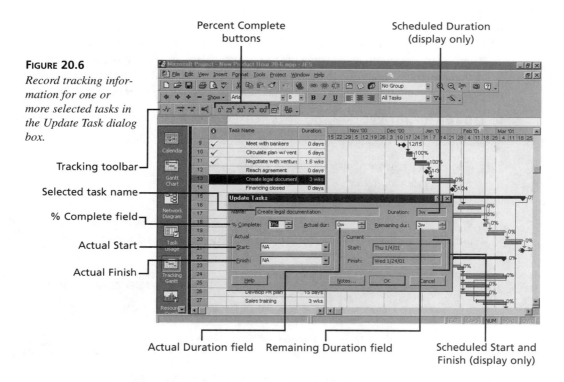

Actual Duration field   Remaining Duration field

Scheduled Start and
Finish (display only)

As was the case with entering an actual finish date and no actual start date, if you enter Actual Duration, Remaining Duration, or % Complete without having entered an actual start date, Project uses the scheduled Start field value, not the Baseline Start, to fill in the actual start date.

Similarly, if you haven't entered an actual finish date when you enter values that imply the task is finished (by entering 100% in the % Complete field, zero in the Remaining Duration field, or an actual duration that's equal to the scheduled duration), Project supplies an actual finish date, based on the actual start date and the actual duration.

20

Recording Actual Work

By default, when you enter values in the actual duration fields (Actual Duration, Remaining Duration, and % Complete) for a task that has resource assignments, Project uses those entries to calculate actual work for each of the assignments. Project then uses the actual work to calculate actual cost, and then sums the assignment work and costs in the task fields.

You can also enter actual work for the assignments manually instead of accepting the values Project creates. This method can add more precision to your records for resource work and costs, especially when some of the resources work more than others on a task. If you enter amounts directly into the assignment's Actual Work field, Project updates the task's Actual Duration and Percent Complete fields to incorporate your entries.

To Do: Entering Work Amounts for Each Resource

To enter total-to-date actual work values for resources on a task, follow these steps:

1. Choose View, More Views and select Task Entry. Click Apply to display the Task Entry combination view.

2. Click anywhere in the bottom half of the screen to activate the Task Form.

3. From the Format menu, choose Details and select Resource Work from the cascading list of options. Figure 20.7 shows the display set up as you need it for entering work values per resource.

FIGURE 20.7

Display a Task Form below a Gantt Chart to allow easy entry of actual work values for each resource.

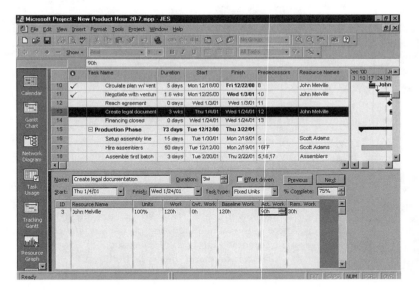

4. In the Gantt Chart, select the task with work amounts to be entered.

5. Activate the bottom Task Form again by clicking anywhere on the form.

6. Enter the latest values you've received in the Act. Work area for each resource on the task.

7. Click OK on the form to lock in your entries.

8. Continue for other tasks by selecting them one at a time in the top view and entering work values in the bottom.

In Figure 20.7, Task 13, "Create legal documentation," has been selected on the Gantt Chart on top of the screen, and the Resource Work values are displayed in the Task Form at the bottom of the screen. Notice that the task is 75 percent complete. Project has entered an Act. Work value of 90 hours (75 percent of the planned 120 hours). To enter your own work value, click in the Act. Work area and type in a number (in hours) or use the spinner control in the cell to find the appropriate number for this resource on this task.

> If you make entries into the task's Actual Duration field (by changing it directly or by changing either the Percent Complete or the Remaining Duration fields), Project recalculates the actual work for assignments and you will lose any actual work amounts you might have entered for the assignments. To avoid this problem, you must remember not to manually update the task's Actual Duration or Percent Complete fields after you have manually entered actual work for an assignment. Or, you can break the computational link between a task's actual duration and an assignment's actual work, as described later in the section "Preserving Manual Work and Cost Entries".

Entering Actual Costs

By default, the Actual Cost fields for tasks and assignments are calculated by Project based on actual work and can't be changed by the user as long as there are unfinished resource assignments. As shown in Figure 20.8, the actual cost details can also be displayed in the Task Form portion of the Task Entry view. Click anywhere on the form, and choose Format, Details, Resource Cost. The dollar amounts were calculated by Project based on the actual work.

Preserving Manual Work and Cost Entries

If you want to keep Project from recalculating the assignment Actual work fields when you change the Actual task duration (with Actual Duration, Remaining Duration, or %Complete), you must break the computational link between the task's actual duration and the assignment's actual work.

Also, if you want to enter cost values yourself (or if you want to import them) even though you have resources assigned, you can allow the Actual Cost fields to be edited.

20

FIGURE 20.8

Change the fields displayed on the Task Form to focus on resource costs.

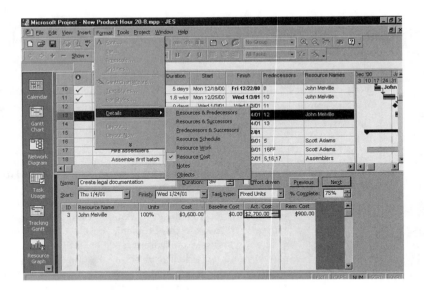

To Do: Preserving Manual Updates to an Assignment's Actual Work and Actual Cost

To break the computational link between task duration and task work, follow these steps:

1. Choose Tools, Options to display the Options dialog box and select the Calculation tab (see Figure 20.9).

FIGURE 20.9

Choose how Project links the task's duration and an assignment's work and cost in the Options dialog box.

Calculation tab

Links the task's actual duration and an assignment's work

Protects actual cost calculations against manual entries

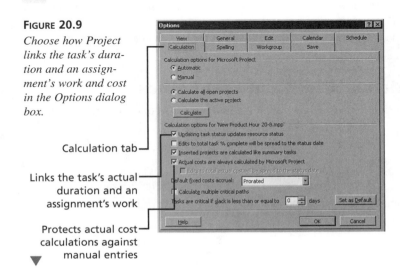

▼ 2. To keep changes in the task's actual duration from changing the resource assignment's actual work, clear the check box labeled Updating task status updates resource status.

Fill the check box to have changes in the task's actual duration calculate changes in the actual work for assignments. Note that this change affects only the current project unless you click the Set as Default button; then it affects only new projects created after this point.

3. To allow direct entries into actual cost fields, clear the check box for Actual costs which are always calculated by Microsoft Project. To have Project calculate these values, fill the check box.

▲ 4. Click OK to close the dialog box.

> If you have been allowing direct entries into Actual Work and Cost fields and decide to revert to having Project calculate the fields, you will lose all the manual entries you have made for actual costs.

If you break the computational link between the task's actual duration and an assignment's actual work, Project will no longer change a resource assignment's actual work values when you update the task's actual duration, nor will it update the task's Actual Duration or Percent Complete fields when you record actual work for the resource assignments. If you break the link, you have to enter the task's Percent Complete values yourself. You just can't have it both ways.

Keep in mind that Duration is a measurement of calendar time in work days. If you mark a task as 75 percent complete, Project understands you to say "75 percent of my allotted calendar time has passed and I have also completed 75% of my assigned work." To truly measure work progress against the amount of time allowed for a task, you must break the calculated link (by choosing Tools, Options, Calculation) and then commit to entering both time consumed (% complete, Actual Duration, and so on) and Actual Work values for each task.

Using the Update Project Command

Ready for a time-saving feature? The remaining tools for tracking that I'm going to show you make life easier, not more complicated.

The Update Project command provides a quick way to update the actual fields for many tasks at once. The command is designed to help you in two specific cases: when you want to show that everything was done as scheduled up to a certain date, or when you need to reschedule the tasks for all or part of a project that was put on hold for a while and is now ready to resume.

20

In the first case, suppose you have been away on vacation and need to bring the tracking for your project up to date. To your utter amazement, you find that everything has been going exactly as scheduled while you were away. Now you want Project to mark as completed all work that was scheduled up to today (or up through some cut-off date you specify), for all tasks or for just some of the tasks. Some of the tasks may be in progress and some may not have started yet. You are looking for an easy way to mark several tasks as being on schedule.

In another situation, some project tasks were put on hold for a period of time while other, more pressing demands occupied your resources. When a date has been selected for resuming work on the delayed parts of the plan, tasks that should have been started by now need to be rescheduled to start on the resumption date, and tasks that were partially completed when work stopped need to have the remainder of their work rescheduled to start on the resumption date.

To Do: Updating or Rescheduling Work on Tasks

▼ To Do

In order to update or reschedule work on tasks, do the following:

1. Choose View, Gantt Chart.
2. If you want to update only specific tasks, select them first.
3. Choose Tools, Tracking, Update Project to display the Update Project dialog box (see Figure 20.10).

FIGURE 20.10

The Update Project command updates progress or reschedules work for many tasks at once.

4. Choose the type of update that you want to perform:

   To make changes to task completion, select Update work as complete through, and then fill in the cut-off date through which the tasks were completed as scheduled.

   - If you select Set 0% - 100% complete, Project calculates the percentage complete for tasks that were scheduled to start but not be finished by the cut-off date.

   - If you select Set 0% or 100% complete only, tasks that were completed by the cut-off date are marked 100% complete and tasks that should have started but not be finished are left with 0% complete

▼   To reschedule work on tasks that have been temporarily halted, or on tasks that have been delayed before they even began, select Reschedule uncompleted work to start after and fill in the date when you want work to resume.

5. If you want to update or reschedule all tasks in the project, select For Entire project. If you have selected just certain tasks to be changed, select For Selected tasks.

▲   6. Click OK to update the tasks and close the dialog box.

Summary

During the planning phase, the time will come when your plan is as good as you can get it, or your customer signs off on the plan, or you simply run out of planning time. Preserve your hard work by capturing the baseline vales for task start, finish, duration, work, and cost. As the project gets underway, but before any changes have been made to the plan, agree on a method for collecting progress information, including the frequencies of updates and the level of detail to be collected.

Keep the plan up to date by making changes to basic task information: start, finish, and so on. After collecting actual progress information, enter that in Project fields such as % Complete, Actual and Remaining Duration, and Actual Work. Viewing the Tracking Gantt to review task progress and slippage is your best project management tool.

Q&A

Q I tried to use the Update Project command to reschedule the remaining work on a dormant task, but it wouldn't do it. Why?

A If you have turned off the Split In-Progress Tasks check box on the Schedule tab of the Options dialog box, Project can't split the task and reschedule the remaining work.

Q Why can't I enter an actual cost for my resources?

A You must disable the check box Actual Costs Are Always Calculated by Microsoft Project on the Calculation tab of the Options dialog box.

Q I entered 50% for a task with a 20-day duration. Then I increased the Remaining Duration to 15 days to reflect changes in the plan. My % Complete figure went down. Why?

A Project is trying to tell you that the current set of numbers does not add up correctly. On a 20-day task, 50 percent completion splits into 10 days Actual Duration and 10 days Remaining Duration. By increasing the Remaining Duration to 15 days, you have increased the total task time to 25 days. Without also changing the Actual Duration, it will remain at 10 days, so 10 completed days out of 25 total is now a 40 percent task completion.

20

Exercises

Your project has been in the planning stages for some time and has gone through team and manager reviews. Before the project gets underway, you know to take the time to save the plan information for future comparisons. At the first meeting of your project team, progress information is provided to you in a variety of ways. Update your plan as instructed in the exercises below. To begin, open the file, New Product Hour 20.MPP. Solutions for the exercises can be found in New Product Hour 20-Exercises.MPP. See the Introduction for instructions to access the sample files and solutions for these exercises on the book's Web page.

1. Save the Baseline information for your plan. Then save the file.

2. View the Gantt Chart and apply the Variance table to verify that all tasks have Baseline Start and Finish dates.

3. Team members have reported the schedule updates below. Change them in the project plan using the Entry table applied to the Gantt Chart.

   Task 4, Test prototype, won't finish until January 31, 2001

   Task 9, Meet with bankers, will now require three days to complete

   Task 11, Negotiate with venture capitalists, is now estimated to take one week but can't begin until January 8, 2001.

4. Use the Tracking toolbar to mark the following completions.

   Tasks 1–5 are 100 percent complete

   Tasks 7, 8, and 10 are 50 percent complete

5. John Melville reported a total of eight hours actual work spent on Task 9, "Meet with bankers." Record his actual hours for the task.

6. Then John Melville picked up a flu bug. Work on some of his tasks needs to be rescheduled. Change Task 10 to resume work on January 2, 2001, and reschedule work on unstarted Task 11 to also resume on January 2, 2001.

7. View the Tracking Gantt to see the effects of the changes on the project plan.

Hour 21

Analyzing Progress and Revising the Schedule

Project management is sometimes compared to risk management. The purpose of tracking, updating, and revising a schedule is to not only meet the stated goals, but also to correct problems quickly along the way. One common analogy is that you, as the project manager and captain of the ship, need to see that hazy object in the distance long before it gets close enough to be recognized as an iceberg about to sink your ocean liner.

What warnings will you have? An overall project report can give you a reading on the pulse as a whole. Also in Project, variances point toward tasks and work drifting off schedule. For detailed assessment of work versus cost, an Earned Value Analysis is included, and there are visual clues to progress available on custom Gantt Charts.

In this hour, you will learn:

- Variance definitions and calculations
- Techniques for investigating task slippage
- Reporting on resource costs
- Steps to creating Earned Value reports
- Methods for rescheduling interrupted tasks
- Techniques for revising a project plan

Analyzing Variances and Revising the Schedule

Despite your best efforts, projects usually do not track exactly as planned. Investigating the difference between the current schedule and the baseline plan is an important part of the project manager's job. The sooner you know how the project is diverging from the original plan, and by how much, the sooner you can take corrective action.

 A *variance* is the calculated difference between a baseline value and the most current data value. See Table 21.1 for several common calculations used to determine the variance.

There are several different types of variances in Project, such as:

- Tasks might not start as planned, creating a *start variance*.
- Tasks might start on time but might not be completed as planned, creating a *finish variance*.
- Certainly costs can exceed estimates, creating *cost variances* for tasks, for individual resources, and for total resource assignments on a task.

> Not all variances are harmful to the overall project. Some tasks might start and finish ahead of schedule, or they might not have required as much time as the original duration estimate. These variances, which will show as negative variance values, won't hurt the project as long as they don't create unproductive gaps in the schedule.

TABLE 21.1   Common Variance Calculations

Value/Field	Calculation
Task Start Variance	Currently scheduled start (the Start field)—Baseline start
Task Finish Variance	Currently scheduled finish (Finish field)—Baseline finish
Task Work Variance	Current total resource work assigned to the task (Work)—Baseline work for the task
Resource Cost Variance	Current cost of the resource over the project—Baseline cost of the resource

Notice that the calculations shown in Table 21.1 can result in negative values. If your current value is less than the baseline, you're ahead (generally speaking)!

Project includes variance fields in several predefined tables. With a task view displayed, such as a Gantt Chart, apply the Variance table to view task start and finish variances, or apply the Work table to view work variances by task. For resource variances, display a resource view, such as the Resource Sheet, and apply the Cost or Work table.

To view a different table onscreen, select View, Table from the menu. Then choose from the cascading table name list, or select More Tables to display the complete list.

Analyzing Progress

How do you measure progress on a project? The first consideration is whether the project will finish on time. Of equal importance for most projects is whether they are staying within budget. You can get this information, and a general feel of the project progress, by examining the overall project summary.

If progress is lacking, however, specific causes need to be investigated. Tasks that are behind schedule, resources that are not completing work in a timely fashion, and general delays caused by competing company projects are all likely causes for a project not meeting its goals. The following sections cover methods for examining these project characteristics.

Reviewing Summary Progress Information

Overall project summary information can give you an indication of the project's general "health." If it's not progressing satisfactorily, you need to investigate further by examining detailed task or resource information.

21

To Do: Getting a Snapshot of the Project's Status

To view overall project statistics, do the following:

1. Choose Project, Project Information.
2. Click the Statistics button. The Project Statistics dialog box is displayed, as shown in Figure 21.1.

FIGURE 21.1

The Project Statistics dialog box gives you a snapshot of your project.

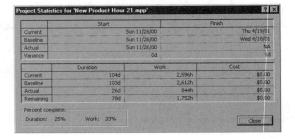

  You can also open the statistics dialog box by clicking the Project Statistics button on the Tracking toolbar.

The Project Statistics dialog box can't be printed directly. Instead, print out a Project Summary report.

To Do: Printing the Project Status Summary

To print a summary of important project statistics, do the following:

1. Choose View, Reports.
2. Double-click the Overview category.
3. Double-click the Project Summary report to preview it.
4. Click Print to print out the report.

Reviewing Progress Information at the Task Level

The task Variance, Cost, and Work tables discussed previously are helpful for viewing progress and variance information at the task level. The entire group of Current Activity reports can also be helpful.

Another way to see whether tasks are progressing on schedule is to display a task *progress line*. Setting a progress date and displaying a progress line causes Project to draw a vertical line on a Gantt Chart on the progress date. The line connects tasks that begin before the progress date or cross the date, and which aren't yet completed. If the line bulges or peaks to the left of the vertical line, that task is behind schedule as of the progress date. These left peaks alert you to progress variances; specifically, tasks with progress behind schedule.

To Do: Displaying a Progress Line

▼ To Do

To draw a vertical line on the Gantt Chart that represents task progress as of a particular date, do the following:

1. Set a progress "as of" date: Choose Project, Project Information and select a Status date. Click OK. If you skip this step, Project notifies you that it will use the current date when you create a progress line.

2. Choose Tools, Tracking, Progress Lines. The Progress Lines dialog box will appear, as shown in Figure 21.2.

FIGURE 21.2

Project progress lines can be displayed for fixed dates or at regular intervals.

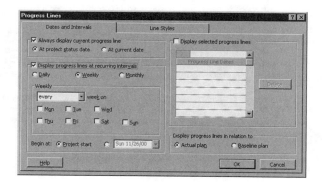

3. On the Dates and Intervals tab, select the dates or intervals for progress lines:

   - Turn on Always Display Current Progress Line for the vertical line to always be visible on the Gantt Chart, either on the current date or the status date you entered in step 1.

   - Enable Display Progress Lines at Recurring Intervals, if you would like more than one progress line displayed at regular intervals on the Gantt Chart. Also, define the interval (daily, weekly, monthly; displayed from the project start date or lines not appearing until later in the project).

   - Turn on Display Selected Progress Lines to show lines at any arbitrary dates you enter in the Progress Line Dates list.

▼ 4. Use the Line Styles tab to adjust progress line formatting.

21

▼   5. Click OK when finished. Progress lines are then displayed on the Gantt Chart, as
        shown in Figure 21.3.

FIGURE 21.3
*Left peaks indicate
tasks that are behind
schedule.*

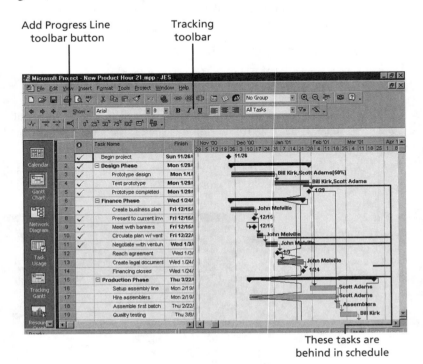

These tasks are
behind in schedule

There is also a quick and easy way to create a progress line on a Gantt Chart using the
▲   mouse and a Tracking Toolbar button.

To Do: Creating Progress Lines With the Mouse

To create a progress line on a specific date using the mouse, follow these steps:

1. Choose View, Toolbars and select Tracking.

2. Click the Add Progress Line toolbar button. The mouse pointer changes
    shape to a vertical angular line with small arrows pointing left and right.

3. Move the mouse to the right side of the Gantt Chart. A pop-up dialog box shows
    which date you are pointing to. Click to display a progress line on that date.

4. Repeat for additional progress lines.

5. To turn these manual progress lines off, choose Tools, Tracking, Progress Lines and
    turn off Display Selected Progress Lines.

▲

The Slipping Tasks Report

Project defines a task as "slipping" if it's currently scheduled to finish after its original, baseline finish date. This assumes that a baseline was set for the project or the task.

To Do: Viewing the Slipping Tasks Report

To view start and finish variances in a report, follow these steps:

1. Choose View, Reports.

2. Double-click the Current Activities category to display icons for reports in that category, as shown in Figure 21.4.

To Do

FIGURE 21.4

Print a list of slipping tasks from the Current Activity Reports dialog box.

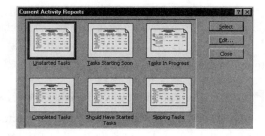

3. Double-click the Slipping Tasks report to preview it.

4. Use the start and finish information provided by the Variance table, and the Successors lists, to analyze the slippages.

5. Click Close to return to the Reports dialog box.

The Overbudget Tasks Report

A task is considered "overbudget" if the current scheduled cost is greater than the baseline cost set for the task. Tasks can become overbudget for a number of reasons:

- More resources have been assigned to the task than anticipated
- More expensive resources have been substituted
- Fixed costs for the task have been modified

To Do: Viewing the Overbudget Tasks Report

To see a reporting list tasks currently scheduled to cost more than their budgeted amounts, do the following:

1. Choose View, Reports.

2. Double-click the Costs category to display icons for reports in that category, as shown in Figure 21.5.

21

FIGURE 21.5
Print a list of tasks currently running over-budget from the Cost Reports dialog box.

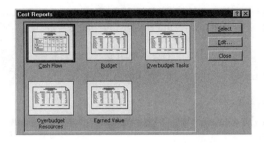

3. Double-click the Overbudget Tasks report to preview it.

4. Review the Cost table information to identify tasks that might need adjustments in the project plan.

5. Click Close to return to the Reports dialog box.

Reviewing Progress Information at the Resource Level

How is a resource's progress measured? Two ways, typically—actual versus scheduled work, and cost versus scheduled cost. The task Work table, discussed previously, shows work variances by task, and the task Cost table shows cost variances by task. If you display a resource view, such as the Resource Sheet, the Work and Cost tables focus on values for each resource instead of by task. The supplied Overbudget Resources report might also help pinpoint resource cost variances.

The Overbudget Resources Report

Typically, resources show as overbudget if they are now assigned to do more work than originally planned. More work means higher costs. It's also possible that a resource got an increase in pay rates in some project period.

To Do: Viewing the Overbudget Resources Report

To view a report listing resources which are currently costing the project more than their budgeted amounts, do the following:

1. Choose View, Reports.

2. Double-click the Costs category.

3. Double-click the Overbudget Resources report to preview it.

4. Review the resource cost information to identify resources who are costing the project more than originally planned.

5. Click Close to return to the Reports dialog box.

The Earned Value Report

Earned value analysis is an underutilized project management tool. It gives the project manager feedback on how the amount of work completed ("earned") compares to the original work plan, and how the cost of the finished work compares to what it was estimated to be worth at the beginning ("value"). In other words, are you getting the productivity you're paying for?

By comparing baseline, scheduled, and actual work and cost values, Earned Value Analysis lets project managers answer three types of questions about their projects:

- Are variances caused by work being behind schedule?
- Are variances caused by tasks requiring more work than was planned for?
- Are variances caused by higher costs than were planned?

 A detailed discussion of Earned Value Analysis is outside the scope of this book. Refer to Project's online Help for a list of the Project fields involved and precise definitions of the fields and calculations. Another resource for Earned Value Analysis is the book, *Special Edition Using Microsoft Project 2000*, published by Que.

The Earned Value table, applied to a task view like the Gantt Chart, lists all the relevant Earned Value data, but these terms aren't familiar to most Project users. General field definitions are given in Table 21.2. Refer to Project's online Help for more precise definitions.

TABLE 21.2 Earned Value Analysis Definitions

Term	Definition
Earned Value	A measure of the cost of work performed up to the status date or today's date. Earned value uses your original cost estimates and your actual work to date to show whether the actual costs incurred are on budget. In other words, earned value indicates how much of the budget should have been spent, in view of the amount of work done so far, and the baseline cost for the task, assignment, or resource. Earned value is also referred to as "budgeted cost of work performed" (BCWP).
BCWS	*Budgeted cost of work scheduled.* The earned value field that indicates how much of the budget should have been spent, in view of the baseline cost of the task, assignment, or resource. BCWS is calculated as the cumulative timephased baseline costs up to the status date or today's date.

continues

TABLE 21.2   continued

Term	Definition
BCWP	*Budgeted cost of work performed* (also the field referred to as the project's Earned Value). The earned value field that indicates how much of the budget should have been spent, in view of the amount of work performed so far and the baseline cost for the task, assignment, or resource. BCWP is calculated as the cumulative value of the timephased percent complete for tasks (or the timephased percent work complete for assignments and resources), multiplied by the timephased baseline cost for the task, assignment, or resource, up to the status date or today's date.
ACWP	*Actual cost of work performed* (ACWP). Shows actual costs incurred for work already performed by a resource on a task, up to the project status date or today's date.
SV	*Earned value schedule variance.* The difference, in cost terms, between the current progress (BCWP) and the baseline schedule (BCWS). If the SV is positive, the project is ahead of schedule in cost terms; if the SV is negative, the project is behind schedule in cost terms. `SV = Budgeted Cost of Work Performed - Budgeted Cost of Work Scheduled`
CV	*Earned value cost variance.* The difference between how much it should have cost to achieve the current level of completion (BCWP) and how much it has actually cost (ACWP), up to the status date or today's date. If the CV is positive, the cost is currently under the budgeted (or baseline) amount; if the CV is negative, the task is currently overbudget. `CV = Budgeted Cost of Work Performed - Actual Cost of Work Performed`
EAC	*Estimate at completion.* The earned value field that shows the total scheduled or projected cost for a task, resource, or assignment. This is based on costs already incurred, in addition to the costs planned for remaining work. EAC is equivalent to the Cost field.
BAC	*Budget at completion.* Also called "baseline cost," the field shows the total planned cost for a task. The baseline cost is calculated as the sum of the planned costs of all the assigned resources, plus any fixed costs associated with the task. `Baseline Cost = (Work * Standard Rate) + (Overtime Work * Overtime Rate) + Resource Per Use Cost + Task Fixed Cost`
VAC	*Variance at completion* (VAC). The earned value field that shows the difference between the estimate at completion (EAC) and the budget at completion (BAC). In Microsoft Project, the EAC is the Total Cost field, the BAC is the Baseline Cost field, and the VAC is the Cost Variance field.

For Earned Value fields to be informative, you need to diligently track task progress, as well as actual work and cost values. See Hour 20, "Tracking Work on the Project," for more information.

With all of this progress comparison data available, you might want to perform statistical or metric analyses on the Earned Value fields. The best way to look at this information is to export it to a spreadsheet application, such as Microsoft Excel.

To Do: Exporting Earned Value Fields to Microsoft Excel

▼ To Do

To send a copy of Earned Value field data into Microsoft Excel, follow these steps:

1. Choose File, Save As.
2. In the Save as type box, select Microsoft Excel Workbook or Microsoft Excel Pivot Table.
3. In the File name box, type a name for the exported file.
4. Click Save to open the Export Mapping dialog box, as shown in Figure 21.6.

FIGURE 21.6

Use a supplied export map to save Project data in an Excel file format.

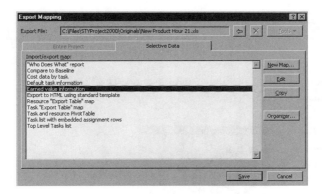

5. In the Import/Export map list, select Earned value information.

▲ 6. Click Save.

Capturing and Reviewing Week-to-Week Trends

By design, Project tracks three sets of fields:

- *Baseline fields* for Start and Finish dates, Duration, Work, and Cost—from the original project plan.

21

- Fields for the *currently scheduled* task Start and Finish dates, Durations, Work, assignments, and others—these are the fields you edit and keep up to date as the project progresses.

- *Actual fields* for what really happened in terms of Actual Start and Finish, Actual Work, and so on—you can enter these directly or let Project provide them, based largely on completion percentages.

As you update the schedule each reporting period, the "current" field data from the previous update will be lost, but you can take steps to capture changes from one period to another. One technique is to save the project plan in separate files from, say, week to week. A standard naming convention should be adopted for this, such as:

`New Widget 8-1-2001.MPP or New Widget August 2001.MPP`

These date-stamped files can then be inserted into a consolidated project to view trends from one period to another.

A second technique for capturing data within reporting periods is to use Project's interim baseline fields. Project copies start and finish dates into reserved start and finish custom fields. There are 10 sets of Start/Finish pairs for you to use.

To Do: Capturing Project Data for Future Reference

To save a copy of current task start and finish dates for future reference, do the following:

1. Choose Tools, Tracking, Save Baseline. The Save Baseline dialog box appears, as shown in Figure 21.7.

FIGURE 21.7

Capture data from this period for later comparisons.

2. Select the Save interim plan option.

3. Choose which start and finish dates to capture and which pair to store them in. By default, Project copies the currently scheduled start and finish date for each task.

   Be sure to keep track of which pairs have already been used, and for which period, so you don't overwrite dates you intended to keep. A task note field is a good choice for this type of documentation.

4. Select an option to copy data for the Entire project or for Selected tasks only.

5. Click OK when finished.

Be aware that capturing interim data in the Start/Finish pairs does not capture data from all Project fields. Work assignments, prorated costs, and values from Actual fields are examples of data not saved with this technique. If you need complete, detailed snapshots of the project over time, use the first method and save a series of files for later comparisons.

Updating the Schedule

The essentials of project tracking were discussed in Hour 20, but sometimes there is a major interruption to a project. Perhaps another company project has become more critical and all resources have been reassigned to it temporarily. Your project plan is still correct, but all or many of its tasks must be postponed. Project has methods for rescheduling uncompleted work on tasks in progress and for postponing tasks that have not yet started. Without these tools, each task would have to be modified manually.

Rescheduling Remaining Work

Tasks that have started but are not yet complete might need to have the unfinished work postponed. You could simply divide the existing task into two separate tasks and track them individually, but another way to represent the interruption is to split the single task into two sections:

- The completed portion
- The portion yet to be done

To Do: Rescheduling Work on a Single Task

To split a task into finished and unfinished portions, follow these steps.

1. Choose View, Gantt Chart.

2. Click the Split Task button on the Standard toolbar.

3. Position the mouse over the bar of the task to be split into finished and remaining work portions.

4. Click on the task bar and drag the unfinished portion to the right. Let the Start and Finish dates in the pop-up dialog box, shown in Figure 21.8, be your guide.

5. Let go of the mouse button when finished.

▲ To Do

21

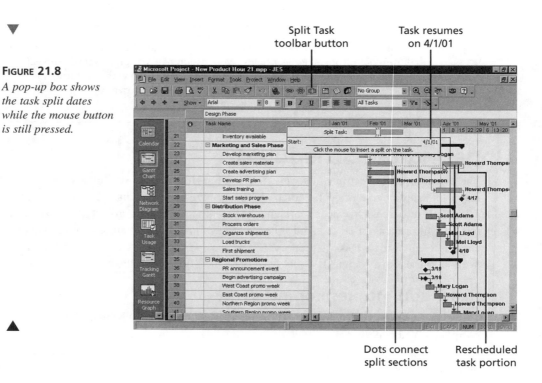

Split Task
toolbar button

Task resumes
on 4/1/01

FIGURE 21.8
*A pop-up box shows
the task split dates
while the mouse button
is still pressed.*

Dots connect
split sections

Rescheduled
task portion

Rescheduling Multiple Tasks

The preceding steps for splitting a task must be followed for each task being rescheduled. If there are several tasks that will be rescheduled to resume at the same time, a dialog box can help you adjust all selected tasks at once.

To Do: Splitting and Rescheduling More Than One Task

To reschedule remaining work on more than one task, do the following:

1. Select all tasks that will resume work at the same point in time.

2. Choose Tools, Tracking, Update Project. The Update Project dialog box will
   appear, as shown in Figure 21.9.

▼ To Do

FIGURE 21.9
*Reschedule remaining
task work for several
tasks at one time.*

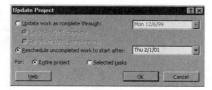

▼ 3. Select the option to Reschedule Uncompleted Work to Start After and choose a date.

4. Select an option to reschedule the Entire project to this date or only Selected tasks.

▲ 5. Click OK when finished.

> Tasks that have not yet started can also be rescheduled using the Project Update dialog box. The complete task is moved to the new start date, keeping the same task duration.

For a visual presentation of the size of delay in the work or how far each complete task had to be postponed, display the Detail Gantt (choose View, More Views, Detail Gantt). For tasks that were completely rescheduled, a narrow line before each task shows the task delay—the current start compared to the baseline start. Tasks that were split to reschedule remaining work will display a gap and a series of periods between the split sections. As shown in Figure 21.10, the amount of delay or size of the gap is also included on the Detail Gantt Chart.

FIGURE 21.10

The Detail Gantt shows the scheduling effects of rescheduling work on tasks.

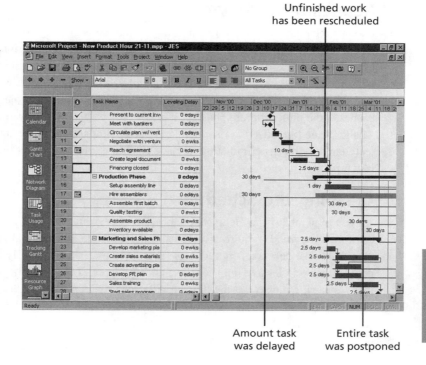

Unfinished work has been rescheduled

Amount task was delayed

Entire task was postponed

21

Revising the Schedule to Finish on Time and on Budget

Your initial project plan is your best guess at the time, and it might be optimistic. Without a bit of luck, or a lot of experience with similar projects, your initial plan probably won't meet certain criteria. Even the best plans, however, rarely progress exactly as initially defined. Hopefully, good project management procedures were in place from the beginning, and the project has a clearly defined goal, realistic assumptions, and well-defined scope. The process of revising a schedule is considerably easier, and more accurate, if basic characteristics were defined early in the process. Even if they weren't, however, Project is a powerful tool for experimenting with "what if" scenarios while revising the plan.

The strategies discussed in Hour 16, "Fine-Tuning the Project Plan," are also effective after the project is underway. The same types of adjustments might be appropriate for revising a project in progress.

Reducing the Scope

Perhaps the plan was simply too ambitious from the beginning. Your dream of launching a national publication might have to begin with the launch of a regional publication, for now. This is an example of reducing the scope of a project. The essential tasks and phases will be very similar for both of the publication projects, but the complexity is reduced for the regional project. A common example of similar projects with varying scopes is the pilot program phase of a major project. The object is to test the plan on a smaller scale to reduce the risk on a larger scale. Put simply, reducing the scope of a project generally means eliminating tasks or phases, particularly repetitive steps, from the initial plan.

Crashing the Schedule

As you remember from Hour 16, the process of revising a project plan is known as *crashing the plan*. It requires you to carefully examine the essential components of the plan and make decisions on tradeoffs. These components are usually described in project management circles as Time, Money, and Resources. If the deadline apparently can't be met, "throwing money" at the project will probably help. You might elect to lease additional equipment, bring in more proficient resources, or hire an outside contractor to perform some tasks. All those options cost money, but save time.

You might also see project components described as Time, Money, Resources, and Quality. The logic here is different from reducing the scope, but might not involve additional money. For example, your initial project plan called for a 2 percent quality control failure rate of the new product off the assembly line. By accepting a 10 percent failure rate, you estimate that you could meet the shipping deadline without redesigning the product. You also realize that the true cost of filling orders will increase because of failures and returns. Is the cost savings up front, from lowered quality standards, greater than the additional cost of order fulfillment? This is a quality and cost tradeoff.

Recall some basic terms from Hour 16. A critical task in a project is any task that can't slip without affecting the project's end date. The critical path, then, is the complete sequence of these critical tasks from the beginning to the end of the project. In Project files, you can adjust each project component—such as time, money, and resources—and review the results. The key to deadline revisions is to focus on critical tasks, tasks that lie on the critical path for the project. These are the tasks, and the only ones, that drive the project's end date, but they may or may not be the most expensive tasks in your project. Viewing cost tables or printing cost category reports can help troubleshoot expenses.

There are a number of options for crashing a plan, depending on your specific needs. A list of the most common planning tactics follows in Table 21.3.

TABLE 21.3 Common Project Revision Strategies

Need/Strategy	In Project
Save time/Shorten the plan	Create overlap (lead time) between sequential tasks.
	Assign Start-to-Start dependencies where possible to remove tasks from the critical path.
	Assign more resources to complete work sooner.
	Reduce durations of critical tasks if possible; there simply might not be as much time available for this task.
	Split complex tasks into a few smaller tasks that are easier to manage.
Save money/Cut costs	Replace expensive resources with less expensive ones (such as senior versus junior programmers).
	Negotiate lower cost fixed price purchases.
Reduce resources/ Use fewer people	Hire fewer, more qualified people.
	Extend the project deadline so fewer resources can perform more work each.

continues

21

TABLE 21.3   continued

Need/Strategy	In Project
Revise scope/ Reduce expectations	Eliminate tasks no longer needed.
	Reduce repetition of tasks.

Some external factors will also guide your choices. Long-term planning, legal obligations, and customer goodwill can't be discounted. Rely on industry practices and experience, yours and others, as much as possible.

Summary

This hour discusses the "manage" in project management. The first step is to analyze the ongoing project for task schedule variances and work progress. Variance tables, activity reports, and project summaries help point to progress and problem areas. Progress lines and custom Gantt Charts offer visual clues to task progress. A sophisticated Earned Value Analysis offers another management tool by comparing work progress and accumulated costs.

The tradeoffs in project tracking are very similar to the tradeoffs originally considered during the planning stage. If all else fails, you might have to reduce the scope of the project or compromise quality to meet other goals.

Q&A

Q What is a pivot table and why might I want to use it?

A A pivot table in Microsoft Excel presents data in a row and column layout that can be rotated, so columns of data in Project can turn into rows in Excel. Pivot tables are useful for creating different summaries of your data, for viewing different levels of detail, and for orienting data for easier graphing. Refer to the Excel documentation for more information.

Q When closing my file I accidentally let the Wizard update the project baseline. Will my variance values now change?

A Yes, they probably will. Any *changes* to baseline values on existing tasks force Project to recalculate other affected fields. Turn that Wizard off (select Don't Tell Me About This Again) after the project is underway, or keep generations of your project files.

Q Can I turn on an audit trail in Project to track changes?

A No. That's another reason why keeping generations of project files can be so important

Q Am I wasting my time using Project if I don't use all of its features, such as Earned Value, or if I don't want to track progress down to each person's hours on each task every day?

A Not at all. Project is a superb planning tool. If you use it to help you create and organize your task list, and nothing else, your project should have a better chance of success simply because you thought through the plan more carefully. But you should, at the very least, capture the baseline information for your plan and enter some type of progress information—even if you do that after project completion—so you can reflect on the quality of the plan later. You will be learning from the experiences in this plan and building the starting point for similar projects in the future.

Exercises

So your boss stops you in the hall and says, How's the project coming? How do you answer that? Do you know if tasks are behind schedule, and if so, which ones? Can you tell your boss which tasks are currently running overbudget, and by how much? Have you adjusted the plan for tasks that were interrupted? The following exercises will help you answer these questions. Begin by opening the file "New Product Hour 21. MPP." The solutions to the exercise can be found in the file "New Product Hour 21-Exercise.MPP." See the Introduction for instructions to access the sample files and solutions for these exercises on the book's Web page.

1. Find out which tasks are currently scheduled to finish late by viewing the Slipping Tasks Report. Which tasks are showing a positive Finish Variance?

2. Some tasks are currently overbudget; that is, they are costing more than originally planned. View the Overbudget Tasks Report to find the cost overrun tasks. Are these tasks overbudget because of an increase in fixed costs or in resource costs?

3. At your last team meeting, you learned that Task 13 will be interrupted while the resource is on another task. Split Task 13 so that it resumes on 2/5/01.

4. You also were informed that the entire Production Phase needs to be postponed until February 2, 2001. Update the plan to reflect the change. Display the Detail Gantt and find out how long you must delay hiring the assemblers (Task 17).

21

PART VII

Beyond One Project, One Application

Hour

Hour **22**

Working with Multiple Projects

In the simplest project management environment, there is a single ongoing project—but life is usually not so simple. A single project might grow so large that it should be broken into discrete phases or task groups, or each department in a company could have a single project to manage, or many departments might have several projects each to track. Projects within and across departments might depend on each other for information, such as completion dates. Instead of creating one huge project across the company, Project allows you to manage smaller files individually and then combine and link them as necessary. These smaller files can be opened one at a time or in a group, and each file can be placed in its own window. A critically important aspect of using multiple project files is balancing workloads for employees or equipment that are assigned between several projects.

I'll show you techniques for consolidating many projects into one and how to share resources between several projects using a resource pool.

In this hour, you will learn:

- How to combine Project files into a consolidated file
- How to link together tasks from separate plans
- What a resource pool is and how to create one
- How to connect files to a resource pool

Consolidating Projects into One Window

Managers tend to want information on the "big picture." How many projects are ongoing? Are they on schedule? Do we have enough resources to meet our goals? Do we have the capacity to take on more projects? Getting the big picture usually requires combining individual active files into one composite file. Once combined, a companywide file can help answer the manager's questions.

NEW TERM *Consolidating* is combining individual project files into one project file.

Files can be combined one of two ways:

- Use the New Window feature to consolidate already open files into a new window and file.
- Manually insert project files into a new or existing file.

Both methods result in consolidated files that can be printed, altered, and used for cross-project linking. You have more control initially with the manual insertion method, but the New Window method is easier to use if project files are already open.

Combining Open Project Files

Files that are already open can quickly be combined into a single file. Perhaps you have been working with several individual files and would like to combine them to print an overall Gantt Chart. The fastest way to combine individual, *open* projects into one file is through the New Window command. Project makes some initial decisions for you, so you have less control when combining files with this method. However, you can make necessary changes after the consolidated file has been created.

To Do: Combining Open Files

To combine open files into a single widow, do the following:

1. Open more than one individual project file.
2. Choose Window, New Window. The New Window dialog box will open and display a list of all open project filenames.

22

▼ 3. In the Projects box, select two or more files to be combined into the new window. Use the Ctrl key to select multiple files that aren't listed consecutively; use the Shift key to select a series of consecutive names in the list.

4. The View option defaults to a Gantt Chart. If you would like the new combined file to open in a different view, select one from the drop-down list, as shown in Figure 22.1. After the new window is onscreen, you can select a view as with any other project file.

FIGURE 22.1

Use the New Window dialog box to select open files for a new combined file.

▲ 5. Click OK when finished.

Saving Combined Projects into One File

By combining open files into a New Window, a new project file is actually created and can be saved for later retrieval. A summary line is displayed at the beginning of each individual project in the combined file. An inserted project icon is also displayed in the Indicators column for each project summary task.

 Be aware that the new combined file is linked to its underlying files. Experiment with the combined file, but think carefully before saving changes to it.

By default, the individual files are linked into the combined file, and that link is read/write. Any changes made in the underlying files affect the combined file, and vice versa. Therefore, when you save or close the new combined file, any modifications, such as schedule changes or resource assignments, actually modify the original individual files unless you answer no to saving *any* changes at the File, Save prompts. Also keep in mind that individual file schedules remain unrelated to each other; no links between the individual projects are created when files are consolidated into one window, unless you create them intentionally as described later in this hour.

Consolidating Inserted Projects

A second method for creating a consolidated project file requires you to open a new or existing file and then insert other project files into it. The individual files don't need to be open; you can browse the folders to find the projects to include. This method gives you more control over the order of the individual projects in the combined file, the ability to set the linking relationship between the individual and combined files, and a choice of whether to insert the files as read only, preventing changes at the consolidated level from being saved back into the underlying files.

In general, projects inserted into a consolidated file behave like "normal" project files. Tasks can be cut, copied, and pasted within the consolidated file. Projects and individual tasks can be linked in any of the four types of linking relationships. With few exceptions, tasks and groups of tasks can also be indented and outdented to alter the outline structure and, therefore, the summary information in the consolidated file.

NEW FEATURE It is not necessary to link project files together to view a critical path across all files. The default setting in Project 2000 computes an overall critical path across all inserted projects. If you would prefer to see a separate critical path for each inserted project, choose Tools, Options, Calculation tab and turn off the feature Inserted Projects Are Calculated Like Summary Tasks.

Working with Inserted Projects

If the projects you would like to see in a consolidated view are not already open, the insertion method for combining projects is your fastest option.

To Do: Creating a Consolidated Project File with the Insertion Method

To insert saved Project files into another file for consolidation, follow these steps:

1. Create a new project file or open an existing file to insert projects into.
2. Display a task view, such as the Gantt Chart.
3. Click on the task where the inserted project should begin.
4. Choose Insert, Project. The Insert Project dialog box will be displayed.
5. If necessary, navigate through file folders to display project filenames.

22

6. Decide how the inserted files will be associated with their original files:
   - Link to Project ensures that the most recently saved versions of the individual files are used in the consolidation (as opposed to a static snapshot of the files which may be outdated), and that individual files *can* be affected by changes at the consolidated level.
   - Under the Insert drop-down list, Read Only inserts the most recently saved version of the file when the consolidated file is opened, but changes at the consolidated level are *not* sent back to the individual file.
7. Click on the name of each file to be inserted into the consolidated file:
   - Use the Ctrl key while clicking to add filenames to the selection.
   - The order in which the filenames are selected determines their order in the consolidated file.
8. When finished selecting files to be inserted, click Insert or Insert Read-Only, as shown in Figure 22.2. The restructured file is then created and displayed, as shown in Figure 22.3. Make column width and timescale adjustments as needed in the combined file.

FIGURE 22.2

Use the Insert Project dialog box to select settings and which projects to insert.

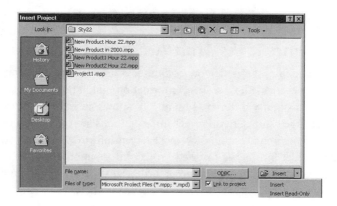

9. Choose File, Save to name and save the consolidated file for future use; otherwise, you must re-create the consolidated file the next time you need it.

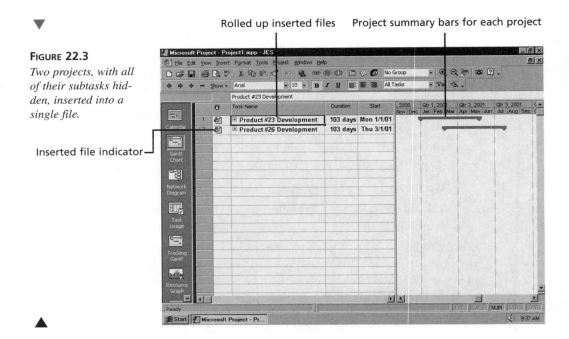

FIGURE 22.3

Two projects, with all of their subtasks hidden, inserted into a single file.

Inserted file indicator

Identifying Tasks That Are Inserted Projects

An icon in the Indicators column identifies a project summary task of an inserted project file. Also, the Task Information dialog box for these inserted project summary tasks is slightly different. Figure 22.4 shows an example of the new dialog box; its name is changed to Inserted Project Information. The Advanced tab allows you to unlink the inserted file and keep only the most recent information in the consolidated file. By clicking Project Info in the Inserted Project Information dialog box, you can view the vital statistics for the individual project file. This feature is particularly convenient for observing the results of "what if" experiments in the consolidated file.

If you are following good project management practices, and refining your projects through experience, templates for similar projects will emerge over time. When similar projects, from similar templates, are consolidated, there will be a repetition of task names. For example, a task named "Prototype design" might appear in more than one project. There's no default method for seeing onscreen which "Prototype design" originated from which underlying project file.

There are several remedies for this confusion. You might already be using a custom field in individual files to assign project names or numbers. If so, display that field by inserting a column for it in the consolidated file. If not, you can use the standard field called "Project" for this purpose. As shown in Figure 22.5, the inserted Project column displays the source filename on each line of the consolidated file.

22

Dialog box name changed to   See schedule information   Change link to underlying
Inserted Project Information   for inserted project   file on Advanced tab

FIGURE 22.4

*The information dia-
log box for inserted
projects is slightly dif-
ferent from the stan-
dard Task Information
dialog box.*

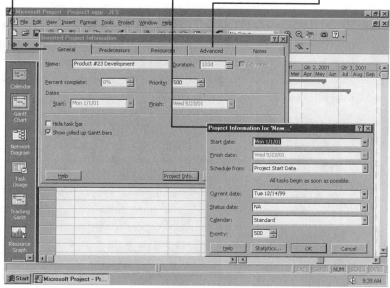

FIGURE 22.5

*The inserted Project
field column identifies
the source file for each
task line.*

Inserted column
shows underlying
file names

Task 3 from the first
New Product file

Task 3 from the second
New Product file

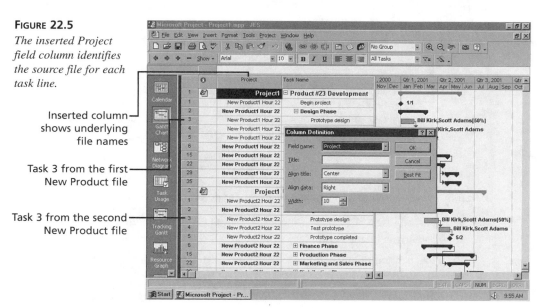

See Hour 18, "Creating Custom Views," for detailed information on inserting columns and customizing tables.

Working with Inserted Projects

Inserted projects in a consolidated file can be manipulated in a number of ways. Individual tasks or groups of tasks can be copied or moved from one project file area into another project, or deleted altogether. Changes such as these affect the individual project files if they are linked into the consolidated file.

 Keep in mind that copying, cutting, or deleting summary tasks also copies, cuts, or deletes the subtasks underneath them.

Tasks can be indented or outdented in the consolidated file outline structure to more accurately represent the relationships between projects. For example, the original file might contain a simple list of major phases of a company's project, such as Design, Finance, Production, and so on. The project manager for the design group can insert his entire project under the Design phase heading in the outline structure of the combined file. He should make sure his entire project was inserted as a subtask under the Design heading; that is, the inserted design project would need to be indented one level farther to the right of the Design phase task.

 Recall from Hour 3, "Starting a New Project and Working with Tasks," that indenting a task one level to the right makes it a subtask and creates a summary task out of the task immediately above it. Outdenting a task moves it one outline level to the left and causes the task above it to no longer be a summary task.

The outline level at which projects are inserted are determined by the following rules:

- Projects are inserted at the outline level of the task immediately above the inserted row if that row is not a summary task.
- Projects inserted below summary tasks are inserted at one outline level to the right, one more indentation.
- Projects inserted at the bottom of a file, where there are only blank rows below them, are inserted at the outline level of the last visible row. If the last row in the consolidated file happens to be a collapsed summary task, the inserted project will assume the outline level of that summary task, not of its hidden subtasks.

One useful feature of consolidation is that a single project can be inserted into more than one consolidated file. This can focus a consolidation on a particular department or manager, for example. Finance and Production projects might be of interest to the financial officer, and the information systems department might need to see Finance and Networking projects combined. A little planning should be done in regards to who has read/write privileges to prevent having "too many cooks in the broth."

> Consolidated files can also be inserted into other consolidated files, which effectively creates a hierarchy of projects. The absolute limit is 1,000 consolidated files; realistically, you will be limited by your computer's capabilities.

Linking Consolidated Projects

Individual tasks and entire projects can be linked within a consolidated file to create true cross-project dependencies. After projects have been consolidated into a single, larger file, they can easily be linked in any of Project's four dependency relationships. It doesn't matter if the consolidation resulted from the New Window method or from inserting projects into another file.

> Recall that the four basic dependency relationships in Project are Finish-to-Start, Start-to-Start, Finish-to-Finish, and Start-to-Finish (rarely used).

See Hour 6, "Linking Tasks in the Correct Sequence," for detailed information on task dependencies.

To Do: Creating File Links in Consolidated Projects

To create links between individual projects, follow these steps:

1. Create a consolidated file by choosing Window, New Window for open files or by choosing Insert, Project to select from lists of files.

2. Link *tasks* in a default Finish-to-Start relationship by the usual linking tech niques. One method is to select the first task name, press and hold the Ctrl key, scroll to see and select the second task name from another project, and click the Link Tasks button on the Standard toolbar. Project will draw the task linking line in the combined file.

   Link *entire projects* by linking the project summary tasks.

▼ 3. To change the type of linking relationship, open the Task or Project Information dialog box for the *successor task* or summary task, move to the Predecessors tab in the dialog box, click in the Type cell, and select a different relationship from the
▲   drop-down list.

As a result of this linking between files, Project will create and insert two new tasks: one in the sending file with the name of the task it sends information to, and one in the receiving file with the name of the external task supplying schedule information. Open one of the inserted files or, if it is already open, make it active by choosing Window, filename. The new, externally linked tasks will be formatted with gray text.

In the individual files, choose Tools, Links Between Projects to examine the links created. The Links Between Projects dialog box will be displayed, as shown in Figure 22.6. The receiving file will have a task listed on the External Predecessors tab. The sending file will have a task listed on the External Successors tab.

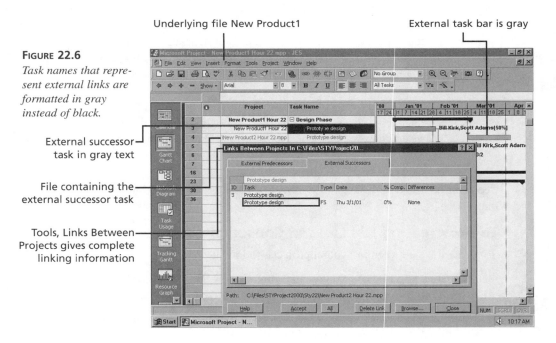

FIGURE 22.6
Task names that represent external links are formatted in gray instead of black.

Notice in Figure 22.6 that Task 4 in the New Product1 file is formatted with a lighter text color. This formatting change indicates that this task is a marker, which points to a task named "Prototype design" in another file (in this example, New Product2). So, Task 4 is an external successor task to Task 3. The two tasks, from different projects, are linked in a Finish-to-Start relationship. Figure 22.6 also presents the detailed linking information in a dialog box. Again, "Prototype design" in New Product2 (with its complete file path given at the bottom of the dialog box) is identified in the Links Between Projects dialog box as an external successor to "Prototype design" in New Product1.

Going the other way, you can investigate the New Product2 file. Task 3 in the New Product1 project is formatted differently, in gray text with a gray Gantt bar, but here it is an external *predecessor* to task 4 in New Product2. This relationship will also be shown in the Links Between Projects dialog box, but on the External Predecessors tab.

> Click the Project Info button in an Inserted Project Information dialog box to see the effects of linking on the successor project's start and finish dates.

Deleting Inserted Projects

What happens if you inserted a project in the wrong spot in the combined file? If it was your last step, you can simply use the Undo command, or you could cut and paste the entire project elsewhere in the outline. If you don't catch your mistake, or simply change your mind later on, delete the inserted project from the combined file.

To Do: Removing a Plan from a Consolidated File

To remove an inserted plan from a consolidated file, follow these steps:

1. Select the project summary task for the inserted project.

2. Press Delete. The project is removed from this consolidation but the underlying file remains stored on disk.

> Make sure you select the summary task for the *entire inserted project* before pressing Delete. By selecting either individual tasks or other summary tasks, you will remove those tasks from the original individual file if it's linked to the consolidated file.

Breaking a Large Project Apart Using Inserted Projects

Projects tend to take on a life of their own as tasks are added or steps to completion modified. It's not uncommon for a simple project to become large and somewhat unwieldy. Even at this point, however, there are usually logical groups of tasks that should be managed together. This type of project is a good candidate for being broken into individual, more manageable files. These smaller files can then be inserted back into a consolidated file for projectwide analysis.

To Do: Breaking a Large Project into Several Inserted Projects

To break a large project into smaller, more manageable files, do the following:

1. Open the large project file.
2. Select a group of tasks that could be logically tracked in a single separate file.
3. Select task ID numbers from the large project and cut the tasks.
4. Create a new file.
5. Paste in the tasks cut from the large project.
6. Save and name the new, smaller file.
7. Repeat for other segments of the original large file.
8. When the large project has been broken into smaller files, use the procedures given previously to create a consolidated file from the new smaller files.
9. Save and name the consolidated file.

Two notes of caution when using this technique:

The start date of the new, smaller files might need to be adjusted (use Project, Project Information).

Also, links between tasks in the original file that would result in links *between* the new files are *not* carried over into the individual files. They need to be re-established as external links to the other small files.

Sharing Resources among Projects with a Resource Pool

A small company or single department might have only one ongoing project that commands all available resources. The Engineering staff could be dedicated to a new product development with the Marketing department focused on selling the new product when it becomes available. It's more likely, however, that even within a single department, there will be several projects in progress or under consideration. Engineering could be developing more than one new product, or different phases of a single product development might be managed by separate project leaders. In this case, several projects in Engineering might require work by the same engineering personnel. This requirement creates a need to manage a list, or pool, of resources.

Project allows you to create a resource pool of all available employees, equipment, or contractors, and maintain the pool separately from individual project files. An individual project file then points to this pool as its source of resources, instead of creating a list of resources within each individual file. With all shared files pointing to the pool, project managers can look across the ongoing projects to make resource assignments and correct allocation problems.

Creating the Resource Pool

Any Project .MPP file containing resource names and other resource information, such as resource calendars, can serve as the resource pool. However, often the resource pool file is simply a Project file that contains resource information and nothing else; that is, there are no tasks in the resource pool file itself. The tasks to which resources are assigned are actually in other, individual files.

To Do: Creating a Separate Resource Pool

To create a pool of resources in a separate Project file, follow these steps:

1. Create a project file by choosing File, New.
2. Choose View, Resource Sheet.
3. Enter resource information, such as name, maximum units, pay rates, and base calendar, for each resource.
4. Choose File, Save, and type a name for this resource file.

The list of resources you want to use might already exist in a project file. If so, there are three additional methods for creating a resource pool:

- Leave the existing file as is but let Project know it will also serve as the resource pool by attaching other files to it. This could create file lock-out problems with other users sharing the pool.
- Open the existing file and save the file under a new name by using File, Save As. This new file will become the resource pool. Then delete all tasks from the file and save it again.
- Open the existing file, copy all resource information, open or switch to a different file, and paste the resource information into the second file. Be sure when copying resource information to either click and drag through the resource ID numbers or select all resources by clicking in the unlabeled Select All cell at the upper-left of the resource sheet. Copying the resource names is not enough!

Sharing the Resource Pool

After the resource pool file has been created and saved, each individual file that will share resource information needs to be attached to the pool. Project describes this as sharing the resource pool. It simply means "don't look for a resource list in this file; look for it in a different file." To set up the sharing, both the pool file and the file with tasks *must* be open. After making the connection, the pool file can be closed to save system overhead.

To Do: Sharing a Resource Pool with an Individual Project

To connect a Project file to a resource pool, follow these steps:

1. Choose File, Open to open the file that's serving as the resource pool (resource file).
2. Choose File, Open again to open the individual project file (task file).
3. Make sure the task file is active.
4. Choose Tools, Resources, Share Resources. The Share Resources dialog box will be displayed, as shown in Figure 22.7.

5. In the Share Resources dialog box, select the Use Resources option.
6. Also select the name of the pool file in the From drop-down list.
7. Click OK when finished.

When sharing has been established, the complete list of resources from the pool is available for task assignments in the attached file. Any assignments made in the task file are automatically updated in the pool file, if the pool is still open. Any other sharing files are also updated.

Project keeps track of which file is serving as a resource pool and which other project files are sharing from the pool. When you later open a file being used as a resource pool, you are given the option of opening the pool as read-only, so others can update the pool while you are working. You can also choose to open the pool file as read-write, which prevents others from updating the pool while you work. The third option is to open the pool and all files attached to it, creating a new consolidated file. Figure 22.8 shows the options available when opening a resource pool file.

FIGURE 22.8

Options when opening a resource pool file.

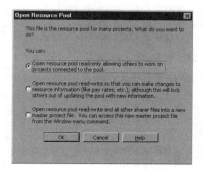

Similarly, when you open a file that's attached to the pool, you have options as to how that sharing file and the pool will be opened. Figure 22.9 shows the options available when opening a file that shares resources with the pool. You can choose to open the pool file, bringing with it the most recent pool information from all other sharing files. The other option is to leave the pool and other sharing files closed. Your computer will work faster that way, but you will need to take an extra step to send out pool update messages periodically.

FIGURE 22.9

Options when opening a connected file if the pool is currently closed.

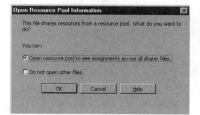

If the pool file was closed while changes were being made to resources in individual files, and then the pool is opened later, you must tell Project to update the pool so that its information stays current for other sharing files and users.

To Do: Manually Updating the Resource Pool

To send your assignment changes to the resource pool while working on your plan, and to receive the latest information from other sharing files, do the following:

1. Open an attached file and choose to Open resource pool to see assignments across all sharer files. Make sure the attached, sharer file is active.

▼ 2. Choose Tools, Resources, Share Resources.

3. On the cascading menu, select Update Resource Pool to *send to the pool* any changes that may have been made that affect the pool.

   To *receive* updated assignment information that other files may have sent to the
▲ pool, select Refresh Resource Pool.

Identifying Resource Pool Links

It's certainly possible that you could lose track of which task files have been set up to share a resource pool, but with Project, you can see a list of all attached files in the Share Resources dialog box of the pool file. The dialog box will be slightly changed from its original appearance when sharing was being established.

To Do: Viewing Resource Pool File Links

To see a list of all files attached to the resource pool, do the following:

1. Open the resource pool file and make it the active file on the screen.

2. Choose Tools, Resources, Share Resources. The Share Resources dialog box will open, as shown in Figure 22.10.

FIGURE 22.10

The Share Resources dialog box in a pool file has a slightly different appearance.

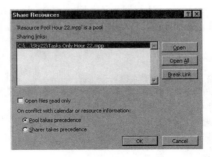

The Share Resources dialog box for an active pool file looks different from the box for a file that's not serving as a pool. Now, a list of all task files sharing the pool is displayed in the Sharing Links area.

3. To open an attached file, click once on its name and click Open. To open all attached files, click Open All.

   You can also indicate that attached files be opened as read-only so that they won't be accidentally altered. Turn on the Open Files Read Only check box before clicking Open or Open All.

   The Share Resources dialog box closes automatically after you click Open or
▲ Open All.

Discontinuing Resource Sharing

A project file does not have to be attached to a resource pool forever. Save system overhead by detaching any completed or inactive project from the pool. Also, you might use the resource pool as a simple repository of resource information, not as the record keeper for resource allocations across many projects. In that case, you can attach a task file to the pool to automatically copy down resource information, instead of having to type it into the file, and then detach from the pool so Project doesn't have to maintain file links.

To Do: Discontinuing Resource Sharing

To break the link between a file and the resource pool, do the following:

1. Open the resource pool file and make it the active file on the screen.

2. Choose Tools, Resources, Share Resources. The Share Resources dialog box will open.

3. In the Sharing links area, click once on the name of the task file that will discontinue sharing.

4. Click Break Link. The resource sharing link will be broken and the dialog box will close.

Summary

A variety of file management techniques and file relationships are possible in Project. You can start with a single file and break it into manageable pieces. Going the other way, several projects can be consolidated into a single window and saved as one file. Within a consolidated file, linking complete projects is as easy as linking tasks within a simple project file. You can also create external predecessor and successor tasks between projects that might otherwise have nothing else in common except dates. By associating projects with a single resource list, you can more easily avoid or correct overallocation of resources.

Q&A

Q I inserted a project into another project, but the inserted file will not move out to a higher outline level. Why not?

A Be careful where you insert projects, and follow the rules given in this hour. The outline level of the task above the insertion point is very important. If you can't restructure the outline as you would like, delete the inserted project and start over, with the following tip in mind: Collapse the outline of the existing file first; then select a row below an existing, visible task that's on the same outline level as where you want to insert the second project; and finally, insert the second project.

For example, if you want the inserted project to be at the first (leftmost) outline level, collapse the existing file outline (you can use the Show button on the Formatting toolbar to chose Outline Level 1), click on the task row under a visible level-one task, and then insert your project.

Q There are tasks in a consolidated file that I didn't want to see, so I deleted them. Now they are missing in the individual project files. What happened to them?

A If the consolidated file has read/write links to the underlying smaller files, changes in the consolidated file will be sent to the underlying files, *including* task deletions. Either create a new consolidated file without the link by using Insert, Project, and clearing the Link to project option, or in the combined file hide (but don't delete) tasks in the existing consolidation by applying filters or collapsing the outline structure.

Q I know I connected my file to the resource pool, but under Share Resources, it says it's using its own resources. Why?

A That happens when the resource pool file is closed. Open the pool file and then check your file's dialog box again. A better approach might be to open the resource pool and check the Share Resources dialog box in that file. It will display a list of all files known to be sharing the pool.

Here's a related question about the Use Own Resources feature. You opened a sharing file without opening the resource pool file, believing this would cut the link and remove the sharing file from the pool. In the Share Resources dialog box, the Use Own Resources option is turned on, so you're sure you are not connected to the pool. But if you actually click on the Use Own Resources button, Project will tell you that you are in fact still connected, and give you the option at that point to force the link to break.

Q My favorite contractors are in the resource sheet in a file I created. I connected to the resource pool to retrieve other resource names, and now my contractors appear in the pool also. Can anybody assign my contractors from the pool?

A Yes they can; there is no resource hiding allowed. Resources local to a file are always added to the pool if that connection is made. This feature can actually be helpful; if you have existing files with different resource lists, create a file for a pool, connect your existing files to it, and Project will sweep in the resource information from all existing files to create the pool.

Exercises

22

You have been working on a project to develop a new product. Another new product has been proposed, and a Project file was created from a template to manage the second product's development. In the following exercise, combine the two product development files into a single file and view the combined Gantt Chart. Make a modification to the combined file to view the supplying file for each task. Finally, link tasks from the two files together.

Also, you have been asked to investigate the possibility of using a single resource list for all active files. The exercise instructs you to attach a file to a pool, assign resources, and save your work. Then you can see for yourself what options are available when you open a pool and an attached file. See the Introduction for instructions to access the sample files and solutions for these exercises on the book's Web page.

1. Use the New Window technique to combine the New Product1 Hour 22 file and the New Product2 Hour 22 file into a consolidated file displaying a Gantt Chart.

2. For clarity, display the Project field in a column before the Task Name column.

3. On the combined Gantt Chart, view outline levels 1 and 2 only. Bring the Gantt bars into view. Change the Timescale to display Quarters and Months.

4. When the Production Phase for New Product1 is complete, the company schedules the Design Phase for New Product2 to begin. Create this Finish-to-Start relationship.

5. Open the Resource Pool file. Open the Tasks Only file. Make the Tasks Only file active. Set up the Tasks Only file to receive its resource list from the Pool file.

6. In the Tasks Only file, assign Mary Logan to tasks 3 and 4. Close and Save both files.

7. Open the Tasks Only file, without opening the other files. How many resources are available on the Resource Sheet?

8. Close the Tasks Only file. Open it again, this time choosing the open resource pool option. Now how many resources are available on the Resource Sheet?

9. Disconnect Tasks Only from the Resource Pool.

HOUR 23

Using Microsoft Project in Workgroups

Communication is the key to a successful project, and Project 2000's Workgroup features enhance and simplify communication among your project team. Typically, the project manager, project team members, and project sponsors all have interests in the progress of the project. Communication is the key to accurate project planning, tracking, and managing. This lesson focuses on electronically communicating Project information such as team member assignments, actual and remaining work, and updated task status. It also looks at methods for circulating the actual Project file electronically.

In this hour, you will learn:

- System considerations for electronic communication
- Methods for communicating with email
- How to use Project Central
- Steps for communicating with team members electronically
- How to set Project task reminders in Microsoft Outlook

Exploring Project's Workgroup Features

A project is only as good as its last update. Out-of-date information can easily lead to poor management decisions, unachievable end dates, and unmanageable resource allocations. Printed reports and information exchanged at team meetings may lose timeliness between reporting periods. Electronic communication of a project's status within a workgroup is the ideal way to keep the project on track.

NEW TERM In the context of this book, a *workgroup* is the group of people directly involved with a project. The workgroup includes the project manager, who typically "owns" the Project file; project resources doing work on the project; affected managers; and possibly external contacts such as customers or contractors.

After your project team has been selected, discussing the project objectives can be advantageous. Use this project kick-off meeting as an opportunity to set up communication and project standards. Decide on a communications medium and determine what tools the project team will need. After the communication process has been determined, the project manager can send out team member work assignments and receive updated actual work reports. The manager and team members can also exchange project updates.

NEW TERM *Actual work* is the amount of time an individual or team has spent on a task to date. This tracking assists in assessing progress of the project.

Another approach is to transmit a complete file to other users who are running Project and ask them to directly modify the project. The problem with this approach is you have no control over what is changed, and there is more opportunity for error by a less experienced Microsoft Project user. Using Microsoft Project in Workgroups can take advantage of email systems, a local intranet, or the World Wide Web on the Internet.

> As a member of a workgroup, you do not need to have Project 2000 installed on your computer in order to communicate via the workgroup function. If project team members do not have Project 2000 installed on their computer, and they are using the email method of workgroup communication, they need to run the `WGSetup.exe` file from the Project 2000 CD.

Deciding on Email, Intranet, or Internet Workgroup Communications

There are two basic options for communicating project information electronically:

- Email
- Intranet or Internet posting

Before deciding on which communication method is best for your team ask yourself a few questions:

- What immediate software, hardware, or network access is available to the project team?
- If the necessary hardware or technical resources for Web-based workgroup communication are not readily available in my organization, does my project have the required budget to procure the needed equipment and technical resources to implement this functionality?

Your existing installations, information system department, or company budget may make the decision for you. While email is the simplest, most commonly used option, the new Web-based workgroup features available in Project Central provide additional functionality beyond the email workgroup capabilities.

Communicating with a Workgroup by Email

To communicate by email, all workgroup members must have access to a 32-bit MAPI-compliant email system. MAPI stands for messaging application programming interface. Most email systems today are MAPI compliant. Acceptable systems include Microsoft Mail, Outlook, and Exchange.

> Check with your system administrator to be sure that your system complies with the specifications mentioned here. Setting up an email server is beyond the scope of this book.

In addition to email access, the workgroup manager must have Project 2000 installed.

Communicating with a Workgroup on an Intranet

You may prefer to communicate project status on an internal Web site, known as an *intranet*. All workgroup members need access to a network and to the network's Web server. The project manager and project team members also need a Web browser such as Microsoft Internet Explorer or Netscape Navigator. Team members once again do not require Project 2000 to be installed on their systems.

Communicating with a Workgroup on the Internet

The same requirements are necessary for communicating on an intranet as on the Internet or the World Wide Web. However, there is one additional requirement: The workgroup must be connected to the Internet. The connection can be through a dedicated server in your company or through an Internet Service Provider (ISP). Check with your systems administrator for more details.

Microsoft Project Central is a companion product to Project 2000. A single Project Central access license is included with each unit of Project 2000. Additional licenses can be purchased for team members. Project Central must be installed on a Web server with connection to an intranet or Internet, which ever is accessible by the entire team. Team members can access project information by logging into the Web server from its Uniform Resource Locator (URL).

Setting Up Project Messaging

After deciding on a messaging method and verifying software and hardware configurations for the workgroup manager and members, you must configure the workgroup settings for your Project file. When using email-based workgroup communication, if a team member's name is the same as his email name, Project 2000 uses that team member's name for communications. Most often, however, you will need to enter each team member's email address in your project. Display the Email Address field on a resource sheet table and enter all the email addresses for the people in the workgroup. To do so, open the Resource Information dialog box by double-clicking a team member in the resource sheet, and enter the team member's email address in this dialog.

Email addresses can be copied from an existing electronic address book and pasted into the Project email field. It's best to do this in a template or resource pool file so that you have to do it only once.

See Hour 22, "Working with Multiple Projects," for information on setting up resource pools.

23

To Do: Setting Up Workgroup Communications in Project

To Do

To set up workgroup communications in Microsoft Project, follow these steps:

1. Select Tools, Options from the menu to display the Options dialog box.
2. Select the Workgroup tab to see the dialog box shown in Figure 23.1.

FIGURE 23.1

Set up workgroup communications in Project by selecting Tools, Options, Workgroup.

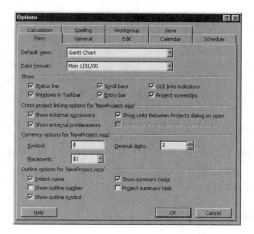

3. Choose an option from the Default Workgroup Messaging for Resources drop-down list box.

4. If you will be using email-based workgroup communication, select Email from the drop-down list box. If you will be communicating using the Internet or intranet, select Web in the drop-down list box. In the Web Server URL (for Resource) field, type the address identification for the Web server and server folder for this workgroup (such as `http://servername/projectcentral`).

5. At the Identification of Web Client Server prompt, either select the Create Account Button or follow the directions on the General tab. Check with your systems administrator regarding setting up new accounts on a server.

▼

▼ 6. If you want an email notification to be sent out to project team members whenever Web-based workgroup messages are sent, check the Notify When New Web Messages Arrive option.

7. Click OK when finished.

> You may want to select a different workgroup messaging option for some team members in your project if they do not have access to email or to the Web. For example, if a team member has Web access but does not have email access, you can set his workgroup messaging option to Web (or vice-versa). Messages may be sent both ways, by selecting both Email and Web. To select a workgroup option for a team member, double-click the team member's name to display the Resource Information dialog box, and from the General tab, select the appropriate setting in the Workgroup drop down list box.

▲

Team members and project managers who use email-based workgroup messaging will communicate using the standard email Inbox and Reply features of their email program. On a Web-based system, two additional messaging features are available: one for project team members and one for the project manager. Team members use Project Central to read, reply to, and track their messages.

To view messages from project team members, the project manager can open the Web Inbox from within Project 2000. The Web Inbox allows the project manager to view team member responses and to update project files with a team member's actual and remaining work.

Sending Task Requests with TeamAssign

When team members have been assigned to tasks in a project, the team members must be notified of those assignments. First, the project manager sends a TeamAssign message to each team member with his or her task assignments. The team member then responds to the manager, either accepting or rejecting the assignments. Finally, the manager opens the response and updates the project with the team member's response.

To Do: Sending a TeamAssign Request

To send a TeamAssign request to a team member, follow these steps:

1. Display a task view, such as the Gantt Chart view.

2. Select Tools, Workgroup, TeamAssign or click the TeamAssign button on the Workgroup toolbar.

▼ To Do

▼   3. Choose an option to send assignments for all tasks or only selected tasks.

4. Click OK. The TeamAssign dialog box appears as shown in Figure 23.2.

FIGURE 23.2

Use the TeamAssign feature to notify team members of their task assignments.

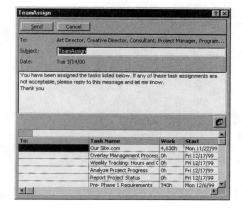

23

5. For the Subject field, accept the default TeamAssign option or type a subject for the message.

6. Accept or modify the text in the message area. It is good practice to give a desired response deadline in the message area.

7. In the list of tasks at the bottom of the dialog box, the To field is the only field you can edit. It is not recommended that you change these fields.

8. Click Send when finished. An icon indicating that a TeamAssign request has been made, but not yet responded to, appears in the Indicators column for the selected
▲   task.

Composing the TeamAssign Form

A standard TeamAssign form is included with Project. It sends and requests information about predefined Project fields. The workgroup manager can add and reorder additional Project fields on the form.

To Do: Adding or Reordering Project Fields

To add or reorder Project fields on a TeamAssign form, follow these steps:

1. Select Tools, Customize, Workgroup. The Customize Workgroup dialog box appears as shown in Figure 23.3.

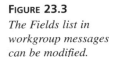

FIGURE 23.3

The Fields list in workgroup messages can be modified.

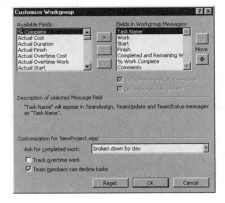

2. Select the desired fields from the Available Fields list and click the arrow to add them to the Fields in Workgroup Message list. Note the description for each field; this text can help you determine the usefulness of each field you might include in the form.

3. Use the Move Up and Move Down buttons to reorder the selected field on the form.

4. If you want the same fields to be listed in the TeamStatus message, select the Include in TeamStatus Message check box.

5. Select a reporting period from the Ask for Completed Work drop-down list box.

6. If you want team members to record overtime work using these forms, select the Track Overtime Work check box.

7. If you are giving team members the option of refusing assignments sent to them using the TeamAssign form, select the Team Members Can Decline Tasks check box.

8. To cancel the changes you have made and close the dialog box, click the Return to Default Settings button.

9. Click OK when finished.

Responding to TeamAssign Requests

If you are a member of a workgroup, it's likely that you'll need to respond to TeamAssign messages from your manager.

To Do: Responding to a TeamAssign Message

To Do ▼

To respond to a TeamAssign message your manager has sent to you, follow these steps:

1. From your email Inbox, select the TeamAssign message to which you want to respond and click Reply.

   Alternatively, Web users can run their Web browsers to display the Workgroup Login box as shown in Figure 23.4.

23

FIGURE 23.4

Display the Workgroup Login screen with your Web browser.

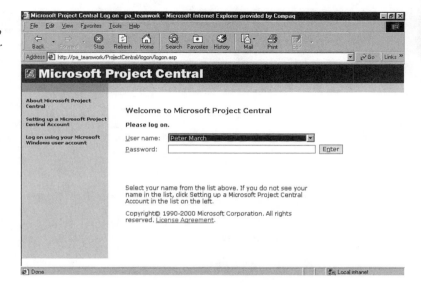

After logging in, a team member's messages are displayed in the TeamInbox, as shown in Figure 23.5. Click the envelope icon next to a TeamAssign message to open that message.

2. If you want, you can type a reply in the message area.

3. Email users can accept or decline the assignment by typing **Yes** or **No** in the Accept? field.

   TeamInbox users can select or deselect the Accept? check box to accept or decline the assignment.

▼ 4. Click Send when finished.

FIGURE 23.5
Web team members
respond to task assign-
ments using a browser
and the TeamInbox.

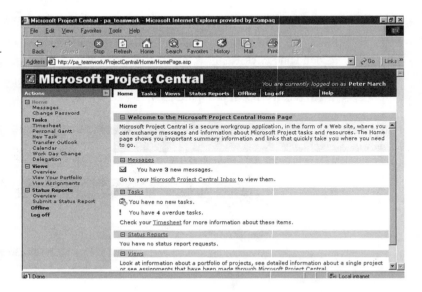

Workgroup Manager Feedback to Team Members

After team members have responded to TeamAssign messages, the manager must incorporate these responses into the Project file. Accepting team member feedback is easy:

- If you are using email-based workgroup messaging, project managers can open the
  email from the mail program's Inbox.

  The project managers can send further communication to the team member by
  Clicking Reply, entering a message, and clicking Send. (The team member's
  response to the task assignment is not entered into the Project file at this point.)

- If you are using Web-based workgroup messaging, project managers can select
  Tools, Workgroup, TeamInbox or click the TeamInbox icon on the Workgroup tool-
  bar. This automatically opens up your browser to the log in screen of Project
  Central.

  The manager should review each team member's message for accuracy and com-
  pleteness before accepting it into the Project file. Choosing Update Project automatically confirms the member's assignments in the Project file. Web managers
  can choose Update All to incorporate all TeamAssign messages into the Project file
  at once. Alternatively, you can choose Cancel to close the message without updating the Project file.

After the Project file is updated with a team member's response, the icon indicating that the manager is waiting for a TeamAssign response disappears from the Indicators column in the Gantt Chart view.

Requesting and Submitting Task Progress with TeamStatus

23

TeamStatus messages allow the workgroup manager to monitor the progress of the project, which includes hours worked and hours remaining. Because the project can be updated with this information at the click of a button, this makes the process of collecting actuals from project team members much less time-consuming. A workgroup member can send a status update on any task assigned to him or her, whether or not the manager has requested a TeamStatus report.

If you want to request a status for a subset of tasks, select these tasks prior to accessing the TeamStatus function.

To Do: Sending a TeamStatus Request

To send a request for a TeamStatus report, follow these steps:

1. In the Project file, select the tasks that you want to update.

2. Select Tools, Workgroup, TeamStatus.

3. Send a request to the members on the selected tasks or on all tasks.

4. If you want, you can make changes to the Subject field and message area.

5. Click Send when finished. An icon indicating that a TeamStatus request has been sent, but not responded to, appears in the Indicators column for the selected task as shown in Figure 23.6.

The project manager can easily see which tasks and team members have responded to the TeamStatus request by viewing the TeamStatus icon in the Indicator column.

FIGURE 23.6

The indicator column shows that there has not been a response to all TeamStatus messages.

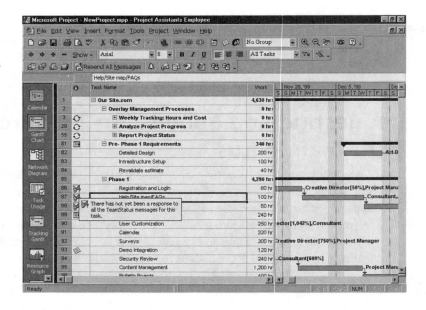

To Do: Responding to a Status Message

For a team member to respond to a status message, follow these steps:

1. Open a TeamStatus message in your email Inbox or the TeamInbox.

2. Enter actual data for the task, including actual hours worked and hours remaining.

3. If you want, modify the message area.

4. Click Send when finished.

If assigned Project tasks are being tracked by members in Microsoft Outlook, task status reports can also be generated there: Use the Tasks, New TeamStatus Report feature in Outlook.

Sending Task Updates with TeamUpdate

TeamUpdate should not be confused with TeamStatus. A *status message* is used to gather hard project data, such as hours worked and hours remaining. An *update message* is used to notify the workgroup of changes that the project manager has already made to the project plan. For example, a task's duration may have changed or the task's start or finish dates have been modified. The team member needs the updated information to keep his or her list of ongoing responsibilities current.

When an update message has to be sent to a team member, an icon appears in the task's Indicators column to remind the manager to send the message. Project managers do not have to continuously review which team members have to be updated about tasks, as Project 2000 keeps track of this information automatically.

When the manager sends an update message for the entire project, all team members who have been affected by the changes are notified.

Workgroup members can respond to the message communicating any concerns or issues regarding the TeamUpdate; however, team members do not have the choice of accepting or declining the change. The reply appears in the manager's Web Inbox along with other messages from the project'steam members.

To Do: Sending a Task Update

To send a task update to a team member after a change to the project, follow these steps:

1. Select Tools, Workgroup, TeamUpdate. The TeamUpdate dialog box appears as shown in Figure 23.7.

FIGURE 23.7

The manager sends a TeamUpdate message to inform a team member of project changes.

2. Enter a Subject for the message.
3. Type the text of the message to be sent.
4. Click Send.

> If no task information has actually changed, and you attempt to send a TeamUpdate message, a dialog box appears to inform you that a TeamUpdate cannot be sent because there is nothing to update!

23

Setting Task Reminders

Microsoft Project tasks can be integrated into your Microsoft Outlook task list. If Outlook is available on your machine, and you use Outlook to receive and respond to your workgroup manager's messages instead of using the TeamInbox, accepted tasks are automatically added to your Outlook task list. Reminders of upcoming dates and deadlines can be set for Project/Outlook tasks. The reminder is actually set from within Project.

To Do: Setting a Task Reminder for Tasks Already Accepted with Outlook

To set a reminder for a Project task you have already accepted using Outlook, follow these steps:

1. From Microsoft Project, choose Tools, Workgroup, Set Reminder. The Set Reminders dialog box appears as shown in Figure 23.8.

FIGURE 23.8

You can set an Outlook reminder for a Project task.

2. Make selections for the reminder time period such as minutes, days, or weeks ahead.

3. Indicate whether the reminder is keyed to the task start date or finish date.

4. Click OK when finished. The task reminders are sent to Outlook, which will then issue the reminder at the appropriate time.

Circulating the Project Schedule for Review

Email and Web users have some additional communication options available to them in Project 2000. Entire Project files can be sent by email for other users to both review and modify. Alternatively, pictures of selected tasks can be sent with email messages to team members and others.

Using the Send Command

The Microsoft Project Send command is similar to the Send command in other applications in the Microsoft Office family. The Send command opens a new email message form where you can compose and address a message, and the current active project is automatically attached. This process requires a 32-bit MAPI compliant email client, as discussed earlier in this hour. Both the sender and the recipient must have Project installed to send or open the file. A single file can be sent to multiple users in one email message.

To Do: Sending a File to a Workgroup Member

To email an entire Microsoft Project file to a member of the workgroup, follow these steps:

1. Select File, Send To.
2. Select Mail Recipient. An email message dialog box opens.
3. Complete the To and CC fields as you would for any email message on your system.
4. Send the message.
5. Close the email dialog box.

Using the Routing Slip

A routing slip allows you to circulate the same project file from one recipient to another, accumulating suggested changes in the project file. The initial sender designates an order in which the file is to be circulated and is notified as each recipient receives the project file. No recipient receives the file until the previous recipient forwards it along; eventually, the file is sent back to the originator.

To Do: Using a Routing Slip

To send a Project file using a routing slip, follow these steps:

1. Select File, Send To.
2. Select Routing Recipient.
3. The Routing Slip dialog box appears. In the To area, fill in the names of the recipients.
4. Modify the order in which the recipients will receive the Project file by using the Move buttons next to the To area.
5. Choose One After Another to have the file travel sequentially to each recipient. The sequence number will appear beside the name of each recipient.
6. To ensure that the file gets back to you when all recipients have passed it along, select the Return When Done check box. See Figure 23.9.

FIGURE 23.9
This figure shows the routing slip with the Creative Director moved to the last position using the Move button.

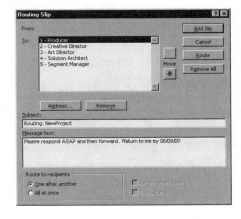

7. Click Add Slip when finished.

> If you are not sure of a person's email address, you can select the Address button. By selecting the button, an Address Book window will open containing your contact list from Outlook. Select the desired recipients and add them to the Message Recipients box.

Sending Schedule Notes

There is an additional email option for communicating Project information. Schedule notes offer a couple of advantages: The manager can optionally include the project file with the message, or can include a picture of only the selected tasks for the recipients to review. The mailing list is generated for you when you select a group of recipients from inside the notes messages.

To Do: Sending a Schedule Note

To send a schedule note, follow these steps:

1. Select Tools, Workgroup, Send Schedule Note. The Send Schedule Note dialog box appears as shown in Figure 23.10.

FIGURE 23.10
The Schedule Notes option lets you send a picture of project tasks.

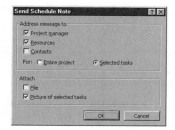

2. Choose the recipients by selecting the appropriate Address Message To area check boxes: Project Manager, Resources, or Contacts, or any combination of these three options.

   In the For area, choose the group for which you want to include all email addresses: the Entire Project or only the team members mentioned in the Selected Tasks.

3. With this note, you can include an attachment of the entire File, a Picture of Selected Tasks, or both, by selecting the appropriate check boxes.

4. Choose OK when finished.

5. An email message dialog box appears. Adjust the addressee list and subject message as necessary.

6. Send the schedule message.

Summary

Communication is the key. Informal communication can get lost or be misunderstood. Microsoft Project provides a variety of ways for a project or workgroup manager to exchange updated project information with team members. For project teams with email access only, team members do not have to have Project 2000 installed on their computers, but they must run a special setup program included on the Project 2000 CD. For Web-based communications, software must be installed on a Web server, and each user must have a Web browser installed on her computer. After the system is in place, the project manager generates TeamAssign notices, TeamStatus requests, and TeamUpdate messages using email or the Web. Team members receive assignments, reply to the manager by accepting or declining the assignments, and submit TeamStatus reports of accomplishments through their email Inbox or Project's TeamInbox. If an email system and a Web server are both available, the team gets the best of both worlds: Internet message posting and complete file transmissions with Send, Route, and Schedule Note message options.

Q&A

Q Under Tools, Workgroup the TeamInbox option is grayed out. What do I change to use this feature?

A The TeamInbox option is grayed out because Web has not been selected as the default for workgroup messages. To do this select Tools, Options, Workgroup and change the Default workgroup message drop-down list box.

Q I'm a team member. Do I have to run Microsoft Outlook to see my task list?

A No. You can track your project assignments using Project Central, the Web-based workgroup messaging application.

Q Each workgroup member prefers to use a different communication type. Is there a way to view each team member's workgroup setting?

A Yes. Go into your Resource Sheet view and insert a column called Workgroup.

Exercises

1. Use Project Central to send a custom status report to your team members automatically on a weekly basis. Create your report to ask for the following information:

   - Major Accomplishments
   - Objectives
   - Issues

   After you have created your report, and sent out your request for status, use Project Central to review all status reports before merging them into one overall team report showing important information, including who wrote the comments and when.

2. Customize your TeamUpdate dialog box to include the Late Start, Late Finish, and Cost fields. Send a TeamUpdate message, requesting they fill in the appropriate information. Upon receiving the updated information make sure your project plan is updated to reflect the late start, finish, and costs.

3. In the Project Central Gantt Chart view create a personal Gantt chart by re-ordering the columns (to suit your present needs), filtering for critical tasks, group them by project name, and then modify your view to show your task list from Microsoft Outlook.

Hour **24**

Exchanging Project Data with Other Applications

In a number of situations, you will find it helpful to be able to export project data to other software applications or import data from other applications into Microsoft Project 2000. For example, you might want to prepare a report or presentation about your project for a Web page or for a Microsoft PowerPoint presentation. You might also want to export a picture of a Project view such as the Gantt Chart or the PERT Chart to be used in another application.

Similarly, you might want to use data already entered in another application as part of your Project document. For example, you could start a new task list by importing a list of tasks and dates created in a Microsoft Access database. You might already have a typed list of resources with their cost rates and email addresses in Microsoft Excel that you would like to include in your resource pool. Importing the data directly into Project prevents typing errors and certainly saves you time. For small amounts of data, you can use the copy and paste facilities of the Windows Clipboard. Keep in mind that pasting data from another application offers you the opportunity to paste dynamic links to the original source so that when the data from the source changes, the pasted copy of the data will reflect those changes. With that technique, you can link resource cost rates in Project to a pay-scale file in Excel or Access.

This hour introduces you to Project's many options for exchanging information with other file formats and software applications. Although this subject is too broad and too detailed to cover in-depth in this book, you will be introduced to a few of the features that you are most likely to use.

In this hour, you will learn:

- The file formats supported by Microsoft Project 2000
- How to save Project 2000 data to older versions of Microsoft Project
- How to export Project 2000 data with other Microsoft applications
- How to customize your importing and exporting of project data through Import/Export Maps
- Steps for linking project data within Project 2000 to external documents using the Paste Special function

File Formats Supported by Microsoft Project 2000

You can import and export entire projects or selected sets of project data with the File, Open and File, Save As menu commands. These commands allow you to read and write the project data in formats other than Project 2000's native MPP format. Some of the formats that you might see in Project 2000 are beyond the scope of this book or are used less frequently these days and will not be covered here.

File formats supported by Project are listed here; their file extensions are given in parentheses:

- **Project Database (*.mpd)**

   This format uses the Microsoft Access 97 and Access 2000 data file format, although it has a proprietary extension (.mpd).

- **Microsoft Project 98 (*.mpp)**

   With this file format you are able to save your Project 2000 plans to be accessible in Project 98. Although they have the same .mpp file extension, beware that there might be inconsistencies between the two.

- **Microsoft Access 8.0 Database (`*.mdb`)**

  You can save all or part of the project data in the Access 97 or Access 2000 format using the `*.mdb` file format. Any application that recognizes this format can open and edit the file or query it for reports.

- **Microsoft Excel Workbook (`*.xls`)**

  Use this format to exchange task, resource, or assignment information with Microsoft Excel. Microsoft Project can import from and export to both the Excel 8.0 and Excel 2000 formats. You can also link field entries in Project with cell values in Excel.

- **Microsoft Excel PivotTable (`*.xls`)**

  This special format is used in both Excel 8.0 and Excel 2000 for its PivotTable functions. Although you can export individual fields of Project data to a PivotTable, you cannot import an Excel PivotTable into Microsoft Project.

- **Hypertext Markup Language (`*.htm`)**

  This is the HTML format used by Web browser programs. You can export Project field data to the HTML format, but you cannot import HTML files into Microsoft Project. Refer to Hour 19, "Publishing Projects on the Web or an Intranet," to learn more on this file format.

24

> The file extensions used in the preceding list and in the following text are visible to you only if Windows is displaying file extensions. To display file extensions in Windows 95, open Windows Explorer and choose View, Options from the menu. On the View tab, clear the check box for Hide MS-DOS File Extensions for File Types That Are Registered. Click the Apply button and then click OK. For other Windows operating systems simply open Windows Explorer and do a Help menu search for information on "viewing file extensions."

As you can see in Figure 24.1, the Open dialog box in Microsoft Project lists by default all files that match the pattern `*.mp*`. Consequently, the list of files you can open directly includes the standard Project documents (`*.mpp`), Project templates (`*.mpt`), and database documents (`*.mpd`). To save a Project file in one of the other file formats, you must explicitly select the file type when you save it (see Figure 24.2).

FIGURE 24.1

All files in native Project formats (*.mp*) are listed by default in the Open dialog box.

FIGURE 24.2

You can save a Project file in other formats with the Save As command.

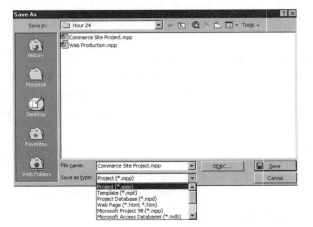

Exporting Project 2000 Data to Older Releases of Microsoft Project

As you have probably already experienced while working with computers, many of the commonly used applications that exist have several versions. You may have had problems opening a Microsoft Word document that someone sent to you in a version of Word that is newer than the one you had available on your system. This same situation holds true for Microsoft Project. Therefore, you need to understand the dynamics of a Project 2000 (*.mpp) file format versus a Project 98 (*.mpp) file format.

Saving a Microsoft Project 2000 Plan in the Project 98 Format

There might be times when you need to hand off Project 2000 data to be accessed by someone using Project 98. In this situation you will need to save the Project 2000 plan with the Project 98 (*.mpp) file format. When executing this operation, make sure that the person who is receiving the Project 98 version understands that some of the incompatible data might be lost during the conversion. If it is necessary to save your plan in the Project 98 format, be sure to compare the two files to check for any inconsistencies.

To Do: Saving a Project 2000 Plan in the Project 98 Format

To save your project in the Project 98 format, follow these steps:

1. Choose File, Save As to display the Save As dialog box.

2. Select the location for the new database file in the Save In box.

3. Pull down the list of file types in the Save As Type list box and select Microsoft Project 98 (*.mpp) and click Save.

4. You will then be prompted in the Planning Wizard dialog box to save your Project 98 plan with or without a baseline.

   In Figure 24.3 you will see a Saving to Microsoft Project 98 Format dialog box that warns you about the possible problems when saving your plan in Project 98.

FIGURE 24.3

From here you can decide whether you would like to continue in the saving process or cancel.

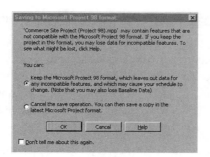

You can open Project 98 documents directly in Project 2000, but some features in Project 2000 might not be applied to your Project 98 document. After you have viewed and made any changes to the Project 98 plan, be sure to save the plan in the proper format. When closing you will be prompted to either overwrite the plan in the latest version, Project 2000, or save it in its existing Project 98 format (see Figure 24.4).

FIGURE 24.4
Simply select the appropriate response to save the Project document.

Routinely using both Project 98 and Project 2000 documents can be tricky. Be sure to keep in mind which version of Project you and others are using and you should have no problem exchanging Project 2000 data with older versions of Project.

Saving the Entire Project in a Database

Microsoft Project 2000 can be saved in two different database formats: the Microsoft Project Database format and the Microsoft Access format. Both formats use the Microsoft Access 8.0 and Access 2000 file format and can be read from either Access or Project. All project data can be saved in the database format, including field data, views, calendars, and formatting. The files can then be queried, opened, modified, and saved either in Microsoft Project or in Microsoft Access. Of course, in Access, the data appears simply as a database, whereas in Project, the data appears in the familiar Project views.

Using the Microsoft Project Database Format

You can only save an entire project in the Microsoft Project database format (*.mpd) and not just parts of a project document. Because you can save multiple projects in the same database file, the Project database is the preferred format to use for a repository or archive of past projects. Saving projects into a database in Microsoft Project allows you to open the archive in Access and analyze patterns of performance for resources or tasks over multiple projects.

To Do: Saving a Project in a Microsoft Project Database

To save an entire project in the Microsoft database format, follow these steps:

1. Choose File, Save As to display the Save As dialog box.
2. Select the location for the newbe database file in the Save In box.
3. Pull down the list of file types in the Save As Type list box and select Project Database (*.mpd).

   The names of the existing MPD files in the selected location appear in the dialog box.

▼   In Figure 24.5, the Project document was originally named COMMERCE SITE
        PROJECT.mpp, but the name changes to COMMERCE SITE PROJECT.mpd when the
        MPD file type is selected. Also notice that an existing Project database named
        INTERNET PROJECTS.mpd appears in the file list.

FIGURE 24.5

*Selecting Project
Database (*.mpd) as
the file type changes
the files that appear in
the list of files and the
extension on the
default filename.*

24

4. If you want to store the project in an existing database, select the database in the
    file list.

    If you are creating a new database, supply the name for the database in the File
    Name text box. The default database name is the same name attached to the
    Project file. To give the database a distinct name, you must type the new name. If
    you plan to store many projects in the new database, be sure to give it a fairly gen-
    eral name that relates to all the projects you will be storing in the database.

5. Click the Save button.

    If you are creating a new database, the Save to Database dialog box appears and
    you can skip to step 7. If you are adding the project to an existing database, con-
    tinue below.

    If you are adding a project to an existing database, Microsoft Project has to know
    whether you are overwriting the existing project(s) in that database or appending
    another project to those already stored there. A dialog box appears to let you
▼   choose the next step (see Figure 24.6).

FIGURE 24.6

You can append the project to an existing database, or you can overwrite all the projects in the existing database with the new project.

6. Click the Append button to either add this project to those already in the database or to replace one of them with the one you are saving. The Save to Database dialog box is then displayed.

Click the Overwrite button only if you want to remove all existing projects from the database and save the new project in that file by itself. The Save to Database dialog box is then displayed.

Click the Cancel button if you want to back up and select a different database name to use, leaving the database you selected unchanged. Return to step 5.

7. When the Save to Database dialog box appears, the Entire Project tab is selected because that is the only option available when you are saving a Microsoft Project database (.mpd) (see Figure 24.7).

Your project's name appears in the text box labeled Project Name by default. If this is a new database, enter a new name or use the existing one.

If this is an existing database, be sure to click the arrow in Project Name box to review the other project names already in the database. If you reuse an existing name, the project you are saving replaces the one already in the database.

FIGURE 24.7

Review the list of projects already stored in the database.

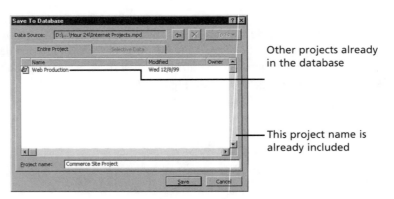

Other projects already in the database

This project name is already included

8. Click Save to begin saving the project in the database.

Opening Projects from a Microsoft Project Database

You can open a project that was saved in the Microsoft Project database file format with the File, Open command.

To Do: Opening a Project from a Microsoft Project Database

To open a project that was saved in a Microsoft Project database, follow these steps:

1. Choose File, Open.

2. Select the location of the database file you want to open from the Look In box. The Microsoft Project database files in that location are displayed along with other Project files stored there.

3. Choose the desired database name from the list and click the Open button. The Open from Database dialog box appears with one or more projects listed within. (see Figure 24.8).

24

FIGURE 24.8

Select the project name to be opened from a Microsoft Project database file.

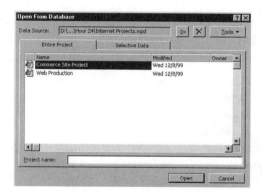

4. Choose the project you want to open from the list.

5. Click the Open button to begin loading the project from the database.

Using the Microsoft Access Format

You can save an entire project in a standard Microsoft Access 97 or Access 2000 database with the extension *.mdb. Although you can only save an entire project in the Project database format, you can save the entire project or just a portion of it in an Access database using the *.mdb file formats. Because the Access format uses the standard Access extension, the file is recognized by more applications than a file saved in the Project database format.

> You mainly use the Access database format when you want to save just parts of a project, as described in the next section.

The steps for saving an entire project in the Access format are virtually the same as those used to save a Microsoft Project database. The only differences are that you select the Access file format type (*.mdb) at the Save As Type drop-down list at the start of the process, and when the Save To Database dialog box appears you have additional options (as explained in the next section).

Using Import/Export Maps to Exchange Project Data with Other File Formats

You can choose to export selected data to other applications. For example, you can export just the task list with selected accompanying fields, or just the resource pool or a list of assignments. In Hour 19, you learned how to export project data to the HTML format for a Web page.

You can also import data from other applications. Suppose that you have been given an Excel workbook that contains a list of tasks with estimated start and finish dates and you have been asked to put together a project plan from this list. You know that the dates will probably change as the project schedule is developed, but the date ranges you've been given can serve as an initial estimate of duration. If you import the task list and the dates into Microsoft Project, Project can calculate the duration for each task from the dates in the list.

> If only selected rows or columns of a Project table are to be exported or imported, you have to use an import/export *map* to match Project fields with the fields in the other format.

NEW TERM In order to place data from another application into the correct fields in Microsoft Project (or vice versa), you must define a *data exchange map* that pairs Project fields with the data location in the other application (for example, a field in Microsoft Access or a column in Microsoft Excel).

Figure 24.9 shows the Excel workbook that you'll import into a new Project document. The column headings in the file PROJECT MANAGER TODO'S.XLS are not the traditional Project field names, but the import map you develop will match them with Project field names.

FIGURE 24.9

The task list and dates in Excel can be imported to form the basis of the project schedule.

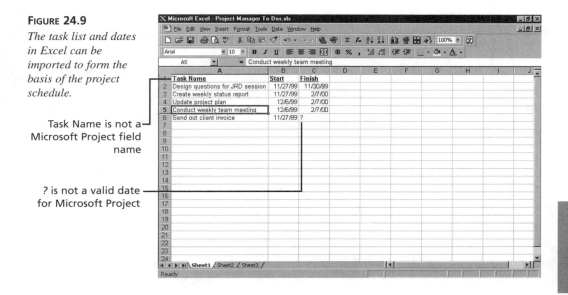

Task Name is not a
Microsoft Project field
name

? is not a valid date
for Microsoft Project

Review the source data carefully before starting the import operation. The source data does not have to contain the correct Project field names. However, invalid data (like the question mark in the finish date column) can cause problems during the import operation. It's easier to correct invalid data types before you start the import operation.

To Do: Importing Excel Data into Microsoft Project 2000

To import data from an Excel workbook into Microsoft Project, follow these steps:

1. From Microsoft Project, choose File, Open to display the File Open dialog box.

2. Use the Look In list box to select the location in which the Excel workbook was saved.

3. Change the Files of Type selection to Microsoft Excel Workbooks.

4. Select the Excel file from the file list and click the Open button to display the Import Mapping dialog box (see Figure 24.10).

5. Click the New Map button in the Import Mapping dialog box to display the Define Import/Export Map dialog box (see Figure 24.11).

6. On the Options tab, in the Import/Export Map Name text box, supply a name for the map you are creating. I suggest that you make the names very descriptive of the purpose of the map.

▲ To Do

24

▼

FIGURE 24.10

*A new map that is cre-
ated can be saved to
your Global.mpt to use
with other project files
and will be listed in
your Import/Export
Map list.*

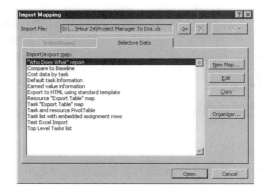

7. Select the check boxes for the type of data you are importing. In this example, you are importing only Task data.

   Also, make sure that there is a check mark in the box labeled Export Header Row/Import Includes Headers. This option ensures that Project will not attempt to treat the column headings as the first task.

   Note that the option to import assignment detail rows is not available. Project has no way of knowing which rows are tasks (or resources) and which are assignment details.

FIGURE 24.11

*You must import the
headers to help you
match the imported
data with Project
fields.*

Be sure that headers
are included so that
you can see column
headings

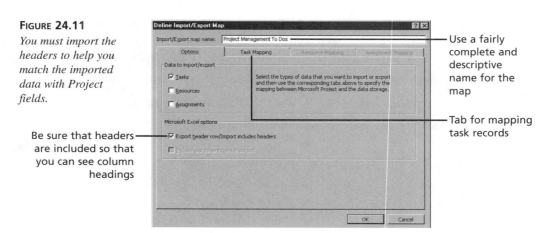

Use a fairly
complete and
descriptive
name for the
map

Tab for mapping
task records

8. Choose the tab for the data types you are importing. In this example, the Task Mapping tab is selected (see Figure 24.12).

▼

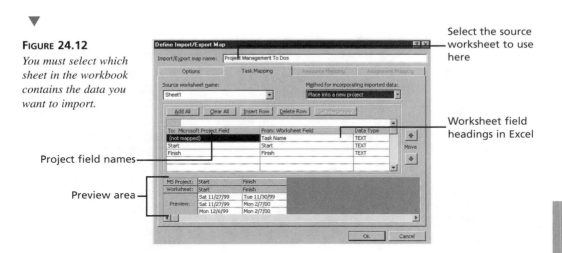

FIGURE 24.12

You must select which sheet in the workbook contains the data you want to import.

Select the source worksheet to use here

Worksheet field headings in Excel

Project field names

Preview area

24

9. Use the list arrow in the Source Worksheet Name list box and select the worksheet you want to use. In this example, you will use Sheet 1.

   When the source worksheet is selected, Project fills the From column in the center of the mapping table with the column headings from the worksheet and attempts to find a matching field name from Project in the left column. In Figure 24.12 above, you can see that Project was not able to find correct matches for all the Project fields.

10. To supply the correct field name in the first column of the mapping table, you can type the field name into the Edit bar just above the table, or you can use the in-place arrow control to display a list of all Project field names and select the correct one from the list.

    In this example, supply **Name** as the Project field for the Excel Tasks column heading. After you identify the first field as Name, Project's preview at the bottom of the dialog box in Figure 24.13 shows how the imported table will look.

11. From the Method for Incorporating Imported Data list box as seen in Figure 24.14, select the appropriate method for importing the data. In this example, the imported data will be placed in a new Project file. You can also append the imported data to an existing Project file, but you don't have the time to cover that in this hour.

12. Click OK to save the import map and return to the Import Format dialog box.

13. Click the Open button in the Import Format dialog box to begin the import process.

▼

FIGURE 24.13

Project cannot match the worksheet column headings with Project field names unless the worksheet contains exact matches for Project's field names.

Select Place into a new project

Edit bar

Field name recognized now

Preview area correct

FIGURE 24.14

You have three options for incorporating imported data from an existing file.

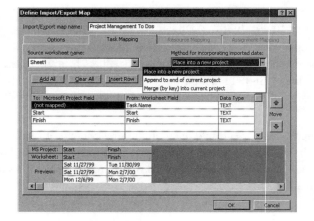

14. If there is a problem with the data types being imported into any field, you have to respond to a warning message like the one displayed in Figure 24.15. Choose one of the following options to respond to the warning:

   • Choose Yes to continue importing and to continue seeing error messages. You should generally choose this option unless you know what the problems are and what corrective action you must take in the Project document as a result.

   • Choose No to continue importing without seeing further error messages.

   • Choose Cancel to stop importing.

▼

FIGURE 24.15

If a data mismatch occurs during importing, Project warns you and allows you to choose how to proceed.

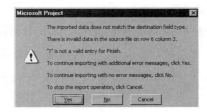

The mismatched data is not imported into Project, and the affected field in Project will display a default value. You will have to find these holes in the data and manually supply the correct information if you choose to continue.

It's a good idea to jot down the source references in the warning message (see Figure 24.15). If you are importing a lot of data at once, the references can help you locate the problem in the source file so that you can determine where you have to look in the Project file to fill in the missing information.

24

15. Review any data type mismatches and correct the entries in the Project file.

The resulting Project file from this import is shown in Figure 24.16. Note that each task has a flexible constraint indicator (because importing tasks with dates is the same as entering fixed dates manually). Note that because the Finish date for the fifth task was a question mark, which is an invalid date, Project supplied its own Finish date for the task Send Out Client Invoice.

FIGURE 24.16

The tasks in a Project file created by importing dates have soft constraints on the tasks.

Tasks with imported dates have soft constraints

Duration is calculated for the date range imported

Default Finish date is supplied because of invalid data

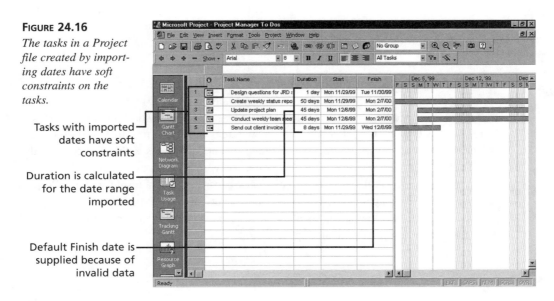

If you do not intend to be tied to the dates in the source data, you will want to remove the constraints from the tasks.

To Do: Removing Date Constraints from Multiple Tasks

To remove date constraints from multiple tasks, follow these steps:

1. Select the tasks for which you want to remove the constraints. In this example, simply select all the tasks by clicking the first row and then pressing Ctrl+Shift+down arrow to select all the rows.

2. Click the Task Information tool to display the Task Information dialog box.

3. Select the Advanced tab.

4. From the Constrain Task Type field, select As Soon As Possible.

5. Click OK to complete the operation.

> When removing a constraint on a task that is not linked to a predecessor or successor task, keep in mind that the task will now have a start date corresponding with the start of the project. The Project Start date was entered in the Project, Project Information menu option.

Copying Selected Data between Applications

In addition to exporting (or importing) data using the File, Open or File, Save As command, you can also use the Edit, Copy and Edit, Paste commands to copy selected data from one document to another and the receiving document can be in the same application or in a different application. For example, you can copy a wage rate from Excel into a Project Resource sheet or copy a picture of a Project Gantt Chart into a PowerPoint slide show.

You can also use the Insert, Object command to insert data that is presented by another application as long as both applications support Microsoft's OLE protocol (Object Linking and Embedding). For example, you can insert an Excel workbook into a task's Notes field or Objects field. If you insert a new Excel workbook file (that is, if you create the document from within Project), the data it contains resides within Project, and the Excel "object" is said to be *embedded* in Project. If you insert an existing Excel file as an object into Project, the object is said to be *linked* because the data resides outside Project and can be edited independently of Project. When you open the Project document, the linked copy of the workbook can be automatically updated to reflect any new values that were created while Project was not open.

NEW TERM *OLE* (Object Linking and Embedding) is a standard that allows you to share information that originates in one document with other documents—even documents in
other applications. However, both applications must support the OLE standard if sharing
is to take place.

Copying Data from Other Applications into Microsoft Project

You can use standard Office hotkeys and menu commands to paste information into
Project from other Office applications. For example, you can select a cell in an Excel
workbook using the Ctrl+C hotkey and then paste the value into a cell in a Microsoft
Project table. If you use the Edit, Paste Special command, you can choose the Paste Link
option to create a link between the copy data you paste in the Project document and the
external cell in Excel. With a link, if the value in the Excel workbook changes, Project
can automatically update the value in the Project document.

To Do: Pasting Linked External Data Into a Project Table

To copy and paste data as a link from an external file into a Project table, follow these steps:

1. Select the data in the external application. Figure 24.17 Shows the Excel worksheet
   from which you will copy data.

FIGURE 24.17

*A separate Excel
spreadsheet of
resources is kept
updated. Any changes
made to this master
list can be reflected
into the Project 2000
resource pool.*

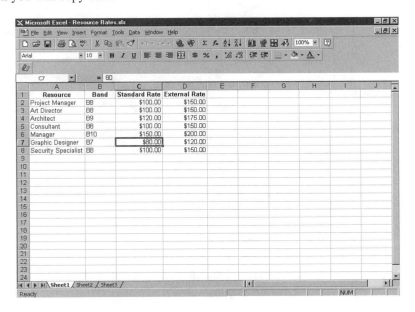

2. Use the Edit, Copy command in that application to put a copy of the data in the
   Windows Clipboard.

▼ 3. Select the location in Project to which the data is to be pasted (see Figure 24.18).

4. Choose Edit, Paste Special to display the Paste Special dialog box.

5. Select the Paste Link radio button; from the As list of data types, select Text Data.

6. Click OK to paste the link. The Graphic Designer resource now shows a standard rate as seen in Figure 24.19.

FIGURE 24.18

The Graphic Designer in the Project 2000 Resource Pool has a Standard Rate of $0.00/hr. You need to paste the correct rate into the resource pool with the Paste Special option to create a link that will automatically update this field.

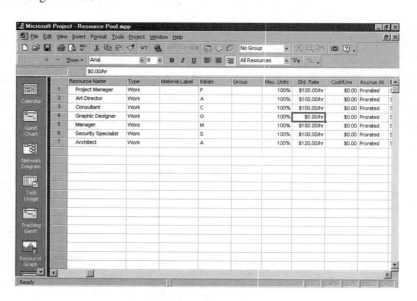

FIGURE 24.19

After creating the link a small gray triangle will appear in the lower-right corner of the cell where the Paste Link was performed.

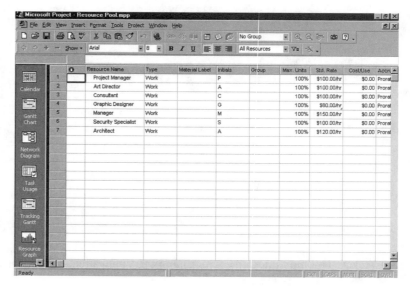

▲

A small gray triangle appears in the lower-right corner of any cell in Project that contains a linked value. When you open the Project file that contains linked data, an alert dialog box appears to warn you that the file contains linked data (see Figure 24.20) and offers you the opportunity to update the display by opening the source of the link and retrieving the current value stored there. Choose Yes to update the linked data now; choose No to avoid waiting for the link to be reestablished at this time.

FIGURE 24.20

You are automatically alerted when a project you open has linked data that might be out of date.

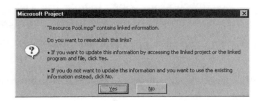

You can update linked data at any time while working with a document. To do so, select the Edit, Links command to display the Links dialog box (see Figure 21.21). Select the link you want to work with from the Links list. Click the link you want to update and then click the Update Now button. You can also disconnect the link from the external source by clicking the Break Link button or change the source links location for any documents that have physically moved by selecting the Change Source button.

FIGURE 24.21

Update links manually at any time with the Edit Links command.

Select link to work with

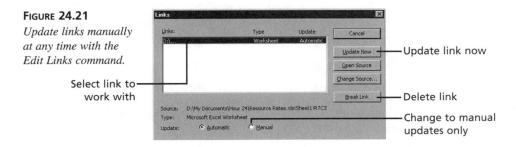

Update link now

Delete link

Change to manual updates only

Copying Microsoft Project Data into Other Applications

You can copy Project data into another Office application by using standard Office techniques for copying with the Windows Clipboard. For example, you can paste a link to the total cost of a project into an Excel workbook that you use to track the cost of all current projects.

To Do: Pasting a Link to the Total Cost of a Project

To paste a link from Microsoft Project into another Office application, follow these steps:

1. Open the project file and display a task view such as the Gantt Chart view.

2. Display the project summary task by choosing Tools, Options. The Options dialog box appears. Select the Project Summary Task option on the View tab.

3. Display the Cost table by choosing View, Table, Cost. The Total Cost column shows the total cost of the project in the row for the project summary task.

4. Press Ctrl+C or select the Edit, Copy command to copy the total cost value to the Clipboard.

5. Open the Excel workbook and choose Edit, Paste Special to display Excel's Paste Special dialog box.

6. Choose Paste Link and select the Text type from the As list box.

7. Click OK to complete the action.

As work on the project progresses, and actual costs update the Total Cost field in Microsoft Project, the Excel file continues to show the most current cost of the project.

Copying Project's Views to Other Applications

Another method of copying Project data allows you to paste a picture of a Project view in another application. For example, you can save a picture of Project's Gantt Chart and paste it into a PowerPoint presentation.

To Do: Saving a Project as a Static Picture

To paste a picture of a Project view into another application, follow these steps:

1. In Microsoft Project, display the view you want to copy and format it to look the way you want the final picture to look.

2. If you want to include only selected tasks in the picture, select those tasks now. You can select tasks that are not adjacent to each other by pressing the Ctrl key and clicking the desired tasks. Those tasks will then appear next to each other in the picture.

3. Click the Copy Picture tool on the Standard toolbar to display the Copy Picture dialog box:

    - If the picture will be viewed only onscreen, choose the For Screen option.

    - The For Printer option is used if you want to proceed in printing your Project view or if you want to optimize the way the picture will look when printed on that printer.

▼

- The option To GIF Image File is mainly for publishing on Web pages, but can be used to insert as a GIF in other documents.

To include in the picture all rows currently visible on your screen, choose Rows On Screen. If you have selected the rows you want to include, choose Selected Rows.

To include the time periods visible on your screen, choose As Shown On Screen. To have the picture cover a specific span of time, enter From and To dates.

4. Click OK to copy the picture to the Clipboard.

5. Open the document into which you want to copy the picture.

▲   6. Choose Edit, Paste or press Ctrl+V to paste the picture into the new document.

Figure 24.22 shows the Project Gantt Chart view inserted into a new PowerPoint slide presentation.

24

FIGURE 24.22

The Gantt Chart from a Project document is displayed in a PowerPoint presentation.

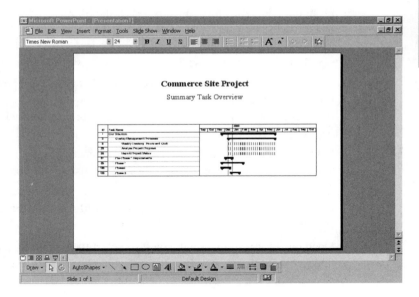

Linking Selected Data Between Applications

If you select the Link check box when pasting an object into a project, the object is linked to its original application and will change if the original object is modified. To copy an object as a linked object rather than an embedded object, follow the instructions for inserting an embedded object but remember to select the Link check box. Alternatively, you can select the object to copy in another application, use File, Copy to copy it to the Clipboard, select Edit, Paste Special, and select the Link check box to insert the object into Project as a linked object.

Summary

In this hour you have seen how Project 2000 data can be exchanged with other applications by using several methods including: Save As, Import/Export maps, cut and paste techniques, and OLE objects. You should now be able to use Project data more efficiently throughout the life of your project by using the many features discussed.

Q&A

Q **I need to send my client a Project 98 version of my project plan, but I only have Project 2000 on my system. How do I go about giving my client the appropriate version that they can access?**

A Open up your Project 2000 plan and go to the File, Save As menu commands. From the File Type drop-down list select the Microsoft Project 98 (*.mpp) file format. Click Save. You will be prompted to save a baseline. Next you will be warned about the issues of saving to a Microsoft Project 98 file format. Select the option you desire. You can now send your client a copy of the plan in Project 98 to view.

Q **I want to be able to link some Project fields to an Excel worksheet, but I update the data only once a month. How can I prevent the fields from updating every time I open the project, but still update them when needed?**

A When you Paste Special project data and select the Link check box to link the data to the original application, also select the Manual Update check box to prevent automatic updating. Then, when you want to update the data, open the Links dialog box and click the Update Now button.

Q **I want to insert photos or art images of products into the Task Notes boxes for Project tasks. How can I do this?**

A Open the Task Information dialog box, select the Notes tab, and use the Insert Object button to open the Insert Object dialog box. With the Insert from File option selected, insert the file that has the product image you want.

Q **I want to put an image of a project's Gantt Chart into a Word specifications document. How can I do this?**

A In Project, arrange the Gantt Chart as you want it to appear in Word, and then click the Copy Picture button. Switch to Word and paste the picture by pressing Ctrl+C.

Exercises

One of your team members does not have access to Project 2000 and needs to give you a list of tasks with start and finish dates for you to incorporate into the overall plan. How would you handle this scenario using what you have learned in Hour 24? Create a list of tasks with start and finish dates in an Excel spreadsheet. Using import/export maps, export the data from the Excel spreadsheet to a Project 2000 plan.

With this new plan you have created above, you will now need to assign resources to the tasks. In doing this you want to make sure that the standard rates for the resources are consistent with the one that Finance keeps in an Access database of employee information. What steps would you need to take to ensure that the resource rate information is accurate and up to date?

24

INDEX

X-Z

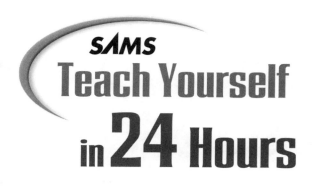

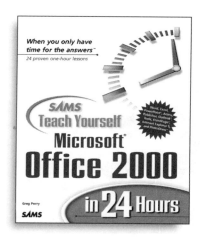